Literary Skinheads?

Contents

Preface

Since World War II, Germany has always looked to Washington for both connections and protection, wanting to insure that the United States remains tightly bound to Europe and European security. The American presence keeps not only French ambitions in check, but German ones too—something of a relief to those Germans who are suspicious of their own impulses.[1]

In the midst of the Second World War, a group of British sociologists and literary scholars met to discuss the "German Mind and Outlook." Their lectures and discussions were documented in a volume that appeared in 1945. The appearance of such a scholarly work was not the rule during wartime, as evidenced by the stamp "Book Production War Economy Standard" opposite the table of contents.[2] In his foreword, G. P. Gooch stated that the project was meant to "aid in the understanding of the gifted, efficient, hardworking, disciplined, romantic, unstable, inflammable and formidable nation with which for the second time in a generation we find ourselves at war."[3] He went on to stress that "German culture is at least as interesting and important a theme as the German state."[4] This is as true today as it was then. In 1989, a new chapter in the long history of this culture began. Reunified Germany is of course not a "new" country, but rather the latest of myriad geographical and political configurations. As can be expected, the culture—including the political culture—of the *Bundesrepublik Deutschland* contains elements whose origins lie in the period before 1945. The present study will concern itself with one of these elements, namely the cultural conceptions and political views of right-wing intellectuals. Very little of the pertinent material is available in English, so one of the purposes of this exercise is to enable those who do not know German to familiarize themselves with a contemporary sociocultural phenomenon of some significance. The main focus will be on literary figures, but it will be necessary to speak of nonliterary intellectuals as well.

In the nineteenth century, and well into the twentieth, Germany was often characterized as the "land of poets and thinkers." With the advent of the mass media, digital culture, and ubiquitous visual images, one might well ask if the literary sphere still carries significant weight in the European Union's most populous country. Although the demise of high culture is regularly bemoaned by German authors and critics, there is a core of support for such culture that has yet to disappear (although it is clearly a minority affair). Since the fall of the Berlin Wall, and to a certain extent even before that momentous event, the advocates of elite culture have been situated on the right, even the far right of the political spectrum. Before 1989, they were not afforded much attention, since blatantly right-wing views had been marginalized in postfascist West Germany. (Such views were of course—officially—nonexistent in East Germany.) This began to change in the course of the Historians' Debate[5] of the 1980s, and the Literature Debate[6] of the early 1990s initiated an assault against the literary left that continues to this day. Simultaneously, a quite different kind of assault has become all too commonplace on German streets, i.e., vicious attacks against non-Germans. Although there is no direct connection between the conservative cultural criticism analyzed in this study and xenophobic violence, the two can be seen as manifestations of a general malaise, a disorientation that may last for quite some time. Migration from impoverished regions to the prosperous West,[7] rising unemployment in Germany (and much of Europe), the much-discussed globalization of the world economy, and the questioning—some would say erosion—of traditional values have helped create a climate of anxiety and apprehension. After reading about this climate for years, I spent six months in Berlin (July 1997 to January 1998) in order to experience it firsthand. While flying back to the United States, I read the banner headline shared by several German newspapers: "German Unemployment Reaches Record Postwar High."

What follows is not a characterization of the Germans per se, but rather an attempt to describe one subgroup in contemporary German society. It remains to be seen whether this subgroup will attain considerable influence in the coming years. One can well imagine, however, that this will depend primarily on the future economic health of Germany. (As of this writing, record unemployment stands in sharp contrast to record highs at the German Stock Exchange.) The anxiety found in today's Germany is at least in part a reaction to the disruptions and (largely self-inflicted) losses suffered by the German people in this century. Roy Pascal, one of the most eminent "foreign" observers of German affairs in our time, wrote an assessment of a central figure in German culture that is an appropriate motto for my own ruminations:

> In peace-time, in a time when social conflicts were not too acute, Nietzsche could inspire an aristocratic seclusion and devotion to the personal life. The brutality of his doctrine could remain as an undercurrent. In times of stress it became an all-powerful swirling torrent.[8]

Such differentiation is clearly more fruitful than a blanket condemnation of the German character before 1945 and a concomitant clean bill of (democratic) health for the subsequent period.[9] The most accurate description of the German nation that I have encountered to date is "stubborn transiency,"[10] a term rejected vigorously by those who believe that a state of normalcy has been attained. I do not proceed from the premise that "Germany will try it again,"[11] but I firmly believe that it would be irresponsible to ignore certain disquieting trends beginning to make an impact between the Rhine and the Oder-Neisse.[12]

The original motivation for this book was my reaction to the appearance of Botho Strauß's polemical essay "Anschwellender Bocksgesang" ("Impending Tragedy") in 1993. I was amazed to discover a number of themes and concerns of the cultural and political right in a text written by a writer long associated with the left. In the process of contextualizing this essay, I turned to the general condition of German intellectuals in the 1980s and 1990s. This in turn led to a look back at the origins and development of conservative-elitist literature in Germany since Romanticism. All this would be more than sufficient to warrant an exercise in literary analysis and cultural history. Over and above such intellectual phenomena, however, it was the abovementioned manifestations of xenophobia in post-1989 Germany that provided a strong motivation to put pen to paper. The availability of the German press via the Internet made it possible to follow developments on a day-to-day basis from abroad. As a non-German who has lived in Germany for extended periods of time over the course of the past thirty years, I have reacted not only intellectually and politically, but also emotionally to each incident of violence, be it the burning of a home for asylum seekers or the beating of a foreigner on a commuter train. In the context of such atrocities, the attempts of right-wing intellectuals to redefine German identity and reinterpret the course of recent German history deserve attention—

especially since problematic exercises in mystification and obfuscation are not limited to Germany, or even Europe.

The characterization of the intellectuals in question as "right wing" — as opposed to "conservative" or "neoconservative" — needs some clarification. In the context of contemporary German politics, it should be taken to mean a position to the right of the Christian Democrats, even to the right of the (Bavarian) Christian Social Union. Although certain representatives of the German New Right have attempted to transform the Free Democratic Party into a conservative nationalist grouping,[13] most of the figures discussed below situate themselves outside the spectrum of the traditional conservative parties in Germany. These people do not, as a rule, cultivate contacts with far-right parties like the National Democratic Party (NPD), the German People's Union (DVU), or the Republicans, either. They form, instead, an extraparliamentary cultural and intellectual opposition. In this they are following in the footsteps of the Conservative Revolution of the Weimar era. They hope to set the stage for a cultural shift that will eventually lead to fundamental changes in the political system and the structure of society.[14] In an essay published in 1983, Jürgen Habermas offered a critique of such agendas.[15] A mere seven years later, the cultural program he analyzed could take on an overtly nationalistic dimension, given that the "German question" had been finally laid to rest. It is reunification that separates the New Right from the "old" neoconservatives: A new self-confidence and openly displayed sense of national pride, unthinkable in the divided country, are now the order of the day.[16] The campaign against a kind of national inferiority complex — the result of Germany's defeat in World War II and the subsequent cultural and political reorientation imposed on the country — would of course be unthinkable in Britain or France. The current situation in Germany is thus *sui generis*.

Since this study is mainly concerned with members of the literary intelligentsia, the construction of an intellectual genealogy is essential. This will be done in abbreviated form, since the emphasis is on contemporary developments. The survey begins with the Romantic poet and political theorist Novalis, whose verses and ideas hold a strong attraction almost two hundred years after their formulation. After an encounter with Nietzsche, we will turn to the messianic poet and prophet Stefan George, a self-styled *Führer* in the cultural sphere of the early twentieth century. Thereafter, Thomas Mann's *Betrachtungen eines Unpolitischen* (Reflections of a non-political man) and the much-discussed Conservative Revolution will be examined. Special attention will be given to the aspect of change, or transformation: Where did these writers begin, and where did they conclude their literary (and political) journeys? Their attitudes toward Western democracy and authoritarianism will be of special interest. Although space will not permit a broadening of this section beyond the German context, the reader may well discover commonalities with authors like Knut Hamsum, Ezra Pound, or Louis Ferdinand Céline. With regard to England, John Carey's provocative *The Intellectuals and the Masses*[17] provides a fascinating comparison with collateral developments in Germany.

The second chapter focuses on the unique partnership of former East German dissident Ulrich Schacht and West German critic Heimo Schwilk as an example of cultural reunification with a decidedly conservative flavor. These two relatively unknown figures achieved a degree of notoriety as editors of the controversial 1994 anthology *Die selbstbewußte Nation* (The self-confident/self-aware nation), and they are now the leading younger representatives of the "literary right." Chapter 3 analyzes the rightward drift of two prominent authors, namely Botho Strauß and Peter Handke. Their recent exercises in cultural and political criticism—revolving around the role of the mass media and the growing dominance of the superficial and the trivial in society as a whole—are the latest salvos in a German debate that began in the Wilhelminian era. An excursus examines the anti-American strain characteristic of the German New Right and discusses one rather questionable method of defending the American—and Western—model. The study originally concluded with an assessment of the present state and future prospects of the neonationalist cultural project in Germany and beyond, but important political events and cultural debates (especially those involving Martin Walser and Peter Handke) necessitated the addition of an epilogue covering the period from September 1998 to May 1999.

Unless otherwise noted, all translations from the German are my own.

I would like to thank Keith Bullivant, Edith Clowes, and Elliot Neaman for their careful reading of the manuscript. Initial thoughts and early versions of my approach to the subject were put in print by Valters Nollendorfs (*Monatshefte*), Klaus Bohnen (*Text & Kontext*), and Keith Bullivant (as editor of the volume *Beyond 1989*). Free time for writing was provided by the

National Endowment for the Humanities and Purdue University. Ernst-Ullrich Pinkert gave me a public forum for airing my views by inviting me to lecture at Aalborg University. Ulrich Profitlich made me feel welcome at the Freie Universität Berlin during my research semester there in 1997–98. Helpful comments and encouragement were given by Michael Geisler, Marc Silberman, Beate Allert, Mechthild Hart, Matthias Konzett, Anton Kaes, Martin Jay, Sibylle Tönnies, Christiane Lemke and Antonia Grunenberg. Margaret Hunt guided me through the various stages of publication at the Purdue University Press, and John McGuigan and Bruce Carpenter made valuable editorial suggestions. I am grateful to the members of my family for their willingness to spend six months in Berlin. Needless to say, I alone am responsible for any errors or misassessments that might be found in the present volume.

Literary Skinheads?

Chapter One

Predecessors and Predilections: A Problematic Legacy

The Enlightenment and the French Revolution were the beginnings of the modern world, and Romanticism was the first reaction to this world. In this first postrevolutionary era, both the idea of conservatism and the image of the writer as first and foremost a unique individual with a highly developed subjectivity made their appearance. At first glance, the two phenomena not only have little to do with each other, they even seem to be diametrically opposed. The single-minded path taken by the modern writer is, after all, hardly an expression of an homage to customs and traditions that evolved over time. The protected and at the same time monitored position of the writer at court in the days of the ancien régime was, in the course of the nineteenth century, consigned to the dustbin of history. Due to censorship and, in some cases, criminal prosecution, not a few wordsmiths had to ply their trade in exile. Making a virtue of necessity, the exiles initiated, or at least accelerated, the process of intercultural communication. The German Romantics, who were reacting to a revolution not at home, but abroad, also went into a kind of exile. They sought out a realm of fantasy in which their spirits could take flight, unfettered by history or politics. One cannot ignore a strain of prorevolutionary radicalism in the early years, embodied by such figures as Friedrich Schlegel or Joseph Görres, but these two—and others like them—later became advocates of the repressive restoration system constructed by Metternich. The "turn to the right" has, at least until recently, put its stamp on the perception of the entire movement, making it the Romantics' fate to have their image "fade extremely one-sidedly into the past."[1] In the context of this study, the Romantic with the most enduring impact is Friedrich von Hardenberg, called Novalis (1772–1801).

Novalis, an aristocrat and landowner's son, studied philosophy with Fichte, law, and mining engineering. His ties with everyday reality were actually quite strong compared to many of those who strove to emulate him: "It is this combination of an active life and poetical contemplation that lends to his work a peculiar tension."[2] Although his views on history and society can be culled from purely literary works such as the novel *Heinrich von Ofterdingen* (1802), it seems expedient to concentrate on his nonfictional writings, namely *Miscellaneous Observations/Pollen* (Vermischte Bemerkungen/ Blüthenstaub, 1797/98), *Belief and Love* (Glauben und Liebe, 1798), *Political Aphorisms* (Politische Aphorismen, 1798), *Universal Sketches* (Das Allgemeine Brouillon, 1798/99) and *Christendom or Europe* (Die Christenheit oder Europa, 1799).[3] One should keep in mind that Novalis did not live to see Napoleon as the imperialist emperor and occupier of Germany and much of continental Europe. He was thus reflecting upon the course of the revolution in France, not upon its later transmutation. As in the case of Georg Büchner, we are dealing with the observations of a rather young author.

Already in *Miscellaneous Observations/Pollen*, one encounters motifs and beliefs that are, even today, part and parcel of the conservative cultural scene. The poet, for example, is given a special status—or rather, it is lamented that such a status has been lost:

> Poets and priests were originally one, and only later times separated them. The true poet is, however, always a priest, just as the true priest has always remained a poet. And should not the future reinstate the old ways? (*Bst*, no. 71, 255 and 257)

The elevation of the poet goes hand in hand with the assertion that most princes, or monarchs, are representatives of the genius of their time (*Bst*, no. 76). One might assume that this would be considered the pinnacle of civilization, but Novalis leaves no doubt that the poet is one step higher, since he has the potential to be "a perfect representative of the genius of humankind" (*Bst*, no. 76, 261), placing him clearly beyond the bounds—and bonds—of any one epoch. Although Edmund Burke is praised, Novalis does not call for a return to pre-1789 conditions. The ideal here is the "poetic state," the only one seen as true and perfect (*VB*, no. 122, 282). This state is a juxtaposition of democracy and monarchy, and it is the poetic spirit which mediates between the masses and the prince. Such a model might be taken for constitutional monarchy or enlightened absolutism, but it is in fact neither, since it contains a utopian element. The poetic spirit is given the task of uniting the past and the future, and the locus of said unification is "the atmosphere of the poet" (*Bst,* no. 109, 283). What might this future be? When it said that children represent a "Golden Age" (*Bst,* no. 97, 273), the implication is that the young, not yet completely integrated into organized society, carry with them not only the shape of the future, but a knowledge of our most ancient origins.[4] One should note that the antithesis of the utopian, i.e., the philistine, also makes an appearance in this work. Novalis makes his disdain for this type utterly clear. The philistine never transcends everyday life, he has little use for poetry, and his religion is little more than an "opiate" (*Bst,* no. 77, 263). The worst of these are apparently the ultra-materialist "revolutionary philistines." The French Revolution is hence set in opposition to the glories of the poetic spirit.

Belief and Love, an apotheosis of King Friedrich Wilhelm III of Prussia and especially of Queen Luise, continues this sort of nonpolitical critique of political developments (underlined by the collection of short poems printed at the beginning). Even more than in *Pollen,*[5] the Germans are portrayed as the saviors of European civilization: "A land that satisfies heart and mind could well be a German invention . . . " (*GuL,* no. 7, 291). To counter the democratic fetish of the philistines ("miserable philistines, devoid of spirit and lacking in heart" — no. 23, 296), Novalis envisions a revitalized — in actuality thoroughly idealized — monarchy. He is not blind to the injustices committed by reigning monarchs, but he is also afraid of majority rule, at least rule by the *existing* majority. The solution is to have the masses educated by the king until they reach the point where they are all "capable of ruling" (no. 18, 294). This would lead to authentic republicanism, characterized by "general participation in all affairs of state, close contact and harmony of all members of the state" (no. 37, 302). As a poetic vision, this is not overly controversial, but there are some aspects that are troublesome. The belief that identification with the state can more than compensate for such trivial concerns as sufficient nourishment (no. 8, 291), and the notion that medals and uniforms should be used to demonstrate that each and every person is a citizen — i.e., someone whose identity is derived primarily from his association with the state (no. 19, 295) — were transformed into social reality during the Third Reich.[6] It is easy to overlook such details, given that the prince is seen as the chief artist in a nation of artists striving to reach the above-mentioned "Golden Age" (nos. 39 and 41, 303f). The mixing of art and politics is alternatively intriguing and maddening.

The *Political Aphorisms* revolve around similar themes, placing love and the family at the center of the state. Novalis restates his fear that the majority—given the less than flattering name "the large crowd" (*PA,* no. 67, 308)—will be manipulated by narrow-minded populist demagogues. Prefigurations of Tocqueville's analysis of American democracy abound. Specific recommendations are only provided in the vaguest form, however: The nature of the state would be irrelevant if only we would be ruled by the original laws of humankind (no. 67, 309). It is never made clear what these laws might be. Those who seek more clarity in *Universal Sketches* will be disappointed. Once again, the high status of the poet, the centrality of religion, and the role of the family are emphasized. It is only in *Christendom or Europe* that a historical dimension is introduced, in the shape of medieval Europe.

As many have remarked, this dimension is in reality no more than a facade. Novalis's portrait of the Middle Ages is no less idealized than his image of monarchy. It is a plea for belief and art set against skepticism and critical thinking, formulated in the hope that the Golden Age (*CoE,* 745), the "holy time of eternal peace" (750), will not forever remain a dream. Surely it is no accident that the words "childlike" and "childish" appear on the first few pages, linked to such words as "trust," "dream," and "innocence." On the path to true humanity, one must rid oneself of the trappings of everyday reality, and this can be most easily accomplished by children—or the "childlike," e.g., the artist—who have not yet been entwined in a web of pragmatic considerations.[7] This smacks of escapism, but it is only one facet of the essay. Novalis is not blind to the conditions that led to the Reformation (clerical laxity and decadence, for example), and he also does not condemn outright the forces of revolution active in his own time. He recognizes that the old politics will no longer suffice, so he proposes a compromise, namely religion as mediator between the political adversaries. His description of the two camps is of no little interest here:

> The old world and the new are battling each other, the deficiencies and insufficiencies of the previous state institutions have become obvious in the form of terrible phenomena. . . . Both sides have great, necessary claims which they must make, driven by the spirit of the world and of humankind. Both are indestructible powers in the human breast; here the reverence toward the ancient, the devotion to that which has evolved over time, the love for the monuments of the forefathers and for the glorious old national family, and friends of obedience; there the rapturous feeling of freedom, the boundless expectation of grand areas of activity, the pleasure in the new and the young, the casual contact with all fellow citizens, the pride in the general validity of humanity, the enjoy-

ment of personal rights and of common property, and the powerful sentiment of citizenship. (*CoE*, 748)[8]

This is anything but a conservative manifesto, but it does not stand alone. When one reads that nature ("so wondrous and incomprehensible, so poetic and endless" — 742) resists all attempts to "modernize" it, and that it is foolish to attempt to "model" history and humanity (744), one wonders if the holder of such views and the author of the just-quoted passage are one and the same.

Taken as a whole, *Christendom or Europe* is a confusing conglomerate bound to frustrate those who would divine one single thrust from it. In one regard, however, it is possible to establish a line of continuity from the earlier aphorisms and observations to this work. Once again, it is the Germans who have been chosen to implement the highest aspirations of the human race. It is in Germany, Novalis proclaims, that signs of a new world (744) can already be discerned, whereas the other European lands are still involved in useless disputes. These disputes are "war, financial speculation, and partisanship" (744). The Germans, in contrast, are occupied with history, the arts, and science, and their endeavors are blessed with "an incomparable diversity, a wonderful profundity..., broad knowledge, and a rich fantasy" (745). Marx could have been thinking of these words when he wrote his "Critique of Hegel's Philosophy of Right" in 1843 (although his assessment of Germany's lot was quite different). There is no doubt that Novalis was idealizing his countrymen, but he was far from nationalist chauvinism. We will never know whether he would have gone in this direction if he had lived until 1815. It was left to others to interpret his fragmentary and often cryptic writings.

The process of interpretation—sometimes reencryption—has been evolving for almost two centuries. Hermann Kurzke has convincingly demonstrated that the use and abuse of Novalis for various kinds of conservative causes is based on a fundamental—whether intentional or not—misreading, one that ignores the utopian impulse of his writings. Even Kurzke, though, admits that the unsystematic nature of Novalis's œuvre lends itself to misinterpretation: The fascination with the irrational is not an end in itself (it is subordinated to the recreation of a Golden Age), but it must be seen as one of the many building blocks of later fascist or totalitarian ideologies.[9] From a liberal perspective, this has been confirmed but excused as the product of a mainly poetic mind-set.[10] From an orthodox Marxist perspective, Novalis is a minor player in the wave of irrationalism that swept Europe for over a century.[11] In the standard collection of the political writings of the German Romantics, Novalis appears as a utopian dreamer who refused to participate in traditional politics—in contrast to some of his contemporaries, who served the cause of restoration rather than utopia.[12] This debate will doubtless continue for some time. For our purposes, it is perhaps most important to place emphasis on two points. First of all, Novalis chose—after the rejection of *Belief and Love*—to ignore the possibility of political activity or change in the framework of the system that existed in his own time. Second, when he did ponder the nature of society and history, he did not separate such themes from his identity as a poet. Since the poet, as we have seen, was placed at the pinnacle of the cultural and social hierarchy, his views were meant to be prescriptive. This is a model that can be encountered again and again in the evolution of modern German culture.

The literary periods following Romanticism contributed little to the genesis of twentieth-century cultural conservatism. This is clearly the case with regard to the representatives of "Junges Deutschland" or the "Vormärz," but it also holds true for the "Biedermeier," a time generally described as conservative. Even a work like Adalbert Stifter's voluminous novel *Indian Summer* (1857), an attempt to defend ethics and idealism against the encroachment of a modern age characterized by industrialism, materialism, and urbanization, was ultimately too escapist and quietistic.[13] The proponents of "Poetic Realism" in the second half of the nineteenth century vacillated between rather mild social criticism and resignation. Not surprisingly, then, the next torchbearer was a not really a literary figure at all, but rather a philosopher who occasionally wrote poetry, namely Friedrich Nietzsche. One must of course speak not of Nietzsche, but of the many Nietzsches.[14] It is difficult to dispute the fact that Nietzsche influenced almost everyone to some degree,[15] but, as in the case of Novalis, many readers—and a number of nonreaders as well[16]—selected certain ideas and simply ignored others. Like Stifter, Nietzsche was reacting to inchoate mass society, albeit in a diametrically opposed manner. His extreme individualism, loathing for conformity, and preference for an existence on the margins of society were the products of a combative, not quiescent nature. Instead of dedicating himself to the preservation of the artifacts and practices of an idealized past, he chose to construct a mode of thinking and living appropriate to the future—as he envisioned it. It is not immediately apparent how the parameters of such a project would jibe with conservatism.

According to Lukács, Nietzsche's "whole life's work was a continuous polemic against Marxism and socialism."[17] This was carried out in a rather roundabout manner, since, as Lukács himself points out, Nietzsche did not read Marx. Said polemic was directed in general terms toward anything that might promote democracy and hinder the rule of the elite. The "democratic movement" is seen as the "heir of the Christian movement,"[18] and Christianity was the target of Nietzsche's most biting comments. This religion, with its "resentment *against* life" and its promotion of guilt and the "herd animal morality,"[19] was his mortal enemy. One dilemma for most conservative readers is already clear: the critique of democracy and socialism must be divorced from the rejection of the Christian religion. The masses must also be convinced that the "master's morality" must guide the cultural and societal elite, whereas they themselves will have to submit to the tenets of the "slave morality." No mean feat!

One method of uniting the elite and the masses would be to place them under the umbrella of the nation or "Volk." This was unexpectedly successful in 1914, for example. Nietzsche's works are, once again, of limited usefulness for such an endeavor. He castigated the cultural decline that accompanied the economic and political ascendancy of the Reich, lamented the "nationalistic squandering of power" after 1871,[20] termed Goethe, the country's greatest writer, "not a German event, but a European one,"[21] often boasted of his purported ancestors in the Polish aristocracy, and spent extended periods of time abroad. He did, however make a disturbing connection between the democratization of Europe and a "physiological process" by which the Europeans would become more alike, gradually losing their ties to the milieu and conditions that had molded them for centuries.[22] This could easily be read as a warning against racial mixing and a justification for ethnocentrism, but it is not a major theme found in a number of his works. The question remains: Which Nietzsche mesmerized German conservative writers—and not a few of their left-leaning colleagues as well?

There seem to be two answers to this. First of all, especially in the years before the First World War, the incomparable aura surrounding Nietzsche was attributable less to his writings than to his life. It was as "an exemplary personality"[23] that he had the most impact. He became known as the ultimate rebel, the outsider utterly disgusted with the trappings of bourgeois society—and one willing to forego the comforts and perquisites of that society. He was part of European decadence, but he strove to overcome it. The "generation of

1914," disgusted with the self-satisfaction of the establishment and the unheroic nature of life, felt a strong affinity with him (or at least with the myth of his life that was being created). When he taught that destruction was not to be feared, but welcomed as a liberation of creative energies, this was what many—especially the young—wanted to hear. The danger inherent in praising the "proud and well-developed human being" and in the same breath detesting the misguided intercession on behalf of "all that is weak, sick, failure, suffering from itself—*all that ought to perish*"[24] only became apparent much later. Secondly, Nietzsche, like Novalis, placed the elite intellectual—whether in his manifestation as philosopher or artist/poet—on a pedestal. (The fact that Nietzsche rejected Romanticism in his later years does not mean that he bade farewell to this particular aspect.) Those who felt a similar calling within themselves could find ample vindication for their strivings in his works. Beginning with the early formulation in the *Birth of Tragedy* ("[I]t is only as an *aesthetic phenomenon* that existence and the world are eternally *justified*"[25]), and continuing until the very end ("Art is the great stimulus to life"[26]), Nietzsche outlined the contours of a new aristocracy. A number of Germans felt that they deserved to be given an entry in the *Gotha* of that select group.

One of the first was the poet Stefan George (1868–1933). In contrast to the creator of Zarathustra, who did not recruit "believers" and feared that he would be "canonized,"[27] George cultivated the image of the prophet and endeavored to surround himself with a circle of disciples. One observer chose the adjective "zarathustraähnlich" (similar to Zarathustra)[28] to describe him. In his poem "Nietzsche," George refers to his mentor as the "thunderer," the "redeemer," and even the Christ-like leader ("führer mit der blutigen krone"). Adulation does not preclude criticism, however: Nietzsche's solitude is contrasted with George's own need to be surrounded by a group, and the philosopher's preference for polemics over poetry is lamented.[29] The differences between the two can be attributed at least in part to the changing times. Whereas Nietzsche lived during the most bombastic and self-congratulatory phase of the *Kaiserreich*, George came of age in a period when symptoms of the crisis that would lead to the outbreak of the First World War were difficult to overlook. Initially, George dealt with these symptoms from an exclusively esthetic perspective—to such a great extent, in fact, that he has been termed the ultimate practitioner of the "esthetic evaluation of social conditions."[30]

George's career is usually divided into two parts. During the first phase, which lasted until the beginning of the twentieth century, he pursued a program of pure estheticism borrowed mainly from Baudelaire and Mallarmé. Traversing Europe in search of poetic perfection and kindred spirits, he strove to renew German as a language of beauty. (It can hardly be denied that this project was a necessary one, since German poetry in the late Wilhelm-inian era was wallowing in an imitative backwater.) Due to the efforts of George, his sometime collaborator Hugo von Hofmannsthal, and others, German poetry did regain its former status. This proved to be merely a pre-lude to a broader cultural mission, however. The purely artistic group origi-nally associated with the journal *Art News* (Blätter für die Kunst) was transformed into a fellowship dedicated to a general cultural renewal. The shift is reflected in the title of the new journal *Yearbooks for the Spiritual Movement* (Jahrbücher für die geistige Bewegung), which appeared from 1910 to 1912. Art was supplanted by a much more ambitious reformational thrust. A new aristocracy was to transform society by means of high culture. After a quasi-religious episode involving the worship of young Maximilian Kronberger as an incarnation of beauty, youth, and the Hellenic ideal — an episode that scandalized many — George and his circle worked to lay the groundwork for a new heroic age set in opposition to degeneracy, democracy, and materialism. Their ideology of "power, service, fellowship, and empire"[31] was not meant to be overtly political, but it was undeniably interpreted that way by those youthful sympathizers who volunteered in 1914 to demon-strate that they were worthy to serve.

George himself did not come out in favor of the war, but he did not de-nounce it publicly either. His long 1917 poem "War" ("Der Krieg") com-posed in typically hermetic language, is a mirror of this ambivalence. On the one hand, the prophet ("Seher") declares that the war is merely the external manifestation and culmination of those currents that only he was capable of feeling. He also shows no enthusiasm for "domestic [i.e., German] virtue" and no disdain for "foreign treachery."[32] In both camps, he asserts, no one senses what is at stake, since both are preoccupied with petty concerns. The only shimmer of hope lies in the reception of the prophet's message about a future on a higher level of being. Unfortunately, the sublimity of the mes-sage is marred by a reference to the desecration of the blood and the warning that those who engage in it deserve to be exterminated — unless they are re-deemed by the actions of the elite.[33]

Even though these lines were written over eighty years ago, it is still chilling to read them in light of what was to follow. After 1918, George came to believe that the Germans, having been cleansed by defeat, were the only people capable of transcending the abominations of the modern age (including feminism and plutocracy). Is this not a modern version of Novalis's dreams for then-"backward" Germany?[34] As has often been pointed out, George was anything but a Nazi (although his elitist rejection of National Socialism had more to do with his disdain for vulgarity and the unwashed masses than with morality or politics).[35] To his credit, he refused to be associated in any way with the NSDAP, turning down the presidency of the "Poets' Academy" in the Prussian Academy of Arts and choosing to die abroad. He was also untainted by anti-Semitism, although it is ironic that his Jewish disciples tended to be more German than the Germans themselves when it came to glorifying Germany's cultural mission. The antidemocratic bias of his circle—which included a streak of anti-Americanism,[36] common to most of the sworn enemies of the Weimar Republic—doubtless contributed to the climate that facilitated Hitler's seizure of power. In the end, he was one of the many who were used by the Nazis and then discarded as soon as real power was within reach.[37] George did not have to reconsider the ramifications of his political naiveté, as he died before the fascist atrocities reached their peak (just as Novalis did not see the rise of German nationalism and Francophobia and Nietzsche did not experience World War I firsthand). Three of the writers considered in the next section did live long enough to engage in retrospective reevaluation.

One of the major reference points for contemporary Germany's New Right is the so-called Conservative Revolution. This movement, once considered a historical footnote to the rise of Nazism, has received much attention in recent years. The ongoing attempts to rehabilitate its representatives and divorce its ideas from the Third Reich will be discussed in chapter 2 of this study. At this juncture, a profile of four major authors will be presented. The term itself was first used by Thomas Mann in his *Russian Anthology* of 1921, after the struggle of conservative intellectuals against the Weimar Republic had begun. In his analysis of Nazism, Karl Dietrich Bracher delineates the cultural and political parameters of a world view to which a rather heterogeneous collection of individuals adhered:

> . . . the *topos* of the incomparable uniqueness and higher quality of German nationalism, its anti-Western mission in the battle against the supposedly subversive effect of liberalism and capitalism with regard to state and community, against miscegenation and emancipation, international socialism, pacifism, and bourgeoisification.[38]

These are the marching orders for the cultural variant of the infamous German "special path" (*Sonderweg*), which left its indelible stamp on the course of the twentieth century.[39] The outlines of this path were discernible in the late nineteenth century, but it was the experience of World War I that brought them to the forefront. In the course of that war, an extended essay on literature and politics was written, one that amazed not only many readers, but also the author himself.

When the guns of August sounded, Thomas Mann was a well-respected writer and financially secure member of the upper middle class. Up until that time, he had been known as the quintessential *homme de lettres*, albeit one who enjoyed a level of material prosperity rarely seen in literary circles. His emergence as a tribune of German nationalism — not the only one from the intellectual elite, to be sure — had two root causes. First of all, he was appalled by the vicious propaganda unleashed by the Allies against Germany. This propaganda in effect situated the homeland of Dürer, Goethe, and Beethoven beyond the pale of civilized (i.e., Western) society. Secondly, Mann's older brother Heinrich, especially in his essay "Zola" (1915), criticized the excessive chauvinism of the Germans in general and (without naming him directly) of Thomas Mann in particular. The Francophile Heinrich not only advocated the politicization of literature, castigated "capitalist militarism" and agitated against the tyranny of the "ultra-patriotic good-for-nothings," he also expressed his disgust for those "creatures of luxury" who live mainly the life of the soul and defined estheticism as "a product of hopeless times, hopeless states."[40] Such epithets were directed not only at Thomas: they were also an exercise in self-criticism, since Heinrich had espoused estheticism, monarchism, and anti-Semitism well into the 1890s. At the time, no one could have imagined that the author of venomous tracts against Jews, liberals, socialists, and suffragettes would later become the leading spokesman of the German literary left.[41] His more famous brother went through a similar (but not identical) transformation, but it occurred much later. On the way, he penned the *Reflections of a Nonpolitical Man* (Betrachtungen eines Unpolitischen).[42]

As a writer, the extremely erudite Thomas Mann had much to say. Unfortunately, he also tended to say too much. In the case of the *Reflections*, there are mitigating circumstances, however. This book was less of a literary exercise than a kind of exorcism. The author had reached a crossroads, and the inability to choose a future direction led to a personal crisis, one that was exacerbated by the war. Mann describes the process of writing the *Reflections* as a "more than two-year intellectual military service" (1). If he suffered ill effects from the war, they lay mainly in the inability to create imaginative works. He thus describes his long essay as an "artist's work" as opposed to a "work of art" (2). His thoughts are directed to a specific audience, namely the "educated bourgeois public sphere" (11), meaning that he is engaging in a dialogue with the intellectual elite of the nation. Most of this elite—including such imposing figures as the philosopher Max Scheler, the economist Werner Sombart, the philosopher and sociologist Georg Simmel, and Rudolf Eucken, winner of the 1908 Nobel Prize for Literature—was clearly, even rabidly in favor of the war. Thomas Mann was no different—or was he?

This self-described "child of the nineteenth century" engaged in a life-long dialogue with the icons of that era, namely "Romanticism, nationalism, middle-class culture and identity ("Bürgerlichkeit"), music, pessimism, and humor" (13–14). There are obviously some icons missing from this list, e.g., industrialization, the idea of progress, and revolution—and that is not an oversight on Mann's part: these are phenomena that not only do not belong to his world, but even militate against it. The opposing forces are masterfully portrayed in the 1901 novel *Buddenbrooks*, where the author's sympathies clearly lie with the older, humanistically educated middle class (*Bildungsbürgertum*). This stratum is doomed by the rise of the new entrepreneurs, the poorly educated parvenus.[43] One could say that Mann never truly accepted the inevitability of this process, even though he was capable of accurately portraying it. In the *Reflections*, he attempted a tour de force: the already marginalized "old" bourgeoisie was to be put forward as one of the bulwarks of the nation. Since it did not produce the weapons of mass destruction needed for modern warfare, it had to produce something less tangible, albeit equally necessary, i.e., ideology. The necessary prerequisite for this enterprise was the bridging of the gap between culture and politics ("Geist und Macht") in Germany (246, 281). To effect this, Mann pursues a two-pronged strategy.

On the one hand, he becomes a mouthpiece for some of the most distasteful propaganda and prejudice gushing forth from Germany at the time. He has no trouble justifying the violation of Belgian sovereignty (142, 178), he stands behind unlimited submarine warfare and has no sympathy for the victims of the sinking of the *Lusitania* (330, 417, 445), wishes for a Europe disgusted by "Negro-like sybaritism" (480),[44] deplores the influence of the Jews (443, 462, 520), recommends the feudal system (!) as an appropriate bulwark against the West (426), and even offers some inane biologistic prattle concerning the drop in the German birth rate as a direct result of the influx of Western "civilization" into Germany (577–578). Should one laugh or cry when one reads that in 1876, the year in which German fertility reached its peak, "there lived in Germany Bismarck, Moltke, Helmholtz, Nietzsche, Wagner, Fontane" (578)? Mann does not hesitate to leave behind the bastions of high culture in search of allies, as evidenced by his praise for Houston Stewart Chamberlain, the British-German advocate of Aryan superiority (554) and his multiple references to the middle-brow fanatic Paul de Lagarde, one of the founders of the Volkish movement.[45] It is shocking enough that Mann would lower himself to de Lagarde's level, but even more incredible that he would term him one of the great men of Germany, on the same plane as Nietzsche and Wagner (268). These passages can surely be regarded as the absolute nadir of Mann's career.

On the other hand, the titanic struggle against Western democracy and civilization that makes up the bulk of the *Reflections* is a half-hearted effort at best. Even though considerable polemical energy is expended countering the alleged "stultification" (Verdummung) of the Germans and their transformation into "social and political [as opposed to cultural] animals" in the process of "de-Germanization" (264), Thomas Mann does not really believe that Germany will win the war. He hastens to distance himself from blood-thirsty "war panegyrists" like D'Annunzio, emphasizing that, far from propagating war, he seeks to support the German people in this conflict that has become its fate (569).[46] (A similar mentality was equally alive and well during World War II, long after Mann had rid himself of it.) The fate of the masses, especially of the troops at the front, is not the main concern, however. The real motivation behind much of Mann's rhetoric is the fear that the coming of democracy will inevitably lead to a culture of mediocrity and with it to the end of the privileged status of the elites. When Mann warns of the demise of the "great man," it is significant that he inserts an excerpt from a poem by Stefan George in which it is asserted that the "noblest of the noble" only flourish in Germany (357). Those who ask wherein this nobility might lie can find the answer in Mann's vision of the peoples of postwar Europe. He imagines an exchange of material and spiritual goods among "the handsome Englishman, the polished Frenchman, the humane Russian and *the wise German*" (481; my emphasis). In this same passage, Mann also dreams of a time when his soul will be "cleansed of politics" (481). Now we have come full circle—back to the "nonpolitical man" of the title. The higher pursuits of the human race have been assigned to the Germans (actually: the German elites), and the nature and organization of life in society are mere bagatelles that distract them from their sublime mission. By the end of the *Reflections*, Mann has retracted almost everything, denying that he is a militarist or nationalist, even claiming that he is not a conservative (577)—after he has argued at length that conservative Russia (as represented by Dostoevsky) is the only true soul mate of Germany. At least Mann did not become afraid of his own courage, as the Germans say. After he had finished his military service with the pen, he shocked everyone and dismayed his erstwhile comrades by transforming himself into perhaps the most prominent supporter of the Weimar Republic.

The nature of this transformation is thrown into relief in the 1922 public address "On German Democracy."[47] In a preface written after the fact, Mann declares that he has *not* had a change of heart. In the speech itself, he repeats this claim, choosing language close to that of Martin Luther: "I retract nothing. I do not take back anything substantial" (829). He had of course already done so in the *Reflections*. (Perhaps he thought that very few Germans had actually read all six hundred pages of that work!) "On German Democracy" is dedicated to the author Gerhart Hauptmann on his sixtieth birthday. Hauptmann had received the Nobel Prize for Literature in 1912, and Mann addresses him here as a "people's king . . . a king of the republic" (812). This is not exactly what one would expect in a text designed to make democracy appealing to the German people. In fact, the main witness called by Mann to defend the idea of democracy is none other than the Romantic Novalis, a "special kind of royalist" who believed that there could be no king without a republic and vice versa (812). There is also praise for Stefan George, who has, according to Mann, transcended his Francophile origins and become a "purely national affair" (814). The Social Democrat president of the republic, Friedrich Ebert, is given the title "father" (i.e., of the nation), but there is no doubt that Mann wishes to provide his listeners primarily, yet again, with an apotheosis of the writer. Literature is, he asserts, "a heroic act, a sanctified life, an overcoming of human frailty, a renunciation of everything conventional and a struggle against it" (823). In a strangely undemocratic manner, then,

Mann has set himself up as a prophet, one who now must preach the doctrine of democracy, a sort of brainwashed Zarathustra. In this role, he actually does criticize Nietzsche: the master race, the blond beast, and the rejection of Christianity are now outdated (836). More significantly, war is rejected as a basis of nationalism. If the Germans are to save the remnants of their national identity, they must, according to Mann, posit as its essence not the "mystical-poetical" element of war, but a "cult of peace" (816). It took no little courage to utter such sentiments in a chaotic time, and Mann risked his prestige as a prominent cultural figure by doing so. One cannot ignore the fact, however, that he couched his remarks in such a way as to make them absolutely inaccessible to the majority of the German people. The symbiotic brew of Hellenic culture, Goethe, Novalis, Nietzsche, and even Walt Whitman that was to yield a "Third Reich of religious humanity under the aegis of Eros" (846–847)[48] could hardly have held an attraction for the disoriented masses thirsting for a way out of the post-Versailles dilemma.

The *Reflections* remain controversial to this day, and this can be attributed to a great extent to the international recognition of Mann as a central figure of world literature in the twentieth century. One observer believes that the book is not a document of the Conservative Revolution,[49] whereas another finds it very significant because of Mann's conscious effort to defend his conservatism while distancing himself from the "radical right."[50] The author of a monumental biography of Mann characterizes the "innermost essence" of the *Reflections* as "the announcement of the revolt of irrationality that was to hurl Germany and Europe into the abyss."[51] The debate will doubtless continue for years to come.

Another text, the one that contributed greatly to the popularization of the term Conservative Revolution, has remained relatively unknown, at least beyond literary circles.[52] It was thus something of a sensation when, in 1997, German officials from the Office for the Protection of the Constitution not only referred to the author of this text as the originator of the Conservative Revolution, but did so in the context of a report about right-wing radicalism in today's Germany.[53] They were referring to a speech entitled "Literature as the Spiritual Sphere of the Nation" that was given by the Austrian author Hugo von Hofmannsthal (1874–1929) at the University of Munich in 1927. Can one imagine the creator of *Everyman* and *Der Rosenkavalier* and cofounder of the Salzburg Festival as an extremist?

If one reads Hofmannsthal's speech after finishing Mann's *Reflections*, the first impression is that the tone and temperament are quite different. Mann is aggressive, combative, and irritated. A cultural manifesto is juxtaposed with a personal vendetta. None of this is evident in Hofmannsthal's 1927 speech, delivered just two years before the author's death. This is an end point, not a phase in intellectual development. Hofmannsthal, an esthete and precocious poet in his youth (Stefan George had attempted without success to win him over for his project of elitist cultural renewal), had gradually turned toward "the idea of Austria" as a model for cultural dialogue, cross-fertilization, and reconciliation. It has not escaped most observers that much of that "idea" was the stuff of myth, but to this day, many Austrians do not share that assessment. During the early years of World War I, Hofmannsthal produced some pieces of patriotic propaganda that were totally out of character for a polyglot reader and critic of world literature.[54] The outcome of the war signaled the end of the old Greater Austria—the one that he had hoped would be a model for all of Europe. He became increasingly conservative and resigned to the eclipse of long-held dreams. The only antidote to resignation was to transfer previous visions from the political to the cultural—especially literary—sphere.

In 1923, Hofmannsthal edited a *German Reader*, a selection of prose written between 1750 and 1850. At the beginning of his preface, he offered a justification for this project that speaks volumes about the construction of German identity:

> It is not insignificant whether or not a nation possesses a keen literary conscience, and this is especially true for our nation, for we do not have a history that could bind us together. As recently as the sixteenth century, there were no deeds and suffering shared by all parts of the people, and even the cultural heritage that stands behind the suffering and could turn it into a common possession is not a common heritage. The distant past, that of the Middle Ages, is too hazy: old fairy tales cannot bind a nation together. It is only in literature that we find our physiognomy. Behind every individual face that gazes upon us meaningfully and honestly, the enigmatic face of the nation appears.[55]

As so often in German[56] history, the clearest contrast can be found in France, and Hofmannsthal speaks admiringly of the self-awareness of the French, whose language has a legitimate claim to global supremacy. This was rather daring at a time when Germany's eternal enemy ("Erbfeind") was reaping the benefits of the hated Treaty of Versailles. In "Literature as the Spiritual Sphere of the Nation," the comparison with France once again is a central component in the analysis of the German condition.

Neither in the preface to the *Reader* nor in the speech does one find a call to imitate the French model, however. Just as the French have created a culture that is suitable for this "most gregarious of nations,"[57] a culture that meshes well with their skepticism and orientation toward the here and now (394), the Germans must strike out on their own. Their primary focus, according to Hofmannsthal, is not the national society, but instead "the refutation of the societal" (397). The "deepest of instincts" counters the mixing of the life of the mind and the life in society in Germany (395). One must keep in mind that this instinct holds sway exclusively in an elite of "seekers" who realize that Germany is a nation with a "tragic bent" (400). The impossibility of constructing a civil society founded upon instinct and the tragic apparently did not occur to Hofmannsthal. He puts forth Nietzsche as a prototypical seeker who rails against the superficiality of the half-educated philistines. The danger, as portrayed here, lies in the possibility that the Germans might lose their "originality" and their dreams (392).[58] If limited to the cultural sphere, this view might well merit serious discussion. Amazingly, Hofmannsthal goes on — despite what he has said previously — to link reverie with the political. An individual figure who emerges from the "chaos" with a claim to the offices of teacher and leader ("Lehrerschaft und Führerschaft") begins to recruit comrades for his "crusade" (401). This figure is not only a true German, but also an "absolutist" with a "titanic" project. He (a "she" would be inconceivable in this context) has a "dangerously hybrid nature" capable of love and hate, teaching and seduction (402). Anyone who has read these citations — but not the entire text — might think of Hitler, who was already a force on the national scene when the speech was written. Hofmannsthal does speak of a "prophet," but this prophet is also a poet who intuitively understands the "healing power of language" (401–402). That description fits a Stefan George better than a Hitler. The image of the prophet eventually gives way to a vision of various elite groups (together more in a spiritual sense than a physical one) who can see into the future, embodying the "[instinctually] perceptive, premonitory German essence" (406).[59] We are now on dangerous ground. Where might this intentionally irrational crusade lead?

If Thomas Mann sought to make democracy attractive to his conservative audience by tracing it back to Novalis and Romanticism, Hofmannsthal chose a very different strategy. Although he did not deny that both the Storm and Stress movement of the 1780s and Romanticism were important initiatives, he distanced himself from these predecessors. He rejected the "confusing hodgepodge of conceptual ephemera" and the "cult of feeling" and was especially critical of the "irresponsible nature" of the first Enlightenment critics (407–408). He called for a "stricter, more manly behavior" and declared that the new seekers were not searching for freedom, but rather commitment (408). Instead of fleeing from life, as the Romantics did, he proclaimed, life is not worth living without "valid ties" (411). At this point in the speech, the listeners must have been at the edge of their seats. Would Hofmannsthal announce a new political movement? Would he declare his allegiance to an existing grouping? In the end, neither happened. The speaker chose to forego concrete proposals, although it is clear that his conclusions could only appeal to one part of the political spectrum. Referring disparagingly to the "convulsions" of the Enlightenment era, he glorified opposition to the Reformation and the Renaissance, an opposition that he named "a conservative revolution" (413). Even though he referred to the goal of such a movement as "a new German reality," there was nothing innovative about it. Like Novalis before him, Hofmannsthal looked back to the medieval period for inspiration. In actuality, his antimodernist fantasies were so hopelessly vague that they precluded any union of culture and politics in the turbulent 1920s. It was left to other, more practically oriented Germans to use his terminology and promotion of German alterity as a facade for an upheaval that led not to the elevation, but the destruction of the old cultural elite. The case of Hofmannsthal demonstrates that encyclopedic learning and cosmopolitanism are no guarantee against self-delusion and political naiveté.[60] It is worthy of mention that this cosmopolitanism had an unexpected, but not inexplicable lacuna. In the 1920s, Hofmannsthal did write a series of articles for the American magazine *The Dial*, but he claimed at the very beginning of his 1927 speech that the United States was nothing like Europe. To him, it was an outwardly powerful young state lacking both an inner sense of spiritual community and a historically rich language transcending everyday communication. There is no doubt that an attitude like this contributed to the German elite's rejection of Enlightenment rationality and political democracy. It would be exaggerated, however, to assert that Hofmannsthal "popularized" the Conservative Revolution.[61] After the war, he was too isolated to exert lasting influence. It was a charismatic figure from the next generation who was destined to take center stage.

The generational dimension appears to be a decisive one vis-à-vis the degree of ferocity with which the conservative cultural critics attacked the Weimar Republic. It has been maintained that Hofmannsthal's image of his time was dominated by the impression that the individual was increasingly helpless in the face of entities and mechanisms beyond his control.[62] This may well have been a feeling characteristic of most of his contemporaries, who had grown up in a relatively stable world. The "angry young men" (once again, women are peripheral to this phenomenon) that followed were born into societies already marked by signs of crisis. The representative of that group who deserves our attention here is Ernst Jünger (1895–1998). Placing Hofmannsthal in a line that leads to Jünger is misleading at best.[63] The younger man's involvement in the events of his age was much more intimate, especially in the military sphere. George did not serve in uniform, and neither Thomas Mann nor Hofmannsthal experienced combat,[64] but Jünger was one of the most highly decorated German soldiers in World War I. He not only spent extended periods at the front, but also went on to mythologize his experiences in several books. These writings, from *Storm of Steel* (1920) and *Battle as an Inner Experience* (1922) to *Copse 125* (1925), *Fire and Blood* (1925), *Total Mobilization* (1931), and beyond, shaped his public image as a writer, even though many volumes were to follow. This observer has great difficulty casting an impartial eye on the man who demonstrated a keen intelligence, gift for language, and ruthlessness bordering on barbarism in these early works. Having said that, I should provide some examples of what disturbs me the most.

Already in the preface to *Storm of Steel*, Jünger takes a position of great distance from the reality of war—and not only war:

> Did it not seem then that life itself was speaking out of the confidence of its savage and visionary heart, knowing very well that in its more secret and essential depths it had nothing to fear from even the deadliest of wars, and going its way quite unaffected by the superficial interchange of peace and war?[65]

On the surface of it, this is just one more expression of the "vitalist" philosophy embodied by Nietzsche and (on a more primitive level) Ludwig Klages. There is one crucial difference, however: Jünger's musings were not merely academic, but rather a reaction to combat. As he goes on to say on the page just cited, "[T]he war, for all its destructiveness, was an incomparable schooling of the heart." This "schooling" was actually a hardening or at least a confirmation of a hardness already there. Jünger, like many (mainly male, one imagines) Europeans of his generation, felt restless in the "long period of law and order" and felt "a real craving for the abnormal" (21). Such sentiments were not foreign to Hermann Hesse, for example, but he chose to spend the war in Swiss exile. Others, like Jünger, sought out combat, only to die or to live to regret their fantasies. Very few men with Jünger's intelligence could look back at life in the trenches and declare: "What is more sublime than to face death at the head of a hundred men?" (25). There are many such noteworthy phrases in *Storm of Steel* that cannot be inventoried here. For our purposes it must suffice to point out that the final passages praise life in the service of ideals and posit war as "an ideal preparation for life" (282). Like Thomas Mann, Jünger asserts that "bodily suffering always increases the sensitivity of the inner being" (280), but unlike him, he pays homage to a "feeling that dwells in the blood" (283). As an aside, one might ponder that until 1999, the German citizenship law was a *ius sanguinis*.

In his first book, Jünger tried to depict "the experience of war purely." In the second, he turned to the "psychology" of war.[66] The essence of this "psychology" is apparent in the introduction and the first chapter—entitled "Blood." We are told that in war, man (and in this case, the translation of "Mensch" as man—as opposed to human being—is accurate[67]) makes up for everything that he has missed out on. His drives, no longer held in check by society and its laws, now become not only all that matters, but even something holy.[68] This sounds almost Freudian, except for one minor detail: Jünger celebrates the "wild orgy" of instinct, whereas Freud recognizes it as a distinct possibility and fears it. Freud feels ambivalent about the constraints placed upon individuals in the name of civilization, but Jünger absolutely revels in the "animalistic," the unbridled "Urmensch," the "cave dweller" (15). No Mann or Hofmannsthal could have written such things. It should be clear that the term "protofascistic" is meaningless if applied to Jünger *and* his predecessors. The older writers, for all of their patriotism, would hardly have praised modern warriors as "a completely new race . . . magnificent predators . . . the keenest juxtaposition of the body, intelligence, the will, and the senses" (37). When one reads that battle is "the male form of procreation" (50), there is no doubt that the zenith (nadir?) of irrationalism has been reached. Perhaps that is an overstatement, since there were many writers much less intelligent than Jünger who espoused such sentiments. In their cases, later enlistment in the Nazi cause was quite logical (if one may use the term in this context). This is exactly what Jünger did *not* do, and for that reason he remains a fascinating figure.[69]

Ernst Jünger died while this chapter was being written. There was an astonishing number of responses to his death, and the critical literature examining his life and works fills many volumes.[70] The image of Jünger—especially the current one—will be examined in chapter 2 as well as in the conclusion. He is indubitably one of the key mentors of the contemporary intellectual New Right. As far as the nature of that mentorship is concerned, he appears to play a role similar to the one that Nietzsche played for those born in the 1890s. His works are read, to be sure (albeit selectively), but it is his image as an outsider that exerts the strongest attraction.[71] This is a bit paradoxical, since it is practically impossible to reconcile the stance of the "great refuser" with enthusiastic participation in war. (Nietzsche, like Hemingway, tended to the wounded.[72]) The solution to the puzzle lies in many observers' tendency—whether conscious or not—to concentrate primarily on Jünger's *inner* life as an aristocratic observer, an elitist "Anarch," as he would say. His turn away from militarism, which most discern in the World War II years, was not accompanied by an embrace of democratic principles or any sudden affinity with the masses. In addition, he accomplished the impressive feat of concealing a strong anti-bourgeois animus within a thoroughly bourgeois facade.[73] In this, he was not unlike the chameleon-like François Mitterand, who congratulated him on his one hundredth birthday.[74]

Before turning to the present scene, it would be instructive to contrast Jünger with the poet Gottfried Benn (1886–1956). Although he was at least as elitist as Jünger, Benn made a fatal miscalculation, one destined to make him a fixture in studies of intellectuals and tyranny:[75] He lent his considerable reputation to the Nazi cause in 1933. Most literary scholars treat his short-term infatuation with fascism as an aberration or a misunderstanding that did not taint the core of his poetic production.[76] There is something to be said for this viewpoint, but by the same token, one could say that Benn also "misunderstood" Nietzsche as a prophet of pure estheticism. For all of his destructiveness, Nietzsche did believe that new ideals must be found after the overcoming of the old, whereas Benn was too much of a nihilist to believe in the necessity or possibility of such a project (except in 1933!). He also was capable of praising Stefan George,[77] although the later George subscribed to fundamental cultural renewal in a way that was foreign to him. The procedure was the same as the one he used when writing laudatory prose about Heinrich Mann: the early l'art pour l'art phase was posited as a constant, rather than a stage later rejected by the politically engaged author.[78] Such myopia had few direct consequences beyond the republic of letters, but Benn's blind spots or distorted vision regarding the nature of the NSDAP enhanced—albeit briefly—the prestige of a regime that he himself came to despise.

On April 24, 1933, not quite two months after the burning of the Reichstag in Berlin, Benn gave a radio speech entitled "The New State and the Intellectuals." The text was published the next day in the *Berliner Börsenzeitung*. Benn begins with a salvo against the "intellectuals," i.e., the leftist intellectuals, who are incapable of seeing that the new system of National Socialism is "anthropologically deeper," since it is making the transition from the "economic to the mythical collective."[79] (This is set up in contrast to the Soviet Union, which is condemned as a "tyrant state" (442), following a line of argument not unknown in the post-1945 period.) It is made very clear that the new state has come into being in opposition to the intellectuals, and Benn applauds that. History, he asserts, is not democratic, but "elemental," and it works by means of a "new biological type" (444). Nietzsche's largely symbolic "blond beast" has apparently become a creature of flesh and blood. This beast has no need of freedom of speech, for "everything that has made the West famous" was created in "slave states" (446–447), claims Benn. Our striving must be directed toward the "absolute" and the "irrational," that is, "that which has not yet been formally destroyed by thought" ["zerdacht"] (448–449). What is strange about such postulates is that they are juxtaposed with sarcastic comments about those who have fled the new state. These émigrés are portrayed as interested only in material possessions, e.g., villas and Mercedes automobiles (449). Benn uses a term to describe their wealth ("das Erraffte"—that which has been "grabbed" in a sinister manner) that was central to the Nazi polemics against Jewish capitalists. Did Benn, who was not anti-Semitic and even defended Jewish Expressionists against Nazi cultural functionaries, simply "misunderstand" the Nazi term? He seems to fit a disconcerting pattern of hyperintellectuality and selective perception of social reality common to a certain type of German writer.

A few weeks after Benn's polemic, one of the émigrés, Thomas Mann's son Klaus, responded in the form of a letter to his attacker.[80] The response was not another polemic, but rather an attempt by an "impassioned and faithful admirer" of Benn's works (74) to understand how a writer as great as Benn could succumb to the lures of fascism. As Peter de Mendelssohn has argued, when a major figure errs, everyone takes notice, and such figures cannot escape this fate.[81] Klaus Mann, for one, could not imagine that Benn, of all people, could make his peace with the barbarians:

> What could have caused you to put your name—that has been for us the embodiment of high standards and a simply fanatical purity—at the disposal of those whose lack of standards is absolutely without parallel in European history and from whose moral impurity the world turns away with disgust? (75)

In the framework of this study, it is important to note that Klaus Mann himself—herein very much his father's son—expresses his own sympathy with the irrational and speaks of its "seductive power" (76). Despite this sympathy, he reaches an insight that recalls the words of Roy Pascal cited above in the preface:

> Today, it seems to be almost an inevitability that an overly strong sympathy with the irrational leads to political reaction, if one does not really watch out. First comes the great gesture against "civilization"—a gesture that, as I can attest, holds a strong attraction for intellectuals—; suddenly one arrives at the cult of violence, and then in no time at Adolf Hitler. (76-77)

Mann pleads with Benn to divorce himself from "hysterical brutality," prophesying that the life of the mind will have no place in the Third Reich. He was right about that, but he was wrong when he claimed that those who did not come out unequivocally against the Nazis would "no longer" be part of the civilized world.

Benn chose to publish Mann's personal letter, using it as a platform to savage the antifascist émigré community. In his "Response to the Literary Émigrés,"[82] he prefigured the postwar debate between those writers who left Nazi Germany and those who chose to remain when he claimed that only those who have experienced "German events" in Germany were capable of comprehending them (239). He repeated his earlier views about a new man arising from the "inexhaustible fount of the race" and declared proudly: "Of course, this view of history is not enlightened or humanistic, but metaphysical, and my conception of man is even more so" (241). Incredibly, Benn attacked the émigrés in exactly the same manner as Thomas Mann had railed against his "democratic" brother in his *Reflections* almost twenty years earlier, dubbing them "amateurs of civilization and troubadours of Western progress" (242-243). Benn had great respect for Thomas Mann, but once again, he was able to engage in a one-sided reception of his works, ignoring the democratic shift of the 1920s. Despite his thoroughgoing antimaterialism and alienation from the masses, he even went so far as to proclaim that German workers were much better off than before, because the socialist project had been put into practice in Nazi Germany (244-245). The new homeland ("Heimat") was a bulwark against "the metropolis, industrialism, and intellectualism" (246). This was dangerous nonsense, but one prophecy did *almost* come true: Benn stated that the entire German people was willing to sacrifice itself ("untergangsbereit") for the Nazi cause (247).

Was all this intellectual and moral confusion the product of thought processes (muddled as they might have been), or was it nothing but opportunism? The "decadent" Benn was ostracized by the Nazi cultural functionaries in the 1930s[83] (he had already emphasized in his "Response" that he did not belong to the NSDAP and had no relationship with its leaders), and as it became apparent that Germany would not win World War II, Benn began searching for ways to change his image. In his autobiography, he expressed amazement at the fact that the younger Klaus Mann had understood the nature of National Socialism better than he.[84] Just the same, he pointed out that his 1933 essay, despite being "Romantic, effusive, melodramatic," contained issues that were still "acute" after 1945 (74). In hardly convincing fashion (at least from the perspective of this reader), Benn argued that he had not been an advocate for the Nazis but instead for something akin to the self-determination of nations (80). As a witness, he called none other than Thomas Mann, comparing his own loyalty to the German people with Mann's patriotism in the *Reflections* (83–84). There is some truth to this, but had history stood still since 1917? Benn portrays the artist and intellectual as one "drawn into the maelstrom" (84). This does not prevent him, however, from criticizing the émigrés (who were, after all, artists and intellectuals themselves) for not saving Germany from the "disaster" (90) before it was too late. The apparent belief that literary intellectuals could have preserved Weimar democracy would be comical if it were not pathetic. (Their efforts to *undermine* democracy were not insignificant, however.) Even *after* the collapse of the Third Reich, Benn failed to come to grips with his own irrationalism or the relationship between politics, economics, and culture.[85] Despite this, he was eventually given exalted status as a paragon of true art, one rigorously divorced from history, society, or any considerations not situated on the metaphysical plane. To be sure, this status was limited to *West* Germany. The representatives of antifascist culture, those who had been vilified by Benn and other "inner émigrés," were generally not welcome in the Western zones of occupation.[86] Many of them settled in the East, and some, like Thomas Mann, never lived in Germany again. They were the heirs of the "other" German tradition,[87] the one beyond the scope of this book.

Chapter Two

Long Forgotten, Now Feisty: Reunification and the Right's Quest for Respectability

After the collapse of the Third Reich, conservative writers found themselves in a difficult—and not wholly undeserved—predicament. Those who had supported the Nazi cause were banned for a time, and those who had remained in Germany but retreated into a tenuous "inner emigration" attempted to portray themselves as patriots and guardians of true culture. (One widely publicized dispute involved attacks on the antifascist Thomas Mann by the relatively unknown "inner émigrés" Walter von Molo and Frank Thiess.[1]) The German literary right might well have disappeared altogether if it had not been for the Cold War. As the Soviet Union went from wartime ally to mortal enemy of the West, anticommunism became not only acceptable, but *de rigueur*—long before Nikita Khrushchev's 1956 "secret speech" about Stalinist atrocities. The course of thoroughgoing Western orientation set by West Germany's first chancellor, Konrad Adenauer, allowed former Nazis to delude themselves into believing that they had been part of a crusade to save the occidental heritage. Ironically, many of the antifascist writers who settled in the Soviet zone of occupation, later to become the German Democratic Republic, were Jewish.[2] (Among them were Anna Seghers, Friedrich Wolf, Stephan Hermlin, Stefan Heym, and Arnold Zweig.) They had avoided death in the concentration camps, only to be declared enemies of the West by some of the same "colleagues" who had gloried in the prospect of an Aryanized German culture.

Benn's first postwar book publication came in 1948, and Jünger was prohibited from publishing until 1949, mainly because he had refused to provide information to the Allies in the course of de-Nazification.[3] A surprising number of "second-rank" Nazi writers (if such a term is conceivable) went on to publish in West Germany, avoiding any blatantly pro-Nazi sentiments. These included Werner Beumelburg, Hans Friedrich Blunck, Edwin Erich Dwinger, Hanns Johst, Erwin Guido Kolbenheyer, and Kurt Ziesel, who achieved dubious postwar notoriety by accusing Günter Grass of purveying "the worst kind of pornographic filth"[4] and leading a campaign against muckraker Günter Wallraff.[5] Even Hans Grimm, the author of the (in-)famous 1926 novel *Volk ohne Raum* (People without space), continued to publish until his death in 1959. A group of traditional conservative writers (e.g., Hans Carossa, Werner Bergengruen, Ernst Wiechert, Reinhold Schneider, Rudolf Hagelstange, and Gertrud von Le Fort) also formed part of the postwar literary scene. Since they wrote mainly poetry — the least-read genre — and prose from a religious or ethical perspective, their influence was rather limited. During the postwar reconstruction period, introspection and meditation about guilt and personal responsibility held little attraction. As I have argued elsewhere,[6] conservative literature was mainly ignored by literary scholars until the fall of the Berlin Wall. The young West German writers who began their careers after World War II by no means viewed themselves primarily as representatives of the left (even in the East, "critical bourgeois humanism" was tolerated in the immediate postwar period), but they generally had no affinity with fascism and cultivated a kind of skeptical individualism.[7] Affiliations with the political left were mainly a product of the social upheavals of the 1960s. Conservative writers who went beyond purportedly timeless ethical humanism or literary expressions of religious faith inhabited a cultural Diaspora for decades. When the Diaspora came to an abrupt and unexpected end in 1989, there remained only one inhabitant, none other than Ernst Jünger.

Up until now, we have focused on literary figures. Their *Weltanschauungen* of course did not evolve in a vacuum, as was demonstrated with reference to Nietzsche. One could easily devote an entire chapter to the influence of Oswald Spengler's *Der Untergang des Abendlandes* (The decline of the West, 1918–22) on Thomas Mann, Jünger, and others. The same is true of the philosopher Martin Heidegger, who not only engaged in a dialogue with Jünger but also became a major force in postwar French culture. Of late, an entire scholarly industry has arisen around the analysis of Heidegger's actions and thoughts in Nazi Germany.[8] The legal theorist Carl Schmitt, who depicted Hitler as the "protector of the law" and praised the 1935 Nuremberg Laws, and the anthropologist Arnold Gehlen, "the most single-minded theorist of counter-Enlightenment institutionalism"[9] as a crutch for fragile human beings, are significant figures as well. All four—Spengler, Heidegger, Schmitt, and Gehlen—have the status of intellectual mentors of the post-1989 New Right. This status is reflected in the pivotal volume *The Self-Confident Nation,* which will be presented below. One way to broach the discussion of the relationship between literature and other areas of human inquiry is to turn to a compelling study originally written in the 1950s and reissued after German reunification.

In 1958, Christian Graf von Krockow, who has since gone on to become one of the most prolific and discussed writers on twentieth-century German political and intellectual history, published a book entitled *Decision: A Study of Ernst Jünger, Carl Schmitt, and Martin Heidegger.*[10] Although this was a scholarly book, Krockow emphasized that the "decisionism" that he described had proved to be in error and should not be tried again (159). The "decisionism" ("Dezisionismus") that he found in the works of the imaginative writer, the legal theorist, and the philosopher is characterized by a separation from material reality, a separation linked to the "general disorientation" of the German populace in the wake of late—but highly accelerated—industrialization and its social consequences (the so-called "special path"[11]) and the lack of exemplary social and political models, especially after 1918 (5). According to Krockow, the nineteenth-century German bourgeoisie, incapable of obtaining political power comparable to its economic influence, committed "ideological class suicide" by turning against the Enlightenment principles that had enabled it to flourish (28). In order to demonstrate the extent of this phenomenon, Krockow points to the antibourgeois stance in Thomas Mann's *Reflections,* a work by an "arch-bourgeois writer" (41).

To illustrate Jünger's perspective, Krockow cites a phrase from *Combat as an Inner Experience*: "It is not *what* we fight for that is important, but *how* we fight."[12] A second, more concrete citation from the 1932 work *The Worker* (Der Arbeiter) provides even more insight into Jünger's thought processes: "The more life is led in a cynical, Spartan, Prussian or Bolshevistic manner, the better it will be."[13] In other words, anything that contributes to the destruction of the supposedly antivitalist bourgeois way of life is to be welcomed, even if it is "foreign"—in the geographical and philosophical sense of the word. Krockow discovers similar assertions in Schmitt, who views the dichotomy of "friend and foe" as the basis of all politics. The identification of the foe cannot be accomplished by endless parliamentary discussions; only the leadership elite can make that determination. Even though Krockow traces the influence of counterrevolutionary theorists like Bonald, de Maistre, and Donoso Cortés on Schmitt, he still seems astounded that a figure of such intelligence could describe dictatorship as "true democracy" in the Germany of 1932 (65). If Heidegger offers a philosophical foundation for Jünger and Schmitt, the latter two provide an "ideological and political commentary" for the philosopher (77). By maintaining that true history, or rather, historicity ("Geschichtlichkeit") takes place without regard for barren, unreflective everyday reality, Heidegger lends an authoritative aura to the real actions and decisions of Jünger (e.g., the apotheosis of combat as one path to true self-knowledge) and Schmitt (the exaltation of dictatorship).

Although Krockow does not fail to mention that all three thinkers distanced themselves from their earlier positions, he is skeptical of such self-interpretations. He finds no room for objectivity in the hermit-like later Jünger (112–115), rejects Schmitt's revamping of irrational dictatorship into an "enlightened, ideology-free" version à la Hobbes (106), and worries about Heidegger's emphasis on the special mission of the "metaphysical" Germans caught between the technology fetishism of the Americans and the social engineering of the Soviets (125). In the earlier and later writings of this unlikely troika, he discovers the internal contradiction of a class that wishes to halt developments at a certain stage and hinder the realization of possibilities that it had once brought forth itself. Krockow's term for this mind-set is "conservative revolution" (157–158). He states bluntly that this way of thinking is faced with two alternatives, neither of which bode well for the future: "ideological flight from reality" or "totalitarian terror" (159). The postwar fantasies of the self-proclaimed elitist Jünger are one illustration of the former, whereas the latter manifested itself—albeit indirectly—both in Schmitt's legal work for the Nazis (who, as in the case of Benn, abandoned him later) and in Heidegger's 1933 speech as rector of the University of Freiburg.

Krockow's point of view was not the only one articulated in the postwar years. Already in 1949, Armin Mohler (b. 1920), who was Ernst Jünger's private secretary from 1949 to 1953, finished a dissertation on the Conservative Revolution.[14] It was published as a book in 1950, and it is still, after two revised editions, the most voluminous work on the subject.[15] In the original version, Mohler criticizes the German intellectual elite for failing to come to terms with what occurred in the first year of the Third Reich, a time, he claims, when it was not possible to clearly separate good from evil (7). By this he means that the Conservative Revolution, although not without responsibility for what was to follow, was in the end distinct from National Socialism. One problem with this view is that Mohler cannot decide what the Conservative Revolution actually was. In the 1950 preface, he provides the following definition:

> [T]hat movement of intellectual renewal that attempted to clean up the field of rubble left behind by the 19th century and to create a new order in life. . . . [I]t already began in the Age of Goethe, and it has not been interrupted by what has happened thus far, but rather has continued on various paths. (8)

This is a vast canvas, and it is indeed stated that it is a phenomenon found not only in Germany, but also in other European countries "and even in some non-European ones" (8).[16] Put this way, it is simply a reaction to modernity. Mohler tries to be more precise by setting the French Revolution as the beginning point, but he must add that not all the counterrevolutionaries are part of his subject, because he is interested only in those who "attack the foundations of the century of progress but do not simply want to restore some Ancien Régime."[17] It turns out that the German version is at the source after all, not only because the intellectual roots of the entire enterprise are to be found in the period "between Herder and German Romanticism,"[18] but also because the German revolt has proved to be the most violent (14).

Mohler makes another distinction which has great relevance for the current situation in Germany: Since the Germans never saw themselves as a nation in the Western European sense—the term refers more to a "frame of mind" (seelischer Zustand) than to politics—the struggle against the French Revolution and the Enlightenment was also a struggle against foreign domination ("Überfremdung") and part of a search for a German, Central European, Nordic, or Germanic identity (15). Mohler does not seem to realize that he is walking a fine line here (like the one between the symbolic blond beast and the biologistic one): Where is the point of transition from exhibiting runic inscriptions to undertaking cranial measurements? His solution—a questionable one—is to limit himself to the Conservative Revolution as expressed in political thought (12). This limitation unfortunately makes the material much drier than it really is, since Mohler admits that parallel manifestations can be found "in all areas of life," including theology, physics, music, urban planning, family structure, bodily care, and the construction of machines (12). (How can one read this list without visualizing the Third Reich, with its German physics, German Christians, new cities courtesy of Albert Speer, and emphasis on physical fitness?) In addition, Mohler himself asserts that the *Weltanschauung* typical of this movement is not produced by philosophers, but by "a new type of author" who is "neither a pure philosopher nor a pure poet . . . a kind of 'poet-thinker,' just as his language is a mixture of the conceptual and the visual" (17). As we will see below, this title was recently bestowed on Jünger by the New Right.

To his credit, Mohler does not avoid an essential fact: The Conservative Revolution, this paradoxical movement of "intellectual anti-intellectualism"[19] driven by the "anti-bourgeois bourgeoisie," has few victories to its credit (19–20). Perhaps its most impressive one to date lies in its contribution to the destruction of the Weimar Republic. Unfortunately, or rather predictably, Mohler chooses to dodge this issue by stating that it is not the purpose of his book "to analyze the weaknesses of the Weimar Republic." He merely informs us that the subjects of his study did not take the republic seriously as an "independent entity" and at times only took it be to the last gasp of the hated Wilhelminian state (38). With such wording, Mohler unwittingly gives up any claim to objectivity. One further example of his affinity with the ideas of the Conservative Revolution deserves to be cited here. In the 1950 conclusion, which is not superseded later, he speaks of our age as an "interregnum" between the collapse of the previous unified worldview of prerevolutionary Christian Europe and a new synthesis that has yet to appear. Instead of terming this view (which he attributes to the Conservative Revolution) a hypothesis or theory, he simply calls it an "insight" (203–204). This is more than an intellectual issue, for Mohler has not remained in his study in recent years: He was an advisor of Franz Josef Strauß, the legendary head of the Bavarian Christian Social Union (CSU), and he has also written for right-wing tabloids like the *Deutsche National-Zeitung* and the *Junge Freiheit*. In a 1995 interview,[20] he openly expressed his sympathy with Italian and Spanish fascism. If this is the kind of new synthesis that he had in mind in 1950, his attempt to salvage the intellectual reputation of the Conservative Revolution was at the very least disingenuous.[21]

A very different and for that reason possibly more disturbing book was published in the early 1960s. Hans-Peter Schwarz, a conservative academic with impeccable credentials, produced a monograph on Jünger with the bland title *The Conservative Anarchist: Ernst Jünger's Politics and Cultural Criticism.*[22] This monograph is a prime example of the "Yes, but . . ." school of criticism. Schwarz examines practically every detail of Jünger's œuvre through 1960, and he makes no attempt to camouflage the most distasteful aspects. Right at the outset, Schwarz postulates that for decades, the German reading public had considered Jünger to be the "authorized speaker for the *Zeitgeist*," a role that he did not relinquish until around 1950, when the paths of the author and the Germans apparently separated (11, 13). After that time, he represented only those who stood in opposition to postwar (West) German society (13). In other words, he was transformed into a voice of the "Ewiggestrige," those who could not come to terms with the German defeat. After 1945, there seemed to be few prospects of reviving the failed project, so Jünger's stance became that of a lonely prophet clinging to his post in hopeless times. Schwarz speaks of a transformation from the "militarist activist" to the "liberal, if not democratic conservative"[23] (15), but he hastens to add that this transformation did not affect the fundament of Jünger's thinking, namely the "deeply seated enmity of the spiritualist metaphysician toward contemporary society" (15). This formulation lends almost a tragic grandeur to a mode of thinking that has in reality been quite calamitous in the context of recent German history.

Here are some of the characteristics of that thinking as elucidated by Schwarz:

1. Transforming history into metaphysics (16).
2. A turn away from empiricism and rationality as products of the hated nineteenth century (23).
3. A fascination with magic, witchcraft, and demonology as witnesses to powers at work beyond our normal perception (30).
4. Plumbing the depths of existence, be it in the ecstasy of battle or creative writing or in quiet contemplation (35).
5. Transcending of the intellect as the hindrance of the kind of holistic experience propagated by the Romantics (42).
6. The propagation of revolutionary elites dedicated to creating the "aristocracy of the future" (104).
7. The theoretical curiosity of a distanced observer (162).
8. Belief in a qualitative difference between the elite and the masses (185).
9. Glorification of "natural" life, small communities, patriarchal order and autarky (186).
10. View of history from the perspective of the ruling classes (220).

This is not a complete list, but these ten points lead inexorably to one question: Must one evaluate this worldview as mere speculation, or is one allowed to ponder its consequences for history and society? Schwarz decides, in the end, to evade this question. He claims that Jünger was basically a nonpolitical man who by chance wandered into the political arena in the 1920s (130). Since he is a "great writer" (126), however, Schwarz feels incapable of judging his impact on politics and society, although he does believe that there is much to learn from Jünger's errors (242). He is absolutely convinced that Jünger will have no successors, so he can strike a conciliatory note at the end: "Let's take him for what he is—not a democrat, but a gentleman with fantasy and character.[24] . . . One is learning and will learn to see him as one of the great eccentrics and outsiders of our literature" (242, 244).[25] Given this degree of sympathy for his subject, it is incredible that Schwarz dares to call Armin Mohler an "apologist" (242). His book is part of a pattern that can be discerned in German scholarship—and society![26]—throughout this century. If a controversial figure belongs even peripherally to the conservative camp, almost anything can be forgiven. Leftist cultural figures are by definition suspect and often seen as foreign elements[27] in Germany. The "Literature Debate" of the 1990s, in which the literary left was excoriated, dwarfs the controversies involving rightist authors after 1945.

A month before the fiftieth anniversary of the capitulation of the Nazi regime, a political advertisement appeared in the *Frankfurter Allgemeine Zeitung*.[28] The brief text began with a quote from Theodor Heuss, a liberal who had been the first president of the Federal Republic. Heuss is quoted as saying that May 8, 1945, was "the most tragic and problematic paradox" for all Germans. The reason was that the Germans had been "saved and destroyed" at the same time. After the citation, whose context is not provided, the rest of the text consists of an attack on "the media and politicians" who speak of May 8 as a day of "liberation." Instead, we are told, "the end of the National Socialist reign of terror" (this is substituted for "liberation") was also the beginning of "the terror of expulsion," new oppression in the East, and the division of Germany. These are not new themes, but the effect of the juxtaposition is to create a nation of victims. In the context of the advertisement, this is rather odd, because the purpose of the exercise is to create the basis for "the self-concept of a self-aware and self-confident nation," which the postwar Germans have allegedly yet to become. Only such a nation could do its part, one reads, to exclude the possibility of "comparable catastrophes" in the future. Which catastrophes are meant actually? There is no reference to the Holocaust in the text,[29] only to the fate of the Germans. Similar views had been purveyed for years, albeit mainly in small journals and newspapers seen only by the already convinced. This particular undertaking was clearly an attempt to get out of the closet and make an impression on the nation as a whole. The publication contains a list of dozens of signatories, two of whom are of special interest in this chapter: Ulrich Schacht and Heimo Schwilk. Their compatriots are politicians from the Christian Democratic Union (CDU), Christian Social Union (CSU), Free Democratic Party (FDP), German Social Union (DSU) (a new right-wing party),[30] one sitting and one former cabinet minister, a former federal prosecutor, active and retired military officers, representatives of the Germans expelled from the East in 1945, a handful of aristocrats (including Prince Ferdinand von Bismarck), and no fewer than eleven of the contributors to the anthology *Die selbstbewußte Nation*, edited by Schacht and Schwilk. Readers are asked to contribute to a so-called "Special Account for Democracy" care of Heimo Schwilk. Aside from the former East German dissident Siegmar Faust, none of the other representatives of the literary sphere have any name recognition. What is unusual about this action is that two conservative literati, Schacht and Schwilk, played a major role in its organization. This would have been inconceivable before 1989, and it harks back to the Weimar Republic.

This has not remained an isolated incident.[31] On May 5, 1995, another advertisement appeared in the *Frankfurter Allgemeine*, decrying the fact that a memorial service planned for May 7, with Christian Democrat Alfred Dregger as the keynote speaker, had had to be canceled due to "an aggressive [defamation] campaign by the leftist media." The five signatories, once again including Schacht and Schwilk, celebrated a sort of victory in defeat, claiming that one of their main goals, namely to break through the all-encompassing rhetoric about the "liberation," had been accomplished. They also stated that they had had expressions of support from all sectors of German society. Their struggle for "freedom of thought" would continue despite defamation campaigns, they assured their adversaries. The word "selbstbewußt" (self-aware, self-confident) is used twice in this brief passage. The group took an almost identical line in yet another advertisement placed in the *Frankfurter Allgemeine* on June 10, 1995. In this case, the bone of contention was the image of June 17, 1953, the day on which the (or rather, some) East Germans rose up against the Communist government and its Soviet backers. The sponsors of the advertisement, among them Schacht and Schwilk, called for the retention of a national holiday on June 17, railed against deserters and pacifists, and linked the 1953 revolt to the 1944 plot against Hitler. In place of Heuss, they chose to quote French historian Joseph Rovan, who believes that the East German patriots belong in the pantheon of the most important Germans. One new element here is the portrayal of National Socialists *and* Communists as the enemies of democracy.[32] We are thus dealing with quite an ephemeral entity here, namely a New Right enamored of democracy and untainted by any association with totalitarianism. Before turning to the hitherto most ambitious attempt to set the parameters of this project, the 1994 book *Die selbstbewußte Nation*, light must be shed on the intellectual development of East German poet and essayist Ulrich Schacht and West German critic and sometime prose writer Heimo Schwilk.

Ulrich Schacht (b. 1951) could probably not have become a "nonpolitical man" even if he had wanted to. His mother was a political prisoner in the GDR, and he was born in the women's prison Hoheneck in Stollberg, Saxony. (One of his books presents the life stories of women imprisoned for political reasons in that penal institution.[33]) The reason for her imprisonment was her relationship with a Soviet officer, Schacht's father, who was sentenced to hard labor and disappeared in the Gulag. When Schacht was seventeen, his opposition to the East German system was crystallized in Prague, where he witnessed the crushing of the "Prague Spring" by Soviet tanks. He became an activist in oppositional groups centered around the Lutheran Church, and his activities led to his arrest in 1973. In 1976, he was released and sent to the West after the government of the Federal Republic had intervened in his behalf. He refers to 1976 as the "year of his second birth."[34] His biography is a German story that would have been very different if his mother had lived in the American zone of occupation and given birth to the child of a G.I. Like many East German dissidents, Schacht studied Lutheran theology at the university. In the West, he turned to political science and philosophy. His writings are eminently political (although his poetry is generally not overtly so[35]), and they are anchored by a strong sense of morality. This is a combination not often found in the West German literary scene, except in the works of "exiled" GDR writers like poet Reiner

Kunze. Like Kunze, Schacht often extols freedom of expression and action with reference to the ideas of Albert Camus.

During the East German "thaw" of the early 1970s, a number of established writers felt able to take more risks with regard to esthetic experimentation and political/social content than before. In contrast to this seeming liberalization, the Socialist Unity Party (SED) gave no quarter to young would-be writers who were involved—however minimally—in underground oppositional politics. The best-known member of this younger group was Jürgen Fuchs (1950–1999), who was arrested after the expatriation of poet-balladeer-social critic Wolf Biermann in 1976. Under duress, Fuchs agreed to leave for the West in 1977. Ulrich Schacht was a known quantity to the Stasi (secret police) *before* he became a writer, so he had no chance of ever publishing in the East.[36] The older GDR writers who were allowed to leave the country after 1976[37] were, in most cases, fairly well known in the West, and they succeeded in continuing their writing careers. Newcomers like Schacht were in limbo from the start. East German dissidents of the stridently anticommunist variety were not popular figures in the West Germany of the 1970s and even 1980s,[38] and such people were more often than not simply ignored, in part because most West Germans were not overly interested in their neighbors to the east. (The gradual "normalization" of relations between the two Germanies and ongoing attempts at rapprochement were also a major factor.) To this day, Schacht, who has published several volumes of poetry and prose and has been awarded literary prizes for his efforts, is an absolute outsider in the German cultural scene. Like other former dissidents, he has been away from the former GDR too long to be a true Easterner ("Ossi"), and Western critics generally disregard him. Few of the leading lexica of literature contain an entry on him, most literary histories mention only that he was one of the many to leave the GDR, and his books are rarely reviewed.[39] One way to gauge a German author's standing in the cultural sphere is to examine the unique annual surveys of contemporary German literature published by Reclam. A perusal of the ten yearbooks published from 1988 to 1997[40] yields the following: None of these volumes contains a review of a book by Schacht. The only piece *by* him is the reprint of a 1995 polemic against Günter Grass and his novel *Ein weites Feld*.[41] In most cases, the references to him do not go beyond bibliographical information about a publication or a brief quotation. The high point is the survey of 1993, in which the volume *Die selbstbewußte Nation* is discussed. Even there, one finds such formulations as "author in the brown [=Nazi] net,"[42] referring not to Schacht, but to Botho Strauß. To put this "limbo" in perspective: In the ten volumes in question, there are over one hundred references to Günter Grass, and almost as many to Peter Handke, Botho Strauß, and Christa Wolf. In recent years, Schacht has been dealing with this situation by moving from literary texts to political essays (in other words, the opposite of the path taken by Jünger in the course of his career).

The development of Schacht's perspective on culture and society can best be traced by analyzing the volume *Gewissen ist Macht* (Conscience is power), which contains essays, speeches, and portraits of contemporary authors (mostly from the GDR) originally published between 1980 and 1991 in newspapers[43] and elsewhere. The back cover provides, in the form of two quotations, an ideological framework for these writings. The first, from 1983, calls for a nonviolent "process of decolonialization" in the "Soviet sphere of influence" as well as "documentary work of mourning" meant to demonstrate the necessity of such decolonialization. The second, from 1989, sounds a triumphant note: "It was worthwhile to believe in the power of the spirit and to deny reverence to the ideology of the status quo." On the one hand, Schacht represents himself as someone who shares a difficult background with many members of his generation, but on the other hand, he states that the East German Lutheran Church was the major influence on his life (30). The latter was typical only of a relatively small number of East Germans, and these people were one of the foci of the opposition.[44] (In West Germany, the—until reunification mainly leftist—opposition to the system was rarely influenced by the established churches, although the peace movement did have a spiritual dimension.) According to Schacht, in the case of any serious poet, "biographical stages" are the "fundamental element" of poetic existence (250). This attitude is far removed from the practice of postmodern identity construction or deconstruction popular in the West, and it explains at least in part the breakdown in communication between the Germans from the "old" and "new" Federal States. To the East Germans, biography—not biology—is fate. Many West Germans, especially those who strive to be "good Europeans," hope that at some point their Germanness will simply be overlooked.

Conscience Is Power has much to say about German cultural and historical identity, although contradictions abound. For example, Schacht writes in 1984 that only part of Germany has been given the chance to prove that

Germans can learn from the past and will not be depraved ("verworfen") forever (38). In the same passage, the GDR is seen as continuing the "barbarism" of the recent past, i.e., German incorrigibility and perniciousness ("Ungeist"). This smacks of the "special path" hypothesis, as does the assertion that for centuries, the Germans' longing for a "perfect world" (heile Welt) has lain at the root of their problems (59). One could imagine Günter Grass making such utterances, but there is a fundamental difference between him and Schacht, who does not at all accept the view that the division of Germany is an appropriate atonement for crimes against humanity. Such crimes, says Schacht, do not, in the long run, justify the perpetuation of Yalta (344–345). In itself, this is not an extremely conservative position (although it was considered to be so before 1989). Another word that Schacht seems to be extremely fond of, however, is a staple of German irredentism, namely "Central Germany" (Mitteldeutschland). The use of this word in postwar Germany—with respect to the territory of the GDR[45]—implies that there is another eastern part of the country that will someday return to the fold.[46] In 1981, Schacht relates the change in his attitude toward Willy Brandt's *Ostpolitik*—from enthusiasm to skepticism—but he declares in the same text that he is still a social democrat (25). On the same page, he uses the term "Central Germans" instead of "East Germans." Anyone who could do that was clearly still searching for a political identity as a West German.[47] His brand of social democracy (or democratic socialism—the two are interchangeable for him) was a throwback to the immediate postwar years, when his idol Kurt Schumacher combined patriotism and a passion for democracy (162). Schacht often refers to the Germans' "inability to mourn" (a concept introduced by the psychoanalysts Alexander and Margarete Mitscherlich[48]), but unlike the West German left, he links it not only to the inability to come to terms with Nazi atrocities, but also with the division of Germany after 1945 (169). His longing for national unity is complemented with a sense of homeland ("Heimat"), another phenomenon long ignored by the left (or rather, consciously avoided, since it was considered to be a smoke screen for nationalist reawakening).[49]

In general, the author of *Conscience Is Power* does not appear to be a candidate for later New Right notoriety. With the benefit of hindsight, however, one can discern a number of incipient indicators. In his rejection of literature as a vehicle for political consciousness-raising (e.g., 231, 240), he is a precursor of the "Literature Debate" of the 1990s. He advocates rationality and Enlightenment (58–59), but almost simultaneously believes that "myths and legends" can tell us more about human beings than any "exact formula" or "ideological definition" (221). He does not deny German "shame," but he characterizes it (years before the "Historians' Debate") as "historical"—albeit "fraught with consequences" (157). He criticizes the homogenizing ("nivellierend") effects of cosmopolitanism (134) and rejects an "aggressive feminism" that thrives on denunciation—an example of "dogmatic self-delusion" (275). Like many anti-Hegelians before him, he repudiates any theory of history that does not place the individual human being at its center (101, 108).[50] In an interview from the year 1990, Schacht even slips into the mantle of the prophet: "That which was seen by me as possible ten, five, or two years ago has now been *real* for over a year" (199). In the meantime, he has turned, with his compatriot Heimo Schwilk (b. 1952), to other possibilities.

Schwilk's background is as different from Schacht's as it could possibly be, and it reflects to no small degree the undramatic biography of most West Germans of his generation, who were never forced to make the kind of existential decisions almost unavoidable for their counterparts in the East.[51] Schwilk was born in Stuttgart, and he studied philosophy, German literature, and history in idyllic Tübingen (finishing with a teacher's certification). From 1972 to 1976, he was a paratroop officer in the Bundeswehr. Like Schacht, he has been a journalist at *Die Welt* for the last few years. Whereas Schacht works in the area of cultural affairs at *Die Welt*, Schwilk has been assigned to the "Berlin and the New Federal States" desk. This fits in well with his interest in the future of the *entire* German nation. He has written and edited books about Ernst Jünger[52] and published articles on literature for the conservative newspaper *Rheinischer Merkur.* The best way to familiarize oneself with his outlook is to analyze the 1991 volume *Wendezeit—Zeitenwende,*[53] which is a collection of essays on contemporary German authors. Most of the essays, written between 1986 and 1991, originally appeared in the *Rheinischer Merkur.* In his preface, Schwilk describes Germany of the 1980s as a "phenomenal success story," one overshadowed, however, by a diffuse anxiety (11). Normally, he says, it would have been the task of culture to thematize such contradictions, but instead, culture became "an object and playground of postmodern arbitrariness, for whom every truth is acceptable, as long as it can be marketed" (11). Despite the "shimmering surface" of consumerism, a cultural crisis could not be overlooked (12). Although the apocalyptic mur-

muring of established writers perturbs Schwilk, he clearly is most disgusted with "West German poet-dandies" who purvey cynicism and narcissism (13). In this, he sounds much like a young disciple of William Bennett or Allan Bloom.

The lead essay, "Mediocrity and the Culinary: A Look Back at the West German Idyll" (from the summer of 1989), dispels this impression immediately. We are very far from the American variety of cultural conservatism. Although Schwilk does express his disdain for the postmodern German retreating into his "Procrustean bed of enjoyment and egocentrism" (18), he bolsters his critique of this state of affairs with references to the *Dialectics of Enlightenment* by the leftist icons Adorno and Horkheimer, Hans Magnus Enzensberger's analysis of the "levelling out of values" in West German society, and Freud's *Civilization and Its Discontents* (18–19, 26). Heidegger and Jünger, as well as the difficult-to-categorize thinker Peter Sloterdijk, are called upon also, leading to a mixed message. When Schwilk decries the role of the mass media and their stultifying effect on the intelligence of the populace, he mentions not only the conservative—and sensationalistic—tabloid *Bild*, but also *Der Spiegel*, the famous left-liberal weekly read by the educated elite (20). Thanks to the "destruction of meaning" undertaken day after day by television (especially the talk show, an American import), all distinctions are being eliminated, including those between "left and right, art and kitsch, action and painting" (23). Unlike American neoliberals, Schwilk does not hesitate to indict the economic system as one of the perpetrators of this travesty. "Irresponsible managers" take advantage of the industriousness, decency, and solidarity of the workers, engaging in shadowy deals like the sale of poison gas factories to Libya and Iraq (19). The fetishization of an ever-higher material standard of living leads to "destruction of the environment and the plundering of natural resources," in a time when "abortion on a mass scale" is systematically destroying life (19). What is most intriguing about this philippic is what is missing, namely a political vision. The politicians are depicted as mere puppets of a system gone wild, who share their ritualized survival behavior with intellectuals (23). The economic elite are the "true politicians and social engineers" of the republic (25). It is an almost automatic reflex to refer to such people as conservatives, and Schwilk also does so—correcting himself immediately: they are actually "Besitzkonservative," i.e., conservatives whose worldview is not determined by a value system, but instead by the drive to retain and increase wealth (25). Without using the term, Schwilk has placed himself squarely in line with the tradition of the Conservative Revolution, collecting some unlikely allies along the way.

After this initial tour de force, the rest of volume offers in the main evidence for the theses put forth. A visit to the mammoth Frankfurt Book Fair confirms Schwilk's suspicion that, in this "era of decline" (Spätzeit, 29),[54] there is no place for serious conflicts, which might darken the mood of the visitors to the literary amusement park. One such conflict would be the question of national unity, and in an essay about this, Schwilk demonstrates how only a few members of the West German cultural elite, like filmmaker Werner Herzog, novelist Martin Walser (who is often quoted by Schacht), or Botho Strauß, dared to challenge the seeming impossibility of reunification. His own program for post-1989 Germany (the essay was first printed in the *Rheinischer Merkur* of September 29, 1989) is not at all what one might expect. Without renouncing Germany's Western "value orientation," he makes the case for a neutral country without arsenals of mass-destruction weapons[55] that could potentially be the main "peace power" in Europe (126). This country would also rid itself of something else, namely "U.S. plastic culture" (127). Cultural self-determination must divorce itself, however, from "saber-rattling visions of German power and importance" à la Fichte, Görres, and others (127). Germany could lead the way in two areas, i.e., "ecological solidarity" (beginning with a cleanup of the polluted areas in the former GDR) and mediation between East and West based on a "free life of the mind" (127–128). The latter formulation is taken from Otto Schily, a former Green who is now a leading—if controversial—Social Democrat. Once again, Schwilk endeavors to build (unlikely) coalitions for the future.

Two portraits of contemporary authors warrant special scrutiny. The first concerns the "neo-Romanticism" of Botho Strauß, whose essay "Impending Tragedy" was to become the centerpiece of *Die selbstbewußte Nation*. Schwilk defines Strauß's project as the construction of an "anarchic" sphere of literature in opposition to a social dynamic that aims at "the self-liquidation of the humane through its technologization and computerization" (141–142). This recalls Heidegger's aversions as well as the self-imposed isolation of the later Jünger (whose name is dropped). Strauß's often opaque language is praised as a counterweight to "jargon and party small talk" (142), and his return to the mystical atmosphere of Novalis is seen as a struggle against the dis-enchantment ("Entzauberung") of the world, a process that has made great strides since the time of the Romantics (143).

The question of the accessibility of a literature so consciously and militantly divorced from the communicative strategies of most "ordinary" people is apparently not an issue for Schwilk. To a certain extent, he accepts a division of labor in literature, and the "other side" is extolled in his portrait of Ulrich Schacht. In reviewing the stories in Schacht's *Brandenburg Concertos*, Schwilk applauds the author for not propagating a form of "escapism that would like to flee from reality to the realm of dreams" (176). The harsh life in a GDR prison is minutely described (and compared to the Third Reich), and Schacht's protagonist Bornholm ponders the nature of human existence in an absurd world — not unlike Camus and Kafka. Since Schacht chooses the parable as the appropriate form for his meditations, the reader may well relate them to similar extreme situations throughout human history. Schwilk clearly approves of this, and his approval is a sign that his conservatism does not entail a return to some imagined premodern idyll. This too is a characteristic stance of the Conservative Revolution (in an updated version for the 1990s).

To date, the coalition-building project initiated by Schwilk and Schacht has had, in terms of impact on the public sphere, one notable success story, namely the publication of the anthology *Die selbstbewußte Nation* in 1994. The reason for giving this title in the original German is that it has — as has been indicated above — a double meaning. In the first sense of "selbstbewußt," the Germans are to become *aware* of their true cultural identity. This is necessary because of postwar "reeducation" in the wake of American predominance in the West. In the second sense, the authors hope that self-awareness will lead to a new self-*confidence*, allowing Germany to play a greater role in world affairs, one befitting its size (the country with the largest population in Europe) and economic might.[56] This was regarded as a taboo until 1989, both because of Germany's tarnished image in the postfascist era and due to the desire to do nothing that might endanger reunification. The two editors of *Die selbstbewußte Nation*[57] demonstrate the kind of self-confidence for which they are striving by printing reactions to their book on the dust cover. The left-liberal camp is represented by citations from the *Frankfurter Rundschau* and *Die Zeit*. The *Rundschau* reporter speaks in a tone of warning of the "moment of self-creation of the intellectual right in Germany," whereas the Zeit commentator views the book as "a declaration of war on the basic consensus of the old Federal Republic." A reporter from Schwilk's *Rheinischer Merkur* declares that the book "deserves real attention," and the political scientist

Arnulf Baring contrasts the authors favorably with "lame leftist public opinion leaders." A blurb from the news magazine *Focus*, the new conservative competitor of *Der Spiegel*, expresses less the real situation than the aspirations of the editors: "The anthology *Die selbstbewußte Nation* is shaking up the German cultural landscape."

When the thirty contributors to this anthology are grouped together in generational cohorts, one finds that fully one-third belong to the "generation of 1968," the makers of the student revolt that shook German society. Eight were born before the Second World War (of these, three during the Weimar period), meaning that they have some direct memory of National Socialism. Eight (including the editors) were born in the 1950s, three in the 1960s, and one in 1970. The composition of the group as a whole makes one wonder just how "new" this New Right is. Another statistic casts doubt on the supposedly forward-looking character of the enterprise: only one of the authors is female, namely Brigitte Seebacher-Brandt, the controversial widow of the most popular postwar German Social Democrat, Willy Brandt. (The Conservative Revolution of Weimar vintage was also almost exclusively a male domain.[58]) Twenty-five of the contributors are West Germans (or have spent most of their lives west of the Elbe), whereas only four are from the former GDR. The only "outsiders" are Austrian Roland Bubik, who works in Berlin, and Michael Wolffsohn, who was born in Tel Aviv and writes on German-Jewish relations. The predominance of Westerners is a reflection of a general cultural trend since reunification: very few Easterners have a voice in national concerns. They are accepted primarily as "experts" on life in the GDR, not as fellow citizens from whom all Germans could learn valuable lessons. In terms of education and profession, the group of thirty comes close to the profile of what Fritz Ringer has called "the mandarin intellectuals."[59] They are all university trained, and the fields of study listed most often are history, literary studies, philosophy, and political science. Journalists form the largest group, followed by free-lance writers, professors, lawyers, civil servants, and teachers. (There are four creative artists: the dramatist Hartmut Lange, the poet Ulrich Schacht, prominent writer Botho Strauß, and the filmmaker Hans Jürgen Syberberg.) To paraphrase Ringer, their status is tied to their academic preparation or cultural production, not to money or prestige passed down through the generations. Their humanistic orientation, that of the *Bildungsbürgertum*, has been under siege since the late nineteenth century and is now relegated to the periphery of a fast-paced consumerist society.

Many of the contributions are reactions to, or continuations of, the polemic "Impending Tragedy" by Botho Strauß (which is reprinted at the beginning of the volume). That particular piece will be scrutinized in the context of Strauß's career in chapter 3 below. (Aside from facilitating a contextualization of "Impending Tragedy," this will direct more attention to the "other twenty-nine" contributors to the volume, who have, taken together, been discussed much less than Strauß.) A logical entry point into the complex of ideas and emotions found in *Die selbstbewußte Nation* can be found in the essays by Schacht and Schwilk, as well as in the introduction that they coauthored. The dedication, to the "patriots of 20 July 1944 and 17 June 1953," reflects the view of recent German history found in the political advertisements discussed above. At the beginning of the introduction — bolstered by a motto about national sentiments from Camus — Schacht and Schwilk provide a definition of "Selbstbewußtsein" that serves as a justification for the entire volume. It is, one learns, an inwardly directed process of finding the "familiar form" of human presence. Individuals who have found self-knowledge can master the future based on their origins and their present existence. The same is true for the "realm of experience and identity" of the family and the nation (11). Such phrases are hardly original or ominous in and of themselves, but this changes when they are tied to the Nazi period. Self-knowledge cannot be obtained without self-confidence ("Selbstvertrauen"), and it is exactly this that today's Germans lack. Why is this the case? Why are they different from other modern nations? The answer lies in the perpetration of the Holocaust, a word that is not used. Instead, the editors speak of an "evil reason" behind the destruction of German self-confidence, related to the "temporary, not lasting German transgression" (11).[60] This is a roundabout way of summarizing the "Historians' Debate" and the attempted historicization of the Holocaust. Specifically, the "transgression" involved allowing the "order-seeking longing for the metaphysical" supposedly so central to German identity to degenerate[61] into "unbounded pursuit of power." It is emphasized that the normalcy of a "selbstbewußte Nation" will not be attainable until the Germans attain deeper self-knowledge and through it "self-purification" (11–12). Now that the postwar status quo has been brought to a conclusion, this goal can be attained, assert Schacht and Schwilk. The manner in which this status quo is described makes it absolutely clear that the message is not directed toward the average German. Instead of simply saying that, in the postwar era, the

Germans were not allowed to be masters of their own affairs because of the crimes that they had committed, the editors state:

> With the 1989 collapse [of the Soviet system], this normalcy, via the irreversible destruction of the postwar status quo, which in turn was attributable to a symbiosis of alienation from self and foreign domination caused by the course of events, has become a historical basis from which one must proceed. (12)

Such rhetorical flourishes, or rather obfuscations, serve no purpose other than to avoid painful historical memories and give the intended elite readership a feeling of superiority. A call for "self-purification" is also much less disruptive than an appeal for regret and remorse.

With amazing panache, Schacht and Schwilk not only declare their opposition to the Enlightenment, but at the same time claim that the political clique running Germany has an understanding of "democracy and civil society" that is limited to staying in power and keeping order by means of increasing prosperity. Allowing free rein to individuals' "self-gratification[62] complex" instead of promoting "nonmaterial values" is not social (see the social welfare state) but asocial (12). The introduction contains no elucidation of these values, concentrating instead on *negativa* like the "hypermoralistic" mass media (Heidegger's "Letter on Humanism" is proffered as a starting point for criticizing such media), ritualized antifascism (that has also been critiqued from a liberal perspective[63]), and contemporary conformism (14–15). The final paragraph has no little import for the entire anthology, however. The two editors emphasize that the "time of German special paths" is over, meaning that the Germans can finally dare once again to go their own way (17). This could be interpreted as a rejection of the cultural and political developments of the nineteenth and twentieth centuries and an appeal to the Germans to return to Romanticism and post-Romantic critiques of the status quo as sources of national identity and spirituality. There is another possible interpretation, but it is not completely convincing. If the "special paths" are taken to be National Socialism and Communism, then the final paragraph postulates a return to conditions prior to 1933. Within the logic of the Conservative Revolution, this would make little sense, since both the Weimar Republic and the *Kaiserreich* are objects of derision, not idealization. The true democracy that is envisioned by the editors is thus not rooted in German political history, but in the dynamic of the present, the potentialities of the future, and the never-realized dreams of Novalis and his heirs. To some observers, this might seem exhilarating, to others profoundly unsettling.

Ulrich Schacht's essay, "Stigma and Concern: German Identity after Auschwitz," pursues an agenda that is not reflected it its title. It is primarily a condemnation of almost every political development since the French Revolution and a scathing critique of political correctness. In contrast to the calm, often contemplative manner of Schacht's poetry and the nostalgic sentimentality of his prose writings about "Heimat," this essay practically leaps off the page with polemic energy. The first sentence contains a key term: "media democracy" ("Mediendemokratie"). This is a system in which those who determine the interpretation of political concepts hold power (57). The fact that this is a view also held by many on the left does not seem to interest Schacht. For him, the domination of the media is simply the most recent chapter in the history of the "fallacious systems of virtue and salvation" that have attempted to achieve power by means of terror (58). Among these are "National Socialism, Communism, Ignorantism, and Costume Humanism" (58–59). The only one that is not taken seriously is "Costume Fascism" (a term borrowed from the writer Martin Walser), i.e., the manifestations of neo-Nazism in reunified Germany. It is difficult to imagine how anyone who would like to be seen as a serious critic of the first four phenomena could dismiss the latter out of hand. It is even more difficult to imagine a milieu that could bring forth the notion that the political class of the Federal Republic is the modern equivalent of the "Committees for Public Safety" from the dark days of the French Revolution (59). What but a raging persecution complex could lead Schacht to speak of "the block-warden system of West German PC society and its PC commissars" that is leading inexorably to "discourse apartheid" (60)? Political correctness has been criticized by many Germans as an unwanted American import,[64] but usually not with such vehemence. The use of the Nazi term "block warden" (Blockwart) also raises the stakes considerably: "PC" is depicted as nothing less than the media democracy's version of fascism.

It is problematic that while this type of "fascism" is placed in the spotlight, the historical manifestation is being "contextualized." As a German, Schacht apparently—unlike some of his compatriots—is apprehensive about undertaking such contextualization without outside help, so he uses a reference to Zygmunt Baumann (sic) as a crutch. The Bauman thesis is that Auschwitz, Kolyma (i.e., the Gulag), and Hiroshima are the triad of horror emanating from the spirit of modernism (58). Such a constellation not only questions the singularity of the Holocaust,[65] but also harks back to

Heidegger's warnings about the American and Soviet models. The problem is that before Germany can resume its mission as the "other" between these models, it has to be cleansed of fascism. To accomplish this feat, Schacht launches an attack on what he calls "post-German, national-suicidal historiography" under the tutelage of said "West German PC commissars" (62). Here, as opposed to other parts of the essay, he names names, castigating the "historical laboratories of Hans-Ulrich Wehler [and] Hagen Schulze" (61) for situating German identity in a community of culture and language rather than in a national state. (The positing of culture as the defining moment is also found in the myriad post-1989 statements by Günter Grass.[66]) The image of national suicide in the form of a verbal perpetuation of Holocaust memories leading to a permanent German self-reproach, if not self-hatred, is taken to its extreme in the assertion that this suicide is "identical with the total will of Nazi Germany to destroy the Jewish people" (63).[67] The use of the term "blindwütig" (in a blind rage) implies that both the Holocaust and its instrumentalization are pathological. Where, then, does Schacht find the seeds of a healthy German self-image? Quoting Hannah Arendt's dictum that it was not a German tradition that led to National Socialism, but rather "the violation of all traditions" (64), Schacht memorializes the representatives of the good Germany "who knew honor and dignity and connected them with Germany" (63). His memorial is a flawed one, however, because he forgoes any differentiation. One finds not only the idealistic Scholl siblings, Dietrich Bonhoeffer, and Georg Elser, the loner who almost assassinated Hitler, but also the members of the July 20, 1944, conspiracy. The latter group had, at least in part, extremely reactionary plans for post-Nazi Germany.[68] This could possibly be overlooked if Schacht's selection criterion had been simply resistance to Hitler, but this is not true, because his list intentionally excludes any resistance by German communists. It also will not do to misuse Thomas Mann as a witness (66), since Mann hardly shared Schacht's vilification of the Communist resistance. Schacht's final sentence ("Hitler is not a symbol of the German character, and Auschwitz is not the logical end point of German history" [68]) is thus less convincing than it could have been. It is one thing to assert—once again, with Camus—that each person has the "absurd freedom" to determine his own identity (57), but he who makes such an assertion should not assume that all observers, especially non-German ones, will look favorably upon an identity that rests upon a questionable reading of the cultural and historical heritage.

Heimo Schwilk's contribution to *Die selbstbewußte Nation* is quite different. Even though he follows his usual practice of drawing from diverse sources (in this case from liberal novelist Siegfried Lenz, sociologist Max Horkheimer, Arnold Gehlen, Carl Schmitt, and Peter Sloderdijk), the core of his essay is the attempt to analyze contemporary Germany through the lens of Ernst Jünger's *On Pain* (1934).[69] Jünger had written that of the measures of human greatness, pain is "the most difficult test in that series of tests that one calls life."[70] He had also spoken — one year after Hitler's seizure of power — of his time as a final "phase of nihilism," one in which most people considered the present order to be merely transitional.[71] Schwilk's "Pain and Morality: On the Ethos of Resistance" moves through similar terrain, with one significant difference: whereas the majority of Jünger's contemporaries may well have felt that change was necessary — although there was certainly no consensus on the nature of that change — Schwilk's contemporaries appear to fear the future, not welcome it. His mission is thus not to offer sustenance, but to shake his fellow Germans out of their stupor. This is anything but a simple task, for, as Schwilk readily admits, the avoidance of pain became "the tacit inner prerequisite for the reconstruction of the [German] state and society after 1945" (394). Here, as in the rest of the essay, he is referring exclusively to West Germany. Pain and sacrifice were the order of the day in the East at least until the 1960s, and that was one of the basic weaknesses of that system, whose people literally had no respite after war's end. In the West, Schwilk discerns an ongoing process of "pacification" that was meant to radically cleanse Germany of "traditional patterns of authority and 'evil' mentality vestiges" (394). The result, according to Schwilk, was to systematically strip the West Germans of their identity, resurrecting them as "constitutional patriots." This term, associated with Jürgen Habermas and Günter Grass, is an object of derision for the New Right. Its replacement of venerable traditions led, according to Schwilk, to "the most extensive neuroticization of generational and authority relationships" in German history. This in turn yielded a society based on self-hatred and material prosperity.

The true national apocalypse was not, it is claimed, really upon the Germans until the 1960s, when the generation of 1968 hoisted banners proclaiming the "total discrediting of all ascetic ideals" (395). Expert testimony is offered by Arnold Gehlen, who warns that societies cannot be built upon the pleasure principle. It is not immediately apparent that this is to be dismissed out of hand (a suitable passage from Freud could have been cited, for example), but when one knows that Gehlen published such theses as a sociology professor during the Third Reich, it is difficult not to have second thoughts. An intellectual discussion of asceticism would not be without merit, but it is instructive to remind oneself how selflessness and renunciation were manipulated by the Nazis for inhuman purposes. In this context, Schwilk's critique of German "self-diminishment" as an eternal reparation for past overbearingness (396) makes one wonder just how much German grandeur might be restored. It is not reassuring when Schwilk tells us, through the words of Carl Schmitt, that "only a political esthetics of the sublime that allows the citizen to transcend his physical existence and risk death" can lead to the discovery of the ability to resist (401). The type of resistance being glorified here is of course not individual resistance, something anathema in the Third Reich (whose laws were formulated in part by Schmitt), but national resistance. But what should reunified Germany resist as a nation? For one thing, it should resist an untrammeled eudaemonism (not just a German failing, we are told, since the "pursuit of happiness" is written into the U.S. constitution!). When Schwilk cites Bertrand Russell on the connection between prosperity and morality, one hears echoes of the pre-1933 German image of British materialism (395). Another bugaboo, possibly the ultimate enemy for Schwilk, is feminism, that is, "the cultural-revolutionary subversion by feminism" (396). The word that is chosen for subversion, "Umtriebe," sounds especially sinister in German. Once again, it is Arnold Gehlen who teaches us that it is the familial "instincts" of women that lead in the end to "a limitless expansion of humanitarianism and eudaemonism" (396). Gehlen's aside that such instincts do, to be sure, have their legitimate place in the family only makes matters worse. His, and Schwilk's, concern is the strengthening of the "counterweights" to such instincts in the realm of the state. If this were to succeed, then many of the problematic aspects of modern Germany would disappear. Among these are road rage ("the venting of aggression by the artificially pacified West German"), "Angst" and a "crisis of orientation," the need for psychiatry, alcohol and drug addiction, crime, vandalism, and, last but not least, abortion (398). Without denying the existence of such phenomena in practically all modern societies, it is clear that a system in which they have been abolished or at least greatly reduced will have to find a higher purpose. Some form of "venting" will no doubt take place, and in the past, authoritarian states have sought to find ways out of economic or political conundrums by engaging in armed conflict.[72] Can Schwilk truly believe that the reduction of consumption and an ethos of service to the community will suffice as bases for social cohesion (402)? The Greens have a similar vision (except for their attitude toward eudaemonism and feminism, and those are not trivial matters), but they are not burdened by a catastrophic realization of the vision in an earlier time.

The essays by Schacht and Schwilk have been highlighted because of their editorial/organizational role and also because they have gone on to amplify their views (in the 1997 book *Für eine Berliner Republik*, which will be discussed below). The contributions to *Die selbstbewußte Nation* are divided into five categories, i.e., "Identity," "Conflict," "Interest," "Resistance," and "Unity." Rather than giving each author equal weight, the individual essays will be viewed with regard to the "German legacy" described in the first chapter and at the beginning of the second chapter of this study. The section "Identity," where Schacht placed himself, is, like much of the volume, a mixed bag. Brigitte Seebacher-Brandt's essay "Norm and Normalcy: On the Love of One's Own Land" is an attack on those who would preserve the "Bonn Republic" and its mentality in reunified Germany. The reason for the attack is that Seebacher-Brandt regards the West German Federal Republic that existed from 1949 until 1990 as an abnormality characterized by "antifascist gibberish," "feigned guilt complexes," and endless "rituals of Enlightenment" (47–48). To counter all-encompassing German self-hatred,[73] she offers countermodels, namely the pre-1933 Social Democrats, the only opponents of Hitler who believed in political freedom (51), and the 20th of July resistance group, whose members were filled with love for their country (53). She constructs a kind of utopian anti-*Volksgemeinschaft* ranging from aristocrats to workers who dreamed of a Germany free of occupying forces, be they enemies or friends. Her belief that Germany wants to be a "normal" democracy (56) is overshadowed by her concern that her country has become too "comfortable," both materially and spiritually (49). In other words, she sees, with no little justification, that most (but by no means all) Germans are less concerned with regaining a sense of national honor than with maintaining their standard of living. Most Europeans are quite content with such a state of affairs.

Seebacher-Brandt's piece is rather pedestrian and was probably included as an attempt at coalition building (i.e., wooing the right wing of the SPD). The rest of the essays in the "Identity" section speak to the question of German *cultural* identity. Reinhart Maurer's "Guilt and Prosperity: On the Western/German General Line," is an attempt to revive "fundamental social criticism" (70) of the kind engaged in by Ernst Jünger and Martin Heidegger in the early 1950s.[74] Maurer laments the fact that talking about nihilism is "out," because the Western general line will have us believe that technology and democracy are "the solution to all problems," rejecting any other lines as "either obsolete or evil or both" (70). The Greens have often been targets of such rejection, and Maurer himself points out with tongue in cheek that all would be well if the per capita energy consumption of the "progressive countries, especially the USA" would be equaled throughout the world (70). He considers the Third Reich to be "at least in part a deviation from the [Western] general line," and defines postwar reeducation as a means to correct this deviation (71). If the Germans are ever to find a way back to this deviation (or at least to a new manifestation of it), they will have to leave behind their "enduring bad conscience" and find a way to a "normal national self-image" (74), the best antidote to an "irrational nationalism" (78). What is fascinating about this view is that Maurer calls for a reevaluation of twentieth-century history that transcends the "perspective of the victors" [of 1945] and takes both fascism and socialism seriously as attempts to deal with "fundamental problems in the force field containing the individual, community, and society, including those that liberalism tries to solve by repressing them" (83). This is quite different from Ernst Nolte's goal of explaining away Nazi excesses by seeing them as a reaction to Stalinism. Paraphrasing Francis Fukuyama,[75] Maurer states that the combination of liberalism and capitalism (he uses the phrase "pursuit of happiness" in English) will indeed lead to the end of history—the absolute end (84). Although Maurer calls—like Seebacher-Brandt—for a normalization of the German self-image, he actually strives to blaze a new "special path," one in which the Germans will have the role of saving the human race from ecological disaster. It is thus not surprising that he disputes any connection between Heidegger and Auschwitz (76), because it is the metaphysical bent of the Germans that supposedly makes them the strongest advocates of environmental protection.

Klaus Rainer Röhl's[76] "Morgenthau and Antifa[scism]: On German Self-Hatred" is a barely coherent tirade against everything from the Morgenthau Plan (which is linked to the visions of today's "fundamentalist Greens" [92]), the taboo placed on any discussion of Allied war crimes (94), the "thought police" enforcing political correctness in Germany (97), and "multicultural buttering-up" ("Anbiederung"[100]). The last point, the alleged (cynical) xenophilia of postwar Germany's ruling class, is a particular concern of the New Right. Although one can easily dismiss Röhl's potpourri, Gerd Bergfleth's "Earth and Homeland: On the End of the Era of Disaster" leads directly to the confluence of Old Right and New Right thinking. Bergfleth (b. 1936), a literary scholar and translator, openly embraces the "antimodern tradition of German thought" (122). He thus chooses to open with a motto taken from Carl Schmitt's *Der Nomos der Erde* about the need for a reorientation of human thought to "the elemental order of [our] terrestrial existence" (101). Bergfleth begins with a horror vision of a world in which the idea of homeland ("Heimat") has been proscribed along with "Volk, fatherland, and nation" (102). Since these have been replaced by "humanitarian dreams and a multicultural-criminal [!] society," the uprootedness analyzed by Heidegger in the postwar period has become much worse. Although this is a universal phenomenon, it is the Germans, robbed of their traditions, who are "broken" and suffer the most (103). Once again, we are told that it is the "leftist intelligentsia" that has sewn the seeds of hatred for everything German, brought about the "fiasco of emancipatory education," cultivated cosmopolitanism instead of love for the homeland, and thus taught a "disdain for the earth" (104). Utilizing the same phrases coined by vitalism and the Conservative Revolution and applied by the Nazis to the Jews, Bergfleth characterizes "the entire culture" of late modernity as "alienated from the homeland, devoid of origins and roots, enlightened, intellectualistic, and cynical" (106). The only way out of this dilemma is through the "antimodern origin" of the homeland, and Bergfleth locates this principally in German Romanticism (106).[77] Romantic "longing for home" (Heimweh) is defined as a striving to return home in contrast to modern rootlessness. As a literary scholar, Bergfleth unfortunately stoops to misusing etymology in the cause of national renewal: even though the word "home" is common to many Germanic languages, "homeland" (Heimat) is found exclusively in German. It is consequently suggested to the reader that only Germans can feel what it really means to have—and lose—one's homeland.[78] (In the *Reflections*, Thomas Mann conceded that Russians might have similar sentiments, and Bergfleth agrees.) This is yet another version of the "special path." In Bergfleth's apocalyptic scenario, a "major collapse" is coming, the result of a nihilism that threads its way through the entire history of the West since Plato, a history that brings with it a "devaluation of man" (113). The only solution is to transcend history, especially the modern nihilistic era with its "ideologies of destruction," i.e., "capitalism, communism, National Socialism, and liberalism" (121). Our sole hope is to renounce the "superficiality of the Enlightenment" and return to the "fundamental knowledge of myth" (121). Only then will we find the "future realm of freedom" — one that is beyond history and society in the "state of nature" (110). As one might expect, it is the Germans, or the "Nordic man," who can understand the "tragic elemental power" of nature (117). One wonders how Seebacher-Brandt's desire for German "normalcy" could possible mesh with such truly frightening doomsday prophecies, how August Bebel or Willy Brandt could find a *modus vivendi* with the Nibelungen. If Bergfleth's mutterings were at all representative, he and any followers that he might have would rate round-the-clock surveillance. Engaging in such mind games in light of twentieth-century history is either a conscious provocation or an expression of a truly eerie perception of reality.

A welcome contrast to Bergfleth's conjuring is found in Hans Jürgen Syberberg's essay, "The Self and the Other: On the Loss of the Tragic." Syberberg emphasizes in his first paragraph that he is speaking not as a theoretician, but as an active artist. His goal is to support new activities in film, the theater, and literature. The "new" that he is striving for is the rebirth of a truly German culture after decades in which the "ward" Germany was subject to the influence of the culture of the occupying powers. According to Syberberg, the end of socialism has brought with it a transitional phase in the old Federal Republic as well, one in which the hegemony of an imported Western morality is beginning to slip (126). On one hand, the filmmaker portrays himself as an artist who was criticized at home and supported from abroad, since the French and American intellectuals saw in his works—for example in the monumental *Hitler* film—the "German soul" that fascinated them (129). On the other hand, he sees the end of an era for those "official" artists who neither caused nor anticipated the events of 1989.[79] For him, art is not a mere provocation, since "esthetics is politics" (132). In other words, he still has a strong sense of identity as a German because it is derived from the esthetic sphere, not quotidian reality. This is why culture is paramount for him, and his vision of Europe's future is far removed from that of his co-contributors:

> If Europe, this stinking fish and maltreated, sore continent, still has — thanks to us — a center, then it is not its military might, not its science, not its economic or consumption-oriented mass, but rather its culture. Even now? It is up to us. (133)

In this vision, the singularity of Germany's tragic fate is the source from which an understanding of and salvation from tragic guilt can be obtained. The other Europeans (with the possible exception of the Italians, who are not mentioned), who feel superior as associates of the victorious Allies, have lost the ability to comprehend tragedy and existential guilt. One may take issue with this claim, but it is clearly on a different plane from the endless mantra of lament and self-hatred found elsewhere in the anthology. As an artist, Syberberg has the opportunity to exorcise his demons by providing them with a form outside himself, rather than watching helplessly while they devour him from within.

In the final contribution to the "Identity" section, Tilman Krause ("Inwardness and Distance from the World: On the German Longing for the Metaphysical") takes up some of Syberberg's themes, including the commonalities between East and West German literature. The sophistication of his approach is reflected in his depiction of Thomas Mann. After praising Mann for his courage in making an "Appeal to Reason" against the Nazis in 1930, Krause relates how the antifascist Mann characterized the Germans in his 1945 speech "Germany and the Germans" (delivered at the Library of Congress) as basically nonpolitical (134). The purpose of this reference to Mann is to demonstrate that one can oppose National Socialism without renouncing that which is "incomparable" in German culture, i.e., "German metaphysics [and] German music" (135; Krause is quoting Mann). Revisiting Syberberg's image of non-Germans who are entranced by the German soul, Krause provides an example from France: Brigitte Sauzay, once François Mitterand's chief interpreter, writes (in 1985) that Germany, once so fascinating and "magical," has become "banal" (135). The reason? It is the "normalization" of Germany after World War II (136). Instead of striking out at those who perpetrated this normalization, Krause admits that a distancing from "German obscurity" was absolutely necessary in 1945. Now, however, after the success of the Westernization process, it is time to overcome the fear of that which has been repressed so long, namely "that complex of melancholy-pensive introversion and turning-away from the world, which can only with difficulty be reconciled with the belief in progress of the rational social culture of the West" (136–137). The justification for such an undertaking lies for Krause in the danger that anything repressed will eventually return "in a destructive form" (136). To illustrate his thesis that the repression of German introspection never was completely successful, Krause praises three of its contemporary literary representatives, namely Botho Strauß, Christa Wolf, and Heiner Müller. The latter two are products of the East German culture and society, one that is seen by Western intellectuals as "premodern" (137). Wolf is defended[80] as a cultural figure who possesses traditionally German characteristics thought to have been overcome:

> [T]oo much serious pensiveness and complicated self-interrogation—very much in the tradition of Pietistic outpouring of the heart and of "Protestant uneasiness." Too much conjuring up of distancing and flight from the world, something unthinkable without the Romanticism that is today felt to be ambivalent. Too much cultural criticism in the garb of the ancients, something that is already problematic in Hölderlin. Too much reveling in the ideals of a fraternal [!] community (rather than society). (138)

When they are formulated in this manner, it is difficult to imagine that these characteristics could ever be cause for yet another crusade against the Germans. Krause is fully aware of this, and he takes great pains to emphasize that the presence of non-Western elements in German *culture* is of no significance for German *politics* (139–141). Let us not forget, however, that Syberberg *equated* esthetics with politics. With his attempt to separate the two, Krause is an outsider in *Die selbstbewußte Nation*. There is no reason to doubt his sincerity, but his presence in dubious company makes one think of Lenin's concept of "useful idiots." Most of the other contributors to the anthology are not interested in enriching German culture for the sake of culture alone. It is hardly fortuitous that the collected essays were not entitled *Treasures of the German Spirit* or *The Unique German Contribution to Global Culture*.

Much of the rest of the volume is repetitious, and many of the essays are not concerned directly with culture and identity, so a critical selection and summary will be provided instead of an exhaustive presentation. In the section "Conflict," there is an outsider somewhat like Krause, namely, Rüdiger Safranski. This literary scholar, once a highly visible representative of the academic left in 1970s Berlin (it is likely that, at least to a certain extent, his politics prevented him from becoming a professor) has written well-received biographies of Arthur Schopenhauer and Martin Heidegger. His essay here ("Destruction and Desire: On the Return of Evil") was a preliminary study for his most recent book.[81] The title refers to the repression of evil in the postwar welfare state, a danger already present in the nineteenth-century America observed by Tocqueville (237). According to Safranski, the events of 1989 and their aftermath have destroyed a world in which the Germans[82] and other Europeans were protected against "intellectual and material risks." The loss of such protection leads people, he claims, to take out their fears on foreigners and "here and there once again on Jews" (238). There is not an emphasis on a specifically German self-hatred, but rather a general diagnosis of "barbarization" manifested as "selfishness, destruction of community spirit, hospitalism, [and] consumerism." This is not new, but an additional ingredient—one which Tocqueville could not foresee—has been added to the mix, i.e., the "brutalization and emptiness" brought about by the media (239). Safranski may sound like a German Neil Postman, but he actually turns to the philosopher Kant for guidance. Civilization is not seen as an end in itself; rather, it is the ongoing attempt to "domesticate" evil (241). Kant believed that the possibility of evil was the price of freedom, but his successors—Safranski names Hegel, Marx, and Habermas and speaks indirectly of Fukuyama—viewed evil as something that could be overcome. In the context of *Die selbstbewußte Nation*, Safranski constructs a unique model, a possibility of a conservatism that does not wholly reject the Enlightenment. Although human beings are made of "crooked timber,"[83] they may still pursue the project of civilization, although there is no guarantee of success. Safranski, who once was no stranger to utopian thinking, now calls upon us to persevere without a gleaming *telos*, and his final sentence demonstrates the distance between his brand of conservatism and that purveyed by many of his coauthors: "We have no choice but to act as if God and our own nature wanted the best for us" (248).

Safranski's assessment of our present condition is the rueful reevaluation of an erstwhile '68er, and its contemplative tone is unusual in this volume. (One wonders why he chose to allow the editors to publish his thoughts, which predate the anthology.) Roland Bubik's[84] essay consists mainly of whining—about the way right-wingers are stigmatized by the media, about the alleged domination of the media by the left, about the secret satisfaction felt by leftists when foreigners are attacked, etc. His improbable vision of Germany's future involves combining a "Dionysian feeling for life" with a "society based on norms" (194). This would involve nothing less than fusing the two Nietzsches into one. Peter Meier-Bergfeld's plea for a Germany more like Austria is chilling. Some of the advantages of the system in place in the Alpine republic that supposedly deserve emulation are: prisons oriented toward retribution, use of the army to keep the peace on the domestic front, a legal system that transcends the "American rhetorical cliché 'rule of law'" (206), reverence for the beautiful (as opposed to the German "conscious cultivation of the ugly" [206]), a paternalistic, premodern, somewhat underdeveloped capitalism with relative autarky, the lack of pornography on television, the homogeneous (i.e., Catholic) religious life, the absence of a revolt of "spoiled children against castrated fathers" (216), a "healthy box on the ears" for misbehaving children (223), and so forth. Perhaps most disturbing is the talk of "Austria's mission" (226). Michael Wolffsohn believes that a traditional German nationalism would be "immoral," whereas an "inwardly directed one" is indispensable (271).[85] He is less worried about the skinheads (who are not particularly German and have no real ideology, he asserts [268]) than about the "global migration" affecting Europe and much of the rest of the world. In listing the growth of the foreign population in Germany since 1958—he calls it a "social revolution"—he does express relief that neither slavery nor the fate of the Jews[86] are conceivable today, although he thinks that it was "mindless" to have brought in millions of "Gastarbeiter" (269). In the course of his often incoherent essay, it never becomes clear just why this might be so. Ansgar Graw, then a journalist at Radio Free Berlin (Sender Freies Berlin), now at *Die Welt*, trots out the usual catalogue of leftist sins (the elimination of taboos, attacks on family and church, pacifism, permissiveness, etc.), only to make an astonishing proposal: "Those who mourn the loss of the organic society from the epoch before the Enlightenment will have to find a historic compromise with those who dream of the omnipotence of emancipatory rationality" (289). The original compromise of this type was of course attempted by the Italian Euro-Communists in the 1970s. What is astonishing about Graw's proposal is that he could make it after laying the responsibility for practically every social problem in today's Germany at the left's door. For Felix Stern, there clearly can be no compromise with his chosen antagonists, i.e., feminists. His title ("Feminism and Apartheid") and first paragraph leave no doubt about that, since he begins with phrases like "sexist virus" and "feminist dead end" (291). Stern fears a "totalitarian language-cleansing" led by feminist linguists, the utilization of sexual abuse charges as "divorce weapons" (he longs for simpler times, when "a little flirt" in the office was taken care of unbureaucratically with a box on the ears [297]), and most of all, "the total separation of men and women"—the "feminist apartheid" (306). Anyone familiar with contemporary Germany knows the feminist movement has made rather modest strides there in comparison to conditions in some other

European countries, not to speak of the U.S. (this is especially true in the areas of work and child care).

Another author who analyzes feminism is the historian Ernst Nolte, who triggered the "Historians' Debate." Much of Nolte's essay is taken up with a reprise of his hypothesis about Italian fascism and National Socialism as (necessary and understandable) reactions to Soviet communism, but there are other aspects as well. Nolte, who portrays himself as a "moderate conservative" (160), does not fear a rebirth of fascism in Europe (if it were to reappear, he predicts, it would be in the U.S. or Russia [161]), but he believes that "liberism," a degenerate form of liberalism, could well destroy nation-states, cause a "gigantic shift in population," and even wipe out the human race (160–161). One effective countermeasure to "consumerism" and "hedonism" would be the conscious choice of well-educated people to dedicate a decade of their lives raising children (and sharing "the burdens and the joys" as equally as possible). This would, he says, not only be beneficial to the environment, it would also realize "the rational and timely core of feminism" (161). If this sounds uncharacteristic of Nolte, widely considered to be one of the most conservative German historians, one should not ignore certain signals embedded in the essay. Nolte discovers "strong leftist features" in the NSDAP (153), and associates both Ludwig Klages and the Nazis with "Green" thinking (159). He intimates that the best ideas of the left will only be realized if put into practice by the responsible right. This is far removed from the compromise proposed by Graw. As a footnote to the Nolte essay, it is not surprising that similar ideas about the relationship of left and right are found in the piece by Rainer Zitelmann,[87] a journalist and historian who is often associated with Nolte. Zitelmann makes the case for a "democratic right" distinct from the "conformist niche conservatives" and the "antidemocratic ghetto[ized] right" (172). This implies that the German government led by Christian Democrat Helmut Kohl[88] from 1982 to 1998 was not a government of the right. Zitelmann in fact uses the word "liberal conservative"[89] to describe this government. For American readers, it is interesting to hear that it takes some "gumption" to say openly that one sympathizes with the right in Germany, whereas one supposedly seldom hears people deny that they are on the left (164). In the world of American culture, it is none other than the "L word" that is rarely heard in public. Postwar reeducation has apparently been, at least when viewed from Zitelmann's perspective, all too successful.

The section "[National] Interest" is not of great relevance here, although there are some notable statements to be found there. Controversial historian Karlheinz Weissmann tells us that "civil society" demands at once too much and too little from human beings, who are not completely rational and are tied to historical tradition (313). If the latter were still quite true, there would have been no reason to publish *Die selbstbewußte Nation*. Former air force officer and former Green Alfred Mechtersheimer characterizes the same Rainer Zitelmann who wishes to construct a "democratic right" as a "leftist" with an enlightened view of nationalism (346). Mechtersheimer also predicts that in the German future, there will be a collision between the "antinationalism of the elites and the nationalism of the masses" (363).[90] The section "Resistance" contains the only essay that offers any criticism of Botho Strauß. Hartmut Lange, a well-known dramatist who left the GDR in 1965, praises the "courageous and very unusual food for thought" found in *Impending Tragedy*, but he warns that Strauß is "playing with fire" (433). He reminds him that dictatorships are more opposed to art (Strauß's raison d'être) than mass democracies with their "anything goes" attitude.[91] Lange's essay is also notable for its separation of Jünger and Heidegger. Citing "Over the Line," Lange claims that Jünger was wrong to think that nihilism could be overcome by positing a new meaning for life ("Sinnstiftung"), whereas Heidegger recognized correctly that nihilism is "immanent" to human beings (442). Lange proceeds to assert that the terms "left" and "right" are irrelevant to culture, pointing to Heidegger's influence on Sartre and Camus (443). This is a line of thinking (one foreign to many of the contributors) that is taken up in the section "Epilogue," which was added after the first edition of the anthology.

Bavarian politician Peter Gauweiler, generally considered to be a representative of the right wing of the CSU, criticizes not the Enlightenment, but its "bending out of shape" and "falsification" at the hands of the left (476–477). He ends his essay not with references to Heidegger, but to Karl Jaspers, Cicero (whose speeches against Catilina are quoted in Latin), and Orwell's *1984*. This attempt at bridge building is also the thrust of Heimo Schwilk's section of the epilogue, although his chosen title, "Mindless Pyromaniacs," suggests something quite different. He does begin with a tirade against the "denunciation" launched against *Die selbstbewußte Nation* by the leftist media, mocking leftists who hold up the banner of Habermasian "nonhegemonic discourse" while condemning those who do not share their views (465–466). He

attests that there is not even a trace of "salon fascism" in his anthology (467).
On the contrary: The book is an illustration of the "freedom of thought" /¹⁰
long opposed by the left (468). He even provides a reading list for those who
would dare to follow him:

> a knowledge of critical theory [i.e., the Frankfurt school], Bloch's utopianism,
> Benjamin's spiritual materialism, Hannah Arendt's analysis of totalitarianism,
> Heidegger's existential ontology, Carl Schmitt's theory of the state, and Ernst
> Jünger's esthetics of the miraculous. (468)

Even more significant than this list is his own comment on it: "As necessary
as a polarization is in the political sphere, it is nonsense in the esthetic
sphere. There are no leftist or rightist metaphors, only good ones and bad
ones" (468). Two things must be said about this dictum: First, it will never
be possible to completely separate politics from culture—especially in Europe, where culture is (still) often highly subsidized—although such a separation has often been posited by both conservative social elites and
conservative artists. (Can one in all good conscience initiate legal proceed-
ings against a Hamsun or Pound?) One should not forget that many of the
same critics—and politicians—who readily accepted the moral authority of
the anti-Soviet[92] Solzhenitsyn were disinclined to accept the possibility of
such a phenomenon (Böll or Grass, for example) vis-à-vis Western society
Second, Schwilk's words are clearly directed to an extremely small elite.
Very few Germans have had the intellectual preparation necessary to tackle
the kind of texts that Schwilk recommends. If the target group consisted exclusively of conservative intellectuals, the number would be even smaller.
One has the impression that the editors of *Die selbstbewußte Nation* feel isolated from the mainstream, and that they have realized the necessity of
reaching out to sectors of (educated) society normally averse to their
Weltanschauung. Only time will tell if their efforts will be crowned with a
modicum of success.

This is not the place to survey the responses to the publication of *Die
selbstbewußte Nation*. Most of them concentrate upon the essay by Botho
Strauß, to which we will soon turn. It would be instructive, however to take
a brief look at the review published in *Der Spiegel*, probably the magazine
most vilified by the intellectual New Right. The title itself is, unfortunately,
an example of the "bending" spoken of by Gauweiler: "Teachers of Hate."[93]
The quotation marks in the title, easily overlooked by the casual reader, refer
to words—quoted in the last part of the review—written by the problematic

Gerd Bergfleth. They refer not to the authors of *Die selbstbewußte Nation*, but rather to leftist intellectuals, who purportedly sow the seeds of (self-) hatred against everything German (104). After this citational sleight of hand, *Spiegel* journalist Martin Doerry uses attributives like these to describe the contributors and contributions to the volume: "scurrilous," "a flood of brownish [i.e., protofascist] prose," "growing enthusiasm for war," and "duds."[94] Any serious analysis of *Die selbstbewußte Nation* must come to the conclusion that the authors are an extremely diverse group and that the views expounded are often contradictory. The harried reader of a newsweekly may not be interested in such fine distinctions, and the editors of the weekly itself are obviously not. Why is this significant? The reason is that very few people have seen lengthy reviews of the anthology, but over a million at least cast a glance at the polemic in *Der Spiegel*. Such are the vagaries of the free and open public sphere.

Three years after their attempt at coalition building,[95] and two years after their spectacular newspaper advertisements,[96] Ulrich Schacht and Heimo Schwilk struck out on their own, publishing a book in tandem for the first time. The work is entitled *Für eine Berliner Republik* (*For a Berlin Republic*), and it contains, as the subtitle informs us, "polemics, speeches, [and] essays after 1989."[97] Only one of the pieces had not been previously published (at least in part), and two are reprints from *Die selbstbewußte Nation*, i.e., Schacht's "Stigma and Tribulation" and Schwilk's "Pain and Morality." No fewer than ten other contributions appeared in the rightist journal *Gegengift* (*Antidote*), which leads one to believe that the authors have come to the conclusion that publication in peripheral journals is not the way to reach one's intended audience. The title refers to the plan to move the German central government from Bonn to Berlin, a move seen by many as a symbolic gesture uniting the old and new member states of the Federal Republic. The essays in *Die selbstbewußte Nation* written by East Germans (and not introduced in this study up until now) demonstrate just how difficult this unifying process might be. Steffen Heitmann, an unsuccessful candidate for federal president in 1993, laments the fact that the East German "revolution" — a term that many would not use without qualifications — has lost its original impetus, which was a "moral" one (450, 447). Having said this, Heitmann has no qualms about citing a polemic by Hans-Dietrich Sander (for Rainer Zitelmann, a representative of the "antidemocratic right" [171]) and then refusing to make a moral judgment about Sander's views. Among the views cited by Heitmann are the depiction of National Socialism as the "failed attempt to liberate at least the Germans from the rule of modernity," the characterization of the Holocaust as "an interlude of unaccustomed brutality for the Germans, for Jews one grisly act of the normalcy of their history," and the "oriental rationalism" of the "assimilated Jews" as the "predecessor of modernity" (435). When Heitmann concludes that "evil is lurking in human beings," that we must thus avoid political "extremes" and preserve the "center" (454–455), then it is clear that his idea of the center is actually somewhere on the right. The essay by former GDR dissident Wolfgang Templin illustrates the tenuous position of oppositional figures from the East who attempt to speak to the entire nation from a position of moral superiority. In the former West Germany, Templin sees an unlikely alliance of '68er leftists and "increasingly unprincipled conservatives" who failed to confront the GDR dictatorship, choosing instead a problematic policy of détente (458).[98] He would like to see a second Historians' Debate, one concentrating this time not on the Third Reich, but on the image of the GDR (459–460). The fundamental problem with his perspective is that neither the majority of Germans nor most non-Germans would place the character and deeds of the "two German dictatorships" on the same plane. Templin seems to acknowledge this when he calls those who *do* share his view a "little band" (462).[99] These are treacherous waters. How are they navigated by the East/West German Schacht and the West German Schwilk in *For a Berlin Republic?*

The lengthy preface written by the two authors gives more than a few hints of what is to come. Before they begin to speak themselves, they attempt to endow their enterprise with the aura of truth-seeking by providing, yet again, a motto from Albert Camus. Camus assures us that the terms "left" or "right" have nothing to do with the verity of a thought and adds that he would be on the right if it seemed to him that truth could be found there. These words are in themselves not without contradictions, but what follows is much worse. After preparing the reader for a nonideological approach, Schacht and Schwilk immediately launch into a polemic against the left. In their view, 1968 was "the beginning of the wanton destruction" of the "political-moral standards" found in the West German constitution (8). In the meantime, they assert, Germany has become "principally and habitually a republic of the '68ers" (9). This phrase will perhaps have the unintended effect of offering a measure of solace to the former student activists who have long since resigned themselves to failure or cynically made their peace with the system. What the authors are in effect saying is that official party politics is absolutely irrelevant, or rather, that the then-reigning Christian Democrats are no less than puppets of the radical left. Although Helmut Kohl is given his due for facilitating reunification, he is also accused of "doing the business of the social liberalism inspired by neo-Marxism and hyper-egotism" (a puzzling juxtaposition, that) and allowing the dissipation of a state sovereignty that had just been recovered (11). In their eyes, Germany is a country where a whole catalogue of horrors makes everyday life practically unbearable. These include crime, limitless self-absorption, political correctness boosted by the mass media, abortion, homosexual marriages, the suicidal abolition of the deutsche mark, pacifistic ideologies, multiethnic clichés, and a politicized legal system. (To express the nature of the latter, a new word is imported from the U.S.: "Simpsonization" [Simpsonisierung] [10].) Even the ancient foe west of the Rhine is resurrected: The French hope to tame the Germans by stripping them of their economic might in the dark corridors of European bureaucracy (12). These present problems are magnified by the past, since German self-hatred is fueled by "campaign-like, ritualized [pre-]occupation with the Third Reich's murder of European Jews" (12). The impersonal formulation ("Third Reich") is immediately dropped in favor of a reference to individual murderers, who are "numerous Germans, but also foreign secret and special policemen, lawyers, and military men acting for German National Socialist politicians" (12–13). In the third paragraph following this formulation, the authors criticize Germany's "destructive immigration policies" and warn: "Whoever is not ready to preserve cultural hegemony in his own country and to undertake the assimilation of immigrants on this basis will also in the future forfeit his own identity" (13). There are ethnic enclaves—some of them quite large—in German cities (at least in the former West Germany), but these are not the places where most Germans live and work. To deny the still-overwhelming Germanness of the reunified country is to have a distorted perception of social reality or to engage in demagoguery. (It goes without saying that Germans of this bent have not a few counterparts in the United States.) One might also ask just what it means to maintain "cultural hegemony" at a time when the habits and lifestyles of the Germans themselves—see the *Excursus* below—are rapidly changing.

In *Die selbstbewußte Nation*, literature did not play a pivotal role, but it had an overarching presence in the form of Botho Strauß's essay "Impending Tragedy." Strauß's canonization of Heidegger and Jünger as "poet-philosophers" (28) was meant to provide legitimization for his own prophecies, and other contributors, including the editors, clearly accepted the significance of prophetic dicta from the mouths of poets. In *For a Berlin Republic*, the emphasis has changed from the past to the future. Now that the historical lineage of the New Right has been traced, it is no longer necessary to dwell upon it. Not only Heidegger and Jünger, but also Gehlen, Schmitt, and Spengler are now peripheral figures. There is one intriguing reference to the literary background, however. In his essay against the project of European integration, Schwilk leaves no doubt that, although he is opposed to a political/bureaucratic Europe, he is very much in favor of a metaphysical Europe representing venerable traditions. To illustrate this viewpoint, he cites both Novalis's *Christendom or Europe* and Jünger's 1944 manifesto *Peace*. His understanding of this tradition in the present context is that Europe must be grounded on values and must also insure that its market economy take "humane and social standards" into account (74). Schacht and Schwilk do not, however, look to contemporary authors[100] for an elucidation of such values and standards. Rather, they expend considerable energy attacking these authors for their shortcomings and problematic role in German reunification.

In a total of four essays, three by Schwilk and one by Schacht, a kind of literary kangaroo court is set up in order to reprise and extend the "Literature Debate" of the early 1990s. In "Clueless in Berlin: German Authors and the Revolution" (1990), Schwilk attempts to relegate authors with a political streak to the dustbin of history, accusing them of "dilettantism" (139), a word strangely absent from his various paeans to Ernst Jünger. Writers are also dismissed as parasites whose opposition to society is "good for publicity" but without consequences for them, since they "profit" from the economic system (139–140). One must take this to mean that only writers who never publish hold serious views worth considering. This is of course the end of literature as we know it. In the swirl of events after 1989, it was somewhat risky to make global pronouncements of any kind, and this essay is a case in point. Schwilk has great praise for novelist Monika Maron and her "irreproachable biography," and he quotes her as saying that she is more afraid of "Grass and Piwitt" than of "Höpcke and Kant,"[101] meaning that the Western [leftist] intellectuals are worse than the Stalinist Eastern variety (141). A few years later, it came out that Maron had been an informant for the secret police while in the GDR.[102] In another 1990 essay, "The Dry Bread of Utopia: The 'Wende' and the Intellectuals," Schwilk seems to despair of finding any writers worthy of serving the cause of conservative culture in reunified Germany:

> Perhaps it is just a waste of time to generally expect from writers and artists that exceptional ethos that distinguishes personalities like Havel, Dinescu, Solzhenitsyn, or Sakharov. The morality of these creative artists is usually found in their works, whose most productive inspirations are vanity and self-portrayal. There are plenty of examples of great writers who are at times opportunists ["Gesinnungslumpen"] and political dilettantes. (163)

The unparalleled models praised here are a Czech, a Romanian, and two Russians. Schwilk seems truly disturbed by the fact that he cannot provide any comparable figures from East Germany, and he tries—rather unconvincingly—to explain their absence by pointing to the special status of the GDR as part of a divided country and to the unusually effective socialist "reeducation" in the GDR. The tortured logic could be symptomatic of the fact that Schwilk himself is not unaffected by a form of German self-hatred, a phenomenon that he and Schacht would like to eliminate.[103]

In his 1995 essay "Too Far Afield: Günter Grass and the Myth of the Nation," Schwilk turns to the favorite literary whipping boy of the New Right. This piece was originally published in November 1995, several months after the controversies surrounding the commemoration of the end of World War II. Schwilk cannot accept the fact that Grass, of all people, presented the country with "*the* novel about German unity," since he views the author as a pathological national pedagogue consumed with his own obsessions (153). Among these are the author's interest in Poland, and Schwilk is outraged that Grass could openly support the emancipation of the Polish[104] nation while rejecting the German drive for reunification from a "racist-determinist" standpoint (i.e., the Germans will never change). Grass's novel *Ein weites Feld* (Too far afield) was esthetically and politically controversial,[105] but it is less the book itself than, yet again, the "German self-hatred" displayed by Grass—and Jürgen Habermas—that raises Schwilk's hackles. He contrasts it with the rebirth of the "myth of the nation . . . a spiritual reality of captivating power" (157), a rebirth that took place in the East German demonstrations of 1989. It does not surprise Schwilk that this "miracle of German national rebirth" (156) took place in the East, for that part of the country had, he intimates, remained more German than the rest. Once again, it is unsettling that he refers to the residents of that part of the country as "Central Germans" (157). These particular Germans exhibit, according to Schwilk, "German virtues like community spirit, solidarity, inwardness, and knowledge of tradition" (158). In the second half of the essay, Schwilk becomes so involved with his project of a "self-aware nation" displaying "purified patriotism" (158-159) that he forgets completely about Grass and his novel. Ironically, this novel, which has been criticized by so many, has probably received more public attention than all of the writings of the New Right put together. Since intellectuals are rarely free of envy, one can imagine that Schwilk's aggressiveness did not stem solely from philosophical disagreements.

Ulrich Schacht's essay "The Strange Freedom: German Poets and German Unity" is intended to show that patriotism was never foreign to German poets. He reviews verses from the Baroque period (Gryphius), the eighteenth century (Wieland, Schiller), the Napoleonic era—when writers took up arms against Napoleon—and the revolution of 1848, when authors contributed to the formulation of the democratic constitution. The survey ends here, and there is a good reason for that—although Schacht does not seem to see it: Once national unity was achieved—not by the democrats of 1848, but by Bismarck—only lowbrow authors continued to sing its praises. Instead of discussing this, Schacht devotes his attention to poems by contemporary authors who are apparently less than enthusiastic about recent German reunification. Schacht discovers the persistence of a longing for a third path between capitalism and Soviet socialism, even in poets that he truly respects, like Volker Braun. To Schacht, the lack of patriotism shown by such figures is the result of an "incomparable process of spiritual desolation" (150). Since Schacht concentrates almost exclusively on East German poets,[106] an unexpected dichotomy is constructed: The former GDR intellectuals must be as alienated from the populace as their West German counterparts, since they clearly do not represent the "German virtues" extolled by Schwilk. Those few East—and West—German writers who do (based upon Schacht's assessment) are purportedly evidence enough that the "humane positive myth of the German" (151) has not been extinguished completely. To an outside observer, this "evidence" does not carry much weight. The intellectuals dedicated to myth-making are and will probably remain a minority.

The question of the role of literati in nation-building may be of peripheral interest to the reader not fixated on the literary sphere, but the first essay

in *For a Berlin Republic* is one that could and should hold the attention of anyone concerned with the future of Germany. It is an analysis of the Goldhagen debate in Germany, and its title is a variation on the young American scholar's own: "Hitler's Willing Executors: On the Logic of Power in the German Goldhagen Debate." Although a summary of the German debate about Goldhagen's book cannot be given here,[107] it should be pointed out that most observers noted a gap between the reaction of professional historians and that of the general reading public. The historians tended to emphasize errors and omissions, whereas the public displayed a mixture of enthusiasm for the relatively young author and a deep sense of remorse for the Holocaust.[108] As one might well imagine, Ulrich Schacht is anything but enthusiastic. His 1997 essay, the only one in *For a Berlin Republic* not published elsewhere, is less a review of Goldhagen's book than a polemic against Goldhagen's German supporters (whom he calls "propagandists and admirers" [16]). Before entering the fray, Schacht musters "politically correct" support in the form of two quotations. The section of the book containing the essay is preceded by a positive assessment of the "truly talented, extraordinary" German people by then U.S. ambassador to Germany Vernon Walters,[109] and the essay itself has as its motto a statement by German-Jewish Holocaust survivor Inge Deutschkron, who compares Goldhagen's generalizations about the Germans to Nazi practices (16). It is thus suggested to the reader that it is not just right-wing conservative Germans who reject Goldhagen, but even Americans and Jews. Schacht's tactic suggests that he might be worried about a backlash that could harm his conservative project in reunified Germany.

Schacht's actual target is not Goldhagen, but rather Jürgen Habermas, the "militant *spiritus rector* with rational-shamanist denunciation rhetoric,"[110] for whom *Hitler's Willing Executioners* is a gift, or, to use Schacht's military imagery, an "impressive delivery of ammunition" (17), an "anachronistic argumentation bomb" (21). If "eliminatory anti-Semitism" did in fact, as Goldhagen claims, permeate every fact of German society before 1933, then the constant resurrection of that phenomenon could have a deleterious effect on the (re-?)construction of a self-confident nation. Instead of engaging in damage control, however, Schacht literally loses control. Habermas is accused of organizing an "institute for applied repressive tolerance" and transforming the social sciences into "police sciences" used to spy on the populace (18). Habermas's "destructive delusions" (i.e., the possibility of a rerun of fascism, the necessity of replacing the old nationalism with constitutional patriotism) are compared with "vampire research" (18). Jan Philipp Reemtsma of the Hamburg Institute for Social Research, who praises Goldhagen, is portrayed as a "quasi-racist" whose "methodological Stalinism" and "orgy of suspicion" are "virulent" (20). What is odd about this is that it was not right-wing historians who criticized Goldhagen, but left-liberals. Were Schacht's compatriots asleep? That is not likely. Instead, one could imagine that the taboo against attacking Jews was still quite effective. Axel Springer, the late publisher of the tabloid *Bildzeitung* and the blandly conservative *Die Welt*, always took a pro-Israeli stance, and Schacht himself has called for German military support for Israel, as we have seen. This position, long a fig leaf hiding other unsavory sentiments like xenophobia and racism, may well lose its effectiveness as a result of Schacht's tirades. It is true that Schacht does stray from his polemical mission by launching into a rather ho-hum review of leftist fascism theories, but before putting down his pen, he takes the offensive again. He revels in the discomfort of the (leftist) German audience (caught up in "anti-German destructive hate") forced to listen to Goldhagen praise postwar West Germany as a great democratic success (29), and he believes that he has witnessed the Waterloo of leftist pseudomorality, one that he describes as "ermächtigungsgesetzlich" (i.e., similar to the Nazi seizure of power in 1933) (30). The real neofascists, he hopes to teach us, are not the right-wingers, but the hypocritical leftists. Before this lesson can sink in, however, Schacht makes yet another tactical error. He describes the Holocaust as "undeniable," only to add that it was perpetrated by

> politicians, policemen, lawyers, secret agents, German soldiers, and SS formations of National Socialist Germany, *and* [my emphasis] their foreign collaborators in the uniforms of the French gendarmerie, Dutch police, Latvian and Lithuanian SS men, or Polish and Ukrainian thugs in this or that garb. (30)

The structure of this sentence leads the reader to the conclusion that the Germans and their collaborators played roughly equal parts in the Holocaust. If Schacht truly does believe this, his criticism of Goldhagen's book ("It is primarily speculative. One just has to believe it." [28]) rings hollow.[111] To lend credence to his argument, he cites Eric Hobsbawm, Ruth Bettina Birn, and Christopher Browning (33). Cite them he may, but he in no shape or form shares the same intellectual and moral universe. He accuses the German intellectual left, his real adversary, of "shameless fornication with the dead of Auschwitz" and an "eliminatory hate" of all that is German, accompanied by "self-righteousness and ice-cold arrogance" (34–35). The essay ends with a rejection of the singularity of the Holocaust. Schacht asserts that the German media are under "almost totalitarian [leftist] control" (17). He should in fact consider himself fortunate that this control—be it "totalitarian" or not—keeps his views from the general public, and, more importantly, from international attention. If the paranoia, projections, and polemics of Schacht and other New Rightists were widely disseminated, the global community would in all likelihood wonder if the granting of full sovereignty to the Federal Republic was somewhat precipitous.[112] One enterprise that could quickly endanger that sovereignty would be the attempt to use Schacht's description of the reunified country as "Rump Germany" ("Restdeutschland" [181]) as the basis of a political program.[113]

Schacht's speech "The Measure of Shock: On the Fiftieth Anniversary of May 8, 1945" is problematic in similar ways. In order to shake up his audience,[114] Schacht once again chooses to use the language of Auschwitz. He compares the leftist intellectuals who mourn the Nazi victims deeply, but the Soviet victims only in passing, to those who decided who should live and who should die in the concentration camps. For him, these people are "the suffering selectors on the ideological ramp of the year 1995" (48). Their supposed hegemony in German society is described as "Gleichschaltung," i.e., a new version of the Nazi homogenization program that no longer (thanks in part to the mass media) needs a one-party dictatorship to succeed. He will have us believe that, fifty years after World War II, Germany is very close to the totalitarian regime depicted in Orwell's *1984* (49). The "cultural officers of the West German special consciousness who profess pacifism" are in actuality the ones bent on destroying German identity (51–52). We are not told just who these people might be,[115] but we do learn that they consider Mickey Mouse cartoons to be a higher form of culture than German Romanticism, simply because the latter was "supposedly prefascist" (52). For those who do not fathom this logic, one could add that Mickey Mouse is a product of Western civilization, and the postwar Germans are accused of fetishizing absolutely anything that emanates from the West. It is arduous to have to wade through such verbiage, and the task is not made easier by Schacht's self-recycling. Instead of editing the material destined for this volume, the individual texts are simply put together between two book covers. The May 8 speech thus parallels Schacht's "Stigma and Tribulation," a reprinted chapter from *Die selbstbewußte Nation* that is placed here cheek-to-jowl with the speech. Both texts have the same quotations from Elias Canetti (44 and 54) and Hannah Arendt (44 and 55), and both discuss "concern" (Sorge) for Israel (45 and 58). The misuse of Canetti is, incidentally, quite distasteful. The 1945 passage in question, from Canetti's *Sketches, 1942–1972* reads as follows:

> When spring comes, the sadness of the Germans will be an inexhaustible well, and not much will still distinguish them from the Jews. Hitler has turned the Germans into Jews in just a few years, and "German" has now become a word as painful as "Jewish." (54)

Schacht laments the fact that this text is not discussed in German schools, but he sees only the second part of it, namely the victimization and stigmatization of the Germans. He has nothing to say about how Canetti's prophecy did *not* come true: in 1945, not endless sadness and mourning were the order of the day in Germany, but rather the beginning of a long-term repression of the immediate past. Given that Schacht is familiar with the work of Alexander and Margarete Mitscherlich (see above), this lacuna is the result either of purely tactical considerations or of ideological blinders. Is Schacht capable of providing a more insightful and straightforward analysis of the former GDR and its legacy?

In the May 8 speech, the one contemporary German who is singled out as a model and named directly is East German Joachim Gauck, the director of the office charged with dealing with the activities and files of the GDR Secret Police. Gauck is viewed by most, though not all, Germans as someone selflessly dedicated to preserving the memory of the GDR past as a warning for future generations. In *For a Berlin Republic*, Schacht contributes several essays to this project. One of these, "We Brandenburgers: Memories of the First Secretary of the Bureaucratic Murderers" [Schreibtischmörder], sheds light on Schacht's innermost motivation as a writer. After the fall of the Berlin Wall, Schacht strolls through East Berlin and buys a copy of the propagandistic biography *Erich Honecker—A Life for the People*. Sitting in a café in Friedrichstraße, he leafs through it and comes across a photo of the prison in Brandenburg-Görden where Honecker was held as a political prisoner by the Nazis from 1937 to 1945. He managed to escape from a work detail outside the prison about two months before the end of the war, but in his official biography, he is said to have been liberated by the Soviets.[116] Schacht is incensed that Honecker could insult the victims (of fascism?) with his "liberation performance" (105). To him, Honecker is yet another embodiment of the "banality of evil"[117] (Hannah Arendt), and he refuses to grant him the status of a resistance fighter who "fought for humanity although threatened with death" (105). To do this is to deny that German communists suffered and died under Nazi terror, and, more significantly, to deny that the personal experiences of these victims played any role in their political and personal behavior after 1945. Schacht effectively engages in dehumanization, despite his partisanship for humanity. This puzzle is solved by Schacht himself, albeit obliquely. When he looks at pictures of the Brandenburg prison, he looks for his own face: "Behind one of the barred windows: 1974, 1975, 1976" (104). He not only provides us with his prisoner identification number, but also recounts the story of his own resistance against the East German communists. The harsh realities of his life as a prisoner are undeniable and inexcusable, but Schacht's prose creates the portrait of a heroic resistance fighter who overcame every obstacle and retained absolute personal integrity to the bitter end. This is indeed a story worth telling, but when it is told by Schacht himself, it smacks of self-elevation. A sense of moral superiority was probably a means of survival in an East German prison, but the same sense can easily be transformed into arrogance in the post-1989 political scene. In addition, when the superiority is not accepted or is even questioned, the result is often aggression, insult, and vitriol. Sadly, Schacht engages in the same "selection of the dead" that he has accused West German leftists of: there are "victims of the purest kind" (108) who deserve our veneration, and pseudo-victims like Honecker. As for Schacht himself, he was "never a victim," he declares, because he never accepted Honecker's system. Ironically, Schacht ends this essay by saying that he is "sorry for" the benighted Honecker (110), who did his duty (like many other Germans of his generation, one might add). It is the West Germans who negotiated with Honecker rather than ostracizing him for whom Schacht's deepest contempt is reserved.

Schacht's essay "The Sacrosanct Dictator: Erich Honecker and His Societal Defenders" continues in the same vein. It need not be discussed here, with the exception of one point that is relevant in another area of the volume. Schacht attacks Rudolf Bahro, one-time prominent GDR dissident and political prisoner, for thinking aloud about a possible historical legitimacy of the GDR. Although Bahro's political activities in the West — he worked with the Greens and was active in the New Age alternative scene — are not the topic at hand, Schacht cannot help but castigate him for his "ecologically oriented totalitarianism" (112). This epithet is developed into a full-blown argument by

Heimo Schwilk in another part of the collection. The title of the essay, "Self-Betrayal as a Virtue: The SED State and Its West German Collaborators," speaks for itself. It is a condemnation of détente as "inhumane and reactionary" (88) and a vilification of its proponents as collaborators. The analogy with the fascist era does not quite fit, however, especially since Schacht chooses to end the piece with another quote from Camus about "leftist collaborators." One of the characteristics of these people, according to Camus, is a toleration or even acceptance of anti-Semitism (92). The détente policymakers have been accused of many things, but this is patently absurd.[118] No less absurd is the misstep involved in quoting Gottfried Benn at the beginning of the section that contains the essay on collaborators. Writing in 1946, the (former Nazi collaborator) Benn expresses surprise that the "so-called intellectuals" fall prey to political ideologies (77). Finally, the brief polemic "Dangerous Legacy: The PDS and Its Clandestine Admirers" warns West Germans not to fraternize with the East German neocommunist Party of Democratic Socialism, since many of its members belonged to the "hard core" of the toppled regime (183). In a strange twist, Schacht criticizes the intellectual supporters of the PDS as "anti-Western . . . anticapitalist, and anti-American" (184). These are positions not unknown among the contributors to *Die selbstbewußte Nation*.

As has been mentioned above, Heimo Schwilk comes from a very different background, and his writings bear the stamp of a corresponding animus. Although he is no stranger to polemics, from time to time he provides the reader with a glimpse of a pessimistic streak. In 1996, for example, he complained that the chance to "turn" the reunited country to a domestic and foreign policy in the national interest, one prepared by a "spiritual, order-oriented, moral-ethical and economic shift," had been "pathetically squandered" (211).[119] A year later, he predicted that even "contemplating" right-wing alternatives could in the future become a punishable offense, and he went on to advise conservative thinkers to become accustomed to "an existence in the catacombs" (180). At the end of that passage, he used the phrase "holding out even though the situation is hopeless." This is a description of the dilemma of the later Jünger,[120] who had given up all hope of seeing a transformation of society in his lifetime. It is far removed from the Camus-inspired stance of absolute freedom and pugnacity favored by Schacht. Schwilk has not given up yet, however. He continues on as a conservative mole, inspired by the Goethe quotation placed before one of his political essays: "One cannot change one's century, but one can stand up against it and lay the groundwork for salutary developments" (175).

What is, however, the nature of this "century" when seen through Schwilk's eyes? It is surely not the one seen by most Germans. First of all, the Social Democrats, who were out of power from 1982 to 1998, and who have only held the chancellorship for a total of fourteen years (out of almost fifty), are the true victors. Schwilk speaks of the "Kohl system," which is none other than the "universal social-democratization" of Germany (175). Whereas some of the other European countries with comparable systems have seen the light of "Thatcherism" (praised as a practical American way of doing things [177]), Germany is in an era of "national decline" (176). This is hardly an original viewpoint, but what distinguishes it from its formulation by less right-wing observers is the insistence that Germany is firmly in the grip of the "'68ers and their profit-seeking fellow travelers," who are responsible for the "nihilism" of public life and the battle against all traditions (177).[121] For Schwilk (and Schacht), a typical representative of this group is Dr. Rita Süssmuth, then the president of the Federal Parliament. Süssmuth, who does believe in equal opportunity for women, was born in 1937, finished her Ph.D. in 1964, and was a young professor long before the students took to the streets. She is considered to be a liberal member of the CDU, but her ideas are not close to those of the Greens' Joschka Fischer (an archetypal '68er, but one without real political power until his appointment as foreign minister in 1998). What "'68er" really means is anyone who does not believe that the only hope for Germany lies in a return to the reigning values of the pre-1933 period. Schwilk cannot reconcile himself to the fact that, since Hitler took advantage of these values (Schwilk's list: "a readiness to take risks, the will to renewal, daring, a readiness to sacrifice, achievement, punctuality, order, loyalty" [178]), they have become discredited. What has in fact changed is something else: in the process of postwar democratization, more ordinary citizens have a voice in determining *what* to take risks and make sacrifices for, *what* to achieve, and *who* deserves their loyalty. This is often a messy business in a democracy, and today's Germans are no less acquisitive or self-centered than anyone else, but the alternative proposed by the New Right—an alternative that is never really fleshed out to any great extent—does not exert any great attraction. At least not so far.[122] One must concur when Schwilk postulates that German immobilism can be primarily attributed to the consequences of National Socialism (179), and these are not likely to disappear in the near future.

important the note there were (really don't yeah well of both.

Schwilk contributes essays on, or rather, against political correctness and United Europe that recapitulate what he and Schacht have said before. His attack on the Greens — "Eco-Pharisees or The German Desire for Destruction" — deserves a closer look, however, since environmental consciousness and the Green Party are factors to be reckoned with in Germany. Schwilk is so anxious to dismantle the ecology movement as a viable political alternative in Germany that he engages in an activity that he (and Schacht) have often condemned, namely, the construction of a catastrophic tradition in German history. The concrete manifestations of German politics have been determined (he does not say *partially determined*) for centuries by ambivalence — a "genuinely German phenomenon" — an ambivalence that burdens the German mentality. Oscillating between "moralism and dreams of destruction, belief and applied rationality, fear and a desire for renewal," the Germans have gravitated toward an "apocalyptic messianism" (195). The explanation for this, according to Schwilk, must be sought in Germany's central geographic location in Europe, religious conflicts, imperial dreams, and in the ambitions of its neighbors. Once again, we have arrived at the "special path." It is, however, difficult to take the construction of this path seriously when one reads that not only the Nazis, but also Kant and German idealism are part of it (196).[123] The most recent manifestation is supposedly the Green movement, which pairs apocalyptic warnings with hypocrisy (i.e., wailing while consuming high-end goods). Reading Schwilk, one gets the impression that all of the Greens are from the upper middle class, "eco-pharisees" who praise asceticism without practicing it themselves. This does not jibe with his claim that, in coalition with the SPD, they use tax money to support the following groups: "gays, lesbians, drug addicts, criminals, autonomous (i.e., left-wing extremist) activists, anarchists ["Chaoten"], communists, and squatters who reject, disregard, or fight against the values and norms of our free society" (198). This confused piece of prose tells us little about the ecology movement, but much about Schwilk's enemies list. At the end, Schwilk reports with obvious satisfaction that the German economic crisis has led to a drop in interest in ecological questions (200). In place of the purportedly inconceivable combination of "emancipation ideology" and "asceticism," he proposes a "controlled modernism" that would give both nature and man their due (201). In his fervor, Schwilk has overlooked something relevant to his own project. Many observers who attempt to come to grips with the Green Party and the ecological movement in Germany discuss the *conservative* roots of the protest against industrialization and the consumer society, beginning with the educated middle class (*Bildungsbürgertum*) in the nineteenth century.[124] One has even asserted that the Greens are the "true conservatives," those who strive to "conserve what is worth conserving and preserve what is worth preserving."[125] It is clear that the title "true conservative" cannot be shared, so Schwilk's vehemence is understandable. His dilemma is unlikely to be resolved in the near future, since the "modernity" of which he speaks has shown few signs of responding to the feeble attempts to "control" it. Given that he has called for some sort of German Thatcherism himself (see above), the phrase "controlled modernity" is a sham.

At the end of *For a Berlin Republic*, Schacht and Schwilk mount the podium once more in order to speak of the future. In "The Answer of History: Will Our System Be Able to Transform Itself?" Schacht labels Habermas a Trotskyite in disguise (240) and produces Jacob Burkhardt as an early witness to the "demagogic core of all Enlightenment philosophy" (241). Despite this, he unexpectedly calls for a dialogue with "the authentic representatives of the '68ers," whom he distinguishes from the "petit-bourgeois imitators" [Epigonen] of that generation (243). Why might he wish to exchange ideas with those whom he has vilified so thoroughly? The answer lies in his fear of a German apocalypse (this is apparently different from the apocalypse envisioned by some Greens and belittled by Schwilk). Schacht warns us that if the "radical transformation within the system" is no longer possible, the "radical change [i.e., replacement] of the system is inevitable" (243). In other words, if the New Right is not given its chance, another model will take over, and this could well be another attempt to save Germany from modernity by means of fascism.[126] Such rhetoric is a variant of the slogans used by left-wing extremists in the 1970s ("First brown, then red!") with the difference that Schacht hopes to prevent the apocalypse by nipping the "brown" phase in the bud. Despite the oil crisis and recessionary retrenchments, the leftist version held little appeal. The new reformulation has not achieved much resonance so far either. In contrast to such forbodings, Schwilk — usually the more pessimistic of the two — chooses to strike an upbeat note by using as a motto a prophecy by U.S. diplomat Richard Holbrooke: "In five years, the entire world will regard Berlin as the capital and center of Europe" (244). In "From the Bonn to the Berlin Republic: Plea for a National Shift ["Wende"] in Germany," Schwilk predicts that the new republic will no longer be able to prolong "national-masochistic pathologies" or the "boundless hedonistic repression of the West German welfare state" (245). One explanation for this is his belief that, whereas "national" projects remain suspect in the West, the revival of national pride could come from the newly incorporated East. (One recalls that Schwilk's focus at *Die Welt* is on the former GDR.) First, however, the alleged hegemony of the ideas of 1968 — "the continuation of 1933 with other means and an especially momentous date of shame in our history" (246) — must be broken.[127] Schwilk is so fixated with this endeavor (despite Schacht's tentative attempts at dialogue just a few pages back!) that he does not hesitate to enlist the aid of liberal academic and journalist Richard Herzinger,[128] who condemns the '68ers as "political enemies of liberal democracy per se" (247). Searching for the roots of German identity, Schwilk quotes Hegel about the "special role" of the Germans in the intellectual sphere and praises the representatives of idealism rejected by Schacht (248). He characterizes the "mass murder of the Jews" as the "nadir of a perverted striving for 'purity' and 'cleansing'" and worries about the "inclination of the Germans toward the ideal, universal, or totalitarian solution" (248). Has Saul suddenly become Paul? Only to a certain extent. Although Schwilk admits that it is difficult to be proud of being a German, he also rejects "ritualized abhorrence or self-hatred" (248-249). If one combines this stance with his praise of German cultural profundity (247), the gulf between him and Günter Grass is no longer unbridgeable. In fact, he almost (at least at the end of the volume) seems closer to Grass than to Schacht.

What is one to make of this? Perhaps sloppy editing and haste have obscured the New Right creed as proclaimed in *For a Berlin Republic*. If this were the case, then more clarity might be expected in the future. A comparison of this volume with *Die selbstbewußte Nation* makes such a prospect unlikely, however. Creative thinking — including a stimulating rethinking of earlier concepts and critiques — can only be encountered rarely, and contradictions can be discovered both within individual contributions and between various contributors. The overriding propensity is toward resentment, resulting in a striking out in all directions. These angry young men — many of whom are graying at the temples — have so far not succeeded in channeling their rage (reminiscent of "white male backlash" in the U.S.) into a coherent program for political action and social change. It is difficult to imagine how such a program might look, given the difficulty of juxtaposing a concern for the entire "Volk" with Thatcherism, a rejection of the mass media with attempts to infiltrate such media, and the advocacy of religiously anchored values with an increasingly secularized populace. In addition, the myriad attempts at *critique* have yet to lead to creative *production* in the culture sphere. A younger generation of conservative authors has not yet made its appearance,[129] and the tastes of the reading public presently run more to Anglo-American middle-brow novels than to Teutonic profundities (whether articulated from left or right). German feature films with themes even marginally relevant to conservative cultural renewal are few and far between.[130] Practically the only conservative art, i.e., art devoted to variations of traditional models, is produced by former GDR painters like Werner Tübke. Can one thus conclude that the New Right has had negligible impact on the cultural sphere in post-Wall Germany? That conclusion would be justified if one examined only the younger generation(s). In actuality, the lion's share of media attention and publicity has not been directed toward the would-be theoreticians of the New Right, but rather to two established writers of the 1968 generation, namely Botho Strauß (b. 1944) and Peter Handke (b. 1942). Might the "right turn" discerned in the writing of these prominent figures be the harbinger of the cultural, political and societal paradigm shift anticipated by Schacht, Schwilk, and others?

Chapter 3

An Unexpected Detour on the Way to the Pantheon: Strauß, Handke, and the Vagaries of High Culture in Germany

The German "Literature Debate" of 1990–1991 was not what the name implies. Although its initial phase centered around the publication of Christa Wolf's prose piece *What Remains*,[1] its real focus was an attempt to discredit leftist intellectuals and their attempts to use cultural discourse to have an impact on politics and society.[2] East German authors who had criticized the GDR system from within, offering critical solidarity in the hope that "socialism with a human face" might still be developed, were characterized as "failures" or "demi-heroes" ("halbe Helden") who had shifted constantly between "hope and fear, doubt and cynicism."[3] Using the epithet "totalitarian" the way leftist critics had long used the term "fascist" (or at least "protofascist") against conservative writers, Frank Schirrmacher of the *Frankfurter Allgemeine Zeitung* condemned German intellectuals—a term seldom applied to conservatives in the postwar period—as corruptible and selectively blind:

> Fond legends, including that of West German identity, have been destroyed. According to the postwar legend of many German writers, artists, and scholars, the writer, in light of National Socialism, has at his disposal a stable, anti-authoritarian, critical ethos that proves itself when tested. The exemplary case of Christa Wolf teaches us not only that the [totalitarian] model was never overcome, but also how perfectly the intellectual can deceive himself about reality. . . . There is some evidence that many do not wish to hear of the second totalitarian fall from grace in the twentieth century. They appear, as the fate of Christa Wolf demonstrates, not even to comprehend that it has occurred.[4]

This citation is taken from the concluding paragraph of Schirrmacher's controversial and much-discussed essay, one which ends with incriminations against West German intellectuals. The subtext is that the end of the so-called socialist experiment in *East* Germany entails the end of the alleged cultural hegemony of the left in the *Western* part of the country. As has been elucidated above, said hegemony is a thorn in the side of right-wing intellectuals, some of whom, like Ulrich Schacht and Siegmar Faust, found their intellectual identity in opposition to the East German state. Schirrmacher and his allies were criticized, to be sure, for distortions and bias, but the "Literature Debate" was in the end a cultural debacle for the left. The leftist intellectuals were faced with two choices: to repent, lick their wounds, and disappear from the public sphere, or to wait for an opportunity to retaliate. This opportunity came first in the form of a reaction to the xenophobic violence that flared up in Germany after the fall of the Berlin Wall (the venerable antifascist project could once again be revived), and then in the innumerable critical rejoinders to Botho Strauß's 1993 essay "Impending Tragedy." It is conceivable that the campaign against Strauß might have been less polemical and strident if the crusade against Christa Wolf and others had not preceded it.

Writing in *Die Zeit* in response to the publication of both *Die selbstbewußte Nation* and "Impending Tragedy," Robert Leicht proclaimed in a front-page editorial that "whoever constantly calls for a German normalcy must be told: It can only be had within the norms of European civilization."[5] Just what are these norms, however? Leicht, although not uncritical of the Enlightenment, was speaking as a liberal, and his perspective on what comprises civilization and how it should be assessed was not shared by his intellectual opponents. In 1993, it seemed as if old certainties had disappeared overnight. The normally left-liberal *Der Spiegel* commissioned three well-known writers with hitherto liberal, if not leftist credentials, namely, Martin Walser (b. 1927), Hans Magnus Enzensberger (b. 1929), and Botho Strauß, to plumb the depths of the new national mood. The three essays produced for the occasion, "Impending Tragedy" (Anschwellender Bocksgesang) by Botho Strauß, "Views of Civil War" (Ausblicke auf den Bürgerkrieg) by Hans Magnus Enzensberger, and "German Concerns" (Deutsche Sorgen) by Martin Walser, had a dual function. On the one hand, they were meant to stimulate debate about the future direction of culture in united Germany. On the other hand, they were clearly to serve notice that *Der Spiegel* aspired to be a major player in the drama of cultural reassessment and renewal. The magazine was faced with the two-pronged task of attracting new readers from the former GDR and maintaining its market share in the face of the founding of the competing conservative weekly *Focus* in 1993. In the announcement "Concerning Intellectuals" at the beginning of issue no. 26, 1993, a kind of contextualizing afterword to the three essays, one finds phrases like "outrageous utterances" and "a number of taboo violations by German intellectuals." Anticipating the key question, the *Spiegel* editors go on to ask it and provide an answer of sorts:

> Has the *Spiegel* lost its leftist, left-liberal grounding too? As much or as little as the entire critical intelligentsia, which has been seeking new values and orientation since the abrupt end of the well-ordered bipolar world divided into East and West.[6]

In this context, "critical" is a synonym for any variety of leftism. Such terminology would of course by rejected by right-wing intellectuals like Schacht and Schwilk, who see themselves as the true critical spirits, whereas the pre-1989 leftists were, in their view, hypercritical of the West and by nature incapable of—or unwilling to—gain insight into the dictatorial nature of state socialism in the Eastern bloc.[7] As far as the "well-ordered bipolar world" is concerned, the dichotomy had been long since undermined by the presence of exiled GDR dissidents in the West and the reformist adherents of the Gorbachev line in the East. To what extent did Enzensberger and Walser, literary mentors of the generation of 1968, and Strauß, who began writing in the late 1960s, discover new fault lines and potentialities?

There are basically two schools of thought regarding Hans Magnus Enzensberger's role as a writer and social commentator in postwar Germany. Some see him as the former *enfant terrible* of the stifling Adenauer years who became one of the driving forces behind the student movement of the 1960s, only to turn his back on it all, becoming ever more conservative or at least apolitical in the course of the 1970s and 1980s. One could express this in shorthand by referring to the titles of his various projects: from the *Kursbuch* and the project boldly termed "the political alphabetization of Germany"[8] to the slippery *TransAtlantik* and the bibliophile *Andere Bibliothek*.[9] Others argue that one can discern a basic continuity from the 1950s to the 1990s. This has been characterized as "the freedom of carefree, independent reflection"[10] or a "humanistic basic conviction in thinking and writing."[11] What can we glean from the essay "Views of Civil War"?

Most of the German readers of this essay, which is part of the 1993 book *Prospects of Civil War* (Aussichten auf den Bürgerkrieg),[12] probably remembered another rather famous *Spiegel* essay by the same author, namely the 1991 piece equating Saddam Hussein with Hitler.[13] Enzensberger spoke at that time of the doomsday program of each of these "enemies of humanity": "His death wish is his motive, his mode of rule is destruction" (26). Ideology is irrelevant to the author's "anthropological" analysis. If the fanatical leader can find followers who wish to die themselves, anything is possible. According to Enzensberger, this is what happened in Germany in the 1930s, and this constellation was duplicated in Iraq in the 1980s.[14] Normal political maneuvering was thus useless, making war an inevitability. This conclusion transformed Enzensberger into one of the despicable warmongers ("Bellizisten") in the eyes of the German left. The essay on civil war takes up many of the same themes, placing more emphasis on the global situation. The "New World Order" is one characterized primarily by civil wars in every corner of the planet, according to Enzensberger. In contrast to the Cold War era, he goes on to assert, none of the participants in these conflicts is motivated by ideals, ideology, or a *Weltanschauung* of any kind. In fact, they have absolutely no convictions at all. One even reads that they are "autistic" and incapable of distinguishing between destruction and self-destruction (171). The actual goal is none other than "collective self-mutilation" (172). In such a climate, none of the political thinkers—from Aristotle to Max Weber—have anything to tell us. Only Hobbes's *bellum omnium contra omnes* remains an accurate, if depressing description of the situation.

Of particular interest is Enzensberger's assessment of the contemporary German scene in the context of his scenario. He refuses to call the perpetrators of violence against foreigners "right-wing radicals" or "neo-Nazis":

> He knows nothing about National Socialism. History does not interest him. The swastika and Hitler salute are mere props. His clothing, music, and video culture are thoroughly American. "Germanness" is a slogan devoid of meaning that only serves to cover up the empty spaces in his brain. (172)

This does not, however, imply that he fails to take these people seriously. On the contrary: He calls for action (without going into specifics) to eliminate the antisocial violence from German society. If the Germans were to refrain from doing so, he says, they would lose every right to criticize conditions in other countries: "It does not befit the Germans to act like guarantors of peace and world champions of human rights as long as gangs of German thugs and arsonists are spreading fear and terror day and night" (175). This is hardly the voice of a conservative. If anything, it is an example of leftist melancholy stemming from the grudging admission that the universalist morality of the Enlightenment is not realizable on any grand scale. It is not stated triumphantly, but rather in a tone of deep sadness. Enzensberger quotes approvingly from Hannah Arendt's totalitarianism theory, but hastens to add that it does not apply to our world. The cultural pessimism we find here is not coupled with a call to return to traditional values, and there is absolutely nothing in the language of the essay which indicates a turn to the right. Since 1993, Enzensberger has expressed his great respect for Denis Diderot, the quintessential representative of the Enlightenment,[15] and in a recent interview, he praised the student movement of the 1960s for finally making West Germany "suitable for habitation."[16]

Martin Walser has been dissecting the old Bundesrepublik since the 1950s, and until the mid-1980s, he was also viewed as a founding member of the left-liberal literary phalanx. Of late, he has complained of isolation and the loss of old friends. This is directly attributable to his changed attitude vis-à-vis German history and national identity. The general public first became aware of the change in 1986, when *Die Welt* published an interview with the writer (September 29). One could venture to say that it was less the content of the interview than the fact that it appeared in the flagship paper of media czar Axel Springer which caused an uproar. Beyond this, a full-page advertisement hyping the interview appeared in *Der Spiegel* (no. 40, 1986) with a photo of Walser and the following quotation in bold type: "I will not become accustomed to the division of Germany." One was not a little surprised to hear such pronouncements from the author of the antifascist plays *The Rabbit Race (Eiche und Angora)* and *The Black Swan,* who had been politicized by the Vietnam War, felt affinity with the West German Communist Party (DKP—Deutsche Kommunistische Partei) for a time (cf. the controversial work *Gallistl's Illness*), and even signed an open letter to Erich Honecker "With socialist greetings."[17] The first literary manifestation of Walser's preoccupation with the German nation was the 1986 novella *Dorle and Wolf,* whose main character makes the following oft-quoted observation at the Bonn train station: "Halved people were hustling back and forth. The other halves were running back and forth in Leipzig."[18] In actuality, Walser had been ruminating about the division of Germany for quite some time, but this had somehow gone unnoticed. In his provocative speech "Speaking about Germany," given in November 1988 as part of the series "Speaking about our Country," he made a point of quoting from remarks which he had made in Bergen-Enkheim in 1977:

> The existence of these two countries is the product of a catastrophe whose causes can be known. I find it unbearable to let German history—as badly as it went in recent times—end as a product of catastrophe. I refuse to participate in the liquidation of history. Within me, another Germany still has a chance.[19]

Walser was not only criticized by Günter Grass and others for relying on a very vague "historical feeling" rather than rational analysis,[20] but also for accepting CSU politician Theo Waigel's invitation to discuss his speech with Waigel's Bavarian party comrades at Franz Josef Strauß's old stomping ground, Wildbad Kreuth.[21] All this had happened before he published the essay "German Concerns" in Der Spiegel. Can one discover an even more pronounced turn toward conservative and patriotic positions in this essay?

This text, like so many of Walser's fictional and nonfictional writings, is an attempt at therapy, including self-therapy. It came about as a reaction to his appearance in Lea Rosh's talk show in February 1989, in the course of which the author was verbally assaulted by Günter Gaus and Klaus Wagenbach, who called his "Speaking about Germany" superficial and no better than "barroom bluster" ("Stammtischreden") (40). The next day, Walser barricaded himself in a Paris hotel room and wondered whether he was still a leftist, since he had just been attacked "in the name of such glorious positions as internationalism, rationality, and enlightenment" (ibid.). He had hoped, he writes, that his call for reunification would not affect his location on the political spectrum ("Links-Rechts-Skala") (47), since his attitude toward the various contradictions and problems in German society had not changed. This turned out to be an illusion, and his ostracism led to a scathing critique of the German left: "Left—now I see that as an assortment of credos put together according to changing fashions that I cannot go along with. [It is] a chic and scurrilous fundamentalism" (ibid.). Having said this, he explains why he considers it to be so important to come to terms with German nationalism. It turns out that, in his opinion, the success of right-wing extremists is directly attributable to both the exclusion of nationalism from societal discourse since 1945 ("for the best of reasons," he hastens to add [41]) and the refusal to engage in dialogue with those who cannot tolerate this exclusion.[22] Instead of the demonization of skinheads and their ilk, Walser calls for a kind of national conversation about German history and identity. This is not, however, because he himself is a nationalist: "If someone has nothing to be proud of but his nationality, he is truly in dire straits [especially] as a German. . . . The nation—that is no one's major concern. And it hasn't been for a long while. And it will never be again" (41–42). Such utterances bear little resemblance to conservative or nationalist rhetoric. Walser may not call himself a leftist anymore, but he still sounds like one more often than not. For example, he still views National Socialism as the worst catastrophe in German history (no trace of Ernst Nolte here), and he castigates the West Germans for profiting from the labor of the *Gastarbeiter*, only to turn against them in times of economic decline. Words like "community," "morality," or "national pride" are absent from his essay, and his critique of the Enlightenment project stems—as does Enzensberger's—from disappointment rather than ideological opposition (47). As a final note, one could point out that Walser has been a vocal supporter of exiled Bangladeshi author Tamila Nasreen, who is anything but a darling of the right.[23]

Walser's 1990 essay "A Writer's Morning" reads like a practice run for "German Concerns." In it, he refers to two writers whose works provide him with great consolation. The two are Peter Handke and Botho Strauß,[24] who are portrayed as transcending the superficial "opinionated style" ("Meinungsstil") that Walser abhors. As an example of poetic profundity, Walser quotes from the 1985 Strauß poem "This Memory of One Who Was a Guest for Only One Day": "Knew no Germany all my life / Only two foreign states who kept me from / Ever being the German in the name of the people. / So much history, only to end like this?"[25] This is more than a random citation. It is meant to illustrate the fact that most of the thoughts and many of the images in "Impending Tragedy" can be found in other works by the same author, such as the 1985 poem, the prose volumes *Rumor* (1980), *Pairs, Passersby* (1981), *The Young Man* (1984), *Fragments of Indistinctness* (1989), *No Beginning* (1992), and *Living, Glimmering, Lying* (1994), as well as in the plays *Choral Finale* (1991) and *Equilibrium* (1993).[26]

What has made "Impending Tragedy" perhaps the most controversial essay written by a German author since the 1950s (Wolf Biermann's "Agitation for War / Agitation for Peace" (Kriegshetze Friedenshetze), Enzensberger's "Hitler Reincarnate," and Heinrich Böll's "Safe Conduct for Ulrike Meinhof" also come to mind)[27] is the fact that Strauß made a conscious choice not to utilize fictional characters or the institution of the theater to transmit his assessment of the contemporary malaise in both Germany and the Western world in general. Until 1993, only a small segment of the population was aware of the direction of his thinking, and this thinking of course took on added significance after the fall of the Berlin Wall. In addition, he was surrounded by a rather mysterious aura, given that he had kept himself out of the public eye as much as possible and refused to participate in the "democratic public sphere" as defined by the visual media. He was vaguely associated with the left, but most people could not point to any concrete actions in this regard. (The anecdote that one sometimes hears about Strauß collecting for the Viet Cong at the Berlin Schaubühne in the early 1970s might well be apocryphal.)

The reliability of apocrypha is questionable, but publications in a major journal are valuable in documenting the evolution of a writer's thinking about culture and politics. Botho Strauß was an active theater critic before he began his own writing career, and his collected essays from *Contemporary Theater* (*Theater heute*, the leading German periodical in the field) have been published in book form as *An Attempt to Think Together Esthetic and Political Events: Texts on the Theater 1967-1986*.[28] The second part of the title is misleading, because with one exception the volume contains pieces originally written between 1967 and 1971. This was the "1968 decade," a time when everything was in flux, so one learns much about the genesis of Strauß's literary and political identity by reading prose composed during the heyday of the student movement. After perusing the volume, one must conclude that Strauß was not a leftist or a rightist, but rather both simultaneously and at times a juxtaposition of the two. That is, his conception of cultural creativity often clashed with his views on history and politics. In the 1970s, this clash led to a new German literary movement, usually termed the "New Subjectivity."

The first two paragraphs of the book reflect the contradiction that puts its stamp on the entire enterprise. Strauß begins by criticizing the Christian Democrats and their "reactionary use of language" but then goes on to warn that the opponents of the system construct alternative models in such a way that they "become binding for everyone else" (9).[29] This was written in 1969, when leftist radicals had already begun to turn toward rigid orthodoxy. Although Strauß did sympathize with them to a certain extent, the inchoate artist in him instinctively rebelled against prescriptive norms—be they esthetic, political, or about the merging of the two. At the time, however, he still used the jargon of the day. Words like "bourgeois consumers,"

"(late) capitalist," "protofascist," "reactionary sentimentality," "counterrev-
olution," "revolutionary struggles," etc. abound. He does not hesitate to
paraphrase Marx (225) or refer to Lenin, "a theoretician and philosopher of
no little status" (183). He even criticizes the production of a Russian drama
from the 1920s because it does not avoid the danger of presenting a "reactionary anti-Soviet play" (229). Although Brecht is clearly not his favorite
playwright, he does agree that his theater esthetics contains "insights from
the science of Marxism-Leninism" (71). He affirms — sounding more like a
bourgeois pacifist than a Leninist — that all power is "evil" and all wars are
"dreadful" (199), a position that would change radically in the 1990s. In opposition to his later disdain for the masses, he attacks esthetic practices that
do not help raise them to a higher level ("volksverdummende Methode"
[203]). Despite such rhetoric, there is another, quite different undercurrent
in many of the theater reviews. Rationality is seen as an insufficient tool for
dealing with the myriad dimensions of human existence, and the power of
myth is praised. Strauß's comments on the American Bread and Puppet
Theater, normally viewed as a leftist group, are a prefiguration of positions
that would come to the fore in "Impending Tragedy":

> We don't like to admit it, but in the near future, our theater will also change to
> the extent that we succeed in developing a somewhat more enlightened rela-
> tionship to the irrational structures of our thinking. . . . [T]he Living Theatre
> and the Bread and Puppet Theatre maintain a very direct contact with irratio-
> nality. The theater of the collectives does not take a stand in order to erect the
> rule of irrationality, but against the dictatorship of technocratic thinking,
> against the self-alienation of rationality as exploitable ("verwertbare") intelli-
> gence. (28–29)

Strauß sensed even at the time that any creative artist in Germany who espoused such views would be excoriated, since (political) irrationality is as a
rule equated with fascism in the post-Hitler era. (Much of the New Right
project entails rehabilitating irrationality in the *cultural* sphere. It remains to
be seen if such a rehabilitation could be limited to that sphere.) Strauß's enthusiasm for the early plays of Peter Handke was clearly based upon an inner
affinity, and he must have cringed when describing the attacks on the already established dramatist: "the purist! the formalist! the fascist!" (176).
Two names, each mentioned twice in *An Attempt*, can now be seen as har-
bingers of things to come: Novalis and Heidegger.

   According to the *Spiegel* editorial staff, the three 1993 essays were meant
to demonstrate "the deep irritation of the German left."[30] Walser's essay was

placed in the section "Germany," whereas the texts by Enzensberger and Strauß were printed under the rubric "Culture." In the table of contents of issue no. 6, "Impending Tragedy" is called a "polemic" as well as a "somber vision." The short summary of the essay emphasizes that the reader will encounter something completely new: "In the theater, Botho Strauß has made a name for himself as a cultural critic. Now he reveals his pessimistic credo: The onslaught of foreigners is overtaxing our political culture, and history is becoming a tragedy." The allegedly sensational nature of this "revelation" is thematized in another editorial note, in which Strauß is portrayed as a mystery man who "consistently avoids appearing in public" and writes plays "from a distance" (202). Even those familiar with and fond of the author of the essay are promised that they will encounter a very different Strauß. (In the world of the media, the curiosity of the reader—even the interested reader—must be piqued by the use of hyperbole.) The essay's layout includes not only a photo of the author, but also some disturbing images. In order to lend credibility to Strauß's theses or at least promote a certain reading, the editors chose pictures of prisoners of war in Tajikistan, a foreign female beggar (wearing a head scarf and sneakers) in Frankfurt am Main, "hooligans" in Dresden, and the mind-numbing TV show "Dream Wedding" from cable giant RTL. In order to attract the nonpolitical fans of Strauß's plays, a photo showing a scene from the play *Choral Finale* (*Schlußchor*) was also added. The presentation of the essay aimed to make it a true media event, something that would have been unthinkable if it had only appeared in the obscure conservative journal *Der Pfahl*.[31]

This "event" does not, however, begin with a fanfare. Strauß introduces himself—following the irritating practice of American media personalities and politicians—in the third person as a shy person who admires "the grandiose and delicate organism of social interaction" (Miteinander). His shyness does not, as one might otherwise expect, derive from an inferiority complex, for one reads that "not even the most universal artist or the most divinely gifted ruler" could "come close to inventing or directing" this organism (19). The two equally exalted representatives of the elite look down upon all others. One of the two is of course not—or no longer—present, for a "ruler" is not a politician, but rather a monarch invested with divine right, and monarchs in possession of full royal powers and prerogatives have long since disappeared from Europe. The initial paragraph of the essay thus has a certain prophetic aura about it, because it is now only the artist who stands at the pinnacle of the social hierarchy.[32] The self-appointed prophet surveys the scene and discovers nothing but disaster. His warnings are not, however, contained in a fire-and-brimstone sermon utilizing all of the rhetorical tools at his disposal. Instead, certain themes are touched upon and revisited several times. Since some critics of the essay have accused Strauß of flirting with fascism, attention should be directed to one important detail of the apocalyptic vision found at the end of the second paragraph. It is a phrase that was not included in the *Spiegel* version of the essay: "Even [the ripping apart] of solidarity and marching columns" (19). It is more than likely that any contemporary German readers of these words would see in their mind's eye either neo-Nazi skinheads or masked ultra-leftists.[33] The paragraph that contains this formulation is constructed in such a way that the author simply describes things that have made an impression on him without taking sides. The danger emanating from a resurrection of fascism or from some form of left-wing terror is perceived, but at this point, Strauß fails to tell us how he might react to either alternative. His apparent passivity or indifference is not what one would expect in a political essay.

After the introductory section, Strauß turns to a discussion of democracy and prosperity—without mentioning capitalism. He speaks of a "system of structured freedoms" in which "economism stands at the center of all motives" (21). (This is of course close to the German view of Anglo-American civilization at the time of World War I.) In the context of "mass democracy," he predicts that the wealth of the people will lead to a corrosion of the cultural "substance" (20). Strauß is hardly the first critic of the superficiality of consumer society, but the manner in which he formulates his criticism is supposed to create the impression that his view is unique. His description of a small street "debased by wealth and ostentation" (20) was not an appropriate metaphor for German society as a whole in 1993, and five years later, after strikes, protest, and endless debates about the crisis of "Germany, Inc." (Standort Deutschland), it is even more off the mark. It is also not the "ignorance" (Nicht-Ahnen) of the masses that makes possible the influence of the "few" who inhabit the "nest of guiding, attracting forces" (20) but rather the lack of a societal alternative after the disappearance of the socialist bloc. An expansion or universal realization of democracy is not, from Strauß's perspective, an alternative worth striving for either: "It remains to be seen if that [the present system] is still democracy or not already democratism: a cybernetic model, a scientific discourse, or a society for the political-technical surveillance of the people by the people" (21). Are these words an expression of indifference or of cultural pessimism? There can be no doubt that Strauß, normally a distanced observer, admires premodern societies that—at least from his perspective—are still based upon old traditions, norms, and customs. Should conflicts arise, such societies might well be superior, he believes, due to their "built-in restrictions on material needs undergirded by religious beliefs" (21). Such views were not unusual in the West before the outbreak of the Gulf War, and even the skeptical Enzensberger made them his own for a time.[34] Strauß is not dismayed by the appearance of "nationalistic currents" in the era after the Cold War (21), because he believes that nationalism can unite a people by means of "moral law" and "ritual sacrifice" (Blutopfer)—something that we Westerners, "in our liberal-libertarian egocentrism," cannot comprehend (21). In this context, Tajikistan is mentioned, although no details are provided. That is unfortunately characteristic of the vagueness of the entire essay. Why does Strauß refrain from depicting, for example, the status of women in Taliban-controlled Afghanistan or in Saudi Arabia? He seems more dedicated to cultivating a feeling for the "tragic dispositions of history" (22) than to upholding human rights.

Given the elusiveness of the text, this assessment could be flawed, however. A quite different interpretation is conceivable, one that discovers in Strauß's praise of the premodern a challenge to the West to revoke the banishment of the tragic from our hyperrationally organized everyday lives and to initiate a search for the primordial forces within us. The justification for such an exercise would be to strengthen our civilization, in order to better defend it against others.[35] This reading assumes, however, that Strauß views the Western model of society as one worth preserving, and there is little evidence of that in the text. Instead of occidental self-respect, Strauß proclaims a doctrine of entropy in which all forms of political action become meaningless: "One can do what one likes, murder or pray, make revolution, or elect free parliaments—at some point, every form falls apart, the vessels fall apart, and time comes to an end" (20). This dictum—which also was not printed in *Der Spiegel*—encompasses criminal behavior, religious fundamentalism, political upheaval, and the practice of democracy. The author apparently believes, like German writer and philosopher Theodor Lessing (1872–1933), that history is the attempt to make sense out of that which is senseless. For Strauß, history is not, however, the only sphere of life where one might search for meaning. For that reason, the artistic (taken to mean all areas of creative cultural production) becomes the focus of his continuing ruminations. He does not limit himself to paeans to art; rather, he mercilessly attacks the enemies of art. In the framework of this attack, he also elucidates the essence of the "foreign" and discusses the ways in which Germans, especially (leftist) intellectuals, react to that which is not German.

The enemies of art, according to Strauß, make up the "cultural majority," and this majority is situated on the "left" (25). If one were to accept this viewpoint, then a true artist would have to gravitate toward the right. Strauß is not thinking of "right" in a political sense, however. He sees politics itself as a mortal enemy of art, because art is "by nature a profound remembering and as such a religious or protopolitical initiation" (25). The main characteristic of his kind of art is less the esthetic than the (retrospectively) visionary, the "fantasy" of the writer (25). The artist's refusal to live in the contemporary world can be traced back to an absolute rejection of the Enlightenment, for it is the Enlightenment that is responsible for the "total hegemony of the present" (24). At this juncture, one must of course interject that the concept of the Enlightenment as it is used here hardly corresponds to the self-image of its adherents. Instead, it refers — whether Strauß realizes it or not — to certain excesses and unexpected collateral effects of technological development, a development that began long before the Enlightenment and went on to become the driving force behind social transformation in the capitalist era. Strauß's critique implies a totalitarian root of the Enlightenment, and if one accepts it, it is clear that modern Western civilization holds little attraction.[36] Unfortunately, the ahistoricity and alienation from "historical evolution" (geschichtlichem Gewordensein [24]) for which Strauß reproaches the left are at the core of his own image of the Enlightenment. One cannot demonstrate one's historical consciousness by characterizing everything that has occurred since the eighteenth century as a deviation from a "long, static time" (25).

Strauß is especially averse to the left's battle against "magical and sacred authority" (25), a battle that inevitably has brought about a "hypocrisy of public morality" that has "always tolerated (if not promoted) the mocking of *eros*, the ridicule of the soldier, [and] the derision of the church, tradition, and authority" (22).[37] Before proceeding to other themes, it must be determined exactly *which* left Strauß is castigating. The "mocking of *eros*" can hardly be considered a main goal of the '68ers (unless one is thinking of the endangered nuclear family, which is rarely praised as an institution worth preserving in Strauß's own works), but if that were in fact the case, then the left would have to be in control of the mass media. (The presence of the financially shaky *tageszeitung* is anything but an expression of such control.) As far as the military is concerned, most postwar German leftists have, it is true, been less than enthusiastic—the parliamentary debate about "out-of-area" forays by the Bundeswehr was a harbinger of change, and German troops are now in Kosovo (cf. the epilogue below)—but that is more than understandable given the German military history of the last one hundred and fifty years. The church is not a leftist domain, although there are a number of "progressive pastors" involved in social activism. Most Germans do not often enter churches anyway, except when sightseeing or learning about architectural history. The left's relation to tradition is more complicated. Although the '68ers prided themselves on breaking taboos (mainly in the area of lifestyle), many of them felt attracted to the traditions of the labor movement. This is a variant of traditionalism that holds no attraction for Strauß. Regarding authority, it cannot be denied that the members of so-called "antiauthoritarian[38] communes" attempted—with questionable results—to dismantle hierarchies, but Strauß seems to forget that the failure of the student movement was followed by a "long march through the institutions" that necessitated compromises with authoritarian structures. At first, these compromises were made grudgingly, but later, they became second nature.[39] These things could be debated endlessly, but that would not be fruitful. It is the vagueness of "Impending Tragedy" that is behind the confusion. Is the leftist adversary crucified in the essay a media czar, a professional politician with pangs of conscience, an unemployed commune member with a worn-out leather jacket, or an intellectual with a civil service job? This question would be of little relevance if the text in question were a story or poem, but Strauß's intentionally public political intervention should be based upon a conceptually and historically solid foundation.

The intellectuals are the key figures (or rather, culprits) in Strauß's comments on xenophobia and xenophilia. They are "the critically enlightened ones who have no sense of fate" (26), and when they are friendly toward foreigners, it is only "because they are furious about existing conditions[40] and welcome everything that might destroy them" (23). If this were true, then self-hatred would have to be factor, and Strauß does believe that he has discovered a "self-conscious German self-hatred" as the source of modern German "tolerance" (23). Since the term "hatred of the father" (26) is also found in the essay, we retrace the steps of the psychological critics of the '68ers: On many occasions, the political activities of the "protest generation" have been described as the expression of inner conflicts (e.g., between "Nazi fathers" and their sons). In the meantime, most observers are capable of differentiation, that is, it is possible to take the psychological factors into account without disregarding other motivations (as the author of "Impending Tragedy" appears to do). Beyond psychology, it is even more problematic when Strauß portrays the intellectuals as isolated from the people, since that brings to mind the infamous Nazi equation "intellectual = Jew." This association, however, is perhaps not appropriate with respect to the essay, because the image of the *average* German that is conjured up is anything but flattering. Although we have seen that Strauß seeks to preserve "our" civilization (see note 40), the "German type as representative of the majority of the people" (23 et passim) is depicted as the archetype of the ugly German. Using attributes like "deformed," "boisterous" (vergnügungslärmig), or "ostentatious" in combination with the epithet "outrageous in their demands" (24), the author makes it abundantly clear that he despises the masses of the affluent society. If that is so, why does it disturb Strauß when "hordes[41] of the unshelterable, the unfeedable are unsuspectingly" allowed to enter the country (34)? Given that the aggressive reaction (by skinheads and others) to these "hordes" is a prerational one, Strauß should actually be in favor of their admission, because it calls up dimensions of human existence for which he otherwise searches in vain in the modern world. Utilizing the theories of anthropologist René Girard, he does in fact assert that "racism and xenophobia" are "'fallen' cult passions" that "originally had a sacred, order-promoting significance" (39).[42] It would be counterproductive to ban the discussion of such theories, but Strauß deserves censure when he plays down xenophobic acts of violence perpetrated by youths wearing Nazi insignias as "initiation by means of the smashing of taboos" (35). The author attempts to avoid sharing responsibility for violent acts by claiming that the "rightist" ("Rechte") that one should emulate is "as far removed from the neo-Nazi as the soccer fan is from the hooligan" (25). This strategy fails, however, because Strauß never really draws clear distinctions between the two groups. If the hazardous intellectual balancing act in this essay is a typical manifestation of the so-called normalization of German cultural discourse after reunification (and after the "Historians' and Literature Debates"), one can almost understand why some observers long for the old "abnormal" state of affairs.[43]

Can one discern a clear agenda in "Impending Tragedy"? Many issues of current interest are touched upon, only to be quickly cast aside. Typical examples would be the limits of growth (Strauß praises "ecologists" without discussing their concrete activities [27]), the character of nationalism, the relationship between native-born citizens and both immigrants and refugees, and the stultification of the masses in the new media age. (Regarding the latter, it is possible to speak of the "intelligence of the masses" without lamenting the fact that "10 million RTL viewers" [31] could probably never be transformed into avid readers of Heidegger!)[44] The real thrust of the essay leads in a different direction. It involves an appeal to an elite group to preserve true living and thinking for a future age. Strauß leaves no doubt that only a select few deserve admission to this exclusive circle: "The minority! Ha! That is by far too many! There is only the little band of scattered individuals. Their only medium is the exclusion of the many" (33). This "exclusion" is different from the "isolation" of the intellectuals that was criticized above, because is a voluntary one. Even the term "elite" is rejected by Strauß, since it is not exclusive enough: "[S]urvival [is] only possible in the most narrow literary-ecological enclaves, in thinking and feeling preserves" (33). One could of course ask to what extent the alternative model of human existence cultivated by the residents of such enclaves would be of interest to the "dull, enlightened mass" (31). Strauß has clearly thought about this question, because he seems to have difficulty coming to terms with the distance between him and the public (33). The cause of his malaise does not, however, lie in the lack of contact and *interchange* with the masses. Rather, he longs for the times when literature "had real power far beyond the confines of the few, when it *ordered* [my emphasis] the world and the powerful to train their capacity to listen and to strengthen wishing, thinking, and remembering" (32–33). Here we have, following the tradition described in chapter 1, not only the conception of the poet as seer, but also the vision of the poet as priest. This is a dream that certain poets have kept alive since the days of Plato, but it is difficult to dispute that the dream has been fading faster in the past fifty years than ever before. One is also justified in asking if the realization of this dream would have been beneficial for humankind. It is highly unlikely that a majority of Strauß's contemporaries would be inclined to follow his bidding after reading his characterization of the human subelite: "The subsoil has always been the same muck" (33).[45] Before joining the intellectual lynch mob that has, in the face of such arrogance, mounted a campaign against Strauß (the author's supporters have not been inactive either), one should determine whether such pronouncements are more than mere language games. To determine that, one must return to the question of cultural pessimism. In his self-portrait as a rightist, Strauß disputes any connection with this worldview: "The cultural pessimist considers destruction to be unavoidable. The rightist, however, hopes for a profound change in mentality born in the face of dangers" (27). A few paragraphs after this statement, the reader learns what the prospects are for such a change: "The paradigm shift (Leitbild-Wechsel) that is long overdue will never take place" (28). *Summa summarum:* "Impending Tragedy" may be an expression of the author's state of mind in 1993, but it is more of a series of diary entries than a political tract. The structure of the text appears to be purely fortuitous (in the two versions, Strauß put together the many textual building blocks in different configurations), and neither conceptual nor political clarity can have been his goal.[46] The fact that the editors of *Die selbstbewußte Nation* chose to reprint "Impending Tragedy" as a sort of credo of the New Right is quite astonishing. Their action can only be explained in one of two ways: Either they were so mesmerized by Strauß's dark labyrinth that their powers of analysis and criticism were benumbed, or they hoped to bask in the glare of publicity attracted by the political coming-out of a prominent writer. Beyond this, one wonders why Strauß himself provided the *Spiegel*—from his perspective an influential representative of deleterious rationalism—with an opportunity for a media coup. Was this nothing but an unabashed publicity stunt? Can the author have believed that the allure of his words would restore the vision of the blinded rationalists, or did German self-hatred claim yet another victim?[47] Similar questions can be put with regard to the political intervention undertaken by Peter Handke two years after the controversy surrounding "Impending Tragedy."

When scholars attempt to describe the nature of various literary periods or movements, they sometimes use pairs of writers as emblems. The chosen figures can represent unity or diversity: Dante and Petrarca, Lope and Calderón, Corneille and Racine, Dostoevsky and Tolstoy, Twain and Whitman, Joyce and Woolf, etc. In German literature, one might think of Goethe and Schiller, Fontane and Keller, Brecht and Mann, or Böll and Grass.[48] With respect to the contemporary period, it has been the names Handke and Strauß that have been often mentioned in the same breath. In most cases, observers point to similarities and parallels between the two writers. If divergencies are discussed, they involve mainly nuances in the esthetic sphere, not the fundamental orientation of the œuvre. Here is a characteristic formulation (that also refers to the novelist Nicolas Born):

> The attempted narrative treatment of the loss of self and the gradual disappearance of the personality is something that they have in common. They differ in the narrative strategies of coming to terms with this and in the use of language to portray it.[49]

Speaking of Handke and Strauß, Lothar Pikulik discusses the "texts of two of the main representatives of the mythical trend" and calls the two authors "the most intelligent and linguistically gifted, though also most controversial representatives of contemporary German literature." He adds that Strauß is close to Handke but writes "very differently."[50] Pia Janke, who begins her voluminous study with a polemic against "journalistic modes of interpretation," focuses on the "path" of the pair "from the absence of meaning to an esthetically grounded meaningfulness."[51] In her book on myth and literature, Susanne Marschall believes that she has discovered "separate paths" that in the end "lead in the same direction," because, she asserts: "The goal of both authors is the reconstruction of the commitment (Verbindlichkeit) of the literary work, the placing of a higher value on the ontological aspect of art, [and] a fine sensitivity for the expressive power of the word."[52]

Most of the scholarly publications on Handke and Strauß revolve around esthetic strategies and the search for identity. Of interest in the present study is the recent shift from predominantly existential themes to overtly political concerns. In the course of their careers, Handke and Strauß have reacted to societal trends and political developments from time to time, but until the 1990s, they generally did so indirectly, i.e., within the framework of their literary works.[53] This sets them apart from the older generation of writers like Enzensberger, Grass, and Walser as well as from '68 era activist and author Peter Schneider (b. 1940). In 1989, critic Bernhard Sorg published an article entitled "Remembrance of Duration: The Poeticization of the World in [the works of] Botho Strauß and Peter Handke." Sorg unearthed in the works of both authors "a disgust with the commercialization and media-friendly packaging of art," emphasizing, however, that such disgust "is in itself not a creative act and also no guarantee of esthetic relevance."[54] In the same vein, one could warn that a disgust with the often pedestrian course of democratic practice and with the banalities uttered by professional politicians in no way guarantees that the writer who feels said disgust will be capable of providing alternatives worthy of consideration.[55] As has been demonstrated in the case of Strauß, the ability to observe and a sensitive nature may or may not be sufficient tools for confronting nonliterary phenomena. They may even act as filters, distorting social and political reality. To what extent does a comparable constellation obtain in Peter Handke's lengthy essays on Bosnia, Serbia, and the West?

At the beginning of 1996, the *Süddeutsche Zeitung*, a newspaper that had not played a major role in the debate about "Impending Tragedy," made a bid for the attention of the culturally and politically interested reader by publishing Handke's "Justice for Serbia" (Gerechtigkeit für Serbien).[56] When Handke began touring Germany, reading the essay to large audiences, the *Spiegel* tried to share the limelight, dubbing the controversy surrounding Handke's essay "the most spectacular battle in the cultural supplements about the poetry and truth of a literary pamphlet since Botho Strauß's 'Impending Tragedy.'"[57] The publication of the Strauß piece had been termed the "media coup of the year," and the *Süddeutsche* was obviously hoping for more of the same.[58] At first, Handke emphasized that he had wanted to take on the media on their home ground rather than publishing another "little book."[59] This plan was later cast aside twice over when two "little books" went to press, namely the *Winter Journey to the Rivers Danube, Sava, Morava and Drina or Justice for Serbia* and, about six months later, the *Summer Supplement to a Winter Journey*. Just as in 1993, neither the marketing nor the reception of the respective writings were left to chance. Despite the similar publishing histories, the actual texts, both of which made headlines, are in actuality quite different.

In the short introduction to "Justice for Serbia," the readers of the *Süddeutsche Zeitung* were informed that they should not expect an objective political analysis by a specialist: "Peter Handke's relationship with Yugoslavia [!] began in his childhood." If Handke had written an essay about Tajikistan, for example, the result would surely have been different. As a travel writer who is always on a voyage of self-discovery (this aspect is sometimes peripheral, sometimes crucial), Handke modulates his narrative tone according to the goal of his journey. Like many European writers, he is very familiar with the U.S., but when he is closer to home, his subjectivity and (childhood) memories are more intensely juxtaposed.[60] In the present instance, he does want to familiarize himself with a foreign culture, but the motivation is less curiosity or wanderlust than defiance: "Primarily because of the wars, I wanted to go to Serbia, to the country of the so-called 'aggressors'" (*WR*, 12–13). The images in the media did not fit in with his 1960s memories of Belgrade and the island Krk, where his first book, *The Hornets*, was written.[61] In addition, Handke's mother was of Slovenian descent. Growing up in Carinthia, he was influenced by the prejudice against the Slovenian minority, but later, the relatively large and exotic region south of the border became for him a refuge from the oppressive atmosphere of postwar Austria:

> If I had the right to call myself a Yugoslavian—a right I can't have, since I am an Austrian citizen—I would gladly characterize myself with respect to my consciousness, intellect, reasoning, soul, and even my sense of space as a Yugoslavian.[62]

In the course of "Justice for Serbia," it becomes clear what Handke means by this and also how he perceives this country. He wants the reader to accompany him on his journey, but not just any reader. Only those who are willing to completely accept his highly personalized kind of "eyewitnessing" (Augenzeugenschaft) are welcome: "And those who now think 'Aha, a pro-Serbian!' or 'Aha, a Yugophile!' need not continue to read" (*WR*, 13).[63] Handke thus integrates not only his own history and identity,[64] but also his resentment against the "wrong" type of reader directly into the text. Nothing comparable can be found in "Impending Tragedy."

The *Winter Journey* is divided into four chapters, namely "Before the Journey" (11–50), "The First Part of the Journey" (51–86), "The Second Part of the Journey" (87–116), and "Epilogue" (117–135). Background and commentary thus take up almost half of the book. One cannot assume, however, that the reader learns how Handke went about his journey or at least how he planned to do it. His remarks on Emir Kusturica's film *Underground* do serve a similar function, though. According to Handke, Kusturica's earlier films did bear the stamp of a "freely flying fantasy," but they lacked "an attachment to the earth, a country, or even the world." That changed in *Underground*, where a "talent for dreaming" allied itself with "a tangible piece of the world and of history" (*WR*, 22–23). The ideal is thus the merging of the imagination and knowledge, whereas knowledge itself exhibits a strong visual component: "What does one know, when one has—connected to networks and online—merely possession of knowledge without that true knowledge that can only come about through *learning, looking, and learning?*" (*WR*, 30). An author who provides the reader with such a definition should not be surprised if he is asked by what criteria one decides *where* to look. Although Handke castigates "the mobs of [journalists] wildly gesticulating from afar who mistake their writing profession for that of the judge or even confuse it with the role of the demagogue" (*WR*, 123), he refrains from providing "intentionally contrasting images" to counter the many "prepunched peep-holes" looking in the direction of Serbia. Hoping to transcend this dichotomy, he wants (following in the footsteps of Hermann Lenz and Edmund Husserl) to illuminate the "third factor" (*WR*, 51). In the end, this entails attempting to show the reader that the Serbs are people like you and me. In and of itself, this is a praiseworthy endeavor, but Handke unfortunately forgets that he is undertaking it in the midst of a war. With no little justification, the world is, under such circumstances, mainly interested in the behavior of the Serbs, as well as the Croats and the Bosnians, as war participants, not as human beings per se. On the one hand, Handke affirms that he "hardly ever found himself so continually drawn in?, tied in?, integrated into the world or world events" as he did on this journey (*WR*, 102–103), but on the other hand, he never remotely considered the possibility of writing as a journalist. In the "Epilogue," he gives us a declaration of his writer's creed that deserves to be cited at some length:

> My task is a different one. Noting down the evil facts is fine. To make peace, something else is necessary that is not less important than the facts. Are you dragging out the poetic now? Yes, if it is understood as the exact opposite of the nebulous. Or let's say instead of the poetic the binding, the encompassing, the impetus for common memory as the only path to reconciliation for a second mutual childhood. . . . based upon the experience that common memory can be awakened in a much more lasting manner through the detour of retaining certain unimportant details rather than by pounding in the major facts. (*WR*, 133–134)

At the end of the same passage, one finds a paean to art that could have been written by Botho Strauß. Art, the "essential diversion," has the power to spirit us away from "our . . . imprisonment in the babbling ("Gerede") about history and current affairs into an incomparably more fruitful present" (*WR*, 134). If one accepts the term "babbling," then this declaration is worthy of support. Unfortunately, Handke overlooks the fact that the people in the former Yugoslavia whom he wishes to help are not caught up in "babbling" about history but rather in history itself, a history that they are shaping themselves. The key event in this history is the war, and peace and reconciliation will not be feasible until those who have—beyond "normal" participation in the war—committed crimes have been brought to justice. The writer is not a judge, but he can be a witness. That is exactly what Handke does *not* do in his essay.

Among the "unimportant details" (see above) reported by Handke are the renaming of a Langenscheidt dictionary (from *Serbo-Croatian* to *Croatian*), the unfinished new buildings, the "black market gasoline peddlers with their plastic canisters" (*WR*, 54–55), the absence of Serbian slivovitz drinkers one evening in Belgrade, old men ("well shaven for Balkan conditions"), the meeting with a Serbian woman who cannot speak Serbian (or can no longer do so), the shape of loaves of bread, homemade wine, eating *palacinke* in an unheated inn, a storm in the mountains, buying winter clothing, a view of the Drina river ("broad, winter-green, constantly fast mountain water" [*WR*, 99]), the connection between the Serbian heroic sagas and the Homeric tradition, a bus station from which it is no longer possible to travel to Srebrenica or Tuzla, and a child's sandal floating in the Drina. Such snapshots can be telling or insignificant, and when pieced together, they form a mosaic of an everyday life tinged with sadness. As justification for the journey of a Western European writer to a war zone (or at least near one), they are hardly sufficient, however. After Handke's polemic against the Western media (especially the *Frankfurter Allgemeine Zeitung, Der Spiegel,* and *Le Monde*) in the first part of the essay, these details are not at all what one might have expected. While it is true that Handke questions the accuracy and objectivity of Western reports about the Balkan conflict, he does not do any investigating of his own, and he refrains from presenting counterexamples to back up his accusations. This contradiction inevitably leads to a discontinuity in the text, in both content and style. A rather picturesque, somewhat melancholy, at times very poetic travel journal is framed by a bitter polemic. At times, it even seems as if the essay were written by two different authors.[65] Handke's odyssey in search of a life that is "less blinded by the quotidian and more poetic" (*WR*, 109), although laudable in itself, leads in this instance to a (self-imposed?) blindness to the *res publica*. This problematic distortion of the poetic quest has a long history in the German cultural tradition.

It would be an exaggeration to characterize the *Winter Journey* as an antimodern tract (Handke does, after all, express enthusiasm for the joys of shopping at a supermarket [*WR*, 110]), but the underlying mood does reflect a certain longing for life in an earlier, simpler age. For example, Belgrade appears at first glance to be a typical southern European metropolis, but the citizens seem to be somehow "more taciturn . . . , more aware . . . , more attentive" (*WR*, 57). The "numerous street vendors" do not praise their wares in stentorian tones, choosing instead to wait "quietly" for their customers (*WR*, 58). The relatively "primitive" exchange of goods holds a unique charm for the visitor from abroad, and this charm makes it into a contrasting model vis-à-vis the consumer societies of Western Europe:

> [There was] something like an ancient and, yes, folksy pleasure in trade . . . . that rubbed off on us as participants in it. . . . Let trade be praised—could you ever have imagined yourself saying something like that (and without being paid to say it)? And I even caught myself wishing that the isolation of the country—no, not the war—would endure; and that the inaccessibility of the Western (or other) world of products and monopolies would also continue. (*WR*, 72)

The person who wrote these lines enjoyed—as a prosperous foreigner—the benefits of this idyll without suffering from its disadvantages. He was able to move about freely and use hard currency to obtain anything that he needed. He also did not have to fear expulsion as an enemy or at least as a member of the "wrong" ethnic group, and he was able to return home knowing that his own four walls were still intact. If it was justified to speak of "revolution tourism" in past years, we have before us a case of "restoration tourism." Is the *Summer Supplement* a further illustration of retrospective fantasies?

In the period between the publication of the *Winter Journey* and its sequel, Handke found himself at the center of a media whirlwind. Sharp criticism of his political essays was disseminated by the mass media, and when he embarked on a long reading tour, he was often confronted with both angry demonstrators and reverential listeners. (One can only speculate about whether Strauß would have caused a tumult by reading "Impending Tragedy" in major cities. In contrast to Handke, he chose not to appear in public.) In the face of protests, Handke could not help but rethink the entire Balkan project. Already in the *Winter Journey*, there were a few instances of self-criticism or at least second thoughts. "It could be," admitted the author, "yes, I am mistaken, the parasite is in *my* eye" (*WR*, 42). "Take notice: this is not at all a matter of 'I accuse.' I am just driven to find justice. Or perhaps merely doubting, contemplation" (*WR*, 124). In the second volume, very little is retracted. The opening statement, namely that a supplement is "perhaps" necessary (*SN*, 9) is not very promising, and one of the listed motivations for the planned journey to Bosnia is expressed in such a flippant manner ("simply because") that one must view it as an example of the "authorial indignation" (*WR*, 11) typical of the *young* Handke. The author of the *Summer Supplement* toys with the reader in the area least suited for coquettishness, i.e., in matters of conscience. After hearing "these and those reactions" to the first volume,

Handke asks himself if he might have "done something incorrect, false, even unjust" (*SN*, 18–19) in writing that book. After playing around with some insignificant details, he only admits to having erred in one particular instance. (He should have "fictionalized" the statement made by a woman whom he encountered [*SN*, 21].) After this extremely perfunctory bit of introspection, the journey can continue.

Once again, the entire report is based upon the memories of the traveler, since there is—for no apparent reason—no written record (*WR*, 134–135; *SN*, 10) in the form of a journal or at least jottings on the back of envelopes. Everything seems to be preprogrammed anyway. Handke picks up his travel documents in the Belgrade office of the "Serbian Republic" (*SN*, 13; the name is not set off by quotation marks in the text) and notices that the walls are decorated not with portraits of "Radovan K. or Ratko M." but rather with a landscape painting depicting "a typically steep Bosnian pasture." The desks are not manned by overweight, sweating bureaucrats, either: "Two women dressed in summer clothes" with an elegance "characteristic of all of Yugoslavia" sit at the office desks. (Bosnian-) Serbian society is thus not represented by men and the military, but by women and pristine nature. The two women also immediately trust the three[66] travelers from the outside world, because they see in them sympathetic figures who do not want to visit their "outlawed country" (i.e., the territory held by the Bosnian Serbs) as "enemies or malevolent people" (*SN*, 13–14). The construction of this friend-foe dichotomy is actually a step backward compared to the *Winter Journey*, where Handke had at least mentioned that a third perspective was conceivable:

> [I have] nothing against some of these journalists who are on the scene (or to express it more clearly: who are involved with the scene and the people on the scene) not to uncover but to *dis*cover. Three cheers for *these* field investigators! (*WR*, 122)

In this second volume, it is Handke himself who represents a "third perspective" (*SN*, 85), but this one has little to do with field investigation in the sense of gathering facts and information. Instead, it is identified with "presentiment" (Ahnung), a capacity which "in my experience points ahead in a very different way than any [mere] knowledge," proclaims Handke. This is the author's esthetic program in a nutshell, but what relevance does it have for a political essay? This question is perhaps misplaced, because in the *Summer Supplement*, the *Winter Journey* is renamed "Winter Story" (*SN*, 30; this new title is also found on the back cover). *Nomen est omen:* As in the case of the retrospective reframing of the political essays from the 1960s (see above), Handke appears to be retreating from the political arena after having been — in his view — misunderstood.

The text of the *Summer Supplement* sometimes resembles a film script ("The border guards, like us, three in number, under the big Western sky, like in Wyoming or Oregon" [29]), a poem (see the image of the wooden boxes originally meant to hold flowers: "filled with earth turned to rubble" [33]), and even the cultural criticism found in "Impending Tragedy." One example of the latter would be the description of the "main street bars" in Bajina Basta: "[It was] stifling to sit there, as it is everywhere in the newly ordered nondescript Europe" (*SN*, 18). The description of a visit to an Orthodox church with a "war casualty cemetery" (*SN*, 46–51) reads like a short story inserted into the travel journal. There is one experience that resists transformation into literature, however, and that is Handke's trip to the destroyed city of Srebrenica. This is the only occasion where the author betrays a degree of inner turmoil. Confronting the aftermath of war — which threatens to "overwhelm the total picture" — firsthand, the author must solve the "problem of how to continue the narrative" (*SN*, 65). This problem proves to be insoluble (no attempt is made to depict the "places where the massacres allegedly occurred" [*SN*, 77]), and it is with a sense of relief that the traveler returns to a Serbia that is "suddenly blossoming, profoundly peaceful, stretching out like a global empire" (*SN*, 79). The observer's inability to deal with the horrors of Srebrenica does leave its mark, however. Upon returning home, Handke is struck by "the intactness here and its opposite there" (*SN*, 88). In his mind's eye, "clouds of soot and sheets of plastic" appear in the tranquil Paris suburbs. Such nightmares soon dissipate, however. To the very end, Handke maintains that he has written "a story without enemies of humanity, without the image of an enemy" (*SN*, 91). This is rather strange, given that the Bosnian Serbs are portrayed as freedom fighters in the tradition of the Native Americans (*SN*, 92). It is difficult not to come away with the impression that the two books on the Balkans are, in the context of Handke's ongoing journey of self-discovery, chapters that went very wrong. Politics and personal concerns do mix, but here the proportions are skewed.[67]

The critical reactions to Strauß's "Impending Tragedy" and Handke's essays on the Balkans in some measure constitute a second "Literature Debate." There were echoes of the past in this event, but not everyone noticed them. Some of the participants even ritually repeated earlier statements without mentioning that they were doing so. One example of this practice can be found in an article by Gerhard Stadelmaier from the *Frankfurter Allgemeine Zeitung*. Both this article and one that responded to it have the following subtitle: "What is Botho Strauß guilty of?"[68] Stadelmaier intends to defend Strauß from his critics, but his manner of doing so is hardly flattering to the writer's ego. In contrast to the "prophet" (Seher und Künder) Handke, Strauß is supposedly incapable of leading anyone down an intellectual path: "He is too indecisive for that, too unclear to himself. He does not precede. . . . He always follows along behind." What could possibly motivate a person to read his texts or attend his plays? The answer is a familiar one: "He is their [i.e., his characters'] seismograph. The seismograph does not cause earthquakes. He registers them."[69] These are of course the words from Ernst Jünger's diaries as quoted above. It is misleading to apply such a characterization to Strauß, because Jünger—despite his protestations to the contrary—was long part and parcel of the earthquakes before deciding to retire to the position of seismographer. Strauß is a purely intellectual phenomenon, and Gustav Seibt, who responded to Stadelmaier, sees this quite clearly. Although Seibt admits that the "reawakening of German traditions" could play a minor role in the populist movement against European integration, he is not overly concerned. After assuring his readers that the controversy surrounding "Impending Tragedy" is nothing radically new, he concludes laconically: "Democracy has withstood it so far." Although Seibt errs egregiously in attempting to effect a total separation between cultural convulsions and sociopolitical trends, his even temper is a welcome exception to the high emotions that at times reigned during the debate.

The question of "guilt" brought up in the *Frankfurter Allgemeine* would in all likelihood never have been articulated if the reactions to "Impending Tragedy" had emanated exclusively from the cultural sphere. The only commentator who was able to move Strauß to make a statement about the reception of his essay was Ignatz Bubis, the prominent spokesman for German Jews. When Bubis asserted in an interview with the Berlin *Tagesspiegel*[70] that Strauß was part of the "phenomenon of right-wing radicalism," and that this phenomenon was at least partially responsible for a climate in which hate crimes (against Jews and others) were perpetrated, Strauß could not help but respond. In the brief text "The Real Scandal" published in *Der Spiegel*, the author claimed that there was no free speech in Germany, especially regarding "the psychopathology of German political biases," and he railed against his critics:

> Whoever even remotely connects the author of "Impending Tragedy," the author of a number of plays and prose volumes, with anti-Semitism and abominable neo-Nazi acts is someone who can no longer bear difference. Thus he is either an idiot, a barbarian, or a political denouncer. Or simply someone who, almost without a will of his own, lets public babbling rush through his own mouth.[71]

It is not the rage behind these words that is surprising, but rather that they were not uttered until a year after the appearance of "Impending Tragedy," after a long period when many provocative formulations were launched against the author. Although Strauß never fails to emphasize that culture is everything to him, that nothing outside the cultural sphere is worthy of notice, he was able to disregard the harsh words spoken by representatives of that sphere. This contradiction can be attributed to the fact that Strauß himself is by no means free of the psychopathology of postwar German life. The liberal entrepreneur Bubis demonstrated that he, at least, did have a "will of his own," and the way in which he reformulated his original criticism of Strauß (and Enzensberger[72]) became part of the assessment of *Die selbstbewußte Nation*. In an interview with *Der Spiegel*, he did not retreat from his belief that there is "a new intellectual right-wing radicalism in Germany," but he offered more differentiation. He included writers in the "general climate change," but no longer associated them with two other, more dangerous groups, i.e., the "intellectual arsonists" like Gerhard Frey of the Deutsche Volksunion or Franz Schönhuber of the Republikaner and the "intellectual trailblazers of intellectual right-wing radicalism" such as Ernst Nolte and Rainer Zitelmann.[73] In this view, the intellectual New Right is placed in the same camp with right-wing politicians (vest-pocket Le Pens, as it were), but the literati are granted the freedom of the court jester. (Bubis later tried to revoke this freedom. See the epilogue below.) These jesters fit Strauß's definition of a tiny elite, but their status is surely not what he had in mind.[74]

The responses of the cultural community ignored by Strauß fall into two major categories, namely critical crusades against "Impending Tragedy" and a variety of counterattacks. The first category was given so much publicity that the second was not given due attention. The title of one early article—"Is Botho Strauß a Fascist?"—became a mantra for those who had "always known" that Strauß was a closet rightist.[75] More damaging was the short article by Peter Glotz, a prominent Social Democrat who later served briefly as president of the new University of Erfurt. Glotz called Strauß a "dangerous muddle-headed fellow" (Wirrkopf) with disturbing views on nationalism, antiauthoritarian child-rearing and xenophobia, but he made it clear that, for him at least, the appearance of Strauß's essay was most important as a symptom of a general reorientation of the German intellectuals: "Take note of the date, friends, it was the *Spiegel* edition of February 8, 1993. It's getting serious."[76] Despite the publication of *Die selbstbewußte Nation*, this warning has proved to be somewhat premature. In *Die Zeit*, Andreas Kilb attacked Strauß as a clone of Oswald Spengler, an opportunist (one who cultivates his art in enclaves provided by the system itself), and a "precentor" (Vorsänger) of a general "moroseness," an "emaciation of feeling and thinking" plaguing German intellectual life in the post-utopian era.[77] The general diagnosis is accurate, but Strauß is the wrong target, since he never seriously sought after any utopias that lay beyond the personal—unlike the '68ers. Other critics turned their wrath toward Strauß's impenetrable style, lambasting him for a "cryptically confusing" use of language.[78] This style was of course characteristic of many of the pre-essay fictional works as well, but it was apparently less of an issue with regard to imaginative writings. Probably the most devastating critique was offered (in the wake of the "Bubis affair") by literary scholar and media critic Klaus Kreimeier. In his polemic, the essayist Strauß is portrayed as someone without a single original idea who limits himself to turning the "prayer wheel" of the pre-1933 "conservative revolutionaries." Like them, asserts Kreimeier, Strauß is not a trailblazer but rather an "indicator." After he has dismissed the author of "Impending Tragedy" as a "low-brow political writer" (Trivialschriftsteller) whose terminology is derived almost exclusively from the "crypto-fascist popular literature between 1920 and 1932," he delivers a backhanded compliment: "All this can be found in Gottfried Benn—clearer, more historically based, 'less capable of being misunderstood,' and, above all: more brilliantly formulated in terms of language."[79] It is not difficult to imagine that this one piece would have been enough to drive the normally withdrawn Strauß out of the political arena for good. Several months after the appearance of Kreimeier's analysis, he did in fact inform Schacht and Schwilk that he continued to be "interested" in their political strategy, but was no longer "personally involved."[80]

Strauß's retreat was no doubt a welcome event in the eyes of many who did not want to believe that "their" author would really associate himself with the figures behind *Die selbstbewußte Nation*. A number of observers did try to effect a separation. Using Leninist jargon, Strauß could be dubbed a "useful idiot" of the *real* rightists behind the volume,[81] or it could be emphasized that he stands head and shoulders above most of the other contributors (who would probably not be capable of truly comprehending him!).[82] Yet another tactic is to make the entire project seem absolutely harmless by pointing out that none of the essays contains an open appeal to racial hatred, a call to drive foreigners out of Germany, or a return to the borders of 1937.[83] Such attempts were problematic at best, and it is not surprising that most of those who sought to defend Strauß realized that it would be counterproductive to put the New Right in the spotlight.[84] Tilman Krause, for example, insisted that Strauß was "never a partisan," and that he is being misunderstood by "overpoliticized literary criticism" (emanating from the left *and* the right).[85] Fellow writer Bodo Kirchhoff said that no one had the right to add Strauß's face to the "wanted poster" for Ernst Jünger and Carl Schmitt,"[86] whereas Eckhard Nordhofen rejected Kilb's attempt to connect Strauß with Spengler: the latter was an "affirmative prophet of doom," but the former is a "contesting" (bestreitend) prophet.[87] Nordhofen is right about Spengler, but he is conveying a false impression of Strauß if one takes him to mean that "Impending Tragedy" was written in the hope that disaster could be prevented.

All of the critics cited above, whether amicable or aggressive toward Strauß, were writing, in the midst of a controversy, for newspapers or magazines with ironclad deadlines. If one turns to responses of more length and depth, one finds that the Strauß supporters are quite well represented. The collected essays found in the 1994 special issue of the literary journal *Weimarer Beiträge* are illustrative of this phenomenon.[88] Moray McGowan concentrates on Strauß's 1989 "Büchner Prize Speech" rather than "Impending Tragedy," because he believes that one can discuss many of the same themes without being distracted by "misleading accusations of fascism" (190). The bulk of his article is, however, devoted to demonstrating that Strauß's image of the writer as hermit—one ultimately derived from Romanticism—is not appropriate for a society that is achieving normalization as a Western democracy. The farewell from the "belated nation" (H. Plessner) must, he believes, but accompanied by a transformation of the writer's role from a premodern one to a modern one (194). It is difficult not to agree with

McGowan that the vision of art as a "higher form of life" still had positive aspects during the Romantic era, but now is too closely associated with a distaste for democracy (200). Harald Weilnböck, who begins his study with a quotation in French from Ernst Jünger,[89] cannot accept the fact that Strauß does not include himself and his activities when analyzing narcissism, "almost the dominating theme of his œuvre" (211). Like Stefan George before him, Strauß is allegedly incapable of direct human contact in "normal" society and at the same time consumed by a longing for such contact. Although Weilnböck does see Strauß as an example of "German masochism," (216), his critical perspective is in the end not fruitful, because he reduces the societal context to a mere stage setting. Some critics basically favorable to Strauß, like Bernd Graff, Bernhard Greiner, Helga Kaußen, or Marieke Krajenbrink, choose to assess his importance by shifting the emphasis away from "Impending Tragedy." It is not clear that this change of focus does service to the author. (It is almost as if Strauß had to be protected against himself.) Krajenbrink admits that some interpretations of "Impending Tragedy" are accurate, but most of them, she claims, are based upon "an inaccurate or even malicious reading" (297). The one point about which there is much disagreement is Strauß's relationship to the Enlightenment. Lutz Hagestedt can state categorically that Strauß has long been an anti-Enlightenment, antidemocratic author who is a model for the intellectual right (266, 279), but Henriette Herwig maintains that Strauß is a representative of the "self-criticism of the Enlightenment." According to Herwig, *all* German intellectuals stand on the foundation of the Enlightenment (286). Anyone who has read Gerd Bergfleth et al. will recognize that this is simply wishful thinking. Herwig's thesis also contrasts with Helga Kaußen's assertion that Strauß already believed in the early 1980s that the Enlightenment had "irreversibly failed" (289). Even Strauß's supporters must admit that it is becoming increasingly difficult to understand his proclamations. These supporters would obviously rather wrestle with the writer's fictional texts than with his attempt at political journalism.

One other piece in the *Weimarer Beiträge* issue must be presented, and its significance lies in its use of the critic as medium. Volker Hage's "The Writer after the Battle," reprinted from *Der Spiegel*,[90] conjures up images of the proselyte sitting at the feet of the master, hanging on his every syllable. This is how it must have been in the "George Circle" at the turn of the century. Since Strauß "hates and fears every public appearance" (140), the critic must convey his thoughts via a sympathetic observer like Hage, who tells us that we might not comprehend everything in Strauß's works because the author has a "greater recall of language" and a larger vocabulary (141). (There is no pause to consider that words can be utilized to hinder communication.) According to Hage, the strength of "Impending Tragedy" lies in the fact that the author does not offer "opinions," but rather "bewilderment" (Verstörung [143]). Lest one disagree, he argues that it is impossible to "contextualize" the essay or the 1993 play *Equilibrium* (Das Gleichgewicht) without a knowledge of the prose works. One has the impression that Strauß never imagined that the reaction to a "journalistic" text (not his métier, he admits [143]) would be different from that of an audience in a theater or the solitary reader of a novel. Is such naiveté conceivable on the part of a prominent author approaching fifty? A rare interview given by Strauß in the summer of 1997 [91] shows that it was the critics who were naive. The interviewer, Tilman Krause (cf. *Die selbstbewußte Nation*) hopes to demonstrate that the author has been misunderstood. To Krause, Strauß is actually more of a '68er (indeed, one who overestimates the impact of that generation[92]) than anything else. The author is allowed to hold forth on this point:

> I would endorse a rightist or new rightist movement? What an absurd idea! As soon as it is a matter of models, I pull back. Thus it is also ridiculous to accuse me of wanting to rise up to be a *vates*, a seer. . . . Of course I am fascinated by George. I am fascinated by thought processes beyond or above the critical. I am also fascinated by the Catholic Church, which has an attraction due to its deep rooting in authority. But that fascinates me because it is foreign to me, not because I could reflect myself in it in an identificatory manner. I will remain a Protestant mystic. As a Catholic, I would have to confess, communicate.

Was "Impending Tragedy" perhaps written by someone else? Strauß reports in the interview that the first version was "much more moderate, unaggressive." It was only the offer from *Der Spiegel* that caused him to transform it into "a manifesto, a pamphlet." In other words, he played the media game in order to attract more publicity. He now admits that much of the essay was mere fireworks ("Theaterdonner") and also that he also enjoys "irritating" people. (Krause adds that these people were the "model pupils of political-esthetic correctness.") After having read this interview, one is left with two possibilities: either Strauß is a "holy fool" who knows little about the world, or he is a cold, calculating manipulator of the public sphere and cultural institutions that are so repugnant to him. (The latter would be incomparably more disturbing than the former.)

One can discern comparable mechanisms and themes in the critical response to Handke's books on the Balkans. There are significant differences between the two "literary scandals," however. First of all, Handke is much less reticent about speaking with the media than Strauß. A number of lengthy interviews are available for perusal, so the interpreter need not rely on conjecture as often as in the case of "Impending Tragedy." Secondly, as has already been mentioned, Handke decided to go on tour with the first volume soon after it was published. His reactions to his audiences and to the protesters who often brought their placards to his readings are a matter of public record. Thirdly, the entire controversy was much more political, because Handke was not engaging in dark musings about a coming apocalypse but rather involving himself in a debate about a contemporary military and political conflict. Finally, the discussion of his image of the Balkans had an international dimension, since observers from abroad offered their viewpoints in the media. (In retrospect, it is remarkable how provincial the "Strauß affair" really was.[93]) Handke, who lives outside Paris, is much more of a known quantity beyond the German-speaking world than Strauß.

In December 1994, Handke was interviewed by *Der Spiegel* about his new novel *My Year in the No-Man's Bay* (Mein Jahr in der Niemandsbucht) and about his views on literature and politics.[94] About a year before his journey to Serbia, Handke announces the end of *littérature engagée*: "The epoch in which literature always had to be factual, honest, enlightening or political is coming to an end" (170). This is the position of the initiators of the "Literature Debate" from the early 1990s. Handke believes that the end of ideologies has come, and he rejects constant categorization and conceptualization as a "German disease" (171). He tells the interviewers that he was never a "'68er," portraying himself as an early target of that generation. When asked a follow-up question about Botho Strauß, Handke makes it clear that although he admires the "subtle" Strauß, he cannot understand how the latter could gravitate toward the "rightists" (171). This is because a writer identifies himself with any one position at his peril: "In any case, he [the writer] is no rightist. And also not a conservative. The writer is everything: conservative and anarchistic" (171). Of even more interest is the way in which Handke describes his relationship with the mass media:

> In the morning, I read *Libération*, in the afternoon, *Le Monde*. You can't escape that. If I ignore the media, the world seems even more oppressive to me, because I know nothing of it. When I see the television news, I am overcome with a feel-

ing of happiness—suddenly, I am in the world. . . . After a long period of disgust with the media, it became clear to me that I cannot in the long run be the enemy of my age or to act as if I were. I don't have to become its buddy, but I would like to—without being conciliatory—get along with it and take part. (176)

A year later, the person who made this statement was to launch bitter polemics against *Le Monde*. Perhaps this was merely an example of the capriciousness of the writer who must be everything and nothing, seeking the public eye in whatever manifestation might suit him at the moment.

Two major interviews granted by Handke in early 1996 provided the writer with an opportunity to react to the criticism of the way in which he was "taking part" in his age by demanding "justice for Serbia." In February, he was interviewed for *Die Zeit* by Willi Winkler, who had three years earlier asked the question: "Is Botho Strauß a Fascist?" The journalist was much more obliging on this occasion, letting the writer state his case without having to deal with troublesome questions. Handke dismissed his critics apodictically: "These people cannot be people of peace. My text is word for word a peace text. Whoever does not see that can't read."[95] Winkler does not ask for clarification, and he simply changes the subject when Handke accuses the *Frankfurter Allgemeine*, *Der Spiegel*, and *Le Monde* of "criminal," even "war-criminal" reporting about Serbia. Later, Handke describes Austria as a country devoid of "self-confidence" (Selbstbewußtsein), much as Schacht and Schwilk speak of Germany. (In 1992, he had described the Germans as being "brutal, inscrutable . . . totally sick."[96]) At the end of the interview, he complains that he is being branded a "nonpolitical author," although he published political texts in the 1960s. One remembers that these essays were intentionally depoliticized in the author's preface to their publication in book form. Winkler has nothing to say about this, either. About a month later, the Austrian journal *profil* provided another forum for the author's ramblings.[97] After claiming—unconvincingly, to this observer—that the Austrian government could have stopped the Yugoslavian tragedy from happening, Handke portrays Germany as a hegemonial power promoting the founding of small states (like the segments of the former Yugoslavia) "capable of being enslaved" in the interests of the German economy (80). Given this mind-set, it is not surprising that he calls the leader of a group of anti-Handke demonstrators a "Capo" (81). (This is an example of the "fascism club" often wielded in German political debates.) In the course of this interview, it becomes clear that the fragmentation of Yugoslavia was a personal trauma for Handke, because he had hoped that the citizens of that country would accomplish what no others in Eastern Europe have done (or wanted to do), namely, to negotiate a third (or "special") path. Ironically, many '68ers (a group to which Handke does not belong, one recalls) may well have had similar hopes and dreams. Perhaps one should not take Handke's political pronouncements too seriously, however. In the *profil* interview, he compares the *Winter Journey* to the ballads of Bruce Springsteen (81) and reveals that the profits gleaned from his reading tour with the book will not be used for "humanitarian purposes," but rather to establish—in the former war zone—a bar "with a jukebox, slot machine, and perhaps even better things" (83). At the end of the *Zeit* interview, Handke asserted that he wanted absolutely nothing to do with political power. Given his pubescent fantasies and lack of any capacity for self-criticism, one can only hope that he will not change *that* position in the future.

Before turning to the numerous commentators who criticized Handke's unexpected exercise in political intervention, one should examine the statements of *support* that were also launched. An unawareness of such statements would make Handke's at times harsh reactions to his critics seem justified, or at least understandable. Even Peter Schneider, an early and sharp critic of the *Winter Journey*, praises the "descriptions of landscapes and people" in the more literary section of the book as examples of "great density of perception and exotic beauty."[98] Schneider's main criticism is that Handke lashes out at the "horde"[99] of foreign correspondents without doing any investigation of his own or providing a single new fact (163). Andreas Kilb, who savaged Strauß's "Impending Tragedy," is impressed with Handke's crusade against the dominant media, and when he expresses his respect for the author's independence, he refers to him as an "extremely dangerous opinion *anarch.*"[100] The final word makes the connection to Ernst Jünger, one that Handke would hardly have made himself. Michael Thumannn defends Handke against Schneider's "one-dimensional perspective," but he is mainly interested in castigating the Germans for the crimes against the Serbs.[101] (In this he is close to Handke's own motivation for writing.) Willi Winkler, once again demonstrating the sympathy found in his interview with Handke, speaks of *Winter Journey* as a "thorough critique of the media" with "philological" accuracy.[102] Winkler's own objectivity comes into question when he denies the right of intellectuals to criticize Handke by pointing out that they have not "bled" (i.e., on a battlefield). The most characteristic position taken by Handke's allies is to separate the literary sections of *Winter Journey* from the journalistic ones. Writer Michael Scharang defends Handke's use of the "anarchy" of narrative as an appropriate method of countering mere "information," which for him is—except for a command—"the most abbreviated form of reality."[103] In a similar vein, Peter Vujica calls Handke's text "a significant piece of a visionary other-world" that has been misunderstood as "reality."[104] It was of course the author himself who caused such misunderstanding by mixing two distinct modes of perception. Even Serbian author Aleksandar Tisma, who does not believe that the *Winter Journey* can help the reader to comprehend the Yugoslavian tragedy, sees nothing objectionable in the book as a literary work:

> Handke did not utilize political argumentation in his book. He did not view Serbia from the perspective of its rulers, but rather with the eyes of a dreaming writer. In my view, Handke is one of the few truly decent writers. Let's let him dream a bit.[105]

It was apparently the age-old French fascination with "German dreaming" (see chapter 1) that led Luc Rosenzweig, despite his rejection of Handke's politics, to see the author's Balkan travels as partly a "German journey of education," one of self-discovery, in which an "empathy for landscapes and people" is deeply felt.[106] Defending Handke was, given the author's fulminant temperament, a difficult task. Austrian writer Peter Turrini, participating in a discussion that followed Handke's reading of *Winter Journey* at the Viennese Akademietheater, called his colleague's prose "a peace text" and "a rational offer to journalists" to rethink their methods. He must have been taken aback when Handke, speaking later in the discussion, referred to the international media as "the Fourth Reich."[107]

Some of Handke's epithets were more personal than that. Audience members who wished to ask questions were dismissed as "assholes" or even "fascist assholes."[108] Continuing to cultivate the Germanic tradition of anal imagery, he told one would-be discussant: "Why don't you stick your dismay (Betroffenheit) up your ass?"[109] The author did resort to more moderate tones during a reading in the hallowed halls of the Austrian parliament. When a Green MP asked him how he would assess a report about Nazi Germany written in "a similarly naive manner," Handke replied: "I hereby sentence you to shame for comparing Serbia with Nazi Germany."[110] Fascism did in fact rear its head at various times during the debate about *Winter Journey*. Gustav Seibt of the *Frankfurter Allgemeine* announced that Handke had "conquered the province of ideological trash" and was an organ for a "mania of blood and soil" (Blut und Boden).[111] A journalist who had worked in Bosnia characterized Handke's prose as "Schreibtischtätertum," i.e., the perpetration of a crime without leaving one's desk (as in the case of Adolf Eichmann).[112] Such extreme formulations were little more than sensationalism. Another critical perspective, one which linked Handke to the tradition described in chapter 1 of this study, was potentially much more damaging. Terming Handke's resentment against the media "predemocratic," philosopher Wolfgang Müller-Funk accused Austrian intellectuals of not accepting the concept of human rights. He also saw in Handke's idealization of supposedly premodern Yugoslavia a "leftist version" of the "Habsburg nostalgia."[113] This is a link to Hofmannsthal's visions of a timeless cultural realm, and one could view "Habsburg" as an Austrian variant of the Middle Ages glorified in Novalis's *Christendom or Europe*. Reinhard Mohr, who called Handke's book tour a "reading procession," believed that he had witnessed the birth of a new "protopolitical atmosphere of awe" (Weihestimmung) in which reality is denied and the audience wishes to be enchanted by the words of the literary prophet.[114] (As has been delineated above, such an atmosphere is hardly "new.") In an ever more complicated world, all too many people seek out a "guru" who will lead them to a "new anti-intellectual bliss or harmony" (217).[115] This is the role that Strauß played in *Die selbstbewußte Nation*, although it could be argued that he was eased into it by his handlers from the New Right rather than selecting it himself. Generally, one has the impression that Handke is a more conscious orchestrator and sociocultural choreographer than Strauß. It is possible to imagine the Austrian as the main character in Thomas Mann's prophetic novella *Mario and the Magician,* but not the anchoritic German.

In late 1996, after the publication of Handke's *Summer Supplement,* critic Gustav Seibt was interviewed about his tenure as chief literary editor of the *Frankfurter Allgemeine*. On that occasion, he declared that the role of literary "guru" was no longer relevant in contemporary German society:

> There is an authorial self-image—that is primarily characteristic of Botho Strauß and Peter Handke—that even now comes down to the conception of the writer as seer or at least as the better perceiver. The striving for better perception should indeed be maintained. In the case of Grass, it's something else. There we have the representational role, the wish to inherit the ermine mantle of Thomas Mann in order to give the nation direction in a political-moral sense.

Both roles, though, entail a prominent public position for authors, one that goes beyond their argumentative potential, and I of course have never been able to believe in that. . . . I don't believe that today any dangers for democracy can arise out of the utterances of a Botho Strauß. Those are hysterical fears.[116]

Seibt spoke in the same interview of a younger generation of authors who "take into account that we have a functioning democratic public sphere," and who are thus "less moralistic, less didactic (präzeptoral)." This was the gist of the "Literature Debate," only this time, Seibt was leading an offensive against authors perceived as being representatives of the right.[117] The problematic nature of both of these campaigns will be addressed at the end of this study. In the context of the "Handke scandal," attention must be turned to a group that still took literary interventions — in contradistinction to Seibt — quite seriously, so seriously in fact, that an anti-Handke book resulted.

In what may well be a unique event in German literary history, Tilman Zülch, the founder, German chairman, and international president of the organization Society for Endangered Peoples (Gesellschaft für bedrohte Völker) collected fifteen "Responses to Peter Handke's Winter Journey to Serbia," added one of his own, and published the lot as the volume *The Writer's Fear of Reality*.[118] The reader has a fair idea of the thrust of the book before even opening it, because the cover shows cellist Vedran Smailovic playing in the ruins of the National Library in Sarajevo. With the exception of Zülch's introductory piece, all of the responses had been published earlier in newspapers or magazines (one was a segment from a television program). The purpose was not to document a cultural debate for future generations — as had been done with the contributions to the "Literature Debate" or the "Historians' Debate" — but rather to place Peter Handke before a kind of ad hoc tribunal. (After the bibliography, one finds a list of addresses and publications from the Society for Endangered Peoples, including one by Zülch about "genocidal crimes" in Srebrenica [136].) Unlike the "Russell Tribunals" of the Vietnam War era, however, the target is not a government or a military force, but an individual writer. This is tantamount to shooting at sparrows with cannons, and it brings to mind other problematic campaigns like the defamation of Brecht in the 1950s Bundestag, the Soviet measures against Solzhenitsyn, or the imprisonment of dissident writers in Eastern Europe. If the goal were a healthy debate, that would be completely in order, but Zülch presents us only with critics, leaving the Handke supporters cited above out in the cold.

Zülch's article, "Speak Finally with the Victims of 'Greater Serbia,' Mr. Handke," provides many grisly details about the Bosnian conflict, including references to violations of human rights perpetrated by Croats and Bosnians. This is helpful, but it is unfortunately supplemented with unnecessary pathos. No purpose is served by asking a rhetorical question like this one: "What might the correspondent of the *Süddeutsche Zeitung*, Egon Scotland — one of over fifty journalists who died in Bosnia up until the beginning of 1996 — have said about Handke's report?" (16). First of all, it was not a "report" at all, and secondly, Zülch's blood reckoning is too similar to the attack on Handke's critics cited above. It also makes no sense to accuse Handke of undertaking a book tour while thousands of Bosnian Serbs are being forced by Radovan Karadzic to evacuate their homes (21). This is reminiscent of a scene in Peter Schneider's 1971 novella *Lenz*, in which the title character is castigated for daring to paint his kitchen during the Vietnam War.[119] More disturbing is Zülch's belated contribution to the "Literature Debate." After categorizing Handke's text as mere "writing" (Schriftstellerei — a less than flattering word for literature [20]), Zülch unexpectedly broadens his scope, placing the author of the *Winter Journey* in the same boat with "many German and European writers" who have "made taboo, covered up, or ignored" the "mass exterminations of National Socialism and Stalinism" (22). His selected list — Hamsun, Hauptmann, Brecht, and Shaw — is not only skewed, it also implies that Handke is working under the same conditions and constraints as his colleagues in the 1930s and 1940s. One could debate the point, but there is no possibility of rational discussion when Zülch asks if Handke might be a "war profiteer" himself (23). One can imagine that literary figures might be "endangered people" if they worked under a régime headed by the confrontational activist.

To be fair, it should be pointed out that most of the other contributors to the volume are literary critics (there is also one filmmaker, Marcel Ophuls, and one author, Günter Kunert), and they are generally also rather harsh in their dealings with the beleaguered Handke. This can be gauged by compiling a list of pejorative terms used to describe Handke's profession and/or his person. He is an "artistic soul" (35), "highly literary nose" (36), a "pale *literatus*" (36), one of the fearful "poets and thinkers" (36; meant pejoratively — see the preface to this study), "snobs, poets, and fellow travelers" (39), a "modern writer" (41; meant ironically), a representative of "blood and soil literature" (49, 71), "diary of Handke's weak nerves" (50), no *poeta doctus*" (52), "intellectual lowlands of politicizing poets" (61), "arrogant sensitivity" (65), "arrogant pride in being a blind seer" (66), "poetry of simple-mindedness" (66), "missionary" (78), "monk" (79), "poet-priest" (81), "hypocrisy" (85), "self-satisfied know-it-all" (85), "exoneration poet" (105), and so forth. This compendium clearly reflects a deep resentment against high culture in general and against Handke in particular. Poet and essayist Günter Kunert (himself a renowned member of the high culture elite), who abhors any mixture of literature and politics, provides us with a sarcastic thumbnail sketch of German literary history:

> The writer, in Germany usually called a "poet" ("Dichter"), even when he produces fat novels, traditionally has had a special position. Since Goethe, the author has expected adoration and subservience. The German poet is a happy coincidence ("Glücksfall") of creation. (62)

This is poppycock, unless one interprets it to mean that not German readers, but German governments have respected and feared writers. Goethe had to flee the oppressive conditions in his homeland from time to time, and after him, many "poets" had no choice but to live as exiles (if they were fortunate enough to cross the border in time). The Pantheon is of course in Paris, not Berlin, Frankfurt, Hamburg, or Munich. Kunert does not provide us with names, but it is clear that he is against the political "escapades" (his word) of both Grass and Handke, two writers whose approaches to politics are diametrically opposed.[120] Kunert's views are put in historical perspective by critic Ralf Caspary, who begins his essay with the following statement:

> Peter Handke is a modern Romantic, a descendant of Novalis and Friedrich Schlegel, and the dispute about his travel report is also a dispute about the political relevance of the Romantic concept of poetry, which these days is taking on strange forms. (77)

According to Caspary, the Serbia described by Handke is the author's own "Romantic utopia," a "premodern idyll in which medieval conditions obtain" (78).[121] The critic is willing to accept this in a purely literary sphere, but when the writer becomes a "missionary" bent on stylizing his texts as a "metaphysical secret code" that transports "truth," he has gone too far. It is not at all difficult to dismantle the self-important Handke,[122] but the subtext of the attacks on him by Caspary and many other observers is that any "truth" that literature might have is necessarily divorced from social and political reality, and that any attempt to link the two domains accomplishes nothing more than the destruction of literature.[123] What is ironic is that not a few of these German critics can hardly contain their enthusiasm when writers from other parts of the world—Salman Rushdie, Gabriel García Márquez, Isabel Allende, Oe Kenzaburo, Nadine Gordimer, Wole Soyinka, Milan Kundera, and many others—construct works based upon such links. One can debate Caspary's assertion that the Romantic concept of literature no longer has any political relevance, but it is a crude distortion of the historical developments to cultivate the myth of a German high culture produced by an elite that consistently enjoys great respect and adulation. Instead, one might consider that the seemingly otherworldly proclamations of that elite are at least partially the result of social isolation, if not hostility or even ostracism. Self-congratulation can be a result of arrogance, but it also can be an attempt to compensate for a lack of attention and respect.

Some of the sharpest criticism of Handke's *Winter Journey* came from abroad. Exiled Bosnian scholar and writer Dzevad Karahasan considers various readings of the text, coming to the conclusion that it is purely literary prose made up of "private gossiping."[124] According to Karahasan, it cannot be a travel report, because Handke knows little about the area he is visiting,[125] and if it were meant to be a "moralistic pamphlet," then it would be "one of the most disgraceful examples of ethical nihilism in our time" (44).[126] Unfortunately, Karahasan disqualifies himself as a judge of moral character by immediately adding that he finds the writer Eduard Limonov less repugnant. It seems that Limonov supported the Serbian siege of Sarajevo with a gun in his hand, an act that makes it easier to see where he stands. This is either ethical nihilism or misplaced irony. Karahasan's critique seems moderate when compared with the fulminations of Marcel Ophuls (whose father had to flee from Nazi Germany). Ophuls comes to the defense of the courageous journalists who risked their lives to report from Bosnia, but his real agenda seems to be an attack on the "political opportunism" of François Mitterand.[127] He even wonders if Handke has enough access to the corridors of power in Paris to cause critical journalists to be transferred to other, less important assignments (37). It is troubling that Ophuls feels the need to construct a dichotomy between the "German writer" on the one hand and the journalists and activist Jewish intellectuals (e.g., Elie Wiesel and Roman Polanski) on the other. The latter are portrayed as calling for intervention against ethnic cleansing despite resistance from "the Elysée Palace, the Pentagon, and the White House" (40). In the end, Handke appears

to be a protofascist at best. This is not the term chosen by André Glucksmann, who speaks of the "monomaniacal terrorist" Handke.[128] Glucksmann
believes that Handke is basically an antifascist and German (self?-)hater
who is primarily interested in besmirching the reputation of the Germans
and Austrians rather than contributing to the understanding of the Balkan
conflict: "Although he is against Hitler, he is, unfortunately, for the Serbs."
Glucksmann's refusal to accept Handke as a "serious intellectual" is an underground continuation of the dispute between Heinrich and Thomas
Mann during World War I. The "serious" intellectual from Paris (or who admires Paris, like Heinrich) relies mainly on rationality (or at least believes
that he does so), whereas the German counterpart is too engulfed in irrationality, antimodernism, and a personal quest to do that. As Glucksmann
puts it in this particular case: "He [Handke] reduces the suffering of the people in the former Yugoslavia to his own psychological drama." Glucksmann
is capable of more differentiation than Ophuls, however. He does not portray
Handke as *the* German intellectual per se. The alternate, more "Parisian"
mode is, he reminds us, represented by figures like "[Günter] Grass,
[Joschka] Fischer, [Jürgen] Habermas, [Daniel] Cohn-Bendit—and when
he was still alive—[Karl] Popper." It is telling that Grass is the only writer on
this list. His model of political intervention based on Enlightenment
principles[129] has been under duress since the beginning of the "Literature
Debate."

Cultural observers in the German-speaking countries could not help
but wonder, after following the course of the debates about Strauß and
Handke, if the postdebate literary careers of the two writers would provide
further evidence of a "veer to the right." Would the seed of a new rightist literature germinate? Strauß's 1994 volume, *Living, Glimmering, Lying*, consisting of thirty-seven short prose pieces, did not offer much clarification.
Written in the style of his earlier *Pairs, Passersby,* it is a postmodern potpourri
of motifs and themes from earlier works as well as from "Impending Tragedy." Among these are the alienation of the writer, the violent undercurrent
and primordial impulses in human relationships, the superficiality of mass
culture, and the inadequacy of reason for plumbing the depths of human experience.[130] This palette only partially corresponds to the concerns of the
New Right. It was not in prose, but rather in texts for the theater and in the
public performance of such texts that the future contours of Strauß's and
Handke's production were to come into focus. This was only fitting, since

both authors had initially come to the attention of the public as representatives of the dramatic genre. Their recognition and success as writers of prose came later and has at times overshadowed their authorial beginnings.

In late 1992, Strauß wrote a play entitled *Equilibrium* (Das Gleichgewicht). It was published in 1993 and first performed at the prestigious Salzburg Festival in July of that same year.[131] It was later staged in several German cities, and it was not a center of controversy, although Strauß did state — in characteristically obscure language — that the play shared "vibrational relationships" (Vibrationsverhältnisse) with "Impending Tragedy."[132] These "vibrations" emanate primarily from the relationship between a father and his son in the post-reunification Berlin of 1992. The father (Christoph Groth), is a dynamic, successful economist who has just returned from a sabbatical in Australia, where he was initiated into both Zen and the art of archery as a therapeutic and athletic exercise. His son Markus is a product of prosperity and liberal upbringing, a rather torpid figure who is not energetic enough to really rebel. His major attempt at countering his father's influence involves arranging a tryst between his stepmother Lilly and Jacques Le Cœur, an aging rock star whom she worships. In the context of this study, the play might be renamed *Liberalism and Its Discontents*. Christoph ponders the ongoing transformation of the world economic system and believes that Eastern Europe has tremendous potential (49). Telling Markus that he plans to open a consulting firm there, he warns his son that only those who act quickly will have a chance to survive. This leads to a heated exchange about morality and society that in all likelihood reflects the reorientation of Strauß's own thinking in the 1990s. After arguing about Iran (Christoph had been a consultant to the shah in prerevolutionary days), the following dialogue ensues:

> **Markus:** At times, people here would also like to the see the hand of the blasphemer cut off. Not the hand of the small-time thieves or prostitutes, but rather the hand of the intellectual scoundrel, the liberal Moloch who is transforming our lives into a stinking garbage heap. Europe is sick. Much sicker than you think.
>
> **Christoph:** What about you? I suppose that you yourself are not liberal?
>
> **Markus:** (forcing a smile): Liberal? No, I'm not. My former best friend is liberal, and I see what has become of him, but I'm not.
>
> **Christoph:** What the devil are you then?
>
> **Markus:** Not at all liberal, more or less. One can be many things, a warrior, an ascetic, a purist, and not approve of everything that is permitted.

Christoph: Hezbollah would be just the thing for you, right?

Markus: One can also believe in Jesus Christ when he says: "I have not come to bring peace, but the sword."

Christoph: Well listen to that: my son is making militant noises! A little bug of a guy, one with stunted growth, a plant that never grew—the weakling is praising moral terror! The coward enthuses about cutting of hands! . . . I'll tell you one thing . . . : the world will be completely liberal, or it will cease to exist. . . .

Markus: . . . Without the revolt of purity, without the cleansing by voices of angels, nothing can be saved.

Christoph: . . . [I]f you hold such views, then go out and take them to the marketplace like all of the fanatics do. You'll soon see that the market decides all by itself if there is a chance for Markus Savonarola." (52-54)

Markus has militaristic fantasies (about Achilles and Hector, for example [62]), but it is Christoph who (accidentally?) hits Lilly with an arrow. The representative of the liberal capitalist establishment, whose egocentrism causes him to overlook the revolting underbelly and dangerous byproducts of the system he defends (criminals, drug addicts, skinheads, violence against foreigners, etc.[133]), is actually more dangerous than his verbally violent son. When Lilly miraculously recovers from the effects of her injury simply by meeting Jacques Le Cœur face to face, the message is clear: It is only outside the parameters of the "enlightened" system, in the realm of the irrational or mythical, that our existential wounds can be healed. In *Equilibrium,* Strauß depicted the contemporary world, providing only brief glimpses of an alternative sphere. In his next play, he left our world completely behind, turning to a literary mentor who portrayed Achilles, Hector, and many others.

Despite the ongoing marginalization of classical studies in the German *Gymnasium*, many Germans are familiar with the literature of ancient Greece and Rome. When Botho Strauß decided to attempt a theatrical adaptation of Homer's *Odyssey,* he knew that he could find an audience with some previous knowledge of the text. A five-part radio play version had been broadcast by South German Radio in 1959, and in 1996, Hessian Radio offered no fewer than twenty-one readings (each forty-five minutes in length) from the epic tale.[134] On that occasion, the reader was none other than the actor Dieter Mann, who was to play the main role in Strauß's *Ithaka*[135] in the 1997-98 production at the Deutsches Theater in Berlin. The July 1996 premiere performance of *Ithaka* in Munich was a media event. Normally, adaptations of classical texts would hardly attract the attention of the mass media, but this was Strauß's first new work for the theater since the controversy surrounding "Impending Tragedy." A special preopening performance was staged for an audience of approximately four hundred critics. Rumors about the play had been circulating since well-known actor Helmut Griem had turned down the role of Odysseus, apparently for political reasons.[136] The question in the critics' minds was not whether Strauß had written a good play, but whether he had decided to amplify his essayistic turn to the right in the form of a purely literary text.

Since Strauß chose to offer an adaptation rather than an original work, one might be justified in assuming that he hoped to deflect any possible political criticism before the fact by taking on a disguise. In a short introductory text printed after the *dramatis personae*, he spoke of transporting the listener into the "childhood of the world."[137] He also modestly described his project as "a translation of reading into a play . . . the long finale of Ithaka, as he [i.e., the reader] imagines it" (9). Beyond selection and rearrangement, his only original contribution was the insertion of three "fragmentary women" (each identifiable by the highlighting of a specific part of the body) as a minimalist Greek chorus. The question remains why a writer who had probably been familiar with the *Odyssey* for decades was motivated to offer his own personal visualization of it in 1996.[138] He could have emulated Wagner by turning to Germanic legends and myths, or he could have reworked one of Goethe's plays satirizing the French Revolution. The first option would probably have brought forth accusations of fascist tendencies, whereas the second would have gone more in the direction of irony and sarcasm than toward the solemnity to which he aspired. Finally, the (re-) elevation of ancient Greece to a model for living implied a critique of the replacement of the old humanistic elite by the new bureaucratic-technological one in the course of the nineteenth century.

Strauß's adaptation of books 13-24 from the *Odyssey* is divided into five parts. The titles of the first four are references to the action on stage ("The Arrival," the "Household of the Suitors," "The Scar [of Odysseus]," and "The Bow of Odysseus"[139]), whereas the superscription preceding part five speaks to the purpose of the enterprise: "The Recognition [of Odysseus by Penelope]. The Contract." This contract (an aspect added by Strauß) is a social one meant to determine power structures and loyalties after the return of the long-absent king. Already in 1.3, Athena decries the "horrifying interregnum" and tells Odysseus that he will put an end to it (18). Throughout the play, it is not the person of the king, but rather the institution of the monarchy that is idealized. As in Novalis, it is actually the queen who symbolizes the institution. (The "Fragmentary Women" describe Penelope as "the pure, the arch-faithful one," terming Odysseus "the often unfaithful one" [14].)[140] Despite this, it is only the return of the king that will "expunge temporality" (13). This can be taken to mean a return to the "long, immobile time" of which Strauß spoke in "Impending Tragedy." As opposed to the suitors, whose activities are limited in scope (they are "soldiers, researchers, merchants, philosophers, statesmen, and athletes" [13]), the king is capable of uniting all for the common good. Before he can accomplish this, however, he must endure innumerable hardships, confront tragedy, and overcome adversity. There is no doubt that Strauß wished to depict this arduous path as a contrast to the modern society that he despises, one which no longer has any appreciation for the tragic dimension of life.

This modern society is of course a democratic one dominated by "pleasure seeking, sports, and boasting," in the words of the swineherd Eumaios (21). In 2.3, the political rhetoric of the suitors can be read as a biting indictment of (pseudo-) democratic practice. Before the audience hears the suitors' views on the nature of government, the "Fragmentary Women" recount the "Argos episode" from the *Odyssey*, thus erecting a monument to faithful service (the dog Argos remains true to his master to the end). Ageláos proposes the election of the king by a council of princes (Strauß uses the word "Gaufürst" as a provocation, since "Gau" was a term from Nazi bureaucratese) and emphasizes that the king must be dependent on the directives of the noble assembly. Leiokritos sees slavery as the basis for increasing prosperity and calls for more military expeditions, and Antinoos, the preeminent suitor, holds forth like a proto–New Dealer: "The goal of all the resolutions of our assembly is the welfare and peace of our peoples." Beyond politics, Amphimedon proclaims that festivals connected with "ancient cults" are to be forbidden and sacrificial offerings of food and drink are to be drastically reduced. Leiokritos also names the Phoenicians as the "main enemy of our trading community," an enemy who supposedly embodies "a lack of character and an unscrupulous pursuit of profit." He adds that the morals and customs of the suitors' peoples are "foreign" to the Phoenicians (38–39). It is the word "foreign" and its variations that are at the center of the rest of this scene. When Odysseus appears, disguised as a beggar, Antinoos uses the occasion as an opportunity to expound on immigration policies: Although he and the other suitors have nothing against foreigners per se, they are upset that "useful foreigners" (e.g., merchants, artisans, doctors, artists, or oracles) rarely appear (40). After Antinoos has insulted Odysseus as an "ugly glutton" (häßlicher Fresser [40]), the beggar responds with an apocalyptic parable about a "false king" (41). This and other comments cause Antinoos to throw a stool at Odysseus, striking the "foreign freak" (Mißgeburt) on the shoulder. Ageláos criticizes Antinoos for acting in this manner, because, he says, the Gods sometimes appear as "lousy foreigners" in order to put people to the test (42). Even the local beggar Iros feels confident enough to call Odysseus a "foreigner and scoundrel" (44). It is only when Odysseus defeats Iros in combat that he is accepted as a "noble foreigner" (47). Playing with language and the audience's expectations again, Strauß has Amphinomos congratulate the victor with "Hail foreigner" (48). Although former Latin students (and readers of the long-running comic *Asterix*) might think of "Ave Caesar," most German spectators would make another anachronistic association, i.e., "Heil Hitler!" Since the faithful swineherd Eumaios greeted the unexpected—and unrecognized—foreign visitor Odysseus with respect and hospitality (see 1.4), the suitors' behavior suggests that the secular democrats pander to foreigners when it suits them, but, barring a fear of heavenly punishment, they will also exploit them to the hilt and discard them. Their humanistic posturing has no real ethical fundament. More apparitions from the Third Reich are conjured up when Antinoos threatens Odysseus: "You know, beggar, what we think here: that which is ugly deserves to be destroyed" (40). After witnessing such abominations, the audience might well be prepared to accept Odysseus's prophecy of a "bloody cleansing" at the end of the scene.

But what would be "cleansed," exactly? In part 3, suitor Eurymachos sounds like a critic of the excesses of the welfare state when he calls Odysseus a "parasite" who knows how to use the system to his advantage (55). He also complains that "vulgarity" is pushing into the upper echelons of society, threatening to submerge the noble suitors in "filth" (56). This is the same distaste for the masses articulated in "Impending Tragedy," and Athena's advice to her hero Odysseus is too similar to the mind-set of contemporary xenophobic hooligans to be understood solely in the (pre-)historical context: "If you do not attack and storm ahead filled with blood lust, hesitation will wreak havoc with you more than the consequences of your deeds" (66). As so often before, Strauß avoids clarity with regard to basic issues. This holds true in part 4 as well. Before the slaughter of the suitors begins, Leiokritos praises war — in this case the Trojan War — as a bringer of prosperity and new skills (70). This recalls the enthusiasm of educated German youth in 1914 and the defense of the soldier in "Impending Tragedy." Demoptolemos spins a tale that sounds like Strauß's view of contemporary Germany: A glutton king ("der Meistesser") is emulated by his subjects, leading to a situation where all will starve unless they work hard, something that none of the decadent people are capable of anymore (71). Shortly afterward, Ktesippos warns his comrades that their prosperity has led them to forget that foreigners should be honored and the needy should be cared for (71–72). In contrast to such insights, Eurymachos rejects the bloody vision of the seer Theoklymenos, calling him "crazy" and a "babbler" whose stories are "foolish" (73). In short, the aristocratic suitors are not a homogenous group. Even Odysseus, who has vowed to destroy them all as revenge for the "period of disorder" (81), spares the singer Phemios and the young herald Medon after Telemachos intervenes in their behalf (85). Odysseus grudgingly admits that they are not "scoundrels," but is still disgusted with them because they did nothing to stop others from committing injustices. They are "fellow travelers" whose ambivalence would make a German audience ponder the role of cultural figures in the Third Reich and the GDR.

Although Strauß made no attempt to eliminate the various contradictions in *Ithaka*, this is not the most problematic aspect of the play. The audience *listens* to the long political debates, but it *reacts* to the violent scenes in parts 4 and 5.[141] Long spears fly through the air, swords are swung, and blood flows freely toward the proscenium. In the midst of the butchery, Athena calls upon Odysseus to become even more enraged, to be unrelenting in his "lust to kill" (83). She also advises him to trust in his own "military strength" (Wehrkraft). This word, which is associated with German martialism from Siegfried to the Nazi Wehrmacht, was cut from the text in the Munich production. There is little consolation in the fact that Odysseus must berate his faithful nanny Eurykleia for enthusing about the "glorious blood bath" (the gods would not want a warrior to rejoice in the presence of corpses [86]). In part 5, the murdered female servants ("whoring maids," in Telemachos's phrase [83]) hang in the background during the recognition scene with Odysseus and Penelope. What is the purpose of such tableaus? Are they little more than the high culture version of Mortal Kombat? Do they offer a thrill to the relatively sheltered Europeans who watch reports about Bosnia or Rwandan genocide on the evening news? Could they cause the audience to consider the many incidents of xenophobic violence in Germany itself? We do not know if Strauß pondered such questions while writing *Ithaka*. We do, however, after witnessing the final scene of the play, know that he took pains to mythologize the ultrarealistic slaughter by ushering in Zeus as a *deus ex machina*. Only a god can stop the violence and reinstitute the "sacred order" (103). To do this, Zeus erases the brutality from the "memory of the people," so that the ruler and his subjects can love each other as they had previously done. This is possible on stage, but not in reality. Neither the memory of the Holocaust nor the images of skinheads attacking foreigners or torching their homes could or should be forgotten. Perhaps *Ithaka* is above all an attempt at self-therapy on the part of the author. The healing that is granted to the ancients remains unrealizable for the contemporary Germans, whose "self-hatred" (cf. *Die selbstbewußte Nation*) is seemingly untreatable. Only flights of fantasy offer a respite—albeit a short-lived one—from its torments.

The critics who reacted to the Munich production of *Ithaka* in 1996 differed with regard to its political significance, but praise for the literary qualities of the work was rare. One called it "not significant" in a literary sense, not worth of any "excitement."[142] Another dismissed the "retelling of . . . absolutely nondramatic material."[143] Rolf Michaelis was not only put off by the brutal murder of Antinoos, "in this Bosnia year one of the most horrifyingly inhuman scenes of the [theater] season," but also by the audience's reaction, applauding the murder "like a trick from Mr. David Copperfield."[144] If this perception is correct (and I believe that it is, given my own experiences as a spectator), then it is not the audience, but rather the "enlightened critics" so vilified by Strauß who take his writing seriously. According to wire service reports, the critics booed the performance, whereas the actual premiere audience was enthusiastic.[145] The critics focused on the content, but the spectators were mainly interested in the star of the show, prize-winning actor Bruno Ganz. Such phenomena are symptomatic of a continuing "Americanization" of German culture, one of the bugaboos of the New Right. Critic Gerhard Stadelmaier, a defender of Strauß, saw this quite clearly when he expressed his amazement that anyone could conceive of a German theatrical production as a danger for democracy. The author of *Ithaka*, in Stadelmaier's view, was in any case "not democratic, not reactionary, but rather simply childlike-fantastic, at worst devout."[146] Richard Herzinger, who contributed the most detailed contextualization of *Ithaka*, came to a very different conclusion: "*Ithaka* renews in a poetic manner the state utopia of political Romanticism."[147] Herzinger depicted Strauß as a latter-day Novalis, who is reviving "cultural criticism anno 1798" and daring to envision the pinnacle of human civilization in a monarchical system. For this reason, asserted Herzinger, the appearance of *Ithaka* is a "far-reaching event in the recent cultural history of the [German] Federal Republic" (8). Another point in Herzinger's article refers back to the traditions described in chapter 1 of this study. Originally, he says, Strauß was a "Zivilisationsliterat" like Heinrich Mann, a "highly sensitive observer of modern everyday life and its subliminal mythical structures." In the meantime, he has supposedly become yet another German intellectual who cannot "endure the limitlessness of irony" and thus attempts to come to terms with the insecurity of modern life by putting forward a "profundity" supported by metaphysics and the philosophy of culture (10).

Herzinger's position vis-à-vis the German revolt against liberal modernity will be examined in the Excursus below. Of interest here is a question which he asks, namely whether Strauß's "prototype of a sublime neo-Romanticism" will succeed in spawning a new antimodern literary movement (7). At the present juncture, this question must be answered in the negative. If even the "elite" audiences that are motivated enough to see live performances of *Ithaka* have difficulty getting beyond fascinating images to confront the real substance of the play, it is unlikely that there will be sufficient interest to support antimodern *literati*. On the one hand, their choice of obscure topics may alienate potential supporters. One example is the cold reception given Strauß's most recent play *Jeffers—Act I and II*[148] in 1998. If the elitist, antidemocratic poet Robinson Jeffers (1887–1962) is a minor figure[149] in American literature, he is practically unknown in Germany. His stance against modern civilization obviously appeals to Strauß, but the affinity between the two is insufficient as a foundation for literature with an appeal to others. On the other hand, in the age of media spotlights, any writer who expresses convictions loses credibility if his own personal life is not an expression of these convictions.[150] When Strauß's book *The Copyist's Errors* (Die Fehler des Kopisten)[151] appeared in 1997, critic Willi Winkler called the author "the most vain writer of our time."[152] This outburst was due at least in part to the way in which *Der Spiegel*—the facilitator of the "Impending Tragedy" controversy—introduced the new work to the public.

The magazine printed an article about Strauß and his newest work as well as a long excerpt.[153] What was sensational about this was that Strauß allowed photographers to take pictures of himself, his son, and his new home in the country outside Berlin. The enemy of the media had decided, even more blatantly than before, to use the marketing mechanisms of the system for his own purposes. It is the ultimate exercise in co-optation when *Der Spiegel* prints an excerpt in which Strauß refers to those who work in the media as "the ruling class" (194). In the book itself, one discovers an absolutely amazing initial paragraph:

> On a hill in the Uckermark [an area northeast of Berlin], I built a white house, and actually there are two, a larger one with a view of a broad meadow hollow, bordering on a forest in the south, the Jakobsdorfer Forest. And a smaller one behind it for guests who never come, with a furnace room and a room for the piano. (7)

Later on, one learns:

> For twenty years I have searched for such a place, where no one lives too close to me. . . . The battle with the beauty [of the landscape] that tries to bring one down, to silence one, is . . . more dignified than the one against boom boxes and neighborhood parties. (13)

From this fortress, tirades are launched against the superficiality of modern life, the ugliness of the city, the corrupting influence of prosperity, the decline of religion, etc. Here is just one key passage:

> I must introduce my little son to a society that I consider to be used up and debilitated. From which I expect nothing but a slow, perhaps, however, an accelerated hemorrhaging.
>
> I cannot perceive anything good or even a prospect, a plan, from any side. It is a matter of nothing but haggling in a moral as well as a strategic sense. (36)

This assessment—which hardly offers succor to the New Right—is by no means an unusual one, but the seriousness of its indictment is undercut by the simple fact that the bearer of the message can afford the luxury of a hermitage only thanks to a prosperity derived from the hated system. As if this were not enough, the packaging of autobiographical snippets to be purchased and consumed by the stultified modern masses[154] is the height of cynicism. It is "haggling" done with an air of superiority. This is definitely not the stuff of which movements are made.

From January to September 1995, Peter Handke worked on a new play. This was the period immediately preceding his journey to Serbia. In contrast to Botho Strauß, who polemicized in essayistic form and then incorporated his viewpoints into a literary work, Handke created a utopian land for the stage and then sought out a possible manifestation of it in social reality. His play, *Preparations for Immortality: A Royal Drama* (Zurüstungen für die Unsterblichkeit. Ein Königsdrama[155]), was published and performed in 1997, about a year after the turmoil surrounding his essays on the Balkans. The front cover of the book version is decorated with a drawing by the author's youngest daughter (Handke's head rests on a fanciful pedestal), and the perspective of the child is often glorified in the play.[156] The back cover offers a passage from the play in which all of human activity is conceived of as a kind of storytelling. As in the *Winter Journey* and its sequel, the ability to see the world and its images clearly without ideological blinders and the power of narration as a counterweight to the mindless chatter of contemporary civilization are at the center of the enterprise. In this case, however, Handke is on familiar terrain: his preferred method of experiencing and describing the world is problematic as a point of departure for political reportage, but not at all unusual in the sphere of literature. It is of course only a basis from which to proceed, not a guarantee of success.

When Handke's monumental (1,072 pages!) 1994 novel *My Year in No-Man's Bay—A Fairy Tale from the New Age*[157] appeared, critic Ulrich Greiner remarked that the author was "on the way to another literature, a Romantic one."[158] The attempt to revive the project of the poeticization of the world, did not, Greiner added, refer back to Novalis and the philosophical concepts of German Romanticism, but rather to the writings of Joseph von Eichendorff[159] and the Austrians Franz Grillparzer and Adalbert Stifter, whose efforts bore the stamp of Catholicism and conservative utopia. Like this troika, Handke hoped to discover beauty and meaning not in catastrophes and violence (cf. *Ithaka!*), but instead in the constant repetitions and rituals of everyday life. *Preparations for Immortality* can be read as an extension of this project in the realm of drama. The following exchange from a 1994 *Spiegel* interview conducted by Volker Hage and Mathias Schreiber after the publication of *My Year in No-Man's Bay* is instructive in this regard:

> **Der Spiegel:** The epoch in which literature always had to be objective, honest, enlightening or political, is nearing its end. . . .
>
> **Handke:** Yes, we are in a promising situation. . . . We have the chance to become universal without all these ideologies.[160]

Although one might at least approximate universality in a novel of over a thousand pages, the attempt to do so on stage in a limited amount of time (most productions of *Preparations* last about four hours) is both a prescription for disaster and an expression of authorial hubris.

The play's intended global reach is emphasized by two quotations used as mottoes. One, about the eternal battle between light and darkness, is taken from the Babylonian *Gilgamesh* epic, whereas the other is a passage from Deuteronomy concerning the transformation of the letter of the law into actual deeds (5). The stage setting depicts an "enclave" that could be in the "mountainous region of Andalusia" but might be anywhere else. Only two of the characters—the cousins Pablo and Felipe Vega—have names; the residents of the enclave and the gang of "Space Eliminators" (Raumverdränger) who threaten them remain nameless. Although numerous allusions make it obvious that the action takes place in our time, the author speaks only of a period "from the last war until now and beyond" (6). The enclave has apparently been terrorized from outside since time immemorial, but its insignificance has allowed it to preserve its own identity. The "World War" (9) did lead to an occupation that left its mark, however. In the night of the invasion, two local women slept with foreign soldiers ("the one supposedly forced to do it, the other supposedly out of burning passion" [9][161]), and nine months later gave birth to sons. Pablo, the son of the rapist, is the "star" (14) who is destined to become king, but Felipe, the love child, is a "little cripple" (15) whose physical deformities do not detract from his happy, friendly temperament. Both boys remain "fatherless," and one of the mothers is convinced that this is for the best: "Good for the present day, good for the present peace, good for the future" (17). As in *Ithaka*, the search for a king is at times strangely antipatriarchal, and the main female figure—for Strauß, Queen Penelope, for Handke the "storyteller"—is idealized.

The nomadic storyteller ("die schöne junge Wandererzählerin") is the key figure in the enclave residents' search for identity and a secure future. The "idiot," who functions as a very inadequate storyteller until the appearance of the real thing, yearns for a king who will bring not "new enslavement, but freedom—no, something for which the word will have to be found . . ." (22). The "people" ("Volk"—played by one actor) have had enough of "idiotic storytellers" and yearn for a new one who will "see and sense" how to proceed (23). The alliance of king and poet (not necessarily in that order) harks back to Novalis. As Pablo and Felipe grow up—encountering the Space Eliminators from time to time—it becomes clear that the former will find himself by leaving the enclave, but the latter will remain in his "element" at home (42).

Handke consciously uses the word "bodenständig" (i.e., rooted in the soil [39]) to characterize Felipe. German audiences who remember the Nazi's euthanasia program will need no explanations for that—especially in a time when the disabled have often been attacked by the same youth who abuse foreigners. Xenophobia was doubtless on the dramatist's mind when he composed the first sentence of the new constitution for the enclave (as proclaimed in the final scene): "Bear in mind that you were once enslaved—bear in mind your own foreignness when you encounter a foreigner!" (123).[162] These are laudable sentiments, but how does one arrive at them, and can they be embellished so as to fill an evening in the theater?

The chieftain of the Space Eliminators has been told that the enclave is "the last bit of nature or naturalness," and that its residents are "the last natural human beings" (Menschennaturen [54]). This is a global statement, but the chieftain and his gang are the only representatives of the "other" who make an appearance in the play, and they are not representative of the rest of the world. Handke may well have intended that, but his model breaks down. The gang members are, in the words of their leader, "heroes of space gulping—the space vacuums, the absorbers of the fake in-between spaces.[163] Our motto: Not space, but stimulus—stimulus instead of space!" (56). This is a caustic portrayal of the contemporary Western model of civilization, what the Germans call the "Erlebnisgesellschaft," or the society that needs ever-changing diversions to keep it functioning. If Handke means that the entire world has embraced or is at least gravitating toward this Western model, then the universality of his message might pass the test. In actuality, the Space Eliminators are not just *any* Westerners, but clearly Germans (just as the enclave residents might be taken for Austrians—or at least idealized Habsburger). When Space Eliminator Three discusses tactics to be used against the enclave, one is transported back to the late 1930s:

> The country must lose its reputation. It should not even have a name anymore. It and its residents are to be reduced to mere numbers. . . . Felipe Vega is to be renamed Franz Apfelbaum, Pablo Vega [renamed] Moses Birnstengel. . . . And the local sparrows are to be marked with a scarlet spot. (93)

Number Three begins to speak of the new "salvation" ("Heil") to be found, but he immediately censors himself: "Pardon me, the use of this word is punished with expulsion from the gang!—, I correct myself: . . . [T]he new drive, the third wind, the unraveling of the knot, the new awakening" (95). If the gang consists of neo-Nazi skinheads (they have been made up to look like that in some productions), then the dichotomy premodern enclave vs. Western materialism breaks down. In the furor of storytelling, the cultural and political lines of demarcation become blurred, much as in *Ithaka*. Perhaps this is less crucial in a modern fairy tale than in a drama purportedly about the "childhood of the human race."

In the end, it is less Handke's imprecision than his obsessive thematization of his esthetic credo and his education—both scholarly and experiential—that submerge the intention to proclaim a humane utopia. Prefiguring the Balkan project, he has the storyteller emphasize that observation ("Anschauung") is paramount: "Who is today still capable of observing? . . . Simple observation has in the meantime become the most difficult thing. It is only through your ability to observe that you will make war impossible" (99). To observe, we must remain as children or become childlike again.[164] The storyteller, who was "still a child this morning" and hopes to again be one "tomorrow morning," fled from "storytelling schools" (46) because they almost ruined her gift. She predicts that the enclave residents will succumb to catastrophe if they do not follow her example: "Your present lack of fantasy, or narrowing of the skull, or congestion of the blood, or weakened ability to dream, or inability to perceive images (Bildunfähigkeit) is one reason for the catastrophe nearing once again" (47). Even a rejuvenated populace would not be entirely inner-directed, however: "Only the storyteller can understand people, or God" (49). German authors have been repeating this message to little avail since Romanticism, and there is hardly reason to expect that Handke's version will be heeded any more than that of his predecessors. To undergird his legitimacy as anointed mediator between the people and the world, the author of *Preparations* literally bombards his audience with examples of his erudition and wit. When the Space Eliminators think that they smell the enclave residents, they are not content to compare the aroma to one or two other smells. Instead, they describe it in the following manner:

> Like cold smoke and moldy straw. . . . Like rotten apples and greasy clothes. . . . Like rusty chains, dried-up inkwells, dried-up holy-water basins, like the farthest village. . . . Like a plugged-up exhaust pipe, trampled beehives, uterine cancer, sweat produced in fear of death, rabbit cages, lions' dens, endless searching for meaning ("Sinnhuberei"). (53)

When the chieftain imagines how he would have destroyed cultural monuments in the past, Handke has the opportunity to demonstrate his intimate acquaintance with these monuments:

If I had been a contemporary of Pythagoras, I would have prevented the [formulation of] the Pythagorean theorem for all time. And in Giotto's day, I would have stopped the painting of his human societies and thus of all human societies after him. And I would have lay in wait for Francesco Petrarca way before the peak of Mont Ventoux, so that no one after him would have said "I" in his discoverer's manner. And Goethe would have been thrown off the [steeple of] Strasbourg Cathedral by me, his natural mortal enemy, and no one after him would have been able to find himself as a Goethean man. (96)

There are many more examples like this in the text. They contribute little to the audience's understanding of the play, and they do much to consign the author's utopian longing to oblivion.

Handke's desire for peace is manifested in the new enclave constitution recited to the people by Pablo. The aforementioned idea of tolerance is complemented by "the daily right to be far away, the daily right to see space, the right to feel the night wind in one's face" and one "new fundamental prohibition: the prohibition of worry" (124). Pablo's vision for the enclave is "dreaming and working" (80),[165] a juxtaposition of Romantic urges and the program of the labor movement that came closest to realization in the Paris uprising of May 1968. Unlike Strauß, Handke does not end his play with the triumph of this new order. With the menacing figures of the Space Eliminators in the background, the storyteller informs the people that a new law and a new order are inevitable, but they might be horrifying rather than uplifting: "Be happy. Be afraid" (134). The stage directions describe the final tableau as motionless, quiet, and dark. Zeus and Athena are nowhere to be seen, and this is not the only difference between *Ithaka* and *Preparations*. Handke's play begins with an act of violence (a paratrooper is attacked by a crowd of "unknowns" with clubs, scythes, pitchforks, and axes [7]), but for the rest of the play, the threat of violence is more of a presence than violence itself. *Ithaka* ends in an orgy of bloodletting that is predicted long before it occurs. Strauß strives to sensitize his audience to the tragic aspects of human existence, whereas Handke goes to great lengths to avert tragedy. Even the chieftain plans to degrade Pablo in such a way as to avoid "even the slightest touch of tragedy" (56), and when the gang goes too far, the storyteller can simply eliminate them from the action ("wegerzählen" [103]).[166] "Cleansing" (Reinigung) is central to *Ithaka*, where the cleaning agent is blood. Handke's storyteller also uses this term (111), but since she herself will be the medium — she announces her desire to be queen — blood will give way to narration. Finally, the role of the people is very different in the two plays. In

Ithaka, they are united by means of a patriarchal order favored by the gods. In the utopian enclave, the people are always hesitant to accept change and skeptical about the pronouncements of Pablo, a.k.a. he who would be king. They are not at all comfortable with the idea of human sacrifice (cf. "Impending Tragedy"!), and in this, they are seconded by the Idiot, who wants to know just *who* would be sacrificed (131). Strauß accepts myth as a valid way of coming to terms with life, but Handke simply uses mythical motifs as one segment of his vast thematic repertory. In a word, irony is inappropriate in *Ithaka* but literally the coin of the realm in *Preparations*.

The critical reception of the Vienna and Berlin productions of *Preparations* mirrors a post-1989 German intellectual life in a state of flux. In general, Handke's text was seen in a more positive light than *Ithaka*, possibly because its message is less offensive (New Right intellectuals would postulate that it is more politically correct). Both dramas have major shortcomings as texts for the theater,[167] but that did not concern most observers. Thomas Assheuer, an important figure in the "Literature Debate," admitted that it was difficult to divorce the literary works from the preceding controversy about the political essays.[168] In *Der Spiegel*, Wolfgang Höbel dismissed *Preparations* as "esoteric kitsch" that need not be taken seriously, but the magazine's editors chose to relativize this judgment by printing an interview with Claus Peymann, the director of Vienna's Burgtheater. Peymann praised Handke for courageously expressing hope "in a society completely rotted out by cynicism and pragmatism."[169] Peymann may be one of the few Germans willing to accept neo-Romantic poets as spiritual and cultural mentors, as evidenced by a statement from the *Spiegel* interview: "We must comprehend that we have to listen to the poets again—sometimes like children [must listen to] their father. . . . Without the poets, we are nothing." (In another interview, Peymann even characterized Handke as an "enlightener" who accepts "mystery."170) Although Benjamin Henrichs correctly discerned in the story of the enclave "the battle of Handke against Handke (singer of peace against madman),"[171] most critics were more interested in comparing Handke with Strauß. Although one incredibly saw both plays as fairy tales,[172] most did not overlook the gap between the two texts and authors. A Strauß partisan provided the following comparison:

> Botho Strauß and Peter Handke are worlds apart. . . . Strauß does not prescribe anything. Strauß does not preach. Handke asserts myths. Strauß shows them. Handke flees into morality and means an ideal present. Strauß rejects all

morality and maintains only a fairy-tale-like presence of mind, into which a story that happened before the beginning of time hurls its lightning bolts and punch lines.[173]

It is true that Handke is more of a preacher than Strauß (albeit a preacher who often undercuts his own sermons), but the latter does preach—not about morality, but (since the campaign against "Impending Tragedy") more and more about nihilism and a retreat from the world. A more widespread assessment than the one cited above contrasts the political Strauß with the naive or "nonpolitical" Handke, who is hardly a reactionary.[174] Another way of putting this is that Handke stands on the "fairy-tale heights," whereas Strauß holds forth from the "marble cliffs"—a reference to the novel by Ernst Jünger.[175] The critic of the *Süddeutsche Zeitung* must have had Jünger in mind when he attempted to portray Handke and Strauß on different paths leading to the same destination. After emphasizing that Strauß "thinks politically," whereas Handke "interprets poetically," he pointed out that both writers were "disgusted" with the present era. They are neither "presumptuous" nor "a danger for democracy," but rather "seismographs" calling for "a new freedom of thought."[176] It is disconcerting that such important matters are couched in imprecise language. There was never a limit to the freedom of *thought* in post-1945 West Germany, although certain thoughts were less welcome as publishable manuscripts than others. (Even this was much less true in literature than in journalism, for example.) There is also nothing "new" about this freedom of thought: it is to a certain extent a return to a mode of thinking that was a powerful cultural presence from the 1870s to 1945. This is also not the first epoch of German history in which intellectuals have been disgusted with their times. ("O tempora! O mores!") One can only hope that in this instance—as opposed to the 1920s—disgust will not cause a critical mass of those with education and sensitivity to conclude that the maintenance and expansion of democracy has no relevance for their lives.

Peter Handke and Botho Strauß belong to a generation that was deeply affected by the culture and politics of the 1960s. Even more so than in the U.S., this generation has had what used to be called "consciousness." Beginning life during World War II and growing up under the shadow of the Nazi legacy, Handke, Strauß, and others have attempted to distance themselves from that legacy. Initially, this involved construction of a leftist or oppositional identity (diffuse as it may have been). The 1970s brought about varying degrees of disillusionment and an inward turn toward self-discovery and subjectivity. After the end of the Cold War and the division of Germany, some have turned to a *Weltanschauung* that fascinated the intellectual elites before 1933. What has remained constant is that this generation has built an identity by utilizing various critical perspectives. The German embodiment of "Generation X"—admittedly not a precise term—has generally shied away from any fixed stance. At the moment, it is thus difficult to imagine that Handke and Strauß will be emulated by a younger generation. The established writers' preference for the bastions of high culture and a highly stylized language laden with centuries of humanistic contemplation are effective barriers to proselytizing. Whatever one might think of the poetic projects of the two, the seemingly irreversible desiccation of traditional cultural wellsprings is not a pretty prospect. Even Schacht, Schwilk, and other New Right intellectuals will be forced to confront the reality of this phenomenon. Latterday Ernst Jüngers, should they appear upon the scene, will probably be ignored by both Enzensberger's "autistic hooligans" and Strauß's lobotomized media consumers. This state of affairs has to date not stopped the flow of words from the gray eminences of post-'89 literature, however. Strauß, as we have seen, continues to provide prestigious theaters with new texts and has begun to offer his readers scenes from his private life. Handke, whose self-image as a writer was apparently shaken by the "Balkan affair," has since recovered. In 1997, he published a three-hundred-page novel with a decidedly nonhomiletic tone,[177] and 1998 saw the appearance of the fourth volume of his journals—a book of over five hundred pages.[178] Disgust with the present and a longing for the simplicity of earlier times may elicit many different reactions from writers, but one premodern response to inner turmoil is apparently not a viable option for them: silence.

Excursus

Attacks on Americanization and Westernization
and One Problematic Line of Defense

Doctor Pusch had once again gotten ready to take off, and he had gone over to America. Yet he found freedom there freer than he liked, and very soon after he had tried living in New York, then in Chicago, he returned to Europe.[1]

The American hemisphere, in the form of metaphor, myth, and utopia, has been a presence in Germany for hundreds of years. Germans, like other Europeans, long projected their dreams and fears onto the *terra incognita* on the other side of the world. After the founding of the United States, myths gradually gave way to new cultural, political, and social realities, to which numerous German immigrants contributed. Reflecting a characteristic ambivalence, German observers have felt both an affinity with and an aversion to the American project more pronounced than any other found on the European continent. The positive feelings about democracy, efficiency, and technology that arose in the nineteenth century have been at times overshadowed by resentments regarding the American role in the military defeat of Germany in the two world wars. In addition, the American popular culture that began to sweep the world in the 1920s and has in the meantime penetrated into almost every corner of the globe has elicited enthusiasm from the masses and skepticism, if not outright scorn, from the educated elite. Postwar attempts at reeducation and the presence of American troops since 1945 have of course also had a tremendous impact. In short, the U.S. has been the most significant "other" in German life for over a half-century. (The Russian presence in the former

GDR, though significant, was not—if one considers the long term—a comparable phenomenon.)

American influence is often discussed on a purely theoretical plane. To illustrate its quotidian ubiquitousness, I have selected a number of passages from *Der Tagesspiegel*, the Berlin daily, from August 1997 to January 1998. They represent only a fraction of the information about, interpretation of, and comparison with America available day in and day out in the print and visual media. An alien reader who knew nothing about the earth's geography might well have the impression that Germany and the U.S. were not separated by an ocean, but rather close neighbors.

- On a tour of the U.S., Dieter Schulte, head of the German Labor Federation (DGB), asserts that wages are too high in Germany, and that the Germans talk things to death rather than acting creatively like the Americans. ("In Amerika wird einfach mal etwas ausprobiert," August 2, 1997.)

- After Brandenburg's prime minister, Manfred Stolpe, publicly worries that Germany will fall apart trying to copy the American system, American historian David Schoenbaum feels the need to lecture him about "American conditions" (excessive energy use, the gap between private wealth and state funding, the love affair with guns, the number of people without health insurance), claiming that "relatively few Americans" are affected by them. ("Amerikanische Zustände," August 9-10, 1997.)

- After wearing a Stetson on a European tour and talking tough, the American secretary of state is dubbed "Sheriff Albright." (Stefan Kornelius, "Der Erste unter Ungleichen," August 9-10, 1997.)

- Reporter Rainer Stadler is not impressed with arguments against affirmative action. His article begins: "Berkeley, of all places." ("Korrekt und ungleich," August 30-31, 1997.)

- Andrew Young speaks in the legendary Nikolai Church in Leipzig, one of the centers of the GDR opposition before 1989. Some listeners leave early, shaking their heads because Young talks not about the civil rights movement they so revere, but rather about business. He characterizes the opening of a Mercedes plant in Alabama as "one of the greatest victories of the civil rights movement." (Paul Stoop, "Big Business: Verbündeter im Kampf für die Menschenrechte," September 5, 1997.)

- Reporter Rüdiger Scheidges is skeptical about trying out the "get tough" policies of U.S. police departments in Germany. He points out that the U.S., "the most industrialized, most capitalist, most technically advanced country in the world," still has a murder rate twenty times higher than Britain and ten times higher than Germany. ("Mit aller Gewalt gegen Gewalt," September 11, 1997.)

- A German expert on labor law wants his colleagues to consider the American method of job creation, "even though . . . it increases the economic inequality in the populace more and more and creates a growing class of marginalized workers." (Martin Gehlen, "Das amerikanische Jobwunder—eine zwiespältige Verheißung," September 21, 1997.)

- The first McDonald's restaurant is opened in Potsdam. Prime Minister Manfred Stolpe (see above!) is photographed taking a big bite out of a hamburger. Preservationists had been against the opening, but youth members of the Christian Democrats applaud it, saying that now the Potsdamers have an alternative to "conservative gastronomy [!]." ("Ein kräftiger Biß in den 'Branden-Burger,'" October 9, 1997.)

- In an article about the Crazy Horse Memorial in South Dakota, an American journalist is quoted as saying that the people behind the memorial are "news Nazis." *Tagesspiegel* reporter Robert von Rimscha explains to his readers: "In contemporary American usage, the suffix '-Nazi' refers to a stubborn ideologue who only accepts his own truths." ("Das größte Denkmal der Welt," October 13, 1997.)

- In a review of the movie *Air Force One,* critic Jan Schulz-Ojala expresses his disgust at the role of German directors in Hollywood: "American directors shy away from making such cineastic stories for first graders. . . . In Roland Emmerich [*Independence Day*] . . . and now Wolfgang Petersen, Hollywood has found two Germans who are willing to deliver crude patriotism —and they're even proud of it." ("Fritzchen spielt Krieg," October 23, 1997.) In an interview with Petersen in the same edition, the director admits that, "as a German," he was not able to try his hand at patriotic films.

- In an interview with American expatriate author Donna Leon, German readers are provided with the following tidbit: "Today, I feel like a foreigner in my own country. . . . Everything there is plastic, everything is garbage . . . I no longer desire to live in the midst of all this cultural trash—and to be constantly subjected to the terror of pseudo-psychological gabbing." ("Kritische Italien-Liebhaberin," November 2, 1997.)

- Gary Smith, the newly appointed founding director of the American Academy in Berlin, tells his interviewer: "This shouldn't sound arrogant, but a half-century after the Berlin Airlift (Luftbrücke), we are initiating a kind of intellectual airlift." ("Eine intellektuelle Luftbrücke," November 12, 1997.)

- Robert von Rimscha describes American anxiety about globalization (the "fast-track" bill had just been voted down) and concludes: "The U.S.A. . . . , which likes to make fun of social-welfare-oriented Frenchmen and Germans because of their timidity and deliberateness, have now demonstrated that fear of the new has a majority at home, too." ("Angst made in U.S.A.," November 12, 1997.)

- In a review of Zbigniew Brzezinski's new book *The Grand Chessboard*, Jacques Schuster states: "After all, the United States is one of the few powerful nations that will finish this century for the most part morally undamaged. Beyond that, its principles are values that are worth living by." ("Kein Interesse an globaler Konkurrenz," December 6, 1997.)

- "America is religious and multiethnic. That won't change, even if the immigration laws become more restrictive and bizarre groups claim the status of religions." (Robert von Rimscha, "Religiös und multiethnisch," December 27, 1997.)

- "Drastic change arouses mistrust in Germany—for understandable historical reasons. However, a dramatic shift is exactly what the world increasingly demands." (Fred Kempe [editor of *Wall Street Journal Europe*], "Der 'German Dream' von Ruhe und Frieden," December 28, 1997.)

- "The puritan esthetic is not permitted to be an end in itself; it must have a message, the most edifying message possible. A Christ figure submerged in urine does not look very edifying. . . . One side calls for political correctness, the other for patriotic correctness. Both are (in the European view) esthetic nonsense. As if nonconformist, disturbing, undemocratic, and message-free content . . . had not always been the privilege of the arts." (Andreas Zielcke, "Frohe Botschaft," December 31, 1997 / January 1, 1998.)

- "No graffiti on the walls of the single-family homes with porches and back yards. The venerable walls of the university are decorated with neither posters nor political slogans. In Princeton, demonstrations don't have to be broken up, for there are none. Whoever lives here is content. Princeton is beautiful, and Princeton is not America." (Hans W. Korfmann, "Hier gibt es keine Demonstrationen," January 2, 1998.)

- "Critics of the gigantic highway expansion are most upset about the shopping malls out in the country. . . . With their dozens of shops and free parking, they cause the traffic problems, they say. But the objections are coming too late. When Berlin and Brandenburg agreed in 1993 not to allow another 'Wild East,' most of the shopping malls were already up and running or under construction." (Claus-Dieter Steyer, "Im Kriechgang zum Einkaufstempel," January 4, 1998.)

The wealth of information about the U.S. might be one reason why the Germans have such strong opinions about the former occupying power. It is certainly indisputable that they know much more about us than we do about them. This has of course always been the lot of small(er) states.

Many of the key figures in the German tradition of conservative cultural criticism, including Nietzsche, George, Hofmannsthal, and Thomas Mann, felt ambivalence, even antipathy toward the United States.[2] Many of the contributors to *Die selbstbewußte Nation* picked up this thread. To bring these sentiments into focus, one might consider the following two statements made in 1925, during the most stable period of the Weimar Republic. The first expresses sympathy, even enthusiasm for the U.S.:

> Concrete and sentimental, thus in a positive sense naïve—such is the method of Americanism, in the life of the soul and the spirit as in practical affairs. No burden of culture weighs this method down. It is young, barbaric, uncultivated, willful. It has that free and strong breath we sense in the poems of Walt Whitman and which already enchanted Baudelaire. It follows no abstract or historical ideal, but instead follows life. Americanism is fanaticism for life, for its worldliness and its present-day forms.
>
> Americanism thus appears as the strongest opponent of romanticism, which sought to flee worldliness. It is the natural enemy of all distraction from the present, whether through a backward-looking conception of history, through the mystical, or through intellectualism.[3]

In this text, America has become an illustration of German vitalist philosophy. The reference to the "burden of culture" also harks back to Goethe's 1827 poem "To the United States," in which the poet envies the people who need not engage in "useless remembering."[4] Those who believe in the inherent superiority of a culture that has evolved over time—despite their veneration of the Goethean icon are of course horrified by this and fear what is to come:

> An equivalence of souls unconsciously arises, a mass soul created by the growing drive toward uniformity, an atrophy of nerves in favor of muscles, the extinction of the individual in favor of the type. Conversation, the art of speaking, is danced and sported away, theater brutalized into cinema; literature becomes the practice of momentary fashions. . . . And since everything is geared to the shortest units of time, consumption increases; thus does genuine education—the patient accumulation of meaning over the course of a lifetime—become a quite rare phenomenon in our time, just like everything else that can be achieved only by individual exertion. . . . What is the source of this terrible wave threatening to wash all the color, everything particular out of life? Everyone who has been there knows: America. The historians of the future will one day mark the page following the great European war as the beginning of the conquest of Europe by America.[5]

Although he perhaps was not aware of it, the author of these lines was not speaking about Europe at all, but rather about the European cultural elite and its conception of what the "Old World" should be. From the perspective of the masses, life had become actually *more* colorful than before thanks to the availability of cheap entertainment in the form of movies, gramophones, radio, competitive sports, dance halls, etc.[6] High culture had not been consumed by the masses in earlier epochs (Shakespeare's Globe Theatre being a notable exception), and that did not change. What did change was the status granted to those who produced works of high culture. Over a period of time, the creators of such culture had to yield their pedestals to technological wizards like Edison, daring adventurers like Lindbergh, and athletes like Joe Louis (or, in the German case, Max Schmeling).

Although the decline of the *Bildungsbürgertum* began in the nineteenth century, it has yet to reach its conclusion. Some conservatives even dream of reversing the process of decline.[7] The lamentations of the last hundred years continue to be repeated with little variation:

> Someone has said that the people ("Volk") is the highest and the lowest. That may be accurate in a historical sense, even more so in a mythical one. Today, however, the German people no longer creates a secret treasure in the soul of the individual, a treasure from which he could derive strength. He [the people] is nothing but a moody, lazy majority potentate. A destroyer of absolutely all intellectual power. He speaks German only out of laziness. Most of his emotions and interests could be better expressed in American [English].[8]

Botho Strauß wrote these words in the 1990s, shortly before the publication of "Impending Tragedy." His vision of the German people in its unspoiled state is a Romantic idealization of a people's community (*Volksgemeinschaft*) that may or may not have existed in a distant past. The idea of a "treasure" produced by a homogenous culture is similar to the "secret Germany" (geheimes Deutschland) yearned for in the George Circle. Peter Handke has expressed similar feelings, but there is one important difference. Whereas Strauß, despite his interest in American literature and theater, never felt especially close to the U.S., Handke did. As a critic has recently pointed out, the protagonist of his 1972 novel *The Short Letter about a Long Good-bye* (Der kurze Brief zum langen Abschied) did not fear that his European identity and artistic sensitivity would be damaged by "eating fast food at some gas station in the U.S.A." Until 1989, when he wrote his *Essay on the Jukebox* (Versuch über die Jukebox), his love of pop culture and "commodity esthetics" remained strong, and anti-American resentments did not appear. It was only the disappearance of the old Yugoslavia that brought forth anti-Western feelings.[9]

German elitist writers and other New Right intellectuals would be less concerned about the infiltration of American mass culture if they were to read — and believe — the analyses of it provided by certain scholars writing in English. Richard Pells, for example, argues that "the 'Americanization' of Europe is a myth. A powerful and enduring myth, often cherished by the Europeans themselves because they can use it to explain how their societies have changed in ways they don't like, but a myth nonetheless." Despite Allied efforts at postwar reeducation, Germany provides, according to Pells, in its "mixture of acquiescence and defiance," an illustration of the European ability to resist outside pressure. The motivation behind Pells's book is a desire to advocate democratic "free choice" as opposed to the "paternalistic prescription" favored by European elites.[10] Similarly, Rob Kroes describes how American cultural products are adapted to European sensibilities, and he celebrates the "resilience [of] . . . the old European cultures that refuses to be washed away easily."[11] Kroes speaks of "cultural appropriation," of "an experiment in creative identification,"[12] but neither he nor Pells has much empathy for those who might chafe at the role of mere adapter.

The same is true for Roger Rollin, who states categorically: "The world has been McDonaldized." From Rollin's perspective, anyone who asks whether this is "progress" is a "cynic."[13] He seems surprised that "those on the receiving end of American exports" seem more interested in the process than the exporters.[14] Stephen Haseler, who rather simple-mindedly equates anti-Americanism with opposition to democracy, discusses "traditional German criticisms of the United States" in the context of the "contemporary search for a separate German identity" and worries that "these deep-seated . . . 'cultural' criticisms could enter mainstream thinking."[15] Haseler wrote this in 1985, and he located the troublesome elements not in the New Right, but rather among the "Greens" and the "peace movement." Perhaps the most thoughtful contribution to this discussion is that of Paul Hollander, who began his study of anti-Americanism with conceptions not unlike those of Pells. Even though Hollander retains his partisanship for the American system, he concludes that "hostility toward the United States, and especially certain aspects of American culture, is not always or entirely irrational, and even some of its irrational manifestations may originate in conditions that warrant concern."[16] Like Haseler, he examines such hostility on the left, not the right (as evidenced by his multiple references to Günter Grass). Despite his capacity for objective analysis, Hollander has a blind spot that distorts his perception:

> [T]he restlessness of estranged intellectuals and the hostility of the adversary culture are in all probability generalized responses to the discontents of life in a thoroughly modernized, wealthy, secular, and individualistic society where

> making life meaningful requires great ongoing effort and remains a nagging problem—*at any rate for those whose attention does not have to be riveted on the necessities of survival.*[17]

German critics of American influence doubtless exhibit the responses described here, but these responses are not completely unrelated to the social conditions referred to at the end of this passage. This is to be expected, since practically the entire German populace has been engaged in a struggle for survival twice in this century. This experience has not disappeared from the German collective consciousness, and there is no reason to believe that it will in the near future. Those who have been pushed to the edge of the abyss in wartime would surely be traumatized if that were to become a real possibility in peacetime.[18]

In his 1993 study of German anti-Americanism,[19] Dan Diner takes a stance similar to Hollander's. Diner, a history professor who teaches in both Tel Aviv and Essen, writes that his study was "triggered by the reactions of the German public to American involvement in the Gulf War of 1991" (ix). As someone who has gained a reputation as a critical intellectual,[20] Diner displays a strange form of self-censorship when writing about German attitudes toward the U.S. On the one hand, he obviously has no sympathy with the "Romantics' clear disapproval of America [that] went hand in hand with general opposition to liberal views" (38). In convincing fashion, he demonstrates why one should reject the modern versions of such disapproval as manifested in such books as Adolf Halfeld's *Amerika und der Amerikanismus* (1927), Leo L. Matthias's *Die Entdeckung Amerikas oder das geordnete Chaos* (The discovery of America or the orderly chaos, 1953) and *Die Kehrseite der USA* (The other side of the USA, 1964), and Caspar Schrenck-Notzing's[21] *Charakterwäsche. Die amerikanische Besatzung in Deutschland und ihre Folgen* (Characterwashing: The American occupation of Germany and its consequences, 1965). On the other hand, he devalues any and all criticism of the U.S. by linking anti-Americanism with anti-Semitism:

> Like a cultural code, it [anti-Americanism] is expressed even by people having neither practical nor theoretical knowledge of America.
> In this way, though not only in this way, anti-Americanism resembles anti-Semitism structurally (as well as in the selection of metaphors). In some respects, anti-Americanism can even be understood as a further stage in the secularized hostility towards Jews. Even though the two phenomena, on account of their different developmental histories, could never be considered identical, they both represent ideologically shaped reactions to modernity. (20)[22]

Although Diner is cautious in his formulations ("in some respects," "even though"), this linking is comparable to the "fascism club" oft wielded by German leftists against their critics. What is strange is that one finds another turn of phrase that sounds much like Hollander: "[N]ot all perceptions are products of irrational spouting of blind figments of the imagination" (12). Diner has no desire to discuss such perceptions, however. When critiquing Rolf Winter's[23] book about the violent nature of U.S. society, for example, he speaks meekly of "facts which are not being contested here individually" (146). When dealing with Hans Magnus Enzensberger, a sometime critic of the U.S. with a formidable intellect, Diner's analysis is more than questionable. He cites a 1968 statement by Enzensberger ("Fascism is not hideous because the Germans practiced it, but because it is possible everywhere."[24]) and interprets it as follows: "The horror of Nazism referred to as fascism thus does not lie in its past reality, but in its future possibility" (129). What Enzensberger meant to say was that it is not the particular perpetrator that makes fascism hideous (a characterization that he would not reject), but rather the realization that this was—and continues to be—a human possibility. As we have seen above, Enzensberger does not view his countrymen through rose-colored glasses, but his 1968 statement does dispute the singularity of the Holocaust, something that Diner cannot accept. In the end, Diner is not sure that Germany has irreversibly become part of the West. His reservations are not his alone, and he cannot be denied the right to be "anxious" (108) about the future. However, he opens himself up to criticism when he asserts that "the stance toward America is an indicator for the Westernization of Germany" (108). This is tantamount to proclaiming that there is only one viable model for modern society, and those who do not embrace it are untrustworthy. Such proclamations are of course welcomed by the New Right, since they support the view that Germany is a mere satellite without its own identity. If Diner refers to American "political culture" as the measure of all things, the authors of another study also include U.S. popular culture, making the mix even more potent.

In the past few years, Germanist Richard Herzinger has become a tribune of liberalism in Germany. His cultural commentary, which has appeared in *Die Zeit, Der Spiegel, Der Tagesspiegel,* and elsewhere, concentrates on themes like human rights, cultural pessimism, the Holocaust, neonationalism, fundamentalism, and utopia.[25] In 1995, he published, together with Hannes Stein (whose field is English literature), a volume entitled *Endzeit-Propheten oder*

Die Offensive der Antiwestler (Apocalyptic prophets or the offensive of the anti-Westerners).[26] The authors' views are close to those of Dan Diner, but they go much farther. In contrast to most of the writers who have been presented in this study, they clearly enjoy utilizing humor and irony to make their points. This can be quite refreshing; unfortunately, there are also instances of unintended humor. These arise mainly when the virtues of mass culture are being praised. The dedication and epigraph of *Apocalyptic Prophets* were carefully chosen to emphasize the direction of the authors' thinking. The book is dedicated to the memory of Karl Popper, whose rejection of nationalism and primitivism are cited in the text (89, 225). The epigraph is a quotation from Robert Kennedy's *To Seek a Newer World:*

> To be an American also means having been ostracized and foreign, it means having gone down the path of exile and knowing that whoever turns away the ostracized, the foreign, and the exiled is also turning away America.[27]

The insertion of this quotation should indicate to the reader that the book in question has less to do with America than with an idealized view of what America should be.

Herzinger and Stein reject pacifism, so it is only logical that they would resort to a scorched-earth policy in their book. After they have attacked representatives and resurrectors of the Conservative Revolution, anti-Semites, regionalists, communitarians, cultural nationalists, tribalists, advocates of political correctness, environmentalists, pacifists, fundamentalists, and others,[28] there are few figures left standing. These include Voltaire, Karl Popper, Albert Camus, Robert Hughes, liberal Israelis ("A miniature version of the U.S.A. has emerged on the Mediterranean." — [43][29]), and Woody Allen.[30] Many of those subjected to scathing criticism (or sarcastically humorous dismissal) are also "red flags" for the New Right. This is because both liberals and rightists reject the world view of the generation of 1968. Herzinger and Stein of course see no common ground, as evidenced by the following statement about the legacy of Romanticism: "The leftists repeated the litany that bourgeois democracy is only a formal one; their rightist *opposite numbers* [the English term is used in the original] decry the absence of values ("Wertevakuum") in mass society" (12). They reject both "progressive" and "reactionary" (195) antiliberals while defending the empty space ("Leerstelle") at the center of liberalism (12). This is not the place to discuss the supposedly nonideological character of liberal thought. Of interest here is the authors' attitude toward American culture, especially popular culture.

That their assessment would be a positive one is a foregone conclusion, given their characterization of the U.S. as "a kind of new founding of the human race . . . a continuing, unfinished experiment with a society that is open to all people of every ethnic and cultural origin" (33). Europe has no right to a separate identity, since it has almost destroyed its own "so highly praised culture" in two wars. (This is a rather strange formulation, given the otherwise sharp criticism directed toward the path of German history in the volume.[31] The two world wars were not initiated by "Europe.") At this historical juncture, "'Americanization' is not an unpleasant secondary effect, but rather the *conditio sine qua non* of European freedom" (34). Herzinger and Stein have no sympathy with European intellectuals who—like theater director Ariane Mnouchkine—see Euro-Disney as a "Chernobyl of culture" (34). More to their liking is the attitude of German-Romanian writer Richard Wagner, who has said that the progress of democratic reforms in Eastern Europe can be measured by "the degree of proliferation of McDonald's restaurants" (35). (In 1995, Romania still did not have one.) They claim that in every anti-American, there is a small voice persistently whispering: "Do it right, go to McDonald's" (24).[32] An explanation of why this is the "right" thing to do is also provided: "McDonald's symbolizes the American experiment of combining equality for all with the profit motive and entrepreneurial initiative" (25). This institution is hated by both right and left, it is claimed, because it has surpassed the fascist notion of "Eintopfsonntag" (people from all walks of National Socialist life came together to eat a simple bowl of soup on Sundays) and also realized the old goal of the labor movement to have the proletarians partake of the culinary bounty of the bourgeoisie. It is difficult to take such (admittedly humorous) statements seriously, but there is no question that the authors are not joking when they contrast the purportedly antimodern, tribalistic comic *Asterix* (in which the last remaining Gallic village defies the modernizers from Rome) with the world of "Entenhausen," the German name for the town where Donald Duck lives.[33] Here we find a "voluntary association of autonomous individuals" that has replaced "tribal ties" (179). Allowance is made for a great variety of lifestyles, and the private sphere is respected. (This was before the advent of Kenneth Starr.) There is no discrimination, since dogs, pigs, and owls can compete with ducks for leading positions in the community. The political system is stable, prosperity has reached (almost) everyone, and Donald is the kind of worker that European entrepreneurs fantasize about: "mobile and willing to retool and unwilling to put up with the lack of opportunities in his profession" (183). Entenhausen even offers niches for the "social-romantic" pigs and the "hypermoralistic collectivist" Bad Boy Club. These outsiders demonstrate that there is no alternative to "modern metropolitan civilization" (184).

Do Herzinger and Stein look up from their comic book and think that they are still in fantasy land? No, they know the difference between fairy tales and reality.[34] They readily admit that the West is not "the best of all worlds." Their commitment to it is, they point out, "nothing more than the cheerful admission that we have no utopia" (11). At the same time, they fear that the West may be once again betraying its universalist roots, as it did when it stood by and let the Holocaust take its course (228–229). This was—and is—a serious matter, but the authors do not convince us that such a betrayal is contrary to the logic of the liberal system. Although they believe that the uniqueness of Western civilization lies in its capacity for self-criticism (230), there is one area of that civilization that is never subjected to scrutiny, namely the economic system. We learn that the residents of Entenhausen are so absorbed in "the joys of the consumer and leisure society" that they have no time to think about something as "boring" as an "identity" (188). Such thoughts might be boring for the authors, who indirectly hint at their own identity as "rootless cosmopolitans who feel absolutely no desire to belong to a community" (80), but for the majority of the human race, self-definition via consumer goods is not an option. If it were, ecological catastrophe would be a probability rather than a possibility. Capitalism can thrive in a society that upholds the universalist rights of the Enlightenment, but these rights are not a precondition of success. Other things are necessary, however, i.e., constant economic growth, increases in productivity, a quick return on investments, and rising profits. These are the "values" (and the cultural, environmental, political, and social ramifications that follow from them) that warrant no attention from Herzinger and Stein, and this omission—be it intentional or not—greatly diminishes the impact of their polemics against the "anti-Westerners." In the final analysis, their offensive backfires and even provides succor to those who strive to discredit the Enlightenment as a sham purveyed by cynics. Unfortunately, their attempt to neutralize anti-Semitism fails as well. The New Europe, they assert, must embrace the "Jewish component of European history," what is described as "the liberating, opening, cultivating effect of capitalism" (92). The "moneyed Jew" (Geldjude—93), personified by the cosmopolitan Rothschild family, is offered as a much better model for the continent than culture, something basically "irrational" that can be used as a springboard for tyranny (94-95). The accompanying portrayal of Switzerland as a model country where money—rather than "mythical origins"—determines identity (91-92) has been rendered especially embarrassing by events of the past few years. This faux pas, together with the implication that "Jewish rootlessness" is an ideal worthy of emulation, will not be quickly forgotten.

Any critique of *Apocalyptic Prophets* undertaken from abroad would be incomplete without an attempt to demonstrate just what Herzinger and Stein are reacting to. Their missionary zeal is at least somewhat more understandable when it is compared to the spoutings of the prophets referred to in their title.[35] Many harrowing accounts of American arrogance, bullying, ignorance, soullessness, etc. have come out of Germany in this century. In this context, one example will have to suffice. It is a 1996 volume entitled *Deutschland—eine amerikanische Provinz. Der große Seelenmord* (Germany—an American province: the great killing of souls).[36] The author, Gustav Sichelschmidt,[37] has done students of anti-Americanism and the German right a great service. They need not scour libraries and archives in search of characteristic themes and formulations. Everything that one needs to know is found in this volume. One can speak of four major questions: 1) Who are the Germans? 2) Who are the Americans? 3) What is the West? 4) What is the shape of the future, and how will it be affected by Europeans (especially Germans), Americans, and Jews?

Germany is, for Sichelschmidt, first and foremost the land of idealism—as opposed to materialism. Goethe is the embodiment of this idealism, and its purpose, already formulated in the Romantic era, is to counter the "disenchantment" (88, 141) of the world typical of our age. This can only be accomplished in the inner realm ("humane[s] Weltinnenreich") that is the true home of the Germans (95, 163). Germany has been prepared for this task by its many trials over the course of history. The project of dismantling the special German identity during and after the Thirty Years' War is compared to the plan for reeducation after 1945. One important vehicle for this was and is the contamination of the German language ("our old honest German" [49]) with foreign words and concepts, leading to a German-American "Mischidiom" (8). The foreseeable end result is cultural genocide: "One does not think in a German manner anymore, and soon one will not feel in a German manner. One speaks the language of our country less and less"

(61). Citing Lamennais, Sichelschmidt wonders if his people is not destined for the role of martyr ("Märtyrervolk") put on earth to preserve true humanity (93). (Germany already saved the West by battling the Red Army, it is emphasized—[18, 98].) Although one stereotype of the "Hun" is the fanatical soldier, his militarism is supposedly a mere invention (angedichtet [46]). Echoing the words of Thomas Mann, Sichelschmidt also asserts that the Germans are basically "nonpolitical" (91). Their main failing, he claims, is that they are too malleable, too ready to become "loyal subjects" (65, 107), "opportunists," and "fellow travelers" (57). This is not a revelation, but another assertion is: the Germans are more "friendly toward foreigners" than anyone else (63). This is the portrait of a nation of victims subjected to innumerable injustices. (The term "castrated" appears four times in the text.) To bolster his case, Sichelschmidt cites positive assessments of German culture ranging from Madame de Staël and Emerson to Knut Hamsun and former Boston University president John Silber. He leaves no doubt that the disappearance of this culture would be "the true German catastrophe," whereas the destruction in 1945 was terrible, but not a threat to German identity (82-83).

An integral segment of victimology is the search for a conspiracy, and Sichelschmidt's description of the United States leads exactly down that path. In his Manichean scheme, America is diametrically opposed to Germany in every possible respect. Symbolized by Hollywood and the "Wall Street mentality" (7), this is a country without culture that represents "the greatest danger for all civilized nations" (39). Educated Germans cannot accept the moralizing tone used by the descendants of both the murderers of the Native Americans and slave owners, according to the author: "How would it be if good old Uncle Sam, instead of putting up Holocaust museums all over, would build memorials to the Indians who were sacrificed on the altar of history or to the (too) many millions of black slaves that died?" (139). (This is the only instance where the world "Holocaust" is used in the book.) Beyond the issue of guilt—Dresden and Hiroshima are mentioned (130) and the conduct of the Vietnam War is termed "bestial" (112)—Sichelschmidt's America is an ametaphysical, conformist, hypermaterialistic, nonreligious, soulless, superficial society that exports catastrophe to the Germans and the rest of the world. The "goods" include

> AIDS, alcoholism, antiauthoritarian education, drug addiction, youth sects, violent crime, the Mafia, cultural decline, pornography, record divorce rates, sexism, terrorism, racism, neuroses, and all kinds of damage to civilization. (45)

This is far from the world of Herzinger/Stein, and it is only logical that the author warns of the "horrible legacy of liberalism" (171) and rejects the "Laissez-faire" attitude of modern intellectuals (71). One "export" not on the above list, simply because it permeates the entire book, is American popular culture, especially popular music. German youth, alienated from "serious German music" (56), welcomes the "invasion of the Afro-American jungle" (9). Sichelschmidt chooses his words carefully here. The word "nigger" only appears twice in his book, and on both occasions, it is contained in a citation or reference. Jazz, we are reminded, was considered to be "nigger music" by the Nazis (56), and an unnamed American is quoted as saying that the rhythms of rock-and-roll are being used to bring the whites down to "the level of a nigger" (60). Such rhetorical strategies lead to the question of whether Sichelschmidt is really against America per se. When he refers to John Kenneth Galbraith's thesis about the "capitulation of the white elite" (118), one can imagine that he sees a conspiracy at work in the U.S. as well.

This is indeed the case, although it is difficult to follow the argument. On the one hand, Sichelschmidt clearly rejects the whole idea of an artificial society that has not evolved organically. On the other hand, one suspects that the "white elite" might have done better if it had not been subject to corrupting influences. Who was, then, actually behind the cosmopolitanism, hedonism, and mammonism that he deplores? This only becomes obvious in the second half of the book, where references to Jews abound. The author readily embraces the highly controversial view that it was primarily Jews who profited from the African slave trade (140, 144), so Jewish infiltration can be posited as appearing very early on. The American variety of capitalism is called "Raffkapitalismus" (33), the term, mentioned above, that was favored by the Nazis. The Americans' notion of being a chosen people may have come from the Jews, who joined them in an "unholy cooperation" (37). Despite the use of the word "cooperation," the general impression is that the Jews have worked behind the scenes. They dominate the media (85), and Hollywood was and is "firmly in the hands of the Jews" (121). It is surely no accident that the only film title that appears in the book is *Schindler's List* ("unspeakable"), and Sichelschmidt blames the "Jewish bosses" in the film industry for cementing the negative image of Germans on the screen (130–131). It is impossible to dispute that such stereotyping exists, but Sichelschmidt does not ask himself if it might at least partially be connected to the course of modern German history. On the contrary: He understands very well, he says, why the German people chose to end the disaster of the Weimar Republic by "opting" (98) for the Nazis, and he theorizes that the Third Reich might have been "a secret revolt against Americanism" (99).

Although the tone of *Germany—An American Province* is generally pessimistic, the author does hope that another "revolt" might still take place. He often compares today's U.S. to the Roman Empire in its decline. The German "historical mission" is to preserve the West in the face of the "great American apocalypse" (141). In contradistinction to Herzinger/Stein, Sichelschmidt speaks of a "specific occidental self-image" that must oppose Americanism (45). In other words, the center of the West is not America, but Europe. Although Sichelschmidt singles out the French for high praise in light of their resistance to American cultural influence (49-51, 119-123), he envisions Germany as the "spiritual leader of Europe" (the phrase comes from writer and Nobel Prize winner Paul Ernst [156]). If one compares this train of thought to Thomas Mann's *Reflections*, it is clear that the West has moved in an eastwardly direction. (The position between East and West no longer exists.) Like Mann, Sichelschmidt has found a soul mate in Russia, where, he claims, opposition to American influence in the post-Soviet era goes hand in hand with homegrown anti-Semitism. He is upset that Germans are still afraid to publicly link the two phenomena (126-127). Given his Russophile stance, it comes as no surprise that his favorite critic of the U.S. is Alexander Solzhenitsyn, who became intimately familiar with U.S. "cultural deficits" (127) while an exile in Vermont. When he praises the "brave and disciplined" Red Army (129) and casts aspersions on the U.S. military (13, 111), the reader might well wonder if yet another world war might be in store. This is a mistaken impression, however. Sichelschmidt does intimate that the Germans have secret strengths (Berserkerkräfte [88]), but he leaves no doubt that Germany will not survive as a recognizable entity unless there is "a decisive collapse" of the United States (157). If this were to come to pass, would it be the end of history? Not in Sichelschmidt's view. Even after the American disappearance from the world stage, the "racially homogeneous Jews" would not stop trying to dominate the world (157-158). In the meantime, the German's duty is to "hate" the Americans (174).

Although Sichelschmidt's book was published in 1996, it reflects the temperament and thinking of the Old Right more than that of the New Right. It is a swan song, not a program for political action. Many younger rightists have realized that it is (politically) suicidal to appear to be loose cannons, and they have decided to transmit their messages in a more subtle manner. In the framework of this *excursus*, a brief look at Heimo Schwilk's thin volume about the Gulf War can illustrate the shift. In his preface to *Was man uns verschwieg. Der Golfkrieg in der Zensur* (What we were not told: the Gulf War and censorship),[38] the author sounds not unlike other German anti-Americans.[39] His thesis is that both Saddam Hussein and George Bush had planned from the beginning to manipulate the press. One might expect from this that the two leaders would be put on the same plane, but that is not the case. Although Schwilk rejects the characterization of Hussein as the "Hitler of Baghdad" (23), he does not hesitate to call him a "notorious brute and inveterate militarist," a dictator who is too impatient to develop the kind of military-industrial complex needed to carry out his threats (25). The Germans are criticized for building chemical plants and bunkers and helping to extend the range of the Scud missiles (26), and the possibility that Israelis could be killed by poison gas provided by the Germans is described as "horrible" (31). At least some of these statements could have been made by German leftists.

Schwilk's real concern is connected to the role of the U.S. in the "New World Order" and the lack of respect given the Germans for their contributions to that order. Although he appears to be against press censorship (and upset about the lack of access granted to German journalists like himself), he actually seems to admire American policy during the war. For him, Bush's plan to co-opt the media is a strategy that may be "questionable with regard to democracy" but "understandable with regard to power politics" (29). The German observer appears to be envious of a country that can successfully pursue such strategies. The patriotism of American reporters (75) is also duly noted (see the statement by Wolfgang Petersen above). In contrast to this, the Germans were subject to attacks in the media for not sending ground troops to the Gulf. Schwilk believes that the U.S. wanted it this way, because German reticence made it easy to portray the European "giant" as a fair-weather ally incapable of being counted on in international affairs (78). He boasts that without German logistical support, the preparation for battle would have been impossible (78). A German chancellor from the New Right, one surmises, would not have hesitated to offer the services of the Bundeswehr.

Schwilk's experiences in Saudi Arabia allow him to demonstrate that his countrymen are not undervalued everywhere. He learns that Germans are treated well there because they are considered to be "honest, capable, and friendly toward the Arabs" (77). When crossing the border into Saudi Arabia, Schwilk has a long conversation with a Saudi officer, and this conversation is the real center of the book. Lt. Abdul Al-Issa first asks for advice about the top Mercedes model, and this is significant, because, we are told, the fabulous wealth of the oil-rich country allows its residents to always choose "only the best" (48). Wealth has of course brought with it an incredible influx of Western goods, as well as "fast-food chains and garishly colorful amusement parks à la Disneyworld" (49–50). Are the Saudis in danger of losing their souls like the Germans portrayed by Sichelschmidt? According to Schwilk, they are not, because they are careful to distinguish between "the material achievements of the West and cultural modernity" (50). The author apparently also believes that it is possible to separate the two, a feat considered impossible by the Old Right. Schwilk leaves no doubt that he sympathizes with the "Saudi experiment of a symbiosis of modernity and tradition" (51). In Germany, there is a group of people who stand in the way of such an experiment. They are only mentioned in a roundabout way in this book about the Gulf War. Schwilk describes how difficult it was for him to obtain a visa for Saudi Arabia, reporting that German journalists were "mistrusted," since they had the reputation of being "hypercritical, moralistic, and undependable" (33). The term "journalist" is actually a code word for "leftists" or "left-liberals," i.e., the generation of 1968. These are also the people who oppose German military operations abroad.[40] With them cast aside (or, more realistically, sent off to retirement homes), the German presence in the Arab world and elsewhere might take on a different dimension. Perhaps this is the subtext of Schwilk's equation of the Arabs' hyperbolic "rhetoric of destruction" with the reunified Germans' "dream of eternal peace" (46): both are mere facades that crumble when tested. Whereas Sichelschmidt's animosity toward America is unequivocal, Schwilk would apparently like to see his country pursue a dual-pronged strategy: While waiting for the collapse of the U.S., Germany can play along with the "Moloch"[41] and regain stature on the international stage.

Conclusions and Prospects

> When one thinks of democracy, Germany is generally not the
> first country that comes to mind.[1]

The words cited above were written by a historian in the late 1990s. They surely resonate differently in a German context than in a non-German one. More than fifty years after World War II, the reliability of the Germans as democratic partners is still in doubt—at least for some observers. It is this doubt, a sword suspended over the head of the German people, that causes establishment politicians to despair (or grovel), rightists to lash out, and elitist writers to retreat into visions of the past. The left, especially the intellectual left, has typically sought to wield this sword itself, perhaps as a compensation for a lack of political influence in postwar German society. The spectre of National Socialism in general and Auschwitz in particular continues to darken the scene in the now reunited country, and there are no signs that it will fade from view in the foreseeable future. (As I write this, the wire services are carrying a story about violence at the 1998 World Cup entitled "In France, Hooligans Are Awakening Memories of a Dark Past."[2]) One can discern two possible reactions to this state of affairs. First of all, Germans can strive to be model democrats and responsible members of the international community (although there is no little disagreement about what that might entail).[3] Second, the very basis for the suspicion directed toward the German people can be reexamined and put in a new light. Aside from fringe groups, there would be little support for the portrayal of the Third Reich as a benign system that went wrong, but a reassessment of the Conservative Revolution and its representatives is much less controversial, simply because this phe-

nomenon is relatively unknown, both at home and abroad. It is just such a reassessment that has been launched in the post-Wall period.

In 1993, the respected Wissenschaftliche Buchgesellschaft published a detailed analysis of the Conservative Revolution.[4] The author, Stefan Breuer,
emphasized that his book was a purely scholarly exercise: "It is not intended as
'an aid to the rightist intelligentsia in Germany' (Mohler 1989, 2:7) . . . or
meant to provide the opposite camp with cheap targets [wohlfeile Feind-
bilder]" (6). The mention of Armin Mohler in the introduction demonstrates
that Breuer feared that he might be dismissed as another partisan like his predecessor. Anyone who has read his study has no trouble distinguishing between the two. Breuer would like to get rid of the term "Conservative
Revolution" altogether, because it is "an untenable concept" that leads to confusion (181). He sees elements like a fascination with the apocalypse, the willingness to use violence, and male bonding as common features (47), but the
only common position that he can discover is opposition to political liberalism
as "a Western phenomenon unsuitable to the German character" (181). Beyond this opposition, he takes pains to make it absolutely clear that the Conservative Revolution was not an attempt to return to the premodern world,
but rather one of many "diverse designs for modernity" that were being discussed in the Weimar Republic (180). Concomitant with this interpretation is
a complete rejection of the "special path" thesis—premodern elites did not
dominate Wilhelminian Germany, he argues against Arno Mayer and others
—and the claim that Weimar Germany was a "bourgeois" society like any
other (15). Its unusual aspects were limited to the heterogeneity of the middle
class (thanks to the presence of the *Bildungsbürgertum*) and the "fixation" with
the state as the "sole guarantor of unity and universality" (18–19). This is indeed rather "academic (6)," especially since Breuer states that the Conservative
Revolution (which he prefers to term the New Nationalism) did not survive the
Third Reich, "despite attempts to revive it" (201). Although he plays with the
idea of a Conservative Revolution that did manage to outmaneuver the Nazis
(it would probably have been a dictatorial and irredentist regime minus the Holocaust and World War II, he thinks [194]), the present relevance of the New
(Charismatic) Nationalism is to be found beyond Western Europe. The "heirs"
to the tradition can be found in Teheran, Baghdad, Black Africa, Southeast
Asia, and the Slavic countries, Breuer tells us (201). This is supposedly an
"echo" of what was "played through" in Germany after 1918 (201). Such a scenario places German nationalism firmly in the past and ignores present resus-

The gist here is that the '90s saw several revisionist intellectual histories of the interwar "Conservative Revolution."

Conclusions and Prospects /// 157

citation efforts. Given the "threat" to the West emanating from the venues just listed, Breuer hopes that the once-virulent German nationalism will in the coming years function not only as an example of the dangers involved in deviating from the Western path, but also as an occasion for reflection about the nature of that path. We might ask ourselves, he suggests, if a "technological civilization" that is "indifferent" to individual traditions that have evolved over time is immune to criticism (202). Writing in the years before 1989, he did not foresee that many representatives of the German New Right would repeatedly ask this question after reunification.

Two studies that appeared in 1995 proceed from assumptions similar, although not identical, to Breuer's. Rolf Peter Sieferle's biographical sketches of five major representatives of the Conservative Revolution (including Ernst Jünger)[5] all portray Germans, but the author emphasizes that the movement was practically "pan-European" (19, 44). Like Breuer, Sieferle views the Conservative Revolution as a thing of the past, a "purely historical phenomenon" that can now be comprehended without fighting it (21). Its protagonists were working on "projects of an alternative modernity" (43), but it was not they, but rather the Nazis who succeeded with their "real Conservative Revolution" (24). According to Sieferle, National Socialism was only one of the "five elements" that coexisted in the 1920s, which he categorizes as the "volkish," the "national Socialist," the "revolutionary nationalist," the "activist-vitalist," and the "biological naturalist." Although Sieferle is not a proponent of these "elements," he is also not an advocate of a one-dimensional model of modernization or a history of the West in which the final result seems inevitable (201). It is perhaps not coincidental that he illustrates this by referring to the United States:

> It can easily be demonstrated that contemporary U.S. society, for example, does not in some ways fulfill the criteria of modernity that were developed in current theories. The ideal of "secularization" is confronted with a widespread religious fundamentalism. "Democratic participation" is realized in an oligarchical party system with low voter turnout. An unpredictable justice system contradicts the rule of law. . . . Instead of growing equality, we find a widening social gap, instead of "rationality," the dominance of the myths of mass culture. The "state monopoly of force" is retreating in the face of growing violent crime. Finally, one can hardly still speak of a "cultural integration" in light of the increasing segmentation of society into races and ethnic groups. (202)

Although such issues also appear in Sichelschmidt's polemic, they are brought up here because Sieferle is unhappy about the direction that U.S. society is taking, not because he is eager to gloat about it. While reconstructing the ideologies of Nazism and the Conservative Revolution, the author acknowledges that the results of such scholarly spadework might be misused by "confused contemporaries" (220). He states unequivocally that both movements were "designs of an alternative modernity" that "fortunately failed" (221). It will not escape a careful reader that this is *not* tantamount to saying that any and all alternatives *should* or *must* fail.

Michael Rupprecht's look back at the "literary civil war" in twentieth-century Germany bears the subtitle "On the Politics of the Nonpolitical in Germany."[6] Thomas Mann's self-description is thus applied to an entire group of intellectuals. Like Breuer, Rupprecht believes that the time has come for an objective reappraisal of the Conservative Revolution. His own purported objectivity is contrasted with "old and new ideologists" (10) who have a distorted view of the past. Even though he clearly rejects such New Rightists as France's Alain de Benoist or Russia's Vladimir Shirinovsky, he claims that figures like Jünger, Spengler, and Schmitt stood "between all ideologies" during the Weimar Republic, although it is admitted that these figures (for no apparent reason, Thomas Mann is included in this group) did contribute to the catastrophic course of German history (9-10). Taking as his point of departure the highly charged German debates regarding the nature of the Gulf War, Rupprecht calls upon his fellow intellectuals to make political discourse more disinterested ("versachlichen") than it has been in the past (29). On the surface, this is laudable enough, given the German proclivity for polemics. Unfortunately, Rupprecht is not an impartial observer himself. Anyone who can compare Ernst Jünger's relationship with democracy to that of Thomas Mann (199), claim that Jünger cleansed the cultural criticism of Spengler and others of "unpleasant antidemocratic overtones" (207) or argue that it is "inappropriate" to compare Botho Strauß with the Conservative Revolution (25) clearly cultivates more than exclusively scholarly interests. His concluding remarks, in which he emphasizes the necessity of reexamining the actions of all intellectuals, both left and right, in our "century of civil wars" (211), suggest that Ernst Nolte's revisionist history is one of his guideposts. In words reminiscent of Sieferle, he describes the Conservative Revolution as one of the projects of "an alternative modernity" (43). He obviously believes that current projects can learn from those predecessors who had difficulty comprehending the dangers of Nazism.

It is noteworthy that those scholars who dedicate their energies to prevent just such "learning" refrain, unlike the three figures just discussed, from declaring their disinterestedness. In their 1997 volume *Vordenker der Neuen Rechten* (Intellectual mentors of the new right),[7] Kurt Lenk and his coauthors introduce the thought of Georges Sorel, Oswald Spengler, Hans Freyer, Carl Schmitt, Martin Heidegger, and Ernst Jünger to a general readership. This is not done as part of the current "philosophical café" fad, but rather to the end of making the German public aware of trends that the authors consider disturbing. It is not disputed that the works of the six intellectuals have been—and continue to be—read and reflected upon by a diverse group of people, but the focus in this case is on the "young-conservative intellectuals who have been trying for some years to make positions to the *right* of the established politics of the large broadly based parties socially acceptable again." What is found disturbing is the attempt to revive the tradition of an "anti-Western, antiliberal, and antiparliamentary right" that had long remained peripheral in West Germany (11). The representatives of the Conservative Revolution are now, in the authors' view, portrayed either as martyrs or as misunderstood loners whose ideas were misused. It is apparently Lenk, a professor emeritus, who is amazed that the younger generation seeks to emancipate itself from a "politically correct" culture by turning to the "weapons of [their] grandfathers" (12). Among these weapons, as described here, are a belief in the power of fate, apocalyptic presentiments, service and discipline, nationalism, heroism, antibourgeois feelings, xenophobia, and many others. (Jürgen Habermas's rather hyperbolic term for all this is "intellectual junk."[8]) The authors see in this arsenal "a declaration of war against civil and bourgeois values" (16), and the international community as a whole will certainly be relieved to know that these values find defenders in today's Germany. In the long term, however, one of the positions taken by these particular defenders is not unproblematic. It is the subliminal tendency to take the alienation characteristic of our modern age less than seriously.

Another 1997 publication[9] is cut from the same cloth, although it is more openly political and less scholarly. (This is not to say that the two areas cannot coexist. It is an author's denial that the former influences the latter that is problematic.) The author, Iris Weber, begins by referring to the 1995 report of the German Constitutional Police, in which the intellectual New Right is given attention for the first time. She wishes to inform her fellow citizens about the "potential danger" to democracy posed by this grouping (7). Her emphasis is somewhat different from that of Lenk et al. A number of pages are devoted to Carl Schmitt and his theory of the state, but Freyer, Jünger, and Spengler are marginal figures. (Heidegger is not mentioned at all.) Instead of concentrating on earlier manifestations of rightist thought, the author discusses more contemporary figures, like Irenäus Eibl-Eibesfeldt, Arthur Jensen, Hans Jürgen Eysenck, and Alain de Benoist. Her differentiation between the various camps within the New Right helps to explain some of the contradictions found in *Die selbstbewußte Nation*. In the context of this study, one aspect that does not interest Weber should be pointed out. Although she provides a detailed presentation of the New Right's plan to gradually achieve "cultural hegemony" (87–90), the role of literature is not considered at all. This was also true of the Lenk volume—with the exception of the chapter on Jünger—and it appears to be characteristic of most observers who are drawn to the topic.[10] Was Botho Strauß's brief encounter with right-wing politics both the beginning and end of the literary right?

At least one critic—like Herzinger, a disciple of Karl Popper—says this and much more. In a breathtaking survey of "two hundred years of the German religion of art," Dirk von Petersdorff equates the end of Soviet socialism with the disappearance of "the last of those counter-modern worlds . . . that had been entwined with bourgeois society since the late eighteenth century."[11] He distances himself from Stefan Breuer, who has analyzed anti-Westernization and a critique of democracy as a phenomenon of the literary right.[12] For Petersdorff, both rightist and leftist German artists (he uses this term to refer mainly to writers and estheticians) have opposed the "open society" and come under the spell of "totalitarian politics" (68). Such statements make his essay appear to be a belated postscript to the Literature Debate, especially since Christa Wolf is criticized for speaking of a "truly democratic society" different from the West German model (71). When Petersdorff portrays Novalis—including the novel *Heinrich von Ofterdingen*—as the beginning of German antimodernism, his comments are somewhat one-sided, but generally not off the mark. With respect to the twentieth century, however, his case is much less convincing. He hesitates to criticize Gottfried Benn, and he seems to forget that Thomas Mann—albeit not without inner conflicts—became an outspoken defender of the Weimar Republic. Worst of all, he sees no great difference between the role of important writers in the GDR (who "had the telephone number of the chairman of the state council") and West German novelists who campaigned for Willy Brandt and the SPD (76). Instead of using the term "novelists," Petersdorff might have specifically mentioned Heinrich Böll and Günter Grass, but this would have undermined his entire argument, since neither Böll nor Grass, despite their often caustic criticism of West German democracy, could be accused of harboring a secret affinity with totalitarian systems. The ongoing interventions of Günter Grass[13] demonstrate that it is possible to envision an incrementally better society without opposing modernity. Petersdorff's plea for an "esthetics that does justice to the freedoms of modernity" (86) is praiseworthy, but his support of Karl-Heinz Bohrer's desire to "free" esthetic modernism from "social criticism, the temptations of totality, [and] the slag of the philosophy of history" (83) is not only a dead end but also a dangerous path for today's Germany.

Why is this so? Imaginative writers (and to a certain extent all true intellectuals) possess a sensitivity that enables them to perceive the normally imperceptible. They are certainly not the only human beings who are capable of this, but they are (almost) the only ones whose main activity consists of observing human actions in the microcosm of everyday life and contextualizing them in the macrocosm of long-term developments. Some would say that this is merely one aspect of literary pursuits, and that is indisputable. There is no dearth of writers who are greatly interested in or even exclusively concerned with the microcosm of their inner selves. In times when cultural and political upheaval is the order of the day (e.g., during the Weimar Republic or the 1960s), the "inner self" is of necessity set upon by external reality and forced to come to terms with that reality. Writers living in such times often produce works that juxtapose the inner and outer worlds, and the reception of such works by contemporary readers can, over time, affect the perception of social reality. In relatively stable or stagnant times (Hegel's description of happiness as the "empty pages of history" comes to mind), few people can discern the currents beneath the calm surface. To accomplish this, one must have an educational background that equips one with the facility to see parallels between the present and past epochs. In Wilhelminian Germany, and even until the 1960s, this background was provided to the extremely small elite that attended the humanistic *Gymnasium*. The postwar democratization and modernization of the German school system has had as one result the virtual disappearance of this background, even among the elite. There can be no doubt that Humboldt's ideal of the well-rounded person is doomed when an intellectual like Stefan Breuer characterizes the traditional *Gymnasium* as "not preparation *for* the world," but instead "*against* the world."[14] Although this preparation is by no means sufficient, it is crucial for the development of an educated citizenry and the survival of civil society. If public support for the humanities (taken to mean critical thinking, esthetic sensitivity, and historical consciousness) continues to wane, there will be only one small cohort of people in a position to perceive the difference between illusion and reality, namely writers and artists. Since the German example has shown that the occupation of such an exclusive position can lead to an unhealthy self-exaltation, the struggles to maintain a critical literature and a critical public are ultimately inseparable.

This is my own subjective judgment, but it is hardly unique. To my own amazement, I have found similar views—albeit from a very different perspective—in the first monograph on the Conservative Revolution, which appeared in 1941. Former Nazi functionary Hermann Rauschning, who, previous and subsequent to his involvement with National Socialism, was a Christian monarchist, had hoped to preserve "human substance" in the face of the destruction caused by the "great secular emancipation movement" that began in the Enlightenment.[15] He lamented the turning away from German idealism ("Weimar and humanism," 180) rejected the stance of both Nietzsche and George, and described Jünger as an "extremist intellect" who played into the hands of the Nazis (72). (The reference to Hofmannsthal at the beginning of the preface set the stage for an alternative vision of culture.) Rauschning saw German literature in the hands of the left, but rather than attacking this camp for monopolizing it, he examined the attitudes of the German elite. His analysis ran as follows: Already before the First World War, the elite had failed in its duty to preserve the "continuity" of "intellectual and political tradition." Even worse, this group had "no real relationship with culture," and this failing had a negative influence on the German people, especially on the middle class, for whom life revolved exclusively around economic success. An untenable situation obtained long before the rise of the NSDAP: "In our political elite, any occupation with intellectual matters was considered to be more or less suspect" (194). The solution, as proposed by Rauschning, is a new kind of elite:

> [W]ithout a stratum that carries the historical, intellectual, and political creativity of the people, even the greatest people falls back onto the level of semiconscious vegetating. Such a stratum should not be confused with any societal upper class based on the nobility of birth or property. (209)

This is tantamount to an elevation of culture, manifested as both a knowledge of tradition and a cultivation of creativity in the present, to equal status with the political and economic system. Equal status does not imply the superiority flaunted by the prophets and seers discussed above, but it does mean that we cannot allow the shape of the future to be determined by forces either unknown to or beyond the reach of the majority of the human race. To do so would be to abdicate all responsibility to coming generations. The realization that such a position might lead to a dialogue between nonfundamentalist elements of the right and the left—not to be confused with the ongoing battle for a middle void of definable characteristics—should not be a hindrance.[16]

Rauschning unwittingly (?) provided the model for such dialogue, even though he was unrelentingly critical of the left as a force for secularization. The model is to be found in his portrayal of the Jews and their role in German society. According to Rauschning, the essence of Jewishness is the combination of critical, dialectical thinking and a conservatism that respects the law, the family, tradition, and a rootedness in the "divine calling" of human beings. As long as the Jew can maintain the creative tension inherent in this constellation, he is "the greatest enrichment within any people (Volk)" (239). (In the case of his own country, Rauschning does not hesitate to characterize the last one hundred and fifty years of German intellectual history as German-Jewish intellectual history[17] [240]!) The antiassimilatory implication of the word "within" is problematic, but one might consider what the future relevance of the model might be if the word "Jew" were replaced by "intellectual." In the twentieth century, most intellectuals on the left have seen tradition as an enemy, whereas most of their counterparts on the right have attempted to defend it or even reinstitute parts of it that had been cast off over time. Leftist critical thinkers have all too frequently been remiss with regard to criticism of their own projects, and their rightist opponents have as a rule viewed tradition as beyond questioning. Certain representatives of the Conservative Revolution attempted to fuse "traditional" concepts such as authority, military virtues, and service with mass society and the use of technology both in industry and as an organizational model for society (i.e., function rather than identity). This alternative failed between the world wars, and there is little reason to believe that it would be more successful now, despite the efforts of such latter-day advocates as Botho Strauß and Heimo Schwilk.

In 1933, some of the ideas of Heidegger, Jünger, Schmitt, et al. were plundered by the Nazis and forced into the Procrustean bed of National Socialist ideology. The contemporary New Right has yet to reach a mass audience,[18] but the relatively sophisticated language in *Die selbstbewußte Nation* has a trivialized counterpart in youth culture (e.g., neo-Nazi racist rock bands, nationalist/xenophobic websites on the Internet,[19] etc.). Until recently, the flurry of intellectual activity and waves of rightist popular culture had not translated into success at the ballot box comparable to that of Jean-Marie Le Pen in France, Jörg Haider in Austria, Gianfranco Fini in Italy, or even Pia Kjærsgaard in Denmark.[20] The right-wing Republikaner have been on the wane, and they have often been involved in turf battles with the German Peoples Union (DVU). In April 1998, the latter unexpectedly won a victory that sent tremors through the entire German political establishment. The DVU captured 13 percent of the vote in the Sachsen-Anhalt state elections. Despite the fact that this impressive figure (about 154,000 votes) was garnered by a "phantom party" with almost no members in the area and made possible by the millions of its founder, Gerhard Frey, there was no ignoring the calculation that a full one-third of male voters between eighteen and twenty-five chose Frey's party.[21] The party program of the DVU, disseminated via the Internet (<www.dvu.net/programm.htm>), demonstrates how the ruminations of intellectuals and the mail-order distribution of CDs with extremist content can be transformed into practical politics. An analysis of the DVU's Twelve Points shows not only how a rightist party attempts to sound like the voice of reason; it also highlights the distance between the German Right and American ultraconservatives.

The preface to the program contains a commitment ("without any reservation") to the German constitution. The individual points begin with a moderate tone, often slipping into right-wing rhetoric at the end. Under "Preservation of the German Identity," for example, there is talk of serving the cause of world peace, but the specific contribution to this noble project is a policy aimed at limiting the number of foreigners in Germany, stopping the abuse of the right to political asylum, and deporting "foreign criminals." The language of Alain de Benoist's ethnopluralism[22] is borrowed here, and France is also set up as a model for stopping the "distortion" of German: the state is called upon to stop the influx of foreign words by means of an institution like the "Académie française."[23] "Self-determination" and the German mark are defended against the bureaucracy of the European Union — a position not unknown even in liberal European Union members like Denmark—but this point is linked to the loss of German territories after World War II. This loss, it is asserted, contradicts the principles of international law. This situation, we are assured, can only be changed by peaceful cooperation, not violence. (One can imagine that the Poles will not be soothed by this addendum.) Collective guilt as a discriminatory measure supposedly used against the German people is rejected, although the crimes of the Nazis are not disputed. It does not inspire confidence, however, when these crimes are depicted as no different than the actions of the Communists,[24] and it is also maintained that "serious war crimes" were also perpetrated by the Allies. German suffering must not be forgotten, and the German soldier (both in his incarnation as a member of the Wehrmacht and today) is to be given due respect. The historical dimension in the first three points yields to questions of social and economic policy in the rest of the document. Subsidies for "German families and mothers," expansion of day care, equality for women, and better health care for all citizens are grouped together with an attack on abortion as both immoral and detrimental to the "preservation of the German people and the securing of the future." Revenues saved by contributing less to international organizations[25] are to be used to guarantee pensions and social programs. Housing and transportation policies are to take the needs of children and youth into account, especially in urban areas. The educational system should offer equal chances to all without promoting pseudo-equality ("Gleichmacherei"). The goals of education are "respect for human dignity and religious conviction, courage, a sense of responsibility, democratic spirit and international understanding, and love for the homeland and the German people." Stricter laws against polluters are called for, and the state is to make the protection of the environment one of its "primary tasks." Experiments using animals are to be kept to a minimum, and those who abuse animals are to be punished more severely. Foreign influences on German culture are to held to a "reasonable level," whereas German artists are to be supported (according to their "achievements"). The mass media are to reflect the "values of the constitution" and the morality of the "majority of the people" and refrain from exerting a negative influence on German rights and concerns. The authors of the program are not unaware of the effects of globalization. They appear to support a limited policy of autarky, one that includes preferential treatment for German firms and farmers (in light of "excessive foreign competition"), a program to renew key domestic industries like shipbuilding and steel, and the use of the "native" energy source, namely coal. All of this is to be accomplished by increased political awareness and participation on the part of the citizenry, channeled through political parties (including new small ones, like the DVU) and referendums.

This vision of a self-aware/self-confident nation contains passages that could have been lifted from speeches by Patrick Buchanan, Jesse Helms, Ross Perot, and many others.[26] It is not surprising to find German versions of isolationism, the V-chip, and "English First," but in the American context, such ideas would hardly be merged with the goal of a strong state that intervenes in the economy, provides myriad forms of social welfare, and lends financial support to artists and writers. The campaign to limit immigration is of course not a unique exercise in the industrialized West. The one aspect of the program that is rooted in the German experience is the effort to restore national pride and patriotism, an effort that must of necessity include a revisionist look at the Third Reich and a plea for the return of lost territories. As was mentioned above, many of the voters who opted for the DVU in Sachsen-Anhalt were young males. They live in one of the "new states" of the Federal Republic, where unemployment is rampant and job security practically nonexistent. Such people could hardly be expected to view globalization as an opportunity or "flexibility" as a virtue.[27] Groups like the DVU may have nothing to offer beyond the tired old recipes of the past, but they are reacting to real social phenomena as well as the perceptions of individuals, as skewed as they may be. If political parties from other segments of the political spectrum in Germany continue to act as if globalization and the gradual disappearance of national identity are not only inevitable but also beneficial, disaffected youth and others may choose to once again follow the "special path." This could have catastrophic consequences for both the Germans themselves and the other residents of the global village.

There are signs that a new type of thinking is emerging in Germany, although it is too early to tell where it might lead. At a meeting of German Catholics, the audience hears criticism of the "uninhibited and shameless egotism" in German society. Delegates also attend a forum about the ecological responsibility of business that includes then Christian Democrat Environmental Minister Angela Merkel and Joschka Fischer, the prominent Green politician.[28] Jürgen Habermas engages in a dialogue with then SPD chancellor candidate Gerhard Schröder and uses the occasion as an opportunity to call for the development of transnational democracy as a reaction to glo-balization and the "strained frivolity of . . . neoliberal politics."[29] Sociologist and legal scholar Sibylle Tönnies (granddaughter of Ferdinand Tönnies, who described the transition from *Gemeinschaft* to *Gesellschaft*) strives to separate Romanticism from the anti-Enlightenment stance of neo-Roman-ticism and advocates a return to "metaphysically motivated Enlightenment" with an emotional component.[30] She also attempts to come to terms with American communitarianism as a possible method for revitalizing the no-tion of community ("Gemeinschaft") long shunned in postwar Germany.[31] Political scientist Antonia Grunenberg supports a concept of freedom that is not equated with material prosperity or social welfare programs. Using the political philosophy of Hannah Arendt as her point of departure, she envi-sions a society in which individuals see themselves in the first instance not as receivers of services provided by the state, but rather as citizens concerned with using and preserving freedom. Knowing that the Germans panic when security and stability are threatened, Grunenberg adds that the stemming of increasing poverty is the *conditio sine qua non* of this model.[32] She has of course read Benjamin Barber, who has issued a trenchant indictment of both "Jihad" (represented in Germany by the xenophobic skinhead, and, on an-other plane, by the elitist intellectual) and "McWorld:"

> Each eschews civil society and belittles democratic citizenship, neither seeks *al-ternative* democratic institutions. . . . Jihad pursues a bloody politics of iden-tity, McWorld a bloodless economics of profit. Belonging by default to McWorld, everyone is a consumer; seeking a repository for identity, everyone belongs to some tribe. But no one is a citizen. Without citizens, how can there be a democracy?[33]

This kind of American export to Germany will one day, one hopes, be as widely accepted as the franchises of McDonald's restaurants, Toys "R" Us or Blockbuster Video found in many cities between the Rhine and the Oder-Neiße.

What of the role of literature in this contemporary constellation? Sibylle Tönnies offers Gotthold Ephraim Lessing (whose drama of tolerance, *Nathan der Weise* [Nathan the wise], was the first play performed in post-fascist Germany) as a model worthy of emulation.[34] Lessing was indeed an exemplary embodiment of intellectual rigor, bourgeois virtues, and human empathy. He was also the product of an era of great upheaval, one far re-moved from our own barely surveyable terrain. Writers like Günter Grass and Christa Wolf are nearing the end of their long—and not uncontroversial

—careers, and the following generation, represented by the now-tainted figures of Botho Strauß and Peter Handke, offers no promising candidates for succession.[35] Few authors desire, or dare, to transcend their own personal concerns, offering a portrait of modern life that might have some impact on more than private life or group identity. Endless debates about whether this is the result of a conscious decision or simply a sign of the (postutopian) times are not likely to be fruitful. Beyond global formulas, the small-scale alternative offered by writer Matthias Altenburg (b. 1958) should perhaps be considered. Unwilling to accept the retreat into elitism and cultural pessimism undertaken by some members of the generation of 1968, Altenburg asks us to at least attempt to resist the "daily evil":

> [A]t least it is possible that this attempt is both the least that must be done and the most that can be done. That would be: an Enlightenment that would not again succumb to the illusion that everything can be illuminated, one that would be aware of the non-enlightenability of most of what exists and would, despite this, doggedly do what it can, knowing that otherwise, only tyranny and resistance would remain.[36]

One cultural figure who apparently thinks along these lines is Hans Jürgen Syberberg (b. 1935). His provocative public statements[37] have made him a favorite target of the cultural left, and his presence in the table of contents of *Die selbstbewußte Nation* has only reinforced his image as a rightist. This is an oversimplification, as a reader of Syberberg's 1981 book *Die freudlose Gesellschaft* (The joyless society)[38] can attest. Many passages of this work appear to be source material for Botho Strauß's essay "Impending Tragedy." The author laments the lack of respect and interest given to culture in democratic society (39), despises television ("Gradual stultification: Television as a drug" [176]), bemoans a youth that has no time to listen and will thus never become wise in old age (190), and values myth as a repository of the "secrets, wishes and the subconscious" of the people (317). At the same time, he does not hesitate to give expression to the contradictions within himself. Although he attacks the "leftist establishment of the intellectuals" (220), he does not conceal his own sometime association with it (231). He is saddened by a loss of German traditions and values (240), but he does not portray these as a racially pure phenomenon:

> Germany without Jews: Loss of intellectual curiosity and the clumsiness of fashions as an inadequate replacement ("Ersatz"). The Jews were our most intellectually vital partners in the modern symbiosis of our culture. This loss is now making its impact felt. We are alone ("unter uns"). (55)

He can laud Ernst Jünger as a writer who dared to be different (221) but go on to compose a list of German cultural icons that includes not only Strauß and Handke, but also leftists and left-liberals like Wolf Biermann, Alexander Kluge, Günter Grass, Heinrich Böll, Bertolt Brecht, Hans Mayer, and Alexander Mitscherlich (381–383). It is not coincidental that Syberberg often emphasizes the human qualities of the people on his list. His main concern, which is reflected in the title of his book, is that the limitless production of material goods in the "consumer society" (he uses the English term) and the removal of obstacles have not yielded a better quality of life: "Are we happier today? Are there more celebrations? Is there more art? Are marriages, social life, living and dying better (190)? These are questions that the left should also be asking, both when analyzing contemporary conditions and proposing alternatives.[39] Once Syberberg's generation of Germans, the last to have consciously experienced both everyday happiness and profound horror, have left the scene, there may be few people disposed to ask such questions, whether in literature or in life. That is a disconcerting prospect.

When Ernst Jünger died on February 17, 1998, at the age of 102, the German print and visual media reacted with an outpouring of appraisals of his life and works.[40] On the evening news (ARD's "Tagesschau"), the one formulation used by many commentators made its debut: "With his voluminous literary œuvre, Jünger evoked great admiration, but also clear rejection." Federal President Herzog was quoted as saying that literature had lost "a unique witness to our time," and Chancellor Kohl added that Jünger had been "an independent and indomitable intellect." (The fact that the two highest representatives of the state would make statements about the passing of a literary figure illustrates the — at least residual — status of high culture in Germany.[41]) The still-controversial discussion of the author's relationship to war and National Socialism was also touched upon during the news broadcast. This was a relatively even-handed portrait provided in a short time slot, and it was probably the one that reached the greatest number of Germans. The many assessments offered by literary scholars, critics, and politicians were actually much more problematic. One would expect a conservative CSU leader like Theo Waigel to call Jünger a "great German" and transform him into an anti-Nazi resistance fighter, but then SPD chairman Oskar Lafontaine's praise of the "stimuli" found in Jünger's works was an example of cynical pandering to the conservative electorate, given the author's distaste for everything that Social Democracy stands (stood?) for.[42] Philosopher Hans Georg Gadamer characterized Jünger's life as "an irrefutable witnessing," granting the author instant status as a monument.[43] (Does "irrefutable" mean "beyond assessment"?) The French—with the exception of Sartre— always more appreciative of Jünger than the Germans, compared the deceased with Hugo and Valéry (*Libération*), asserted that he represented "intellectual freedom" vis-à-vis "subjugation and barbarism" (*Le Figaro*), saw him as a latter-day Roman—"proud, unpretentious, unshakable" (François Mitterand—not from the grave, but in an earlier statement), someone capable of "deciphering" the secrets of modern man (Jack Lang), a writer who sought not military, but rather "literary" salvation (Michel Tournier).[44] Even Jean-Marie Le Pen praised Jünger's patriotism and "chivalrous conduct."[45] It is one thing for outside observers (including former Spanish premier Felipe González, who memorialized Jünger's "human sensitivity"[46]) to make such pronouncements, but quite another for today's Germans to accept an antidemocratic (or at least democratically disinterested) intellectual as a figure worthy of emulation. The *Süddeutsche Zeitung* published articles that contributed to such acceptance, but at least that newspaper also offered a selection of Jünger's own thoughts—from 1982— about subjects like democracy: "I do not advocate any one constitutional form. . . . In Venice, in Greece, in Rome, in various German principalities, there were various forms of human existence. Some succeeded, some did not"; or anti-Semitism: "Who didn't say something against the Jews from time to time back then? Especially the Jews themselves. Take Heine, take Marx."[47] Such details are reduced to insignificance by the eulogizers who wish to exalt Jünger. Writer and essayist Curt Hohoff, who sees Jünger misinterpreted by "politically fanatical ideologists," claims that the author's cultural criticism was on the level of Hegel, Nietzsche, Jacob Burkhardt, and Karl Jaspers.[48] Germanist Harro Segeberg begins his portrait of Jünger with a list of the various manifestations of the centenarian, a list so long that no one phrase stands out. (Strangely enough, the first item on the list is not "enthusiastic soldier," but rather "author of military analyses of the First World War.") Segeberg finds Jünger's purported resistance to "ideological-political" seduction—at least until his final years—admirable, but he is more fascinated with than concerned about the "dangers" inherent in his world view.[49] Critic Wolfram Schütte does not attempt to transform Jünger into a democrat or a humanist, calling him "the only contemporary reactionary with true literary merits," but he in the end describes him as a "fearlessly curious intellectual."[50] Thomas Assheuer finds Jünger's "tirades" against the Weimar Republic "incomprehensible," but he calls him a "genius of perception" who undertook a moral—if not democratic—"turn" (Kehre) during World War II. If Jünger was in fact the "biographer and chronicler of the century,"[51] how would one categorize those figures like Anna Seghers or Heinrich Mann, who experienced a very different *saeculum?* The best advice comes from East German writer Rolf Schneider, who suggests that we use Jünger's diaries as one—not *the*—documentary source on the history of our times.[52] In general, the reactions to Jünger's death are not the expression of a vibrant democratic culture[53] in Germany (at least in my view). They are also not merely a heeding of the old custom of not speaking disparagingly about the dead (*De mortuis nil nisi bene*). The willingness on the part of intellectuals (quite surprising, in some cases) to divorce esthetic sensitivity and sophisticated—if skewed—perception from life in society and the lot of the majority could once again be manipulated in times of crisis. No one should wish that such a test will come.

For the past few years, the Munich publishing house C. H. Beck has offered a series of small paperbacks under the title "The Most Important Knowledge." Three of the recent additions to this series, *The Era of Enlightenment, Romanticism*, and *Good and Evil*, delineate the general context of the present study. Gerhard Schulz, the author of the *Romanticism* survey (which, flouting chronology, came out first), tells the intended general readership that the Romantic is "not a German characteristic and especially not a German fate."[54] Although he does not mention Goldhagen (whose book was yet to come), he sharply criticizes historian Gordon Craig for emphasizing an alleged German affinity with Romanticism's more pathological facets and denies that the discussion of national character has any scientific basis (134). Werner Schneiders, who is responsible for presenting the Enlightenment, has a much easier time of it, since he is not confronted with a primarily German phenomenon (logically enough, the chapter on Germany follows those on England and France). To the probable dismay of the New Right, Schneiders does not refrain from emphasizing that the German version of the Enlightenment had a strong religious dimension.[55] Lessing's juxtaposition of religious conviction with an optimistic philosophy of history is also given its due. On the negative side, the author does not omit a reference to the "long alliance between [German] Enlightenment and absolutism"[56] and the reluctance of the *Aufklärer* to push for political reforms (114). Schneiders discusses many critiques of the Enlightenment, but asks in the end: "What is the alternative?" (133). (*Die selbstbewußte Nation* is not included in the selections for further reading.) Annemarie Pieper, who traces the scientific and philosophical attempts to explain the existence of good and evil, cannot find any one explanation that could claim universal validity.[57] As might be expected in a book written for a German audience, Hitler, Eichmann, and Goldhagen appear on the first pages of the introduction. Pieper is convinced that evil is often more attractive than good, but she tends to side with Hannah Arendt rather than Goldhagen with regard to the crimes of the Holocaust (9). Good and evil remain a "puzzle" to her (119), but she does not hesitate to advocate a "freedom-based constitution" (120) as an absolute necessity. In a passage analyzing utopian dreams, she presents her own personal view of humanity. Her words are a fitting expression of the motivation behind my own investigations:

> [I]n the end, the humanity project always seems to be endangered when one of the basic human capacities — sensuality, common sense, reason, rationality — is deemed absolute and elevated to the sole measure of good and evil. The consequence is an inner disruption of humaneness that leads to brutalization. (113)

Epilogue

Schröder, Walser, Bubis, and the
Ongoing German Quest for Normalcy

No country (or political regime) has a corner on complexity or inner contradictions, but some countries (and regimes) are psychologically more stressful to study than others. Germany is a stressful country to study.[1]

After this study was completed, several events occurred in Germany which had an impact on the sociocultural landscape of the country. This is neither the time nor the place for an in-depth analysis of these events, but a brief survey can shed light on the prospects of the intellectual New Right. In the political sphere, it was the defeat of Helmut Kohl in the September 1998 national elections that was—at least initially—viewed by both political observers and large segments of the populace as a watershed in postwar German affairs. In the cultural sphere, it was the October 1998 speech made by Martin Walser (cf. chapter 3) and the response to it by German-Jewish spokesman Ignatz Bubis and many others that held the attention of the public for several months. The "Walser-Bubis debate" was accompanied by the continuing controversy surrounding design and erection of a Holocaust memorial in Berlin. In the spring of 1999, the "ethnic cleansing" of Kosovo and the participation of the Bundeswehr in military action against Yugoslavia stirred up memories of the 1940s. Finally, there were occurrences in Germany itself whose "normalcy," rather than exceptionality, provided a disturbing backdrop to all of the above, i.e., violent attacks against foreigners.

When Social Democrat Gerhard Schröder was elected chancellor in 1998, it was—incredibly—the first time in the history of the Federal Republic that a government has been voted out of power. Such ultra-stability has been attributed by some to the economic success of the (West) German model, by others to a fear of change stemming mainly from the experience of pre-1945 upheavals. (As the Italians have demonstrated, such fear is not the only possible response to the fascist era.) When Kohl's sixteen-year tenure was brought to an end, commentators were unsure of what to make of the unseating of the Christian Democrats (and their coalition partners, the increasingly neoliberal Free Democrats). One recalls that the editors of *Die selbstbewußte Nation* saw the "generation of 1968" as the root of all evil in postwar German society. For them, Helmut Kohl was a "stealth" Social Democrat who maintained a conservative facade while allowing the left to infiltrate all areas of society. Kohl's talk of an "intellectual-moral shift" was, in their view, a mere sham. Now the reins of power have been taken over by a '68er who was once a member of the Young Socialists (the youth wing of the SPD).[2] The (traditionally) conservative newspaper *Die Welt*, employer of Ulrich Schacht, Heimo Schwilk, and Rainer Zitelmann, did not, however, react to the election results with the publication of a jeremiad:

> The 27th of September is a day of triumph for the '68 generation. With Schröder, the fighters from the extra-parliamentary opposition will occupy the highest offices of the state for the first time.
>   The "march through the institutions" was successful. . . . However, Schröder's election victory is a structural one, not one of the ideology of '68. That was quietly disposed of. In the place of change, though, there appeared in many cases a kind of philosophical ["weltanschauliches"] vacuum. . . . That makes the victory of the ['68] generation into something hollow. A victory without substance?[3]

This question became the order of the day after the new chancellor presented his government's agenda (Regierungserklärung) to parliament on November 10, 1998. A brief summary of this agenda would be instructive here.

Those who expected a blueprint for sweeping changes were doubtless disappointed by the words of the new chancellor. He told his audience that unemployment was Germany's "most pressing and painful problem," emphasizing that "economic productivity is the beginning of everything."[4] Such assertions surely reminded the listeners more of Christian Democrat Ludwig Erhard (the architect of the "Wirtschaftswunder") than of Schröder's charismatic Social Democrat predecessor, Willy Brandt. This was not a critique of the system, but rather of stagnation within the system. Lamenting that the

Germans were no longer "innovative" enough, Schröder called upon his fellow countrymen to make themselves "fit for the European info-society"
("Wissensgesellschaft")" by, among other things, accepting the necessary role
of elites and reforming the university system. He called for a tax reform that
would combine "modern pragmatism" with "a strong sense of social fairness"
and at the same time spoke out against the "abuse of state services." He also
promised to fight crime and pay more attention to the rights of victims. The
term coined for the agenda so described was "politics of the New Center." In
reality, this meant that the SPD was attempting to occupy the middle, pushing the CDU onto the political fringes. Given this core project, references to
cultural matters in Schröder's speech seemed to be mere window dressing.[5]
Kohl would surely not have cited Habermas's vision of civil and cosmopolitan
society, but this was not more than a passing reference. Although Schröder
spoke of the election outcome as a "generational shift in the life of [the] nation" and praised his own generation (in both East and West Germany) as
torchbearers of "civic virtue," "civil courage," and opposition to "authoritarian structures," he emphasized that there would be no attempt to escape Germany's "historical responsibility," i.e., the commitment to building and
broadening democracy. It is telling that the one statement in the address that
had an old-fashioned social-democratic ring to it, namely the proclamation
that everyone has a "moral right" to employment and training, was modified
by an addendum stating that the unemployed have a "duty" to accept any opportunity for training offered them. While denying that his government
wanted to perpetuate a "paternalistic" state (Bevormundungsstaat), he made
it clear that personal choices would have to be subordinated to the goal of a
"leaner, more efficient," less bureaucratized government.

No one was moved to describe the bearer of these sober tidings as a charismatic figure ("A visionary he's not."[6]; "This chancellor will not become a philosopher for red-green visions."[7]). The would-be visionaries, namely those of
the extreme right, were the real losers of the election — or were they? In his pro-
grammatic speech, Schröder made a point of emphasizing that the German
people had "clearly rejected extreme-right and xenophobic tendencies" at the
ballot box. They should be proud of this, he said. A brief glance at the election
results does provide a basis for this pride: Taken together, the three main right-
wing parties (Republikaner, DVU, NPD) received only 3.3 percent of the
vote. The Republikaner garnered 0.1 percent less than in 1994. The collective
figure was still far below the 5 percent required for representation in parlia-

ment, but it was higher than in the previous election. More significant were the regional results of the far right, especially in Berlin and the former East Germany (in percentages)[8]:

	1994	1998
Berlin	1.9	4.9
Saxony	1.4	5.7
Saxony-Anhalt	1.0	4.1
Brandenburg	1.1	5.2
Thüringen	1.4	4.5

These results suggest that the attraction of nationalistic rhetoric and (informal) "ethnic cleansing" in the eastern states should not be dismissed out of hand. This impression was strengthened in March 1999 when the Office for the Protection of the Constitution issued its report for 1998. Although the number of violent incidents involving right-wing extremists dropped by 5.7 percent vis-à-vis 1997, the number of persons considered part of the "scene" grew from 48,400 to 53,600. The number of those considered violent also rose from 7,600 to 8,200.[9] One can quibble about the figures or question — as many have — the criteria utilized by the Office, but the trend is a clear one.

Probably the most disturbing aspect of this trend — at least to this observer — is the growing readiness to use violence against foreigners. More than half of the violent incidents involved attacks on foreigners, and half of these occurred in the former GDR, where youth employment was a major factor, according to Interior Minister Otto Schily.[10] One can by now speak of an endless series:[11] Just weeks before this epilogue was written, Ghanian writer Amma Darko was taunted by about ten youths, who then used beer bottles to emphasize their racial epithets. This occurred on the Baltic-coast island of Rügen.[12] In the same week, three foreign students were insulted and attacked in nearby Greifswald (the word "nigger" was used, although the injured student was from Syria), and two African students were injured in Köthen (where Bach composed his Brandenburg Concertos).[13] Such atrocities led Schily and Justice Minister Herta Däubler-Gmelin to call for an "Alliance Against Xenophobia" ("Bündnis gegen Fremdenhaß").[14] Although it is impossible to determine which of the many incidents of the past few years were the most despicable, the death in February 1999 of Algerian asylum seeker Farid Guendoul in Guben, a city on the Polish border, was perhaps the most shocking to broad segments of the German populace. Guendoul bled to death while fleeing from over a dozen violent youths associated with the extreme right. Even the tabloid *Bildzeitung* spoke of an "incomprehensible battue" (Treibjagd).[15] There was bitter irony in the fact that the societal elites in both Guben and the Polish city of Gubin, across the Neiße river, have long been planning a merging of the two towns in the framework of European unification. (One asks oneself whether the elites or the youthful extremists are isolated from society.) Guben also has more social workers than the typical East German municipality.[16] Shocked citizens took part in memorial services, but politicians attempted to make political capital out of the affair. The party chairman of the Brandenburg CDU, Jörg Schönbohm, accused the reigning SPD of hoping for right-wing electoral successes as a way to weaken the CDU. (He said this on the day of a march organized by concerned citizens in Guben.)[17] Two days later, the Brandenburg minister for economic affairs, Burkhard Dreher (SPD), warned of the economic ramifications of xenophobia: "Although investors have not spoken to me directly about this topic up until now, I know that xenophobia and right-wing radicalism are a hindrance of the highest order for investments." He added that all citizens of Brandenburg should know that by advocating xenophobia, they were "sawing off the branch that they are sitting on."[18] There is doubtless no little truth in this statement, but one must question the ethical principles of a politician who chooses to speak of such things during a period of trauma and mourning. Any public official primarily concerned with his country's image abroad rather than with the serious social problems that affect that image is sending out all the wrong signals. On another level, one must ask to what extent the attitudes exhibited by Schönbohm and Dreher in this particular case are representative of the German political class as a whole. Renowned psychotherapist Hans-Joachim Maaz, upset about the stigmatizing of his fellow East Germans, has recently put forward the hypothesis that, although special circumstances in the former GDR tend to exacerbate antisocial behavior, what is happening in Guben and elsewhere is not unrelated to German society in the West as well:

> [T]he data [concerning] growing violence in the new federal states give us some indications about conditions in all of Germany, and they could warn us about the danger that threatens when the prosperity that has become a given for most of the citizens of the old Federal Republic becomes less and less certain.[19]

One need not accept Maaz's generalizations about the East Germans' "readiness to conform and subjugate [themselves]" and the West German "domination and doer ["Macher"] mentality" to consider the import of the above statement.

In the weeks before the 1998 election, the venerable German discourse about the relationship between thinking and acting, intellectuals and politicians, surfaced yet again. In late August, Berlin witnessed a meeting of minds, the tenth in a series of brainstorming sessions about almost anything under the sun (this one was entitled "10. Ideentreff—Eurovisionen"). Among the organizers of the event were the political artist Klaus Staeck and sociologist Oskar Negt. The point of the exercise was to formulate a manifesto that would provide "a political perspective for a cultural and social Europe."[20] This turn of phrase sounds as strange in English as it does in German: What Europe would not be "cultural" and "social"? The actual intent was to defend the (postwar) European project of social justice and a unique (i.e., non-American) culture. One could not help but reminisce about the—in the meantime highly mythologized—alliance between critical intellectuals and Willy Brandt in the 1960s. In comparison to those days, when the views of writers like Günter Grass were taken seriously (or at least given a requisite hearing), the Kohl era had seemed to be a sort of black hole that swallowed up any incipient dialogue between the pensive and the pragmatic.[21] Ironically, Grass did not come to Berlin this time. If he had been a one-man grassroots movement in 1965, now he chose to appear on a mere four occasions for the SPD, all of them in the East. He was still upset about Social Democrat support for restrictions on the influx of asylum seekers and for broadened surveillance powers for the police.

The chautauqua about "European visions" brought together celebrities like actor Ben Kingsley, film director Constantin Costa-Gavras, writer Elie Wiesel, philosopher Bernard-Henri Lévy, Michael Naumann (later to become Schröder's cultural minister; listed here as "publisher from Berlin"), and former French cultural minister Jack Lang, who, in an subsequent interview, said something that no German intellectual would have dared to say at the time:

> Society has changed. Germany cannot let itself be eternally enslaved by the memory of the Hitler dictatorship. The new Berlin no longer has anything to do with the Berlin of the "Third Reich." I have also already heard that people reject [the idea of] a federal cultural minister, because it reminds them of Goebbels. One is still giving power to Goebbels and Hitler fifty years after their iniquitous deeds.[22]

A German version of this lament was to appear not long after the election. Before turning to it, however, it should be pointed out that Gerhard Schröder, although not a dominating figure at the Berlin conference, did make a statement of some relevance for the present study. After characterizing the Kohl era as "one and a half decades of silence between politics and culture," he proclaimed: "Now we want European high culture."[23] Although it remains unclear just what this might mean (perhaps Pavarotti singing the role of Siegfried at Covent Garden?), one possible subtext could be the hope that Europe could maintain its identity by shoring up the cultural elite as a bulwark against the increasingly ubiquitous mass culture emanating from America.

On October 11, 1998, Martin Walser, a card-carrying member of that elite (albeit one who enjoys extended sojourns in America[24]), delivered an address that spoke to the long-suppressed sentiments of a substantial segment of the German populace. The occasion was the awarding of the 1998 Peace Prize of the German Book Trade. This prestigious honor, presented to persons who have made an outstanding contribution to promoting the idea of peace, had previously been given to such well-known figures as Albert Schweitzer, Ernst Bloch, Max Frisch, Astrid Lindgren, Yehudi Menuhin, and Václav Havel. In 1997, the winner was Turkish novelist and civil rights activist Yasar Kemal. Kemal was introduced by Günter Grass, who provoked many by using the occasion to criticize the German government's policies toward asylum seekers. The *laudatio* for Walser was delivered by none other than Frank Schirrmacher,[25] who had done his best to discredit the leftist literary intelligentsia in the "Literature Debate" of the early 1990s (see chapter 3). In contrast to the immediate postreunification controversy, the purpose was not to destroy the reputation of writers—like Christa Wolf—with a certain political bent, but rather to elevate one author to the status of a model worthy of emulation. Schirrmacher constructs the image of an eccentric who does not fit into everyday reality, but who nonetheless "sees clearer than others things left over, things left undone, legacies (Hinterlassenschaften)."[26] This special vision is made possible by contemplation untainted by any ideology, since Walser— "this great utopia skeptic"—believes in only one utopia, namely narration. The point of all this is to mold the author's entire career into a logical progression culminating in a project of remembering the German past in a highly personal manner. This is not meant to be ahistorical or antihistorical, however. According to Schirrmacher, it is "easy to detest and morally condemn National Socialism" but much more difficult to grasp how "misfortune and crime can rise up all around a person without him noticing it." Ironically, the first part of this statement is wishful thinking (i.e., quite utopian). The second part refers to Walser's 1998 novel *Ein springender Brunnen* (A gushing fountain),[27] in which an attempt is made to rescue a German childhood from the supposedly all-encompassing context of the Nazi period (Walser was six years old when Hitler took power). When Schirrmacher tells us that Walser's politics "stand on poetic feet," we have returned to the perspective of the Romantic Novalis. The problem with this portrait, which is meant to be laudatory, is that it has less to do with Walser's life and career than with the way in which the honoree, who was seventy-one at the time of the ceremony, might now want to (re-)interpret what has come before. As a young(er) man, he challenged the legitimacy of the Christian Democratic government of Konrad Adenauer, followed the Frankfurt Auschwitz trials very closely, and protested against the Vietnam War. As mentioned in chapter 3, he even flirted with orthodox communism for a time. It is clear that Schirrmacher would like to use Walser's reputation and stylized biography as a tool to recast the role of literature in reunified Germany. Although his notion that the gift of seeing can only be realized through a literary mind devoid of ideological and political concerns is highly problematic in the German context, he does direct us toward the core of Walser's acceptance speech. Speaking of *A Gushing Fountain*, Schirrmacher points out the "great paradox" of the author's generation: "to have been objectively innocent, possibly even happy, and simultaneously, thanks to the birth certificate, part of a whole that has become guilty."

When Walser went to the podium in the Frankfurt Paulskirche — where Germany's first democratic constitution was drafted — he began by telling his audience that it was not easy to decide what kind of speech to deliver. Those who congratulated him when the prize was announced seemed to expect a "critical" speech, something that Walser had already done,[28] a "critical sermon" based on the "bad news" ("unguten Meldungen") of the given day. Such sermons usually give the media something to chew on for "two, or even two and a half days." This time, he wanted to "say only nice things, i.e., things that feel good, stimulating things, things appropriate for a peace prize." But how would he be able to justify such a speech? One way would be to confess his weaknesses, especially one of relatively recent vintage:

> I seal myself off from evils in whose elimination I cannot participate. I have several refuges ("Fluchtwinkel") into which my glance immediately flees when the [TV] screen[29] shows me the world as an unbearable place. I consider my reaction to be appropriate. I should not have to be able to bear something unbearable. I am also experienced in thinking the other way ("Wegdenken"). Without

looking the other way and thinking the other way, I would not get through the day, let alone the night. I am also not of the opinion that everything has to be atoned for. I could not live in a world where everything had to be atoned for.

These words were interpreted by many as a license for repression, as a kind of absolution for the Germans, who have had to look at horrible images — specifically those from Auschwitz — over and over since 1945. Such positions have been taken on numerous occasions by the right-wing intellectuals discussed above. Had Walser suddenly decided to join them? Was his long-time advocacy of reunification, a position that had caused him to be ostracized from some segments of the intellectual community, a Trojan horse concealing reactionary sentiments? This statement, along with others in the speech, was clearly provocative, and it had the — surely unintended — effect of rendering some listeners incapable of keeping an open mind until the end (a phenomenon all too prevalent in critical discourse in postwar Germany).

Most of Walser's speech revolves around the tension between the conscience of the individual and the societal rituals that speak — with varying degrees of success — to that conscience. Every German of Walser's generation has experienced decades of public penance for the crimes of the Nazis, but not all Germans have internalized the message or even paid attention. Some, mainly on the fringes of the right wing, have vigorously denied the necessity of such public *mea culpa* declarations. (The official antifascism of the East German state was quite another matter.) Walser himself has not only been conscious of the dilemma of postfascist Germans seeking a "normal" identity, he has pondered the question at great length and written about it.[30] If he now admits that he is compelled to "look the other way," this comes after a long period of self-examination in search of his "share" (cf. Schirrmacher's title) in the horror that was Auschwitz.[31] Many Germans (especially, in Walser's view, representatives of the media and the intellectual left), simply cannot accept the fact that an individual could be absolutely overwhelmed by the shadows of the Holocaust. Some of these people, he intimates, attempt to join the ranks of the victims by taking on the mantle of the indefatigable antifascist.[32] Walser himself makes his stance perfectly clear: "I have never considered it possible to leave the side of the accused (Beschuldigten)." This is not the position of someone acting as an advocate for repression or forgetting. The message is not problematic, but the choice of venue was perhaps inappropriate: The author was mapping out a very personal journey in a very public space.

Walser was doubtless aware of this dilemma, but he was also upset that he, as a German, had to weigh every word carefully. (Already in 1994, he had delivered a public address in which he railed against "new German taboos" and the evils of "political correctness."[33]) Something in him rebelled against a half-century of self-censorship, and his soul was "thirsty for freedom," as he put it. The result was a rhetorical tightrope act. One sentence in particular demonstrates the perils involved in such an exercise:

> No one who can be taken seriously denies Auschwitz; no one still in full possession of his faculties splits hairs regarding the horror of Auschwitz; when in the media, however, this past is held up to me every day, I notice that something inside me resists this continuous presentation of our shame.

This resistance is then connected to the belief that this shame is being "instrumentalized" for some current ends. (Walser added that these ends are "always good ones, honorable ones," but this was generally ignored.) The general impression is that the postwar Germans have been assigned a special status on the periphery of the inner circle of civilized nations. Walser spoke of the "suspicion" that arises whenever anyone asserts that his countrymen now comprise "a completely normal people, a completely ordinary society." In the period after the Frankfurt speech, he was to reiterate his conviction that the Germans have done enough to demonstrate their transformation into a normal democratic nation. On the political plane, Chancellor Schröder was echoing these sentiments, creating an unusual harmony between culture and power.[34]

Although one of Walser's main aims in Frankfurt was to celebrate the emancipatory power of literature and literary language, this was practically ignored in the ensuing debate. The critics focused mainly on two aspects. In defending the sanctity of personal conscience, Walser criticized the planned Holocaust memorial[35] as a "paving over of the center of the capital with a nightmare as big as a soccer field," a "monumentalization of [our] shame." This would send the message that the interaction between Germans and Jews had to end in Auschwitz (in other words, that Goldhagen was right).[36] In addition, he utilized an entire series of epithets to characterize the abuse of Auschwitz for purely political purposes: "routine of threats," "means of intimidation," "moral cudgel," "ritual exercise." Such phrases were not unknown in the Federal Republic, but they had hitherto been used solely by the extreme right outside the public sphere in which most Germans were involved. Walser apparently believed that his impeccable credentials as a progressive intellectual who had dissected not only the fascist mentality, but also the problems of West German society, would shield him from accusations of retrogression and facilitate an open discussion of future prospects. This was a fatal misestimation of the temper of the times.

The major response to Walser's speech was mounted by Ignatz Bubis (1927–1999), a Holocaust survivor and chairman of the Central Council of Jews in Germany. Judging from videotapes of the Frankfurt event, he and his wife were the only members of the audience to refrain from applauding at the end of the speech. If Walser had hoped for an intellectual discussion about the nature of German identity in the new millennium, his hopes were dashed when Bubis became his main respondent. This very public figure was not an intellectual, but rather a businessman, politician (as a member of the FDP), Jewish activist, and voice of the survivors. One would expect a "gut reaction" to Walser's ponderings and provocations, and that is exactly what happened. To lend his critique the weight of history and symbolism, Bubis chose to express it on November 9 at a memorial service for the sixtieth anniversary of the "Kristallnacht." This was actually Bubis's second intervention into cultural affairs: He was the driving force behind the protest that stopped the performance of Rainer Werner Fassbinder's play *Der Müll, die Stadt und der Tod* (Garbage, the city, and death) in 1985. In his autobiography, he stated that the "fundamental question" at the time was "whether one can, in the mid-1980s in Germany, allow an anti-Jewish play to be performed, one that hurts the feelings of the survivors in an extreme manner."[37] In 1998, Bubis did not prevent Walser from speaking (he of course had not seen the text beforehand), but he attempted to discredit the speaker after the fact.

Already on the day after Walser's speech, Bubis had accused the author of "mental arson" (geistige Brandstiftung) and compared him with right-wing politicians like Gerhard Frey of the DVU and Franz Schönhuber, the former leader of the Republikaner.[38] On November 9, he revisited this accusation and amplified it. Martin Walser was not mentioned until the thirteenth paragraph. In the first twelve, one finds a catalogue of horrors: a description of the 1938 pogrom and thoughts on the nature of anti-Semitism in Germany and elsewhere, the Nazi racial laws, the Wannsee Conference, contemporary German racism, anti-Semitism and xenophobia, revisionist historians, the 1995 newspaper advertisements about Germany's 1945 capitulation (see chapter 2) and even the Fassbinder play referred to above. The next link in this gruesome chain, as it were, is Walser:

> The most recent attempt to repress history or to extinguish memory was undertaken by Martin Walser in his gratulatory speech ["Dankesrede"] on the occasion of the awarding of the Peace Prize of the German Book Trade to him on October 11 of this year.[39]

This is guilt by association of the most primitive kind. If Walser was upset when former friends and colleagues shunned him for advocating reunification and "expelled" him from the community of leftists, how must he have felt when Bubis portrayed him as an enemy of democracy, even humanity? It was little consolation that the accuser blatantly misinterpreted some statements, including a passage from Walser's 1978 text "Our Auschwitz." This is not to say that all parts of the Frankfurt speech were perfectly clear (the passage about his attitude toward xenophobic violence is especially vague, as is the nature of the "instrumentalization" of the Holocaust), and Bubis recognized that Walser's highly personal meditation could be taken as a model for others, something that ran contrary to the speaker's intention but was not explicitly excluded, either. In this regard, Walser displayed the kind of naiveté characteristic of Strauß and Handke: One can certainly stand on "poetic feet," as Schirrmacher put it, but one cannot expect to be answered in a poetic manner when speaking about politics. This "blind spot" is one of the few commonalities held by the three authors.

Bubis proved to be naive himself, or at least it seemed to be so. Toward the end of his speech, he emphasized that "he alone" was responsible for what was being said, not "all Jews," just as "only Walser" was responsible for his speech, not "all Germans." Even over fifty years after the collapse of the Third Reich, it is simply not possible for a German Jew—a prominent one, at that—to speak as an individual. This was especially true for Bubis, although he had been the prototype of the assimilated Jew for most of the postwar period.[40] His desire to be a German citizen of the Jewish faith, as he called himself, was much like that of Victor Klemperer, whom Walser admires as a model of the cultured German Jew. When Bubis stated that "we [i.e., the Germans, both Jewish and non-Jewish] have to confront history," he pointed to Goethe, Schiller, Beethoven, and Bismarck as examples of the positive side of that (German) history. This is not the world of contemporary reunified Germany, but rather the sphere of the pre-1933 *Bildungsbürgertum,* which now almost disappeared. Walser also feels at home in this sphere, so his confrontation with Bubis was sadly ironic.[41] Bubis was, and Walser is also patriotic in an old-fashioned manner, something that many Germans are not. The difference lay in personal agendas: Walser hopes for a *future* Germany whose citizens will not feel stigmatized because of their origin, whereas Bubis strove to preserve the memory of *past* horrors in a time when none of the survivors are alive. Unfortunately, two aspects of the Kristallnacht speech made dialogue almost impossible. Firstly, Walser was accused of being part of a growing trend of "intellectual nationalism" tainted by "subliminal anti-Semitism." (Bubis had made similar accusations with respect to Strauß and Enzensberger a few years earlier.[42]) This would place Walser in the midst of the contributors to *Die selbstbewußte Nation*, where he does not belong. Secondly, the final paragraph of Bubis's speech was delivered in the tone of an Old Testament prophet: "We owe it to the victims of the Shoah not to forget them! Whoever forgets these victims kills them once again!" How could anyone respond to such an admonition? And how could Walser pursue a rapprochement with someone who had presented him to the German people—and the world—as an arsonist and potential murderer?

In the weeks after Bubis's speech, hundreds of articles were published about the affair in German newspapers, and television interviews were also conducted. The controversy dominated the cultural scene for the last quarter of 1998, which was of course also the first quarter-year of the Schröder government. A detailed analysis of the positions taken by Jewish and non-Jewish Germans, by intellectuals, politicians, and ordinary citizens will be undertaken in a future publication.[43] In this context, it must suffice to describe the role of Klaus von Dohnanyi, a prominent Social Democrat and son of an antifascist executed by the Nazis, the attempted mediation by former federal president Richard von Weizsäcker, and the face-to-face discussion between Walser and Bubis in late 1998.

Dohnanyi published an essay in the *Frankfurter Allgemeine Zeitung* five days after Bubis had castigated Walser on November 9. He chose the title "Eine Friedensrede" (A peace speech), emphasizing his view that Walser had indeed earned his prize and made a speech worthy of it. Although he reproduced, almost ritualistically, the idea of German crimes and German guilt, he also did something unheard of in postwar Germany: He openly criticized the main spokesperson for the Jewish community while defending Walser. In addition, he left no doubt that Germany was still anything but a "normal" country. After asserting that Bubis did not understand Walser, he added that perhaps such understanding was an impossibility, since "Walser's speech was the lament of a German—a non-Jewish German, though—about the much too frequent attempts by others to gain advantages from our conscience. To abuse it, yes, to manipulate it."[44] This sounds as vague as Walser, but specifics are supplied, above all in the person of U.S. Senator D'Amato, who is portrayed as trying to better his reelection chances by pandering to those who demand compensation from the German government and German firms. Other examples are given, e.g., German schoolchildren being insulted as Nazis in Holland, caricatures of Helmut Kohl as a new Hitler in British tabloids, and knee-jerk negative reactions when German politicians make proposals regarding the Balkan crisis. What is intriguing is that Dohnanyi does not believe that such things can be changed: "Germany is stigmatized, and we Germans carry this mark of Cain. Thus nothing molds German consciousness more profoundly than knowing this and experiencing it." He is convinced that nothing determines Germany identity more than "our common descent from this shameful time" (i.e., the Third Reich). This is actually quite different from the position of a Walser, who, while denying no responsibility or shame, strives to help future generations extract themselves from this conundrum. As writer Peter Schneider has put it:

> We shouldn't let our children grow up with only images of mass murderers in their minds. . . . We have no "normal history," no argument there. But where would we end up if the first thing that we teach our children is this: You are not normal, you do not belong to a normal people. We would surely breed monsters.[45]

Dohnanyi hopes for no more than an increased sensitivity on the part of Jews when they deal with Germans, an acknowledgment of the latter's emotional wounds. Unfortunately, his own emotions got the better of him, and he made a statement that will probably be remembered long after the controversy has faded from memory:

> [T]he Jewish citizens in Germany of course should also ask themselves if they would have behaved much more courageously than most of the other Germans if, after 1933, "only" the disabled, the homosexuals, or the Romanies had been dragged away to death camps. Everyone should attempt to answer this question honestly for himself.[46]

In reality, most Germans did not resist fascism, and most Jews did not become antifascist partisans. Such utterances thus serve no purpose other than to open up old wounds and inflict new ones.

Dohnanyi and Bubis exchanged open letters in subsequent issues of the *Frankfurter Allgemeine*. Despite mutual accusations and insinuations—

Bubis, for example, termed the hypothetical situation cited above "malicious" (bösartig)[47] — they did meet and resolve their differences. Walser and Bubis did not sit down for an open-ended debate until December 13. Walser had felt rather beleaguered in the weeks after his speech: His public appearances were disturbed by demonstrators, Elie Wiesel had asked him to tell his readers that the preservation of memory was part of a dignified life (something that Walser would never dispute),[48] and even the Israeli ambassador to Germany, Avi Primor, had called upon him to supply the clarification that would free his speech from the accusation of anti-Semitism."[49] (In a "normal" country, a foreign diplomat would not have become involved in a domestic cultural row.) Richard von Weizsäcker had defended the integrity of all three "highly respected personalities" (i.e., Walser, Bubis, and Dohnanyi) and expressed the fear that, among other things, "concerned questions" were being asked abroad.[50] Through all this, Walser had remained obstinate, demanding that Bubis retract the characterization "mental arson" before a meeting could be arranged. When the encounter did occur in Frankfurt, the two septuagenarian adversaries were joined by Frank Schirrmacher and Salomon Korn, an architect and member of the Central Council of Jews in Germany. The *Frankfurter Allgemeine* published the entire transcript of the long (almost four hours) discussion on the next day.[51]

The headline that the newspaper chose to place above the transcript — "We need a new language of remembrance" — was an allusion to a speech made by federal president Roman Herzog on November 9, in which he attempted to reconcile the positions of Walser and Bubis without mentioning them by name. Herzog called for a "vital form of remembrance" that would express not only sadness regarding past sufferings but also the necessity of maintaining "democracy, freedom, and human dignity" for future generations.[52] He agreed with Bubis when he emphasized the necessity of remembering the victims of the Holocaust, but he was closer to Walser when he warned that constant reiteration of the message could be counterproductive. He also rejected — again, without providing the source — Goldhagen's term "eliminatory [German] anti-Semitism," as Walser had done in Frankfurt. Did this rhetorical effort facilitate détente between the writer and his critic?

The answer to this question is "yes and no," or as the Germans would say, "jein." The photographs printed along with the transcript lend graphic expression to the course of the discussion. More than once, Bubis is shown pointing his index finger at Walser, who reacts by "defending" himself with an open hand. This constellation can be attributed to the fact that Bubis utilized not only political arguments, but also the weight of his biography, something that Walser could not do. In his long opening statement, Bubis not only criticized "mental arson" and talk of "instrumentalization," but also offered personal narration about the Holocaust, including his father's death in Treblinka and the discovery of information about the murder of other family members in the archives at Yad Vashem. Given this mixing of the personal and the political, Walser was left with three choices: He could simply refuse to listen, but this was not a viable option, since he is not a right-wing Holocaust denier. Alternatively, he could apologize for any grief that he might have caused; this would probably also have ended the discussion. Finally, he could mount a defense based on the premise that Bubis had misinterpreted what he said in Frankfurt. This is the path that he chose.

To accomplish this, Walser had to amplify what he had said before. With regard to "instrumentalization" of the Holocaust, he now provided three concrete examples: 1) "The division [of Germany seen as] rational because of Auschwitz." 2) "The practice of reunification will lead to a new Auschwitz." 3) Literary critics condemning a novel "because Auschwitz does not appear in it." The last point refers to criticism of the 1998 novel *A Gushing Fountain*, which led the German best-seller lists for a long period after its publication. What he did not speak of was the question of compensation for Holocaust victims and forced laborers—in contrast to Dohnanyi. He was thus able to portray his concerns as that of a patriot who believed that his countrymen had a right to be reunited,[53] and an author whose pride had been wounded when political criteria were applied to a work of fiction. Bubis had nothing to do with these issues, so here Walser was speaking to the nation, not to his individual adversary. On the question of "looking away" from the horrible images of the Holocaust, the one that disturbed Bubis the most, Walser reformulated his earlier statement:

> I have looked away at least twenty times when scenes from the concentration camps are shown on television. Why? Because I cannot endure them. In this case, it is physically and psychologically impossible for me to look. I concluded from this that these scenes perhaps—as far as I am concerned—appear too often. However, I did not recommend to anyone that they have to feel as I do about it.

As anyone familiar with the German media knows, if Walser looked away only twenty times, he was in all likelihood *exposed* to these images hundreds of times. In fact, he said that he was "incensed" to hear himself portrayed as someone calling for a termination ("Schlußstrich") of dialogue about the Holocaust, since he had engaged in this dialogue for a long time—much longer than the survivor Bubis, he added. The latter reacted to this insult by asserting that he could not have "continued to live" if he had studied the Holocaust in the postwar years. Later on, Walser cited an insult launched earlier by Bubis ("If his [i.e., Walser's] forebears had kept the Jews from being killed, he would have his [peace of mind].")), but in general a civil tone prevailed.[54]

Even after several hours of give and take, one major point of contention remained, and it was one of some significance with respect to the future activities of German right-wing intellectuals. Bubis maintained doggedly that Walser's public remarks had "opened a gate for others," whereas the author countered that it was "high time . . . that this gate was opened." What was behind this metaphor? The Jewish leader was shocked that a respected figure from the democratic cultural community would express doubts about the necessity for routine, ritual ceremonies commemorating the victims of the Holocaust. For decades, everyone—with the exception of the extreme right— had upheld this taboo. Walser has believed for some time that the radical fringes actually prosper when the representatives of democracy shy away from dealing with delicate matters like patriotism, national identity, and the weight of the past. He also has taken the position—as he did once again in his discussion with Bubis—that National Socialism is by now no more than an "apparition" (Spuk).[55] To him, the social problems in Germany are the same as those in France, Italy, the U.S. and other countries. Only in the German case, however, do the media connect them to Nazism. Such a "connection" can lead to self-hatred (as described in *Die selbstbewußte Nation*), denial of national identity in favor of an abstract cosmopolitanism, or aggressive nationalism. Any and all of these could, in Walser's view, prevent Germany from becoming a nation like any other, forcing the country to remain "a convict let out on parole." To him, the chance of one's remarks being misused by the forces of reaction is less of a danger than the stagnation of public discurse in the face of myriad prohibitions.

German reactions to the Kosovo crisis demonstrate that the public sphere is now much more multidimensional than it once was, and that it is no longer easy to determine an individual's position based on his or her association with a certain camp. Before 1989, the intellectual left and the peace movement were generally opposed to any armed conflict[56] and any use of the

German military. The intellectual right tended to praise the Bundeswehr without calling for its use in a real conflict. This began to change in the Gulf War, when long-time leftists like Wolf Biermann and Hans Magnus Enzensberger came out in favor of Operation Desert Storm. In the present conflict with Milosevic, strange alliances have been formed. In 1999, it was the Social Democrats and Greens who were committed to the NATO bombing, and the once reigning Christian Democrats who were skeptical. (The rightist DVU saw the Germans as puppets of the Americans.) The Greens came to close to a split at their special party congress in May 1999, but in the end, Green foreign minister Joschka Fischer gained the support he needed to continue in office.[57] No consensus has emerged from the intellectual community. Biermann wrote a poem in support of the bombing,[58] and Enzensberger criticized the peace movement: "I was never a pacifist, because I owe my existence to the victors of the Second World War."[59] Grass sided with NATO but also criticized Western support for the breakup of Yugoslavia. [60] *Der Spiegel*, which published statements by a number of writers, summed up the situation as follows:

> The Cold Warrior Alfred Dregger [a veteran CDU politician] united with ex-RAF [Red Army Faction] *guerrillero* Horst Mahler, Pastor Schorlemmer [of the former GDR human rights movement], and Gregor Gysi [chair of the post-communist PDS] for an immediate stop to the bombing; Erhard Eppler [from the SPD left wing] and Bärbel Bohley, once representatives of the West and East German peace movement, [are] for the bombing. . . . Ex-chancellor Helmut Schmidt, advocate of NATO rearming, rejects the military action, as does the leftist investigative author Günter Wallraff.[61]

The Viennese daily *Der Standard* drew up a kind of scorecard of proponents (including Grass, Enzensberger, and Bubis), doubters (including Walser, Christa Wolf, Christoph Hein, and Elfriede Jelinek) and opponents (including Alexander Solzhenitsyn and Peter Handke).[62]

The *Spiegel* article cited above contains a rather apodictic proclamation announcing the death of the critical intellectual who appeared on the scene during the so-called Dreyfus affair in France a century ago. If this were true, high culture would be a hermetic exercise accessible to only a few. Martin Walser may concur that intellectuals have no monopoly on conscience, but he continues to offer comments—some would say sermons[63]—on the state of the world, albeit in literary language. Peter Handke also seems determined to cling to the once-acknowledged role of the writer as truthsayer and prophet.[64] Unlike Botho Strauß, who has stayed away from public scrutiny in the past few years, Handke has sought out opportunities for confrontation, bringing the (or rather, one) voice of high culture to the marketplace of ideas. This demonstrates that temperament is no insignificant factor in the activities of intellectuals (literary or otherwise): Whereas Strauß has—at least for the moment—reacted to sharp public criticism by returning to the role of the "pure" author, Handke still feels the need to take on the Western media and Western cultural hegemony.

It was mentioned in chapter 3 that Handke planned to publish a book about Kosovo as the third volume in his series about the Balkans. For now, he has written an essay describing his experiences in Serbia in early and late April.[65] In February 1999, Handke had said, in an interview with Serbian television conducted in Rambouillet, that "no people in Europe have suffered as much in this century as the Serbs have been suffering for [the past] eight years."[66] In March, he wrote to the magazine *Focus* and explained that he had misspoken: He had meant to say that "[t]he people who . . . have suffered (at the hands of the Germans, the Austrians, the Catholic Ustasha-Croats) the most in Europe in this century (after the Jews), for me, is the Serbs."[67] When the NATO bombing campaign began, Handke wrote an open letter to the world that was published in the Belgrade daily *Politika* on March 26. The most quoted passage from that letter is as follows: "Mars is attacking, and since the 24th of March Serbia, Montenegro, (the Bosnian) Republic Srpska, and Yugoslavia are the fatherland for all those who have not become Martians and green butchers."[68] At the beginning of April, the writer traveled to Belgrade, where he was inducted into the order of "Serbian Knights" for his courage in the face of the "bestial and brutal NATO aggression."[69] After his return home, he announced that he would leave the Catholic Church and return the money awarded as part of his 1973 Büchner Prize.

At this writing, the picture of what happened in the province of Kosovo is still incomplete. Of interest here is Handke's ongoing campaign against the Western media and the scorn that he has been heaping on the principles of the Enlightenment,[70] since this smacks of the "special path" discussed above. Evidence of this can be found in two interviews that he granted in May 1999. In the first, he characterized the "anti-Serbians" as "just as evil and unbearable as the anti-Semites in their worst time."[71] Since he went on to say that "since Hitler, nothing so catastrophically dirty has happened [as has happened here]," one must state that Handke has been engaging in exactly the kind of "instrumentalization" that Walser criticized in Frankfurt.

For him, it is not today's "right-wing radicals" who are the living offspring of Nazism ("to me, they're stillborn, dangerous only like ptomaine"), but rather the generation of 1968 and the leaders it has produced: "The American filthy swine, the English gymnast, all these criminal types." Their German counterparts, i.e., Schröder and Fischer, represent for Handke "eternally horrifying Germany." (By means of a sleight of hand, Austria is exonerated, since it does not allow NATO bombers to fly over its territory.) In the second interview, Handke went much farther. He asserted that NATO has achieved "a new Auschwitz. . . . Back then it was gas valves; today it's computer killers from a height of 5,000 meters."[72] This statement was outrageous enough, but more was to come. The interviewer mentioned that Daniel Goldhagen would like to "reeducate" the Serbs,[73] a proposal that has been criticized by many observers. Handke went beyond mere criticism when he called the Jew Goldhagen, son of a Holocaust survivor, a "Pimpf"—i.e., a member of the Hitler Youth.[74] Walser's (and Dohnanyi's) manner of dealing with Ignatz Bubis might be described as abrasive and at times insensitive, but Handke's epithet was so unconscionable that it may severely damage the prospects of any intellectual "special path" or volkish revival for the foreseeable future. Psychohistorians will no doubt want to analyze Handke's mélange of a nostalgic yearning for the premodern past and the use of modern demagogic rhetoric.[75]

Lest Handke's influence on coming intellectual and literary trends be overemphasized, it should be pointed out that two other factors will be extremely significant. One is the fate of the Berlin Holocaust memorial. After endless discussions and multiple proposals for design and redesign, including those put forth by cultural minister Michael Naumann, a decision was finally made on June 25, 1999. The Bundestag voted 314 to 209 in favor of a modified version by U.S. architect Peter Eisenman, consisting of 2,700 gravestone-like slabs and a documentation center.[76] Now that this "monumental" version has been chosen, only time will tell if such an edifice is destined to become a rendezvous for xenophobic skinheads and their "autonomous" opponents. Were that to happen, it could be a major irritant in the body politic of the Berlin Republic. Secondly, the reaction of the populace to the new citizenship law—a limited version of the *ius soli* finally passed by the Bundestag and Bundesrat in May 1999 after months of heated debate[77]—will be monitored carefully by the extreme right. The CDU/CSU had collected five million signatures against the original plan of the Schröder government, and the SPD-led state government of Hesse was defeated in the state elections of February 1999 when the Christian Democrats made opposition to dual citizenship the main issue in the campaign. Bavaria is considering an appeal to the Federal Constitutional Court. If the watered-down legislation (which only permits lifelong dual citizenship in special cases) were declared unconstitutional, or if the new legal status did not lead to real integration and assimilation in the long term, there would be no lack of fertile ground for those who would strive to (re-) plant the ideas of the Conservative Revolution and of ethnic homogeneity. Could such ideas really take root? Recent trends make this unlikely, but for all the wrong reasons: In the course of the Walser-Bubis debate, almost no one from the younger generation chose to enter the fray. Female voices were also noticeably silent (one notable exception was novelist Monika Maron). The media often portrayed the entire affair as one last standoff between two elderly men attempting to prolong the postwar period, but few opined as to what might follow. On another front, there seems to be mounting evidence that right-wing youth are oblivious to any ideas at all (cf. Enzensberger!). According to the Thuringian Office for the Protection of the Constitution, most reactionary young people are under twenty, and they seem to think that being a rightist is "cool." These people apparently are also attracted to the new strategy   of groups like the NPD, which no longer deny the Holocaust but glorify it. This has given the movement a "totally new character."[78] After presenting these findings, the President of the Thuringian Office made a recommendation that deserves to be heeded: "[German] society will have to grapple with this [phenomenon] much more vigorously than before." It is only through such grappling that Walser's "parolee" will ever be truly free.

Notes

Preface

1. Steven Erlanger, "Germany Sits in with a New Team," *New York Times*, April 12, 1998. In the same issue of the *Times*, it is reported that total German spending on tourism is a close second to that of the United States, making the Germans by far the biggest spenders per capita in travel abroad. This means that while some Germans — the ones discussed in this study — are turning inward, many others are seeking solace and stimulation outside the borders of the country. See Barbara Crossette, "Surprises in the Global Tourism Boom," *New York Times*, April 12, 1998.

2. G. P. Gooch et al., *The German Mind and Outlook* (London: Chapman and Hall, 1945). The other contributors were E. M. Butler, Alexander Farquharson, Morris Ginsberg, Roy Pascal, S. D. Stirk, and L. A. Willoughby.

3. Gooch, vii. Compare this image of the Germans with the recent one from Thomas Sowell: "In the long view of history, few peoples have made such cultural and economic contributions to so many lands in so many parts of the planet as the Germans." Thomas Sowell, *Migrations and Cultures: A World View* (New York: Basic Books, 1996), 104.

4. Gooch, viii. Compare the following statement: "Despite the bluster of recent advocates of 'structural' analysis, the evidence returns us to the view that political ideas and cultural traditions are not of lesser significance than structures of classes or states." See Jeffrey Herf, *Reactionary Modernism: Technology, Culture, and Politics in Weimar and the Third Reich* (Cambridge: Cambridge University Press, 1984), x.

5. See *Ist der Nationalsozialismus Geschichte? Zu Historisierung und Historikerstreit*, ed. Dan Diner (Frankfurt am Main: Fischer, 1987); Charles S. Maier, *The Unmasterable Past: History, Holocaust and German National Identity* (Cambridge, Mass.: Harvard University Press, 1988); Special Issue on the Historikerstreit, ed. Anson Rabinbach, *New German Critique*, no. 44 (Spring/Summer 1988); *The Unresolved Past: A Debate in German History*, ed. Gina Thomas (New York: St. Martin's Press,

1990), and *Reworking the Past: Hitler, the Holocaust, and the Historians' Debate*, ed. Peter Baldwin (Boston: Beacon Press, 1990).

6. This debate is documented in *"Es geht nicht um Christa Wolf" Der Literaturstreit im vereinten Deutschland*, ed. Thomas Anz (München: Edition Spangenberg, 1991) and *Der deutsch-deutsche Literaturstreit oder "Freunde, es spricht sich schlecht mit gebundener Zunge." Analysen und Materialien*, ed. Karl Deiritz and Hannes Krauss (Hamburg and Zürich: Luchterhand Literaturverlag, 1991). For an interpretation of the debate(s) as a generational phenomenon, see the following two articles by Stephen Brockmann: "A Literary Civil War," *The Germanic Review* 68.2 (Spring 1993): 69–78 and "German Literary Debates after the Collapse," *German Life and Letters* 47.2 (April 1994): 201–210.

7. A not unrelated phenomenon is the emigration of Germans to other countries. In 1995, the number of those willing to begin a new life abroad had reached 130,000, and it has stayed at that level since then. See Burkhard Riedel, "Woanders sein Glück versuchen," *Süddeutsche Zeitung*, June 13, 1998.

8. Pascal in Gooch, 183. As Steven E. Aschheim puts it: "Whether one approves of the fact, a variety of movements and ideologies did annex (or actively resist) Nietzsche." See Aschheim's *The Nietzsche Legacy in Germany 1890–1990* (Berkeley and Los Angeles, Oxford: University of California Press, 1992), 309.

9. Cf. Daniel Jonah Goldhagen, *Hitler's Willing Executioners* (1996; New York: Vintage, 1997). Here are three characteristic formulations from the book:

> What conditions of cognition and value made genocidal motivations plausible in this period of German history? . . . The structure of cognition and value was located in and integral to German culture. (24)

> This book is ultimately not only about the perpetrators of the Holocaust. Because the perpetrators of the Holocaust were Germany's representative citizens, this book is about Germany during the Nazi period and before, its people and its culture. (456)

> The reception that this book has received tells us a great deal about what is positive in Germany today. For Germans to confront this horrific part of their past is unpleasant in the extreme. That so many are willing to do so is yet another indication of *how radically transformed democratic Germany has become in the second half of the twentieth century.* (466; my emphasis)

10. Rudy Koshar, *Germany's Transient Pasts* (Chapel Hill and London: The University of North Carolina Press, 1998), 330. The author speaks of "the indeterminacy, the quality of not leading to a definitive end or result, of German national identity" (330).

11. Sigrid Schultz, *Germany Will Do It Again* (New York: Reynal and Hitchcock, 1944). This book was published in the U.S. during World War II. Like the British volume mentioned above, it was "produced in full compliance with the government's regulations for conserving paper and other essential materials." The journalistic account contains the following conclusion: "We will have to remember that Nazism will retain a great appeal for the Germans, even in defeat. . . . Their decent, humanitarian in-

stincts have been buried in decades of wrong teaching, wrong thinking" (238). Echoes and permutations of this teaching and thinking are the subject of this book.

12. The Eastern border, once dubbed the "peace border" (*Friedensgrenze*) by the East German communists, is being—quietly—put into question again. This will be discussed below. For a description of postwar debates about the nature of that border, see Timothy Garton Ash, *In Europe's Name: Germany and the Divided Continent* (New York: Random House, 1993), 224–227.

13. For a summary of these attempts, see Barbara Junge et al., *RechtsSchreiber. Wie ein Netzwerk in Medien und Politik an der Restauration des Nationalen arbeitet* (Berlin: Elefanten Press, 1997), 46–55. See also "Rexrodt warnt vor rechts und greift von Stahl an," *Die Welt*, January 9, 1996, and Evelyn Roll, "Weich wie Stahl," *Süddeutsche Zeitung*, January 12, 1996.

14. After writing this, I discovered a very similar description of the New Right in the U.S. and Britain: "The New Right represents that section of the right wing distinct from both traditional conservatism and from more extreme Far Right groupings." Amy Elizabeth Ansell, *New Right, New Racism: Race and Reaction in the United States and Britain* (New York: New York University Press, 1997), 30. The ideology that Ansell analyzes is, however, somewhat different from the German version.

15. Jürgen Habermas, "Die Kulturkritik der Neokonservativen in den U.S.A. und in der Bundesrepublik," *Die Moderne— ein unvollendetes Projekt* (Leipzig: Reclam, 1994), 75–104.

16. The difficulties involved in finding an accurate term to describe the conservative intellectuals discussed in this book are reflected in Anthony Giddens's *Beyond Left and Right: The Future of Radical Politics* (Stanford: Stanford University Press, 1994). The German neoconservatives that he refers to (31) are close to what I have called the German New Right; Giddens, however, uses this term to describe Thatcherite neoliberalism, which is quite different.

Elliot Neaman has divided the "generation of 1989" into four groups: 1) the "ethnopluralist New Right"; 2) the "theorists of a strong state" influenced by Carl Schmitt; 3) the "spiritual reactionaries" (a term taken from Diederich Diederichsen); and 4) promoters of "neonationalist historiography" such as Ernst Nolte. See Elliot Neaman, "A New Conservative Revolution? Neo-Nationalism, Collective Memory, and the New Right since Unification," *Antisemitism and Xenophobia in Germany after Unification*, ed. Hermann Kürthen et al. (New York and Oxford: Oxford University Press, 1997), 192–197. Botho Strauß is found in the third group—the focus of the present study—along with filmmaker Hans Jürgen Syberberg. These two figures are actually quite different, and the term "spiritual reactionary" is, in my view, too narrow as a characterization of the cultural tradition described in chapter 1 below. Neaman's categories are useful nonetheless.

In 1999, Neaman published an important book on Ernst Jünger, *A Dubious Past: Ernst Jünger and the Politics of Literature after Nazism* (Berkeley, Los Angeles and London: University of California Press). I was not able to read it until after finishing the present study, but I recommend it highly as a thought-provoking complement to my own work. Whereas I am a literary scholar examining the interplay of cultural history and politics, Neaman is a historian who takes seriously the impact of the cultural sphere on political developments. He goes into more depth regarding figures such as Gehlen, Heidegger, and Schmitt (see chapter 2 below), but does not discuss contemporary literary figures like Handke or Walser. As his title indicates, he provides much more detail with respect to Jünger than I do here. Our intentions are similar, but our conclusions are not always the same.

17. John Carey, *The Intellectuals and the Masses: Pride and Prejudice among the Literary Intelligentsia, 1980-1939* (New York: St. Martin's Press, 1993). Carey's book has been translated into German as *Haß auf die Massen. Intellektuelle 1880-1939* (Göttingen: Steidl, 1996). Given the topic, Carey may well have more readers in Germany than in Britain or the U.S.

Chapter 1

1. Ricarda Huch, *Die Romantik* (1899-1902), *Gesammelte Werke*, ed. Wilhelm Emmerich (Köln, Berlin: Kiepenheuer and Witsch, 1969), 6:619. Huch of course views this as an injustice, since in her eyes, it was the ideal of German Romanticism "to encompass everything, the North Pole and the South Pole, within and without, the historical and the radical" (619). Hans Joachim Mähl, speaking of the recent overcoming of this one-sided reception, has said that he is skeptical of contemporary attempts to transform Novalis into a predecessor of postmodern theories and post-structural methods. Cf. Mähl, *Die Idee des goldenen Zeitalters im Werk des Novalis. Studien zur Wesensbestimmung der frühromantischen Utopie und zu ihren ideegeschichtlichen Voraussetzungen* (1965; Tübingen: Max Niemeyer, 1994), vii-viii.

2. Maren Jochimsen, *Die Poetisierung der Ökonomie. Novalis' Thesen im* Heinrich von Ofterdingen *als Anregungen zu einer ökologieorientierten Ökonomie* (Stuttgart: Verlag Hans-Dieter Heinz, 1994), 91.

3. Unless otherwise noted, all of these works will be cited from the following edition: Novalis, *Werke, Tagebücher und Brief Friedrich von Hardenbergs*, ed. Hans-Joachim Mähl and Richard Samuel (München, Wien: Hanser, 1978-1987), vol. 2: *Das philosophisch-theoretische Werk* (1978). References in the text will use these abbreviations: VB=Vermischte Bemerkungen; Bst=Blüthenstaub; GuL=Glauben und Liebe; PA=Politische Aphorismen; and CoE=Die Christenheit oder Europa.

For a selection of Novalis's works in English translation, see *Pollen and Fragments: Selected Poetry and Prose of Novalis*, trans. with an introduction by Arthur Versluis (Grand Rapids, Mich.: Phanes Press, 1989).

4. This is possibly a prefiguration of Hofmannsthal's notion of "preexistence" (Präexistenz), and the inability — or unwillingness — of poets to "grow up" is a topos of Western modernism.

5. No. 61 contains a disturbing prophecy about the Germans: "The German has long been the little guy. Soon, however, he is likely to become the king of the hill. His fate is that of many dumb kids: he will be alive and clever and head of the household long after his precocious siblings have decayed." ("Der Deutsche ist lange das Hänschen gewesen. Er dürfte aber wohl bald der Hans aller Hänse werden. Es geht ihm, wie es vielen dummen Kindern gehn soll: er wird leben und klug seyn, wenn seine frühklugen Geschwister längst vermodert sind, und er nun allein Herr im Hause ist" [251].) This is very close to a prophetic poem by Heinrich Heine, although Heine is not enthusiastic, but rather concerned by his prophetic vision. Cf. H. Heine, "Deutschland" (1840), *Heines Werke in fünf Bänden*, ed. Helmut Holtzhauer (Berlin und Weimar: Aufbau Verlag, 1974), 1:154f. Heine's third stanza reads as follows: "He is a clumsy little giant, / [who] tears the oak out of the ground, / and beats your backs until you're sore / and your heads till they're soft." ("Es ist ein täppisches Rieselein, / Reißt aus dem Boden die Eiche, / Und schlägt euch damit den Rücken wund / Und die Köpfe windelweiche.") Both poetic texts refer to the "belated nation" (verspätete Nation) described much later by Helmuth Plessner.

6. The idea that "commendable housewives" (verdienstvolle Hausfrauen) should be given a medal (*Glaube und Liebe*, no. 26, 297) became the "Mutterkreuz" in the 1930s. The description of the role of women in no. 27 is also very close to "Kinder, Kirche, Küche." Similarities to the Soviet system should not be ignored either.

Interestingly, Novalis is also not "soft on crime," as evidenced by the comments in *Blüthenstaub*, no. 100: "A criminal cannot complain about injustice when he is treated harshly and inhumanely. His crime was an entry into the realm of violence and tyranny. There is no measure or proportion in this world, thus the disproportionateness of the countermeasure should not surprise him." ("Ein Verbrecher kann sich über Unrecht nicht beklagen, wenn man ihn hart und unmenschlich behandelt. Sein Verbrechen war ein Eintritt ins Reich der Gewalt, der Tyranney. Maß und Proporzion giebt es nicht in dieser Welt, daher darf ihn die Unverhältnißmäßigkeit der Gegenwirkung nicht befremden" [273].) The less than harsh treatment of Hitler by the justice system of the Weimar Republic unfortunately did not fit into this model.

7. The role of the child has been described as "a seed that has become visible between nature and the mind." Mähl, *Die Idee des goldenen Zeitalters*, 366.

8. A similar passage is found at the end of the *Politische Aphorismen* (no. 68, 309). At the end of this section, Novalis calls for political and religious tolerance, and in doing so, he sounds more like a representative of the Enlightenment than the quintessential Romantic.

9. Hermann Kurzke, *Romantik und Konservatismus. Das "politische" Werk Friedrich von Hardenbergs (Novalis) im Horizont seiner Wirkungsgeschichte* (München: Fink, 1983), 260 and 171. Kurzke has been criticized for going beyond Novalis's own intentions in his interpretation. Such criticism is extremely problematic, because it assumes that it is only such intentions that determine the way in which a work may be used—or abused. Cf. Herbert Uerlings, *Friedrich von Hardenberg, genannt Novalis. Werk und Forschung* (Stuttgart: Metzler, 1991), 591-593. It is telling that Uerlings

puts the term "political" between quotation marks when referring to Novalis. His final chapter is thus called "'Politisches' Werk und Geschichtsphilosophie." One has the impression that Uerlings wishes to eliminate any considerations that would stand in the way of a canonization of the author. Kurzke of course uses quotation marks in his own title, but for a different reason: He views Novalis as a political dilettante whose writings did, however, have real political impact. This impact is more significant than the fact that he might have been misread.

George Mosse begins the first chapter of his book on German ideology with a broadside ("The intellectual and ideological character of Volkish thought was *a direct product* [my emphasis] of the romantic movement of nineteenth-century Europe. Like romanticism, Volkish ideas showed a distinct tendency toward the irrational and the emotional . . ."), but he does not refer to any Romantic writers by name. George Mosse, *The Crisis of German Ideology: Intellectual Origins of the Third Reich* (New York: Grosset and Dunlap, 1964), 13.

10. Hans Kohn, *The Mind of Germany: The Education of a Nation* (1960; New York: Harper Torchbooks, 1965), 52–55.

At the other extreme, the "poetic" Novalis has been portrayed as a revolutionary opposed not to the ideas of 1789 but rather to the political methods used to realize them. Cf. Wilfried Malsch, *"Europa." Poetische Rede des Novalis. Deutung der Französischen Revolution und Reflexion auf die Poesie in der Geschichte* (Stuttgart: Metzler, 1965). The author undertook his study to counter the "common misjudgment" of Novalis and his epoch as reactionary (vi–vii).

11. Georg Lukács, *The Destruction of Reason* (1962; Atlantic Highlands: Humanities Press, 1981).

12. *Die politische Romantik in Deutschland. Eine Textsammlung*, ed. Klaus Peter (Stuttgart: Reclam, 1985), 31–35, 42–47. In the first English-language collection of this kind, Novalis is a relatively minor figure. The editor provides only the essay "Christendom or Europe." Most of the volume is taken up with excerpts from Fichte. Cf. H. S. Reiss, *The Political Thought of the German Romantics 1793–1815* (Oxford: Basil Blackwell, 1955). In his introduction, however, the editor does state the following: "The work of Novalis constitutes a quarry from which others, such as Adam Müller and Friedrich Schlegel, have hewn stones with which to build their systems" (27).

13. One notable exception is the Thomas Mann of *Reflections of a Non-Political Man*. To enlist Stifter in his version of the conservative cause, Mann had to ignore Stifter's complete lack of irony—a major feature of Mann's own work.

14. A review of new books on Nietzsche is appropriately titled: James Joll, "Nietzsche vs. Nietzsche," *New York Review of Books,* February 11, 1993, 20–23. Joll writes: "There will be no end to the differing interpretations of Nietzsche because the core of each of them can be found in Nietzsche himself" (23). For a critique of the view that Nietzsche was "unequivocally the philosopher of the German right," see Seth Taylor, *Left-Wing Nietzscheans: The Politics of German Expressionism 1910-1920* (Berlin and New York: de Gruyter, 1990), 230.

15. Erich Heller is one who makes such a claim. He is, however, quite selective when it comes to determining what is true literature. In his *The Importance of Nietzsche* (Chicago and London: University of Chicago Press, 1988), he makes the following statement: "Name almost any poet, man of letters, philosopher, who wrote in German during the twentieth century and attained to stature and influence — Rilke, George, Kafka, Thomas Mann, Ernst Jünger, Musil, Benn, Heidegger or Jaspers — and you name at the same time Friedrich Nietzsche" (2). Peter Pütz has said basically the same thing: "Nietzsche has left the clearest traces in literature and existential philosophy," in *Friedrich Nietzsche* (Stuttgart: Metzler, 1967), 58.

16. Even the extraordinarily erudite historian Eric Hobsbawm refers to *The Will to Power* as Nietzsche's "most ambitious work." Eric Hobsbawm, *The Age of Empire, 1875–1914* (New York: Pantheon, 1987), 252. That may be, but Nietzsche never completed it.

17. Lukács, 313.

18. Friedrich Nietzsche, *Philosophical Writings*, The German Library 48, ed. Reinhold Grimm and Caroline Molina y Vedia (New York: Continuum, 1995), 171

19. Nietzsche, *Philosophical Writings,* 210, 170.

20. *The Portable Nietzsche*, ed. Walter Kaufmann (1954; New York: Viking Press, 1968), 442.

21. Nietzsche, *Philosophical Writings,* 204.

22. Nietzsche, "Beyond Good and Evil," section 242, *The Philosophy of Nietzsche* (New York: The Modern Library, 1954), 551–552.

23. R. H. Hollingdale, *Nietzsche*, Routledge Author Guides (London and Boston: Routledge and Kegan Paul, 1973), 195.

24. Nietzsche, *Philosophical Writings,* 235. This is not the kind of productive suffering that Nietzsche went through himself: "Only great pain is the ultimate liberator of the spirit . . ." *The Portable Nietzsche*, 680.

25. Nietzsche, *Philosophical Writings,* 30.

26. Nietzsche, *Philosophical Writings,* 204.

27. Nietzsche, *Philosophical Writings,* 228.

28. Julius Wiegand, *Deutsche Geistesgeschichte* (Frankfurt am Main: Diesterweg, 1932), 231.

29. Stefan George, "Nietzsche," *Werke*, vol. 1 (München and Düsseldorf: Helmut Küpper, 1958), 231–232. See also Frank Weber, *Die Bedeutung Nietzsches für Stefan George und seinen Kreis* (Frankfurt am Main, Bern, New York, and Paris: Peter Lang, 1989).

30. *Die Zerstörung der deutschen Politik. Dokumente 1871–1933*, ed. Harry Pross (1959; Frankfurt am Main: Fischer, 1983), 154. Pross speaks of the "esthetic assessment of social conditions" as a characteristic of the Youth Movement. For a profound study of the limits of "esthetic rationality," see Cornelia Klinger, *Flucht Trost Revolte. Die Moderne und ihre ästhetischen Gegenwelten* (München and Wien: Hanser, 1995).

31. Hermann Glaser, *Spießer-Ideologie. Von der Zerstörung des deutschen Geistes im*

19. und 20. Jahrhundert und dem Aufstieg des Nationalsozialismus (1964; Frankfurt am Main: Fischer, 1985), 100. The German phrase is "Herrschafts-, Dienst-, Bund- und Reichsideologie."

32. Stefan George, *Werke*, 1:410–411.

33. George, *Werke*, 1:411.

34. One of George's early poems could be read as an elaboration of the Novalis aphorism on hunger and freedom (see page 5 above): "You learn: only the house of privation knows melancholy- / Now see in the splendor of the columns the *more bitter* melancholy . . ." [My emphasis.] ("Ihr lernt: das haus des mangels nur kenne die schwermut- / Nun seht im prunke der säulen die *herbere* schwermut . . .") George, *Werke*, 1:139. It is always dangerous to generalize from individual passages, but it is also problematic to ignore such passages. Unfortunately, George's defenders tend to view a "reverence" for the entire work as a necessary prerequisite for the interpretation of any one idea or image. See for example Dominik Jost, *Stefan George und seine Elite. Eine Studie zur Geschichte der Eliten* (Zürich: Speer-Verlag, 1949), 9.

35. With good cause, George's contemporary Soergel begins his chapter on George and his circle with reference to the oft-quoted Horatian dictum: "Odi profanum vulgus et arceo." ("I hate and avoid the base people.') Albert Soergel, *Dichtung und Dichter der Zeit. Eine Schilderung der deutschen Literatur der letzten Jahrzehnte* (1911; Leipzig: R. Voigtländer, 1921), 557.

36. In the introduction to the third *Jahrbuch für die geistige Bewegung*, one finds a passage in which the "Amerikawelt" is equated with both the world of Satan and the world of ants. This passage, which has drawn the attention of many critics, can be found in Christian Graf von Krockow, *Die Deutschen in ihrem Jahrhundert 1980–1990* (1990; Reinbek: Rowohlt, 1992), 56–57.

Krockow also provides the reader with a quote from Rilke decrying the "illusions" ("Schein-Dinge") emanating from superficial America (389).

37. For a fascinating presentation of George's fate in the Third Reich, see Michael Petrow, *Der Dichter als Führer? Zur Wirkung Stefan Georges im "Dritten Reich"* (Marburg: Tectum, 1995). In one of the first exercises in German cultural studies in English, the name Stefan George is not found in the index, although the "George-Kreis" is included as "perhaps the most notable, but most exclusive, manifestation of cultural-conservative opposition" in the Wilhelmine period. This truncation misleads the reader into believing that the group was insignificant after 1918. *German Cultural Studies. An Introduction*, ed. Rob Burns (New York: Oxford University Press, 1995), 20.

In a widely-read survey of German history, the "Kreis" is omitted, but George is listed as a famous poet. Cf. Mary Fulbrook, *A Concise History of Germany* (1990; Cambridge: Cambridge University Press, 1994), 169.

38. Karl Dietrich Bracher, *Die deutsche Diktatur. Entstehung, Struktur, Folgen des Nationalsozialismus* (1969; Köln: Kiepenheuer and Witsch, 1972), 155. Bracher refers to this world view as "romantic-irrationalist reveries" (155).

39. The term *Sonderweg* has been called into question by a number of historians. There

is no doubt that similar ideas can be found beyond the borders of Germany, but nowhere else were they put into practice with such rigor. (It is not surprising that the present-day media image of Italians is not intimately linked to the fascist era, current neofascist political successes notwithstanding. There is a difference in degree that cannot be overlooked.) Thomas Mann's biographer Klaus Harpprecht entitles his chapter on Mann's *Reflections of a Non-Political Man* "On the German Special Path" ("Auf dem deutschen Sonderweg"). Klaus Harpprecht, *Thomas Mann* (Reinbek: Rowohlt, 1995), 400.

The main points of the *Sonderweg* model have been summarized as follows: ". . . the belief in direct continuities between Bismarck and Hitler; the idea of a fundamental contradiction between economic modernity and political backwardness leading to the empire's structural instability; the view that Germany lacked the emancipatory experience of a successful bourgeois revolution, falling prey instead to the continued dominance of old-style 'preindustrial elites' in the political system; the notion that these elites exercised their power by repressive forms of social control and manipulative techniques of rule; and the belief that German history was the site of an exceptional 'misdevelopment' by comparison to the healthier trajectories of the societies of 'the West.'" All this amounts to a "teleology of German exceptionalism." See Geoff Eley, "Introduction 1," *Society, Culture, and the State in Germany, 1870–1930*, ed. Geoff Eley (Ann Arbor: University of Michigan Press, 1996), 3. This summary does not address itself directly to cultural concerns, which are the focus of the present study.

40. Heinrich Mann, "Zola," *Geist und Tat* (Frankfurt am Main: Suhrkamp, 1981), 164, 184, 216, 166, 167. A new American edition of the correspondence of the two brothers has just appeared: *Letters of Heinrich and Thomas Mann, 1900–1949*, ed. Hans Wysling, trans. Don Reneau (Berkeley: University of California Press, 1998). See the following review: John Simon, "Mann and Super Mann," *New York Times Book Review*, April 12, 1998, 12–13. Simon's statement that the brothers were "farthest apart politically" is only partially accurate.

41. From April 1885 to March 1886, Heinrich Mann was editor of the reactionary monthly *Das Zwanzigste Jahrhundert. Blätter für deutsche Art und Wohlfahrt*. One of the contributors was Thomas Mann. For an assessment of this phase in Heinrich Mann's development, see Bernd M. Kraske, "Heinrich Mann als Herausgeber der Zeitschrift *Das Zwanzigste Jahrhundert*," *Heinrich Mann. Das essayistische Werk*, ed. Rudolf Wolff (Bonn: Bouvier, 1986), 7–24. See also Alfred Kantorowicz, "Zola-Essay—Betrachtungen eines Unpolitischen. Die paradigmatische Auseinandersetzung zwischen Heinrich und Thomas Mann," *Heinrich Mann. Werk und Wirkung*, ed. Rudolf Wolff (Bonn: Bouvier, 1984), 54–76.

42. Thomas Mann, *Betrachtungen eines Unpolitischen* (1918; Frankfurt am Main: Fischer, 1983). All citations will be made from this edition. The *Betrachtungen* are also in volume 12 of the *Gesammelte Werke* (Frankfurt am Main: Fischer, 1960).

43. Mann claims that he "almost slept through" the transformation of the German *Bürger* into a bourgeois. *Betrachtungen*, 130.

44. This does not stop him from criticizing the imperialist British for using the term "nigger"! *Betrachtungen*, 441.

45. On de Lagarde, see Mosse, 31–39. For literary manifestations of the fantasies of de Lagarde and his ilk, see Jost Hermand, *Old Dreams of a New Reich: Volkish Utopias and National Socialism* (1988; Bloomington and Indianapolis: Indiana University Press, 1992).

46. Despite his protestations to the contrary, Mann does, incredibly, indulge in the glorification of war as a path to ennoblement (453), claim that suffering brings forth true grandeur (451), and comment sarcastically that it can be as horrible to die in bed as on the field of battle (450). We are all condemned to "bitter death" anyway, he philosophizes (450).

47. Thomas Mann, "Von deutscher Republik," *Gesammelte Werke in 12 Bänden* (Frankfurt am Main: Fischer, 1960), 12:809–852. Page references from this edition in the text. Not all scholars believe that a real "transformation" took place, at least in the realm of ideas—as opposed to practical politics. See Martin Flinker, *Thomas Mann's politische Betrachtungen im Lichte der heutigen Zeit* ('s-Gravenhage: Mouton, 1959), and Ernst Keller, *Der unpolitische Deutsche. Eine Studie zu den "Betrachtungen eines Unpolitischen" von Thomas Mann* (Bern and München: Francke, 1965).

48. It has been pointed out that Mann already used the term "Third Reich" in 1912. At that early stage, it was defined as "the reconciliation of the mind ["Geist"] and art, of knowledge and creativity, of intellectualism and simplicity, of rationality and the demonic, of asceticism and beauty." Thomas Mann, *Gesammelte Werke*, 11:564. The passage is discussed in Hermann Kurzke, *Auf der Suche nach der verlorenen Irrationalität. Thomas Mann und der Konservatismus* (Würzburg: Königshausen und Neumann, 1980), 141.

49. Michael Rupprecht, *Der literarische Bürgerkrieg. Zur Unpolitik der Unpolitischen in Deutschland* (Frankfurt am Main: Josef Knecht, 1995), 48. The subtitle of this study applies Mann's term to a large group of twentieth-century German writers.

50. Bernhard Weyergraf, "Konservative Wandlungen," *Literatur der Weimarer Republik 1918–1933*, ed. Bernhard Weyergraf, *Hansers Sozialgeschichte der deutschen Literatur vom 16. Jahrundert bis zur Gegenwart*, ed. Rolf Grimminger (München and Wien: Hanser, 1995), 8:281.

51. Harpprecht, 429. Georg Lukács criticizes the "romantic anti-capitalism" of the *Reflections*, but praises Mann for his continuing "skepticism with regard to Western bourgeois democracy." Lukács, *Destruction*, 71. He ignores Hofmannsthal completely.

52. Characteristically, a new introduction to today's Germany contains multiple references to Thomas Mann, but not a single one to Hofmannsthal. Cf. Stuart Parkes, *Understanding Contemporary Germany* (London and New York: Routledge, 1997). The first reference to Mann is at the very beginning of a chapter on the political system—not in one on literary history. And what work is mentioned there? None other than the *Reflections* (33).

In a weighty anthology about the Weimar Republic, readers are provided with a four-page excerpt from Thomas Mann's *On German Democracy*, whereas the passage from Hofmannsthal's speech is less than one page long. *The Weimar Republik Source-*

book, ed. Anton Kaes, Martin Jay, and Edward Dimendberg (Berkeley and Los Angeles, London: University of California Press, 1994), 105–109 and 341.

A standard history of ideas in English provides an article about conservatism that links Hofmannsthal to the term "conservative revolution" and mentions de Lagarde, but omits reference to Thomas Mann. Rudolf Vierhaus, "Conservatism," *Dictionary of the History of Ideas*, ed. Philip P. Wiener (1968; New York: Charles Scribner's Sons, 1973), 1:480a and 483a.

53. Johann Hinrich Claussen, "Politik der Unpolitischen. Konservative Revolution: Hofmannsthal und Thomas Mann," *Frankfurter Allgemeine Zeitung*, June 4, 1997. For an article on Hofmannsthal that begins with a report on the 1995 discussion about the Conservative Revolution in the German parliament, see Ute and Helmut Nicolaus, "Hofmannsthal, der Staat und die 'konservative Revolution.' Aktuelle Bemerkungen anläßlich einer parlamentarischen Anfrage," *Politisches Denken. Jahrbuch 1997* (Stuttgart and Weimar: Metzler, 1997), 141–174.

54. These pieces have been described as "embarrassing." Cf. Mathias Mayer, *Hugo von Hofmannsthal* (Stuttgart: Metzler, 1993), 161. For a detailed analysis, see Heinz Lunzer, *Hofmannsthals politische Tätigkeit in den Jahren 1914–1917* (Frankfurt am Main, Bern, and Cirencester: Peter Lang, 1981), esp. 179–181.

55. "Vorrede des Herausgebers," *Deutsches Lesebuch. Eine Auswahl deutscher Prosastücke aus dem Jahrhundert 1750–1850*, ed. Hugo von Hofmannsthal (1923; Frankfurt am Main: Fischer, 1952), vii.

56. Although Hofmannsthal promoted the idea of Austria, he did not believe that there was such a thing as an Austrian literature. The *Reader* includes authors from all of the German-speaking countries, and Austrians are a distinct minority.

57. Hugo von Hofmannsthal, "Das Schrifttum als geistiger Raum der Nation," *Gesammelte Werke in Einzelausgaben*, ed. Herbert Steiner (Frankfurt am Main: Fischer, 1955), 6:392. Further references to this edition in the text.

58. French literature is described as "full of life," but also "devoid of dreams" ["traumlos"]. Hofmannsthal, "Das Schrifttum," 395.

59. Despite such rhetoric, there is no trace of anti-Semitism in the speech (in contrast to the *Reflections*). The *German Reader* includes selections from the German Jews Heinrich Heine and Ferdinand Lassalle. Hofmannsthal was himself part Jewish, but that is of course no barrier to anti-Semitism. One of the most conservative "German" writers in the first half of the twentieth century, Rudolf Borchardt (who corresponded with Hofmannsthal), was also Jewish.

60. As Hans Kohn has put it: "In the Europe after 1918 he [Hofmannsthal] no longer felt at home. The democratization of the world which set in after the First World War was beyond Hofmannsthal's perceptive powers." If one were to replace 1918 with 1945 or even 1989, a similar statement could be made about the contemporary heirs of the Conservative Revolution. Cf. Kohn, *The Mind of Germany*, 250.

61. *The Weimar Republic Sourcebook*, 330.

62. Hermann Rudolph, *Kulturkritik und konservative Revolution. Zum kulturell-politischen Denken Hofmannsthals und seinem problemgeschichtlichen Kontext* (Tübingen: Max Niemeyer, 1971), 21.

63. Kurzke, *Auf der Suche*, 26.

64. In 1900, Thomas Mann served a total of two and one-half months in the infantry (*Leib-Infanterieregiment*). He was released from the military for medical reasons, thanks to the intervention of a friend of his mother. Hofmannsthal served a full year as a cadet (*Einjährig-Freiwilliger*) in 1894–95. He was called up in 1914 and sent to Istria, but after a few weeks, he was sent back to Vienna to work in the War Ministry.

65. Ernst Jünger, *Storm of Steel*, trans. Basil Creighton (Garden City: Doubleday, Doran & Company, 1929), xi. The original German edition was published in 1920. See also Ernst Jünger, *Sämtliche Werke* (Stuttgart: Klett-Cotta, 1978–1983), vol. 1. Further page references from the English edition in the text.

My own copy of *In Stahlgewittern* was a 1943 Christmas present from the commander of the "4.Pion.Lehr.Batl.4" to his men. The title page has the inscription "Kriegs-Weihnacht 1943," the signature of the company commander, and the Wehrmacht symbol.

66. Jünger, *Storm,* 21, footnote (added to later editions).

67. When away from the front, Jünger can fantasize about "women's hands and a good thousand superfluous things . . . that make our lives colorful"! *Der Kampf als inneres Erlebnis, Sämtliche Werke,* 7:24. Further citations in the body of the text.

68. Jünger, *Der Kampf,* 13. To ward off criticism, Jünger asserts that only those who have directly experienced combat have the right to speak about it (22).

69. Like Nietzsche and George, Jünger was neither anti-Semitic nor racist. He was also too much of a connoisseur of French culture and savoir vivre to be a true German nationalist. Richard Herzinger speaks of an "intellectual" anti-Semitism in Jünger: "Jünger's anti-Semitism was not based on race, but rather on ideas. He considered the Jews to be representatives, not creators, of liberalism. For him, the 'Jewish question' was thus not the central problem of the 'national revolution.' Just the same, he believed that Jewishness and 'Germanness' were irreconcilable." See Richard Herzinger, "'Der Sieg der Deutschheit über die Erde.' 'Die Nation' zwischen Mythos und Utopie im Denken der politischen Romantik, der Konservativen Revolution und der Neuen Rechten," *Neonationalismus. Neokonservatismus. Sondierungen und Analysen,* ed. Michael Kessler et al. (Tübingen: Stauffenburg, 1997), 31, n. 27.

70. Here are three recent works in English: Marcus Paul Bullock, *The Violent Eye. Ernst Jünger's Visions and Revisions on the European Right* (Detroit: Wayne State University Press, 1992), Thomas Nevin, *Ernst Jünger and Germany: Into the Abyss, 1914–1945* (Durham: Duke University Press, 1996), and Elliot Y. Neaman, *A Dubious Past: Ernst Jünger and the Politics of Literature after Nazism* (Berkeley: University of California Press, 1999).

Although this is not the place for a research report, it is difficult not to respond to one of the most recent essays on Jünger. The author is concerned that the reader might not perceive the true complexity of the material, but he ends by justifying both Jünger's pessimism and his positive attitude toward the near-apocalyptic effects of World War II by pointing out that many others held similar views. One of these was supposedly Bertolt Brecht, who wrote in 1944 that he was ready to support Hitler in his liquidation of the aristocratic officers who attempted to assassinate him. This is indeed "complex," but not in the way intended by the author of the essay. One small footnote to this is that Jünger spent his twilight years in a house owned by the Stauffenberg family, one of whose members was in fact executed as one of the aristocratic plotters. Cf. Helmuth Kiesel, "Zwischen Kritik und Affirmation. Ernst Jüngers Auseinandersetzung mit dem Nationalsozialismus," *Literatur in der Diktatur. Schreiben im Nationalsozialismus und DDR-Sozialismus*, ed. Günther Rüther (Paderborn, München, Wien, and Zürich: Ferdinand Schöningh, 1997), 163–172, esp. 170–172. Since Kiesel's title does not follow the alphabet ("criticism" is placed before "affirmation"), one must assume that Jünger was mainly critical toward the Third Reich. His wartime service in the Wehrmacht was apparently not related to the "ideals" that he spoke of in his early writings.

71. Jünger's own self-image—at least the one for public consumption—was that of a passive observer rather than an activist. See the famous passage in the preface to his wartime diaries: "After the earthquake, one strikes out at the seismograph. However, one cannot make the barometer atone for the typhoons, unless one wishes to be considered a primitive." Ernst Jünger, "Vorwort," *Strahlungen. Erster Teil. Werke* (Stuttgart: Klett, 1960), 2:13. The "primitive" was hardly a negative term in the earlier Jünger.

72. After a riding accident, Nietzsche was not able to finish his one year of military service (1867–1868). In the Franco-Prussian War, he briefly volunteered as a medic until turning ill himself. Hemingway volunteered as a Red Cross ambulance driver in Italy in World War I. During a brief stint as an officer in 1918, he sustained shrapnel wounds.

73. Karl Heinz Bohrer has described how the post-1945 German middle class could bring Jünger into the cultural fold by concentrating on the later works and ignoring the early ones that contained attacks on the morality and politics of their parents. See Karl Heinz Bohrer, *Die Ästhetik des Schreckens. Die pessimistische Romantik und Ernst Jüngers Frühwerk* (München and Wien: Hanser, 1978), 13.

74. Jünger was also saluted by Helmut Kohl, but this was clearly a misunderstanding on Kohl's part! Jünger accepted the respectful greetings from the head of state just the same, as they could only enhance his aura as a kind of conservative Voltaire.

75. For example, see the following: Peter de Mendelssohn, "Das Verharren vor dem Unvereinbaren. Versuch über Gottfried Benn," *Der Geist in der Despotie. Versuche über die Möglichkeiten des Intellektuellen in der totalitären Gesellschaft* (1953; Frankfurt am Main: Fischer, 1987), 236–282; Jürgen Schröder, "Benn in den

dreißiger Jahren," *Intellektuelle im Bann des Nationalsozialismus*, ed. Karl Corino (Hamburg: Hoffmann und Campe, 1980), 48–60; Jürgen Schröder, "'Wer über Deutschland reden und richten will, muß hier geblieben sein.' Gottfried Benn als Emigrant nach innen," *Literatur in der Diktatur*, 131–144.

76. Dieter Wellershoff, the editor of Benn's collected works, criticizes the irrationalism that led Benn to sympathize with the Nazis, but he also asserts that Benn is "an exemplary figure of recent German intellectual history" whose œuvre is "a concentrated expression of the nature of the era." Cf. Wellershoff, *Gottfried Benn. Phänotyp dieser Stunde* (1958; Frankfurt am Main and Berlin: Ullstein, 1964), 8.

77. Gottfried Benn, "Rede auf Stefan George," *Gesammelte Werke in vier Bänden*, ed. Dieter Wellershoff (1959; Wiesbaden: Limes Verlag, 1962), 1:464–477. Harry Pross refers to this speech at the very beginning of his book on the destruction of German politics. Cf. Pross, 11. In this speech, Benn speaks of his time as the "age of storms of steel and imperial horizons." It is difficult to imagine a relationship between George and Jünger.

78. Benn, "Rede auf Heinrich Mann," *Gesammelte Werke*, 1:410–418. The epigraph of this speech is "Nihilism is a feeling of happiness" (!).

79. Benn, *Gesammelte Werke*, 1:440. Further citations in the body of the text. The "higher form" of collectivity can be characterized as National Socialism or the system described in Ernst Jünger's *Der Arbeiter* (1932), according to Benn. This passage must not have pleased Jünger, who believed that his system was "higher" than that of the Nazis.

80. Klaus Mann's letter is included in Benn's autobiography *Doppelleben*. Cf. Benn, *Gesammelte Werke*, 4:74–78. Page references to this letter in the body of the text.

In 1937, Klaus Mann published an article about Benn ("The History of an Aberration") in the émigré journal *Das Wort*. Even in this text, Mann confesses that he still has a weakness for certain verses by Benn. He goes on to say: "His 'case' is still interesting, only because he was the *only* [my emphasis] German writer of any stature who seriously and with no little intellectual resolution went astray into the camp of National Socialism." KM, "Gottfried Benn. Die Geschichte einer Verirrung," *Die Expressionismusdebatte. Materialien zu einer marxistischen Realismuskonzeption*, ed. Hans-Jürgen Schmitt (1973; Frankfurt am Main: Suhrkamp, 1976), 39–40.

81. De Mendelssohn, 237.

82. Benn, "Antwort an die literarischen Emigranten," *Gesammelte Werke*, 4:239–248. Page references in the body of the text.

83. Despite such attacks, Benn was actually defended by none other than Heinrich Himmler. In a 1937 letter, Himmler stated: "From a national point of view, Benn's behavior has been absolutely beyond reproach since 1933 and even earlier. I consider it to be unnecessary and nonsensical to now run amok against this man who has—especially in the international arena—represented Germany impeccably. I have prohibited all of my subordinates from getting involved in the Benn case." Heinrich Himmler, "Letter to Wolfgang Willrich, Sept. 18, 1937," *Literatur und Dichtung im*

Dritten Reich, ed. Joseph Wulf, *Kultur im Dritten Reich*, ed. Joseph Wulf (1982; Frankfurt am Main and Berlin: Ullstein, 1989), 2:144.

84. Benn, *Doppelleben*, 74. Further page references in the body of the text.

85. His lack of insight was, characteristically, no hindrance when it came to "placing his name at the disposal" of the anticommunist crusade during the Cold War.

86. See the volume *Und das wurde nicht ihr Staat. Erfahrungen emigrierter Schriftsteller mit Westdeutschland*, ed. Peter Mertz (München: C. H. Beck, 1985).

87. Those interested in this other tradition could begin by perusing the works of G. E. Lessing, G. C. Lichtenberg, Georg Forster, Georg Büchner, Bettine von Arnim, Ludwig Börne, Heinrich Heine, Georg Herwegh, Ferdinand Freiligrath, Gottfried Keller, Heinrich Mann, Karl Kraus, Kurt Tucholsky, Ernst Toller, and Bertolt Brecht. This particular stream of German literature is not devoid of contradictions, but it clearly represents a view of the human condition and a concept of history which I, for one, find much more appealing. For a critical assessment of the initial phase of this tradition, see W. Daniel Wilson and Robert C. Holub, eds., *Impure Reason: Dialectic of Enlightenment in Germany* (Detroit: Wayne State University Press, 1993).

Chapter 2

1. Cf. Egbert Krispyn, *Anti-Nazi Writers in Exile* (Athens: University of Georgia Press, 1978), 151–158.

2. See the following books on the situation of Jews in the former GDR: Lothar Mertens, *Davidstern unter Hammer und Zirkel. Die jüdischen Gemeinden in der SBZ/DDR und ihre Behandlung durch Partei und Staat 1945–1990* (Hildesheim: Olms, 1998); Angelika Timm, *Hammer, Zirkel, Davidstern. Das gestörte Verhältnis in der DDR zu Zionismus und Staat Israel* (Bonn: Bouvier, 1998). See also the following review: Peter Dittmar, "'Diese Waffen sind in der Lage, israelische Panzer zu durchschlagen,'" *Die Welt*, May 2, 1998.

3. The form that Jünger declined to fill out was the basis for a postwar novel (*Der Fragebogen* [1951]) by the former militant right-wing author Ernst von Salomon.

4. Franz Lennartz, "Günter Grass," *Deutsche Schriftsteller des 20. Jahrhunderts im Spiegel der Kritik* (Stuttgart: Kröner, 1984), 1:596. The conflict between Grass and Ziesel—including legal action—is documented in *Kunst oder Pornographie? Der Prozess Grass gegen Ziesel* (München: Lehmann, 1969). See also *Günter Grass. Die Blechtrommel. Erläuterungen und Dokumente*, ed. Volker Neuhaus (Stuttgart: Reclam, 1997), 177–180. Ziesel's mission has recently been taken up in the U.S., where the video of Volker Schlöndorff's film version of *The Tin Drum* has been denounced as pornography.

5. Keith Bullivant, "Literatur und Politik," *Gegenwartsliteratur seit 1968*, ed. Klaus Briegleb and Sigrid Weigel, *Hansers Sozialgeschichte der deutschen Literatur vom 16.*

Jahrhundert bis zur Gegenwart, ed. Rolf Grimminger (München and Wien: Hanser, 1992), 12:285.

6. Jay Rosellini, "A Revival of Conservative Literature? The *'Spiegel*-Symposium 1993' and Beyond," *Beyond 1989: Re-reading German Literature since 1945,* ed. Keith Bullivant (Providence and Oxford: Berghahn Books, 1997), 109–110.

Keith Bullivant has asserted that conservative writing, i.e., "the German idealist tradition," exhibited great staying power even after 1945. He is one of the few observers to postulate that "the apparent gulf between an older, apparently conservative generation of writers and critics and the younger, post-war one was far less than it seemed then and has since been perceived." (*The Future of German Literature* [Oxford and Providence: Berg, 1994], 23 and 28).

7. Those who wished to enlist postwar youth in the anticommunist crusade were not pleased with such skepticism. Cf. Helmut Schelsky, *Die skeptische Generation. Eine Soziologie der deutschen Jugend* (Düsseldorf and Köln: Diederichs, 1957). For a (surprisingly) sympathetic portrayal of such youthful skepticism, see the character Manfred Herrfurth in Christa Wolf's first novel, *Divided Heaven.*

8. Some examples: Victor Farías, *Heidegger and Nazism,* trans. Gabriel R. Ricci (1987; Philadelphia: Temple University Press, 1989); Hugo Ott, *Martin Heidegger: Unterwegs zu seiner Biographie* (Frankfurt am Main and New York: Campus, 1988); Philippe Lacoue-Labarthe, *Heidegger, Art and Politics,* trans. Chris Turner (Oxford: Blackwell, 1990); Peter Kemper, ed., *Martin Heidegger—Faszination und Schrecken. Die politische Dimension einer Philosophie* (Frankfurt am Main and New York: Campus, 1990); Günther Neske and Emil Kettering, eds., *Martin Heidegger and National Socialism: Questions and Answers* (New York: Paragon House, 1990); Tom Rockmore and Joseph Margolis, eds., *The Heidegger Case: On Philosophy and Politics* (Philadelphia: Temple University Press, 1992); Alan Milchman and Alan Rosenberg, eds., *Martin Heidegger and the Holocaust* (Atlantic Highlands, N.J.: Humanities Press International, 1996).

The volume by Neske and Kettering contains, in English translation, the 1933 Freiburg speech "The Self-Assertion of the German University" as well as the legendary 1966 interview with *Der Spiegel.*

9. Jürgen Habermas, *Philosophisch-politische Profile,* 3rd rev. ed. (1981; Frankfurt am Main: Suhrkamp, 1984), 107.

10. Christian Graf von Krockow, *Die Entscheidung. Eine Untersuchung über Ernst Jünger, Carl Schmitt, Martin Heidegger* (1958; Frankfurt am Main and New York: Campus, 1990). Page references in the body of the text.

11. Historian Heinrich August Winkler has said the following about this path: "The anti-Western 'special path' of Germany definitively ended with the 1945 collapse of the German Reich. . . . The process of 'Westernization' that has taken place in the 'Bonn Republic' will continue in the 'Berlin Republic,' because historically speaking, there is only one political culture of democracy, and that is the Western one": "Zwei Zusammenbrüche," *Süddeutsche Zeitung,* October 15, 1997. The writ-

ings of the New Right intellectuals discussed in this study demonstrate that, at least in the cultural sphere, the "special path" is by no means a thing of the past.

12. Krockow, *Entscheidung*, 47. The quote is taken from the 1922 edition of Jünger's book (p. 76).

13. Krockow, *Entscheidung*, 54. The quote is taken from the 1932 edition of *Der Arbeiter* that appeared in Hamburg (p. 201). The emphases are mine.

14. One of the readers at the Universität Basel (where Nietzsche had taught in the 1870s) was Karl Jaspers, a leading critic of the intellectual right.

15. Armin Mohler, *Die Konservative Revolution in Deutschland 1918-1932. Grundriß ihrer Weltanschauungen* (Stuttgart: Friedrich Vorwerk, 1950). Unless otherwise noted, the citations in this section will be taken from the second edition: *Die Konservative Revolution in Deutschland 1918-1932. Ein Handbuch* (Darmstadt: Wissenschaftliche Buchgesellschaft, 1972). The publication of this second edition by the prestigious Wissenschaftliche Buchgesellschaft lent an aura of academic respectability to Mohler's work.

16. Mohler discovers similarities to the German movement in Russia, France, Spain, Italy, England (like John Carey, he discusses D. H. Lawrence), and the U.S. Even in the African liberation movements, he maintains, one finds "the mixture of national liberation struggle, social revolution, and rediscovery of identity characteristic of the Conservative Revolution." Mohler, *Die Konservative Revolution* (1972), 13.

17. This quotation and all those which follow come—unless otherwise noted—from the 1972 edition.

18. Krockow also devotes a large section of *Die Entscheidung* to an analysis of Romanticism.

19. A review of Irving Kristol's *Neoconservatism: The Autobiography of an Idea* by Theodore Draper is entitled "An Anti-Intellectual Intellectual." The review was printed in the *New York Review of Books*, November 2, 1995.

20. Iris Weber, *Nation, Staat und Elite. Die Ideologie der Neuen Rechten* (Köln: PapyRossa, 1997), 20 n. 40.

21. In his 1989 third edition, Mohler provides some interesting autobiographical background: "First of all, I wanted to correct a personal error: When I got to know the Third Reich in 1942 [under what circumstances one wonders!], I still naively identified National Socialism with the Conservative Revolution. Soon, however, that turned out to be wrong, and I wanted to discern the difference between the two mentalities. Secondly, my book was meant to be of help to the right-wing ["rechte"] intellectuals in Germany. I had become acquainted with a number of them personally or by reading their works. The way in which they were discriminated against across the board disgusted me—especially since these men had no opportunity to defend themselves. I was always on the side of the people who had the 'compact majority' against them." Vol. 2, 7. There were of course other underdogs to defend, but that is another story.

It was reported in *Die Zeit* that Mohler, a Swiss citizen, volunteered for the Waffen-SS. (He was not accepted.) See Marko Martin, "Stramm zur Sache," *Die Zeit*, no. 33, 1993. The article is about the right-wing newspaper *Junge Freiheit* and the emergence of a new generation of right-wing intellectuals whose models are not "Hitler or Himmler, but rather Carl Schmitt and Oswald Spengler." For a biographical profile of Mohler, who has been a sort of mentor for Alain de Benoist and the French New Right, see *Antifa Reader*, ed. Jens Mecklenburg (Berlin: Elefanten Press, 1996), 104.

22. Hans-Peter Schwarz, *Der konservative Anarchist. Politik und Zeitkritik Ernst Jüngers* (Freiburg: Rombach, 1962). Citations from this work in the body of the text.

23. Schwarz criticizes Krockow (*Die Entscheidung*) for describing Jünger as a passive figure (e.g., one unwilling to actively support the attempts of the resistance to assassinate Hitler on July 20, 1944). According to Schwarz, Jünger used his pen as a weapon, acting as an "extremely uncomfortable critic" of three successive political systems (300 n. 12). One can only accept such a statement if it is made clear that Jünger's critiques had an incomparably more devastating effect on the Weimar Republic than on the Nazi state or West Germany. If Jünger had been such a thorn in the side of the Nazis, his books would not have appeared until the early 1940s. (Even the "resistance parable" *Auf den Marmorklippen* was actually printed in an edition for the Wehrmacht in 1942!) If he had shaken things up so much in the Federal Republic, he hardly would have been presented with the prestigious Goethe Prize in 1982 or the *Bundesverdienstkreuz* in 1985.

24. A fascinating sketch of Jünger's postwar "character" is provided by the poet Stephen Spender, himself an admirer of Jünger's works. When Spender, then on duty in Germany purging the libraries of Nazi literature, met with him in 1945 in his study ("a comfortable room with leathern armchairs and lined with beautiful books"), Jünger not only held forth about the childishness of the French but also spoke of war as "a necessary stage of my experiences." Cf. Stephen Spender, *European Witness* (New York: Reynal and Hitchcock, 1946), 215 and 219. Contrast this with the sickeningly sweet portrait of Jünger presented by historical dramatist (!) Rolf Hochhuth in his *Und Brecht sah das Tragische nicht. Plädoyers, Polemiken, Profile* (München: Knesebeck, 1996), 83–101. Hochhuth pays homage to Gottfried Benn in the same volume.

25. In the definitive biography of Jünger, which appeared after the fall of the Berlin Wall, a similar perspective can be found. The author quotes an infamous phrase from *Copse 125* ("We cannot be national, yes, nationalistic enough."), pointing out that Jünger was reformulating the ideas of Spengler, Niekisch, and Moeller van den Bruck for a reading public "for whom democracy had long since become obsolete." He goes on to say: "For the work in its *literary* physiognomy, such speculations, no matter how alarming they might be in their politicization effect, remain inconsequential [*nicht entscheidend*]." Cf. Martin Meyer, *Ernst Jünger* (München and Wien: Hanser, 1990), 83.

In one of the standard works on twentieth-century German literature, the chapter on Jünger concentrates almost exclusively on essayistic style, disregarding content (and history) to the greatest extent possible. Cf. Hans Schumacher, "Exkurs über Ernst Jünger," *Deutsche Literatur im 20. Jahrhundert. Strukturen und Gestalten*, ed. Otto Mann and Wolfgang Rothe (Bern and München: Francke, 1967), 1:285-296.

26. In the Weimar Republic, the judiciary dealt much more harshly with politically motivated crime from the left than that from the right. The classic example is the nine-month imprisonment of Hitler in relatively comfortable quarters and the five-year prison ordeal of poet-dramatist Ernst Toller.

In West Germany, the state often played down the activities of the extraparliamentary right, while investing considerable resources to counter such activities emanating from the left. The scales have tipped in the other direction since the early 1990s, simply because the number of incidents of xenophobic violence perpetrated by the right has skyrocketed, whereas leftist terrorists like the Baader-Meinhof group have all but disappeared from view. The "Soviet threat" is also no longer relevant (whether most West German leftists were ever attracted to the Soviet model is another question).

27. One explosive factor in this equation lies in the fact that a great number of leftist writers — Heine, Kraus, Tucholsky, Benjamin, and many others — were Jewish. Cf. Bernt Engelmann, *Deutschland ohne Juden. Eine Bilanz* (Köln: Pahl-Rugenstein, 1988). One historian has portrayed the German Jews as the "outsiders" who unexpectedly became the "insiders" of Weimar culture. These "new insiders" — "foreign and irrepressibly modernist" — became the prime target of the reactionary forces. Cf. Avraham Barkai and Paul Mendes-Flohr [said historian], *Aufbruch und Zerstörung 1918-1945, Deutsch-jüdische Geschichte in der Neuzeit*, vol. 4, ed. Michael A. Meyer (München: C. H. Beck, 1997), 167.

The archetypal German leftist writer Bertolt Brecht was not Jewish (although his wife and collaborator, Helene Weigel, was), but the attempts to devalue his literary production by delving into his private — especially sex — life would be inconceivable vis-à-vis a conservative writer. (One example: Jünger's experimentation with mindaltering drugs does not seem to bother his German disciples, although they would certainly castigate President Clinton for his "no-inhaling" rhetoric.)

28. "8. Mai 1945 — Gegen das Vergessen," *Frankfurter Allgemeine Zeitung*, April 7, 1995, 3. The *FAZ* published a front-page editorial with the telling title "Überwunden, nicht befreit" ("Overcome, not Liberated") on April 11. In that editorial, Ignatz Bubis, the then leader of the German Jewish community, was criticized for implying that conservatives are "Nazis minus genocide."

Bubis answered with his own letter to the editor on April 19. (In a radio interview, he had stated that the signatories "were consciously or unconsciously laying the intellectual groundwork for the rise of a dangerous German nationalism." Cf. the Reuters news dispatch by Michael Shields from April 8, 1995.) Additional letters about the affair were published on April 20. On May 6, the *FAZ* published a statement by

Helmut Kohl about the fiftieth anniversary of the capitulation ("Jedem einzelnen Schicksal schulden wir Achtung"). Although Kohl expressed his respect for the human dignity of every person, he lumped together those sent to concentration camps, soldiers, and those driven from their homelands after the German defeat. This was reminiscent of Ronald Reagan's comments in Bitburg in 1985. Rudolf Scharping, then the SPD Chairman, said that it was "intolerable" that cabinet ministers had signed the advertisement published on April 7. Cf. "Scharping: Der 8. Mai 1945 war die Geburtsstunde der Freiheit," *FAZ*, May 5, 1995. Scharping did not mention that Hans Apel (SPD) had been one of the original signatories.

29. This omission was attacked in the counter-advertisement "WIDER DAS VERGESSEN, denn wie sollte man vergessen," placed by the prominent German-Jewish Brauner family in the May 5 edition of the *Frankfurter Allgemeine*. In this text, three figures are singled out for sharp criticism, namely the historian Ernst Nolte, the journalist and historian Rainer Zitelmann, and the Christian Democrat politician Alfred Dregger.

30. The one Social Democrat on the list, former defense minister Hans Apel, removed his name after its presence had caused him — and his party — considerable embarrassment.

31. For more information about this and other advertisements, including the 1994 *Berliner Appell*, see Weber, *Nation, Staat und Elite*, 96–97.

32. This does not imply that the two faces of totalitarianism are identical in the view of the New Right. Brown is still better than red, an argument forcefully presented by historian Ernst Nolte. In his controversial opus on National Socialism and Bolshevism, Nolte describes the Nazi seizure of power ("Machtergreifung," the standard term) as an "anti-Marxist takeover of power" (antimarxistische Machtübernahme), a much more positive formulation. Cf. Ernst Nolte, *Der europäische Bürgerkrieg 1917–1945. Nationalsozialismus und Bolschewismus* (Frankfurt am Main and Berlin: Propyläen/Ullstein, 1987), 28. For a contemporary German review of totalitarianism theories, see Wolfgang Wippermann, *Totalitarismustheorien. Die Entwicklung der Diskussion von den Anfängen bis heute* (Darmstadt: Primus Verlag, 1997).

33. Ulrich Schacht, ed., *Hohenecker Protokolle. Aussagen zur Geschichte der politischen Verfolgung von Frauen in der DDR* (Zürich: Ammann Verlag, 1984).

34. Ulrich Schacht, *Gewissen ist Macht. Notwendige Reden, Essays, Kritiken zur Literatur und Politik in Deutschland* (München and Zürich: Piper, 1992), 30. Further page references in the body of the text.

35. Although it is problematic to judge literature using the criteria of the secret police, one Stasi informant did opine that Schacht's poems were "very abstract" and would probably not have any "mass appeal." This assessment is found in Stasi documents provided by Schacht himself. Cf. Ulrich Schacht, "Versteinerte 'Quellen.' Fragmente zu einer politischen Fossilienkunde im Fundhorizont des Elbe-Oder-Gebietes," *Aktenkundig*, ed. Hans Joachim Schädlich (Reinbek: Rowohlt, 1993), 212. At least in this publication, Schacht's tone is humorous and ironic rather than bitter.

36. The young Schacht did nonetheless *write* quite a bit in the East. The circulation of these writings was limited to showing them to a few trusted friends, however. Some of these "friends" later turned out to be Stasi informants. A detailed list of the preprison writings can be found in court documents relating to the justification of sentencing him to prison. Cf. "Dissidenten? Texte und Dokumente zur DDR— 'Exil'—Literatur," *Deutschunterricht* 43.10 (Sonderheft 1990):522-526. According to the documents, Schacht was viewed as a "democratic socialist" in the tradition of the Prague Spring. One ironic twist: one of the confiscated writings, "The country in which I live," was not held against him, because it was only meant for his diary!

37. These included poets Sarah Kirsch, Günter Kunert, and Reiner Kunze and novelists Jurek Becker, Erich Loest, Hans-Joachim Schädlich, and Rolf Schneider. Jurek Becker may be the only former East German writer who was completely accepted in the West and achieved broad popularity.

38. "Among Western leftists, criticism of the GDR had been seen since the 1950s as an activity engaged in by Christian Democrats, as a theme of the Cold War that did not mesh with détente, as an anti-Communist argument." Jürgen Große, "Politische Verantwortung und moralische Schuld: Aspekte des intellektuellen Diskurses," *German Studies Review*, special issue on "Totalitäre Herrschaft—totalitäres Erbe" (Fall 1994), 176.

39. The only serious attempt to introduce the poet Schacht to the reading public is found in Birgit Lermen and Matthias Loewen, *Lyrik aus der DDR. Exemplarische Analysen* (Paderborn: Schöningh, 1987), 404-424. Schacht himself is probably not, however, enthusiastic about being categorized as a GDR poet, since most of his poems have been written in the West. In a 1989 letter, Schacht said himself that he could not live well if the money from his book publications in the West were his only source of income. An excerpt from the letter is printed in *Sie kommen aus Deutschland. DDR-Schriftsteller in der Bundesrepublik* (Worms: Stadtbibliothek, 1989), 112. It is of course true that before and after 1989, very few East *or* West German writers could devote themselves exclusively to their writing careers.

40. *Deutsche Literatur 19—. Jahresüberblick*, ed. Franz Josef Görtz, Volker Hage et al. (Stuttgart: Reclam, 1981-.) The volume printed in any given year covers the literature of the previous year.

41. Ulrich Schacht, "Ein 784-Seiten-Roman gegen die Wiedervereinigung," *Deutsche Literatur 1995*, 289-293.

42. Roland Müller, "Dichter im braunen Netz," *Deutsche Literatur 1994*, 315-319.

43. No fewer than twenty of the pieces were published in *Die Welt*, the newspaper that has employed Schacht since 1987.

44. See John Torpey, *Intellectuals, Socialism, and Dissent: The East German Opposition and Its Legacy* (Minneapolis: University of Minnesota Press, 1995).

45. Or rather, the "GDR." The Axel Springer newspapers routinely placed the abbreviation for the "other" German state in quotes.

46. In a speech given less than a month before the fall of the Berlin Wall, Schacht described a reunified Germany made up of the FRG and GDR as "the smallest possible Germany" (Kleinst-Deutschland). *Gewissen ist Macht,* 96. In the same speech, he said that Germany should be reunified even if "a majority of Europeans" were against it. (97)

47. Schacht does not hesitate to use the word "liberation" to describe how he was released from prison in the GDR and allowed to settle in West Germany (*Conscience Is Power,* 26), but he and his group now refuse to use it vis-à-vis 1945.

48. Alexander and Margarete Mitscherlich, *Die Unfähigkeit zu trauern. Grundlagen kollektiven Verhaltens* (1967; München: Piper, 1970).

49. Schacht does not always make a clear distinction between the two: "Homeland is, to be sure, always less than the nation, but it is not worth less to the individual. Often it is more essential and valuable to him. . . . Homeland is the foundation of the individual. The nation is the foundation of all the people: in that regard, homeland awareness is foundational, and national awareness is liberating." *Gewissen ist Macht,* 164.

50. Ironically, the SED often put up propaganda posters with the phrase "The human being is at the center [of our endeavors]" (Im Mittelpunkt steht der Mensch).

51. The major decision—at least for most males—was whether to move to West Berlin to avoid induction into the Bundeswehr.

52. See Heimo Schwilk, *Ernst Jünger. Leben und Werk in Bildern und Texten* (Stuttgart: Klett-Cotta, 1988); Heimo Schwilk, ed., *Das Echo der Bilder. Ernst Jünger zu Ehren* (Stuttgart: Klett-Cotta, 1990); Günter Figal and Heimo Schwilk, eds., *Magie der Heiterkeit. Ernst Jünger zum Hundertsten* (Stuttgart: Klett-Cotta, 1995).

53. Heimo Schwilk, *Wendezeit—Zeitenwende. Beiträge zur Literatur der achtziger Jahre* (Bonn, Berlin: Bouvier, 1991). Page references in the body of the text. The title is a play on words: "Wende" is the term denoting the collapse of the GDR and the beginning of reunification, whereas "Zeitenwende" is any turning point in history.

54. The word reminds one of the leftist term "late capitalism."

55. In place of cruise missiles and the like, Schwilk recommends national defense centered around popular resistance, a model based on Ernst Jünger's "Der Waldgang."

56. An essay in which the growing influence of Germany and its link to the so-called "post-Auschwitz paradigm" are discussed was written from a perspective far to the left of Schacht and Schwilk. See Andrei S. Markovits and Simon Reich, "Should Europe Fear the Germans?" *German Politics and Society* 23 (Summer 1994). Reprinted in *Germany, Volume II,* ed. Klaus H. Goetz. The International Library of Politics and Comparative Government, ed. David Arter (Aldershot: Dartmouth and Brookfield, Vt.: Ashgate, 1997), 1–20. The authors state: "We agree with the optimists that the Federal Republic's greatest achievement is its *eradication* of most factors that could lead to yet another Auschwitz. Where we part ways with the optimists is in their view of a democratic Germany with virtually no exercise of power in Europe

and the world." (1–2; my emphasis.) This is similar to Goldhagen's view of today's Germany.

57. All page references will be taken from the 1995 edition: Heimo Schwilk and Ulrich Schacht, eds., *Die selbstbewußte Nation. "Anschwellender Bocksgesang" und weitere Beiträge zu einer deutschen Debatte* (Frankfurt am Main and Berlin: Ullstein, 1995). The first edition was published in September 1994, the second revised and expanded edition in December 1994, and the third expanded edition in February 1995.

58. In his lengthy bibliography, Armin Mohler lists only one group of seven women associated with the Conservative Revolution. He calls them "weibliche Völkische," i.e., women who believed in the movement to return the German people to their true "pure" origins. See Mohler, *Die Konservative Revolution*, 3rd ed. 1989, 1:361–362. Mohler makes a point of mentioning that one of the women, Gertrud Prellwitz (1869–1942), was a "true philosemite" (361). The other women on his list are Edith Gräfin Salburg (1868–1942), Leonore Kühn (1878–?), Sophie Rogge-Börner (1878–?), Maria Grunewald (1875–?), Marie Eckert (no dates), and Ursula Zabel (1908–?).

59. Fritz Ringer, *The Decline of the German Mandarins* (Cambridge, Mass.: Harvard University Press, 1969), 6. Ringer excludes scientists and engineers from his study.

60. The word used is actually "Selbstverfehlung," which contains the word for transgression ("Verfehlung"). Together with "selbst" (self), it means something akin to "alienation from one's true self."

61. Did the editors consciously choose the term "degenerate" (entarten) in this context? It was an often-used word in the Third Reich, for example in the title of the infamous exhibition of "degenerate art" (entartete Kunst) staged by the Nazis.

62. This word ("Selbstbefriedigung") also means masturbation.

63. See Antonia Grunenberg, *Antifaschismus — ein deutscher Mythos* (Reinbek: Rowohlt, 1993).

64. See for example Jörg von Uthmann, "Körper und Lehrkörper. Amerikas Universitäten streiten über 'political correctness'," *Frankfurter Allgemeine Zeitung*, February 19, 1992; Henning Ritter, "Erziehungssucht. Was ist politisch korrekt?" *Frankfurter Allgemeine Zeitung*, April 22, 1992; Jörg von Uthmann, "PC vs. PC. Die Scheindebatte über das multikulturelle Amerika," *Frankfurter Allgemeine Zeitung*, January 7, 1993; Matthias Matussek, "Kunst als Schauprozeß," *Der Spiegel*, no. 15, 1993, 228–232; Ingo von Münch, "Die preußische Großmutter darf nicht fiepen . . . Anmerkungen zur Political correctness in Deutschland," *Die Welt*, July 3, 1997; Diederich Diederichsen, *Politische Korrekturen* (Köln: Kiepenheuer & Witsch, 1996); Stephan Wackwitz, "Stoff für die Lichterketten. Diederich Diederichsen und die politische Korrektheit," *Süddeutsche Zeitung*, October 28, 1996; Thomas Groß, "Tugendterrors Geistermarsch. PC im Zeitalter ihrer medialen Vermonsterung. Das neue Buch des Polit-DJs Diederich Diederichsen . . ." *Tageszeitung*, November 2, 1996.

65. In Schacht's words, Auschwitz was "not unique, but a human possibility" (66).

66. See his *Ein Schnäppchen namens DDR. Letzte Reden vorm Glockengeläut* (München: Deutscher Taschenbuch Verlag, 1993). The first piece (from February 1990) in this collection, entitled "Brief Speech by a Man without a Fatherland," begins with a description of how Grass was accosted by a young man at the Hamburg train station. The man not only called him a "traitor to the fatherland" but also warned that it was time to get rid of people like him (7). Grass goes on to say: "That's the way it is: I not only fear the Germany that has been simplified out of two states into one, I also reject the unified state" (7).

67. In calling for German defense of Israel as a true atonement for the Holocaust, Schacht is echoing the line of the late conservative publisher Axel Springer.

68. Stauffenberg, whom Schacht mentions, was also associated with the "George-Kreis." For a study of the illiberal and antidemocratic political philosophy of some resistance circles as a continuation of Germany's "special path," see Nicolai Hammersen, *Politisches Denken im Widerstand. Ein Beitrag zur Wirkungsgeschichte neokonservativer Ideologien 1914-1944.* Beiträge zur Politischen Wissenschaft, vol. 67 (Berlin: Duncker & Humblot, 1993). See also Gordon A. Craig's review essay "Good Germans," *New York Review of Books*, December 17, 1992, 38-44.

69. Ernst Jünger, "Über den Schmerz," *Sämtliche Werke*, 7:143-191.

70. Jünger, "Über den Schmerz," 145.

71. Jünger, "Über den Schmerz," 190.

72. Without comment, Schwilk offers a quotation from Carl Schmitt about the horrors of a world without metaphysics and "existential enmity" (401).

73. Many of the authors speak of this, but no one offers any empirical evidence for it. My suspicion is that it is more prevalent among intellectuals than among the masses of the people. This would not bother the authors of *Die selbstbewußte Nation*, however, since they are speaking to an elite, at least a potential one.

74. See Jünger, "Über die Linie," *Sämtliche Werke*, 7:237-279. Jünger dedicated this text to Heidegger on his sixtieth birthday. The final section contains a brash rewriting of Jünger's biography: "He who has not experienced the overwhelming power of nothingness ("das Nichts") in himself and resisted the temptation knows the least about his time" (279). Heidegger answered with a 1955 essay also entitled "Über die Linie." A slightly expanded version of this essay can be found in the *Complete Works:* Martin Heidegger, "Zur Seinsfrage," *Gesamtausgabe*, Abt. 1, Bd. 9 (Frankfurt am Main: Klostermann, 1976), 385-426. At one point, Heidegger relates the following: "In the Winter of 1939-40, I discussed the *Worker* [i.e., Jünger's *Der Arbeiter*] in a small group of professors. They were amazed that such a perceptive book had been around for years" (390).

75. Francis Fukuyama, *The End of History and The Last Man* (New York: The Free Press, 1992). Fukuyama does not envision any "special paths" for the Germans: "After the great events of the fall of 1989 in Eastern Europe, a significant number of Germans had doubts about the wisdom of reunification *because it would cost too much.* These are not the hallmarks of a civilization wound tight like a spring, ready to im-

molate itself on the pyre of new and unforeseen fanaticisms, but rather of one quite satisfied with what is and will be" (337). Maurer—and he is not alone in this belief—clearly believes that "what will be" will not be a cause for celebration.

76. Röhl was once publisher of the leftist journal *konkret*, and he was married to Ulrike Meinhof of the Baader-Meinhof terrorist group. His rantings are clearly related to his autobiography or rather his attempts to come to terms with it.

77. Bergfleth praises Tieck, Kerner, and Eichendorff as well as their supposed heirs Gustav Fechner, Johann Bachofen, and Ludwig Klages.

78. As a non-Jewish reader of Bergfleth's essay, I can only imagine what a Jew might feel when reading these words.

The British would surely by astonished to learn that liberalism is of "maritime origin" and is tied to a "disdain for the earth," which in turn leads to a disdain for "homeland, Volk and fatherland" (105–106). It is certainly a mystery that the seafaring British insisted on defending their own patch of *earth* against the Germans.

79. This might sound like a rehashing of the Literature Debate, but Syberberg is actually not at all judgmental regarding the writers from the former GDR. He has no desire to take Christa Wolf (referred to in the essay as Christa W.) to task for her role as a leading GDR author. Perhaps this is because he senses more vestiges of an acknowledgment of the tragic in the East than in the West.

80. With reference to the "Literature Debate" (the term itself is not mentioned directly), Krause calls Wolf's critics "conservative and left-liberal opinion leaders" (137). What might Krause's own stance be? Perhaps that of a cultural conservative and political liberal? This is a rare breed. Although Krause and Syberberg feel no need to condemn Wolf, Heimo Schwilk does so with relish, devaluing her entire œuvre as the work of a totalitarian collaborator. See Schwilk, *Wendezeit—Zeitenwende*, 177–182.

81. Rüdiger Safranski, *Das Böse oder Das Drama der Freiheit* (München and Wien: Hanser, 1997). The biographies are *Schopenhauer and the Wild Years of Philosophy* (1987; Cambridge, Mass.: Harvard University Press, 1990) and *Ein Meister aus Deutschland. Heidegger und seine Zeit* (München and Wien: Hanser, 1994). The latter has now been translated as *Martin Heidegger: Between Good and Evil* (Cambridge, Mass.: Harvard University Press, 1998).

82. Safranski sees similar mechanisms at work in East *and* West Germany. He refrains from using the totalitarianism theory to analyze the former GDR, since he is concerned more with ethical questions and psychological states.

83. Kant used this phrase in his *Idea for a General History with Cosmopolitan Intention* (1784), and it is also in the title of a fascinating book on liberalism. See Isaiah Berlin, *The Crooked Timber of Humanity* (New York: Vintage, 1992).

84. Bubik writes for the most provocative and unorthodox right-wing newspaper, *Junge Freiheit*, that has been under observation by constitutional police. See Burkhard Schröder, "Falsches Kaliber. NRW—Verfassungsschutz observiert 'Junge Freiheit,'" *tageszeitung*, May 29, 1996. Schröder makes a connection between the newspaper and Armin Mohler, whom he dubs "the Nestor of the 'new' fascists." See

also Bubik's "generational manifesto" *Wir '89er. Wer wir sind und was wir wollen* (Berlin and Frankfurt am Main: Ullstein, 1995).

85. See also his attempt to define the differences between right and left: Michael Wolffsohn, "Rebellion der konservativen Querköpfe der Nation," *Hamburger Abendblatt*, June 16–17, 1994. In this article, Wolffsohn asserts that the "New Right" is antitotalitarian and includes people like Armin Mohler and Botho Strauß, who are not associated with the Old Right. It is unlikely that Strauß was pleased to be grouped together with Mohler.

86. Wolffsohn, the only Jewish contributor to the anthology, does not believe in the singularity of the Holocaust. He compares it to similar state-controlled genocides in the Soviet Union, China, and Cambodia (273). (In 1998, the French parliament passed a resolution officially recognizing the 1915 massacre of the Armenians at the hand of the Turks as "genocide.") In doing so, he functions as a token Jew in more than one sense. See his book *Meine Juden—Eure Juden* (München and Zürich: Piper, 1997).

87. Zitelmann is one of the conservatives who have tried to push the FDP to the right (see the preface to this study). In his biography of Hitler, Zitelmann states: "An image of Hitler freed from . . . legends and prejudices can possibly contribute to making it more understandable why not only millions of people, but also intelligent persons from the areas of politics, the military, and even the cultural sphere succumbed to him." See R. Z., *Adolf Hitler. Eine politische Biographie* (Göttingen and Zürich: Muster-Schmidt, 1989), 9.

Zitelmann was also one of the editors of a volume that might be viewed as a "trial run" for *Die selbstbewußte Nation*. See Rainer Zitelmann, Karlheinz Weißmann and Michael Großheim, eds., *Westbindung. Chancen und Risiken für Deutschland* (Frankfurt am Main and Berlin: Ullstein/Propyläen, 1993). The cultural considerations that are emphasized in *Die selbstbewußte Nation* are peripheral in *Westbindung*.

88. Recent biographies of Helmut Kohl, written before his defeat in the 1998 national elections, suggest that he is very close to the mind-set of most contemporary Germans (at least those who vote), and a reviewer cites Margaret Thatcher's pronouncement after a visit with Kohl in his home at Oggersheim: "Oh, this man is sooo German!" See Richard Meng, "Der Kanzler und die Macht, die Macht und der Kanzler. Vier Journalisten widmen sich in vier Büchern der Geschichte und den Geschichten des Dauerregenten Helmut Kohl," *Frankfurter Rundschau*, April 2, 1998.

89. "Rockefeller Republican" might be an equivalent term in the context of U.S. politics.

90. Also in *Die selbstbewußte Nation*, Jochen Thies makes the case for the formation of *new* national elites in Germany. These would not be antinationalistic. Compare this to Christopher Lasch's *The Revolt of the Elites* (New York: Norton, 1995). Michiko Kakutani's review of the book in the *New York Times* (January 13, 1995) denigrates Lasch by placing him on a level with Dan Quayle. Many of the problems that bother Lasch are the ones that bother the German New Right. This does not mean, however, that Lasch is an archconservative. The ideological blinders worn by critics like Kakutani will be discussed at the end this study.

91. Given the recent controversies involving the National Endowment for the Arts, it is clear that Lange's comments do not apply to the American form of mass democracy.

92. Solzhenitsyn's dim view of Western decadence and moral decline was only accepted by the far right.

93. Martin Doerry, "'Lehrmeister des Hasses,'" *Der Spiegel*, October 17, 1994, no. 42, 239–243. The German word "Lehrmeister" includes the meaning of "mentor," making the title even more provocative than it is in English.

94. The German word is "Blindgänger," the term for an unexploded shell. It is ironic that a word taken from military parlance would be used against people accused of an infatuation with militarism and war.

Doerry also offers a critique of the antifeminism in the anthology. The irony here is that even though *Der Spiegel* is generally sympathetic toward feminism and women's rights, it regularly uses female nudity to boost sales among its — mainly male — readers.

95. When I attended a lecture by one of the contributors to *Die selbstbewußte Nation* in the fall of 1997 in Berlin, an acquaintance from the local cultural scene opined that the speaker "probably was sorry that he ever had allowed his essay to be published in that collection."

96. Already in 1994, a "Berlin Appeal" was published as a complement to the appearance of *Die selbstbewußte Nation*. It first was printed in the *Süddeutsche Zeitung* of September 28, 1994, and then reprinted in other newspapers. The text of the appeal is found on page 220 of *Für eine Berliner Republik*. In it, attention is called to a new generation, the conservative "'89ers," who strive to take over cultural hegemony from the '68ers. As has been mentioned above, a number of the '89ers belong to the same generation as the '68ers.

97. Ulrich Schacht and Heimo Schwilk, *Für eine Berliner Republik. Streitschriften, Reden, Essays nach 1989* (München: Langen Müller, 1997).

98. For a Western discussion of this question, see Timothy Garton Ash, *In Europe's Name: Germany and the Divided Continent* (New York: Random House, 1993).

99. The German word is "Häuflein." In English, this would be akin to "Robin Hood's merry men," and Templin is thinking of a group of outsiders upholding the ideals of freedom and justice.

100. Schwilk does however, praise Enzensberger as "one of the few writers critical of Europe" (74).

Schacht criticizes Enzensberger for misinterpreting the "Prague Spring" as an attempt to democratize socialism instead of seeing it for what it — allegedly — really was, namely an attempt to introduce Western European democracy (82).

101. This refers to famed novelist Günter Grass, minor West German writer Hermann Peter Piwitt, who was associated with the orthodox Marxist journal *konkret*, former East German literature czar Klaus Höpcke, and GDR author Hermann Kant, long a cultural functionary (and still unrepentant). Placing Grass in this company is no less than scandalous.

102. I do not agree with those who would like to see the works of Maron and others like her pulped, but I do believe that those works must be read in a different light
given the revelations about collaboration with the Stasi. For Maron's (prerevelation)
critique of the East German mentality, see Monika Maron, "Das neue Elend der Intellektuellen," *tageszeitung*, 6 February 1990 and "'Peinlich, blamabel, lächerlich,'"
Der Spiegel, no. 35, 1992. Maron's later explanation of her own activities—"Man hat
manches Bekloppte gemacht in dieser DDR"—was printed in *Der Spiegel*, no. 32,
1995. GDR dissident Wolf Biermann reacted to this article with his own: "Verlogene
Treue," *Der Spiegel*, no. 43, 1995. For an assessment of the options open to GDR intellectuals, see Wolfgang Engler, "Jenseits des Machtprinzips," *Die Zeit*, no. 15,
1993.

103. The successful (left-liberal) theater director Peter Stein, who has staged many
of Botho Strauß's plays, recently made a statement guaranteed to raise the hackles of
the New Right: "I have always had problems with being German. Like *all Germans*.
I don't like the Germans." (My emphasis.) See Wolfgang Kralicek, "Ich mag die
Deutschen auch nicht," *Der Tagesspiegel*, June 6, 1998.

104. In this passage, Schwilk mentions that "it is considered to be historically
proven" that the Poles were partially to be blamed for German aggression against
them in 1939 (154).

105. The discussion is documented in *Deutsche Literatur 1995. Jahresrückblick,*
288–359. The first review printed there is the one by Ulrich Schacht, who sees the
book as a novel against reunification. Tilman Krause and Hartmut Lange (cf. *Die
selbstbewußte Nation*) are also among the reviewers. For an example of the kind of
prose by Grass that irritates Schacht and Schwilk the most, see Günter Grass,
"Schreiben nach Auschwitz," *Die Zeit*, no. 9, 1990.

106. He does manage to include a stab at Grass as one of the "poets of West German special consciousness" (150). In another essay in the same volume, Schacht
characterizes Grass as "this *spiritus rector* of the intellectual version of the classic German movement for self-hatred" (80). It is noteworthy that in this passage, Schacht
admits that Grass has been esthetically innovative as a novelist. This separation of
content and form was not typical of the "Literature Debate."

107. A thought-provoking analysis and summary (one which is scholarly and subjective at the same time) is provided by Wolfgang Wippermann in his book *Wessen
Schuld? Vom Historikerstreit zur Goldhagen-Kontroverse* (Berlin: Elefanten Press,
1997). One of the first collections of Germans reactions to Goldhagen was edited by
Julius H. Schoeps: *Ein Volk von Mördern? Die Dokumentation zur Goldhagen-Kontroverse um die Rolle der Deutschen im Holocaust* (Hamburg: Hoffmann und Campe,
1996). The liberal weekly *Die Zeit* and *Der Spiegel* loomed large in the debate. See
the following articles from *Die Zeit:* Volker Ullrich, "Hitlers willige Mordgesellen,"
no. 16, 1996 (prepublication excerpts from the German edition of Goldhagen's book
are found in the same issue); Christopher Browning, "Dämonisierung erklärt
nichts," no. 17, 1996; Julius H. Schoeps, "Vom Rufmord zum Massenmord," no. 18,

1996; Gordon A. Craig, "Ein Volk von Antisemiten," no. 20, 1996; Hans-Ulrich Wehler, "Wie ein Stachel im Fleisch," no. 22, 1996; Hans Mommsen, "Die dünne Patina der Zivilisation," no. 36, 1996; Robert Leicht, "Ein Urteil, kein Gutachten," and Marion Gräfin Dönhoff, "Mit fragwürdiger Methode," both in no. 37, 1996; Volker Ullrich, "Goldhagen und die Deutschen," no. 38, 1996. *Der Spiegel* printed the lengthy article "Ein Volk von Dämonen?" as well as a portrait of Goldhagen and his father by German/Israeli journalist Henryk M. Broder in no. 21, 1996. In no. 33, 1996, *Spiegel* publisher Rudolf Augstein published an article entitled "Todbringende Humanisten" and an interview with Goldhagen ("Was dachten die Mörder?).

The Berlin daily *Der Tagesspiegel* published an interview with Goldhagen ("Können Sie wie ein Nazi fühlen?") on September 6, 1996. *Die Welt*, the employer of Schacht and Schwilk, published a review by Manfred Rowold entitled "Das ganze deutsche Volk als Hitlers willige Scharfrichter?" on April 17, 1996. See also the following contributions from the *Süddeutsche Zeitung*, the leading liberal daily: Norbert Frei, "Ein Volk von 'Endlösern'? Daniel Goldhagen bringt eine alte These in neuem Gewand," April 13, 1996; Josef Joffe, "Hitlers willfährige Henker. Oder: Die 'gewöhnlichen Deutschen' und der Holocaust," April 13, 1996; Jan Philipp Reemtsma, "Die Mörder waren unter uns. Überlegungen zu Daniel Goldhagens Buch 'Hitlers willige Vollstrecker,'" August 24, 1996. Here is a sampling of American reactions to Goldhagen: Jerry Adler, "Just Following Orders? A New Book Blames 'Ordinary Germans,'" *Newsweek*, April 15, 1996; Gordon A. Craig, "How Hell Worked," *New York Review of Books*, April 18, 1996; Clive James, "Blaming the Germans," *The New Yorker*, April 22, 1996; Thomas M. Disch, "A Nation and People Accursed," *The Nation*, May 6, 1996; Alan Cowell, "Holocaust Writer Debates Irate Historians in Berlin," *New York Times*, September 8, 1996, Christopher R. Browning, "Human Nature, Culture, and the Holocaust," *Chronicle of Higher Education*, October 18, 1996, and Russell Berman, "Goldhagen's Germany," *Telos*, no. 109 (Fall 1996), 131–140. A psychoanalytic perspective is found in Alice Miller, "Schrebers mörderische Kinder. Wie Haß entsteht: Die schwarze Pädagogik der Deutschen oder die Erziehung der Menschen zu willigen Helfern Hitlers," *Süddeutsche Zeitung*, March 14, 1998.

In 1997, *Der Spiegel* continued the debate with the following publications: "'Ein Anschein von Unsauberkeit.' Interview mit Christopher Browning," no. 31, 164–165; "Goldhagen—ein Quellentrickser?" no. 33, 156–158; "'Alles und nichts erklärt,'" [excerpts from an article by Norman Finkelstein criticizing Goldhagen], no. 34, 56–62; various letters to the editor about Finkelstein's theses in no. 35, 12, and "'Holocaust als Andachtsbild.' Interview mit NS-Expertin Ruth Bettina Birn über Goldhagens Attacken auf Kritiker," no. 46, 266–267.

On September 4, 1997, the Berlin *Tagesspiegel* published a long essay—"Angerührt und aufgerührt"— written by Goldhagen himself to his German readers.

108. It is of course extremely difficult to gauge the reaction of the public as a whole. When I attended a lecture by historian Wolfgang Wippermann in Berlin in October 1997 (the title was "People or Structures? The 'Goldhagen Effect' and the

Crisis of German Historiography"), I was amazed to hear that literally everyone in the room agreed with Wippermann that Goldhagen's thesis was correct. (Wippermann also spoke of some of the problems with *Hitler's Willing Executioners*, but this did not change his overall assessment.) Most of the members of the audience were under fifty. In a discussion with young Germans published by the weekly *Der Stern*, on the other hand, many of the young people felt that Goldhagen's portrayal of the Germans was too one-sided and even racist. See "Ich fühle mich durch dieses Buch angegriffen. Fünf junge Deutsche über Goldhagen, Antisemitismus und die Zukunft," *Der Stern*, no. 40, 1996.

A collection of contributions to the Goldhagen debate has now appeared in English. See Robert R. Shandley, ed., *Unwilling Germans? The Goldhagen Debate* (Minneapolis and London: University of Minnesota Press, 1998).

109. Walters says that one should not overlook the rest of German history when concentrating on the "twelve years of the National Socialist reign of terror" (15).

110. This phrase provides a taste of Schacht's often impenetrable style, which is almost more of a hindrance than the supposed leftist media monopoly.

111. Actually, Schacht sees some good in the Goldhagen debate, namely that it demonstrated the self-hatred and anti-German sentiment of the leftist intellectuals (36).

112. CSU politician Peter Gauweiler, who, as a public figure, has access to the media, does not shy away from drastic formulations. In the CSU newspaper *Bayernkurier*, Gauweiler called Goldhagen a "judge of the [German] people" and accused him of "reverse racism." Incredibly, he mentioned that the book had provided Goldhagen with "over a million Deutschmarks in profit." In a country where the image of Shylock has not disappeared, such statements keep alive the Nazi portrayal of the Jews. The *Bayernkurier* article is summarized in "Für Gauweiler ist Goldhagen ein 'Volksrichter.' Der CSU-Politiker beschimpft den Historiker auch als antideutschen 'Rassisten,'" *tageszeitung*, October 10, 1996.

113. Compare this to Federal President Herzog's 1996 statement at a meeting of the Germans driven from their homes in the East: The territories now part of Poland and Russia belong "to our historical and cultural legacy, but no longer to our state." Cited in "Herzog: Kein Anspruch auf frühere Ostgebiete," *Süddeutsche Zeitung*, September 9, 1996.

114. The speech had originally been planned as part of the May 7, 1995, program in the Munich Philharmonic Hall that was linked to the newspaper campaign "Against Forgetting" (see above). That program was canceled, and Schacht then delivered the speech in more friendly territory, namely at the conservative think tank in Weikersheim near Stuttgart.

115. For example, Schacht criticizes the legendary 1985 speech by Federal President Richard von Weizsäcker—a Christian Democrat—without naming the speaker (49–50). The speech is contained in Richard von Weizsäcker, *Von Deutschland aus* (Berlin: Siedler, 1985), 13–35. In his speech, Weizsäcker spoke of the 8th of May as

"a day of liberation" for the Germans (15), one that freed them from the National Socialist system of terror. This implies that not all Germans were Nazis, something with which Schacht agrees. The problem is that Weizsäcker commemorated not only the victims of Nazism but also the German resistance, and he dared to include the Communist resistance. This was and is not acceptable to the former East German Schacht.

116. See Heinz Lippmann, *Honecker and the New Politics of Europe*, trans. Helen Sebba (New York: Macmillan, 1972), 31–35. The scientist and later dissident-to-be Robert Havemann was held in the same prison.

117. Schacht calls Honecker one of the most "horrifying petit bourgeois figures" (113) ever to exercise power in German history. One wonders if he could produce a list of other representatives of the German petite bourgeoisie who have been given major political responsibility. By referring to the proletarian Honecker as a petit bourgeois, Schacht unwittingly concurs with Lenin, whose skepticism about the possibility of revolution in Germany stemmed from his view that the German workers were too tame, i.e., petit-bourgeoisified.

118. In another essay, Schacht refers the reader to journalist Henryk M. Broder's book *The Eternal Anti-Semite* (193). Schacht asserts that anyone who does not embrace Zionism "loves dead Jews, in order to be able to hate the living ones" (192).

119. This phrase is also found on p. 73.

120. One other example of the traces of Jünger in Schwilk's essays: Helmut Kohl is referred to as the "Head Forester" ("Oberförster" [175]), the title of the brutal leader in Jünger's *On the Marble Cliffs*.

121. In contrast to this, leading left-liberal critic Ulrich Greiner, a key figure in the "Literature Debate," declared in 1992 that the left no longer exists. See Ulrich Greiner, "Flucht in die Trauer," *Die Zeit*, no. 39, 1992.

122. National pride, for example, does not mesmerize the upper two-thirds of Germany society. It does, however, hold an attraction for the "losers" of the present system. Whoever asks about the attraction of the New Right must simultaneously ask how many more "losers" there might be in the future.

123. It might be recalled that "Goethe Communities" were a solution proposed by historian Friedrich Meinecke to set the Germans back on the path to civilization after 1945. Meinecke's thoughts on the subject are excerpted in: Hermann Glaser, *Die Kulturgeschichte der Bundesrepublik Deutschland* (Frankfurt am Main: Fischer, 1990), 3:100–102. The excerpts are taken from Meinecke's 1946 book *Die deutsche Katastrophe*. See the English translation *The German Catastrophe. Reflections and Recollections*, trans. Sidney B. Fay (Cambridge, Mass.: Harvard University Press, 1950), 119–121.

124. Contrast this with Peter Gauweiler's skewed assessment: "Like the '68ers, the Greens are the party of generational conflict and of disagreement with everything that was learned and lived before them." See Gauweiler's "'Ich will kein Held sein!' oder Machtgestöber," *Die wilden 40er. Porträt einer pubertären Generation*, ed. Peter Roos (Düsseldorf: Econ, 1992), 304.

125. P. C. Mayer-Tasch, *Aus dem Wörterbuch der Politischen Ökologie* (München: Deutscher Taschenbuch Verlag, 1985), 79. See also Ulrich Linse, *Ökopaxe und Anarchie. Eine Geschichte der ökologischen Bewegungen in Deutschland* (München: Deutscher Taschenbuch Verlag, 1986). Linse disputes the claim that the Greens are the heirs of a German tradition of Romantic anticapitalism and prefascist irrationalism (154). Neofascists who tried to gain a foothold in the Greens were unsuccessful. See Richard Stöss, *Politics against Democracy. Right-Wing Extremism in West Germany* (New York and Oxford: Berg, 1991) 162–163. For a now somewhat dated assessment of the Greens as an expression of New Age activism, see Fritjof Capra and Charlene Spretnak, *Green Politics. The Global Promise* (New York: Dutton, 1984). In a review of this book, Kirkpatrick Sale stated: "The Green movement is an amalgam of many groups from all parts of the political spectrum (even conservatives)." See "Greener Pastures," *The Nation*, June 23, 1984, 776. For a detailed analysis of Green politics, see Joachim Raschke, *Die Grünen. Wie sie wurden, was sie sind* (Köln: Bund Verlag, 1993).

126. This is of course not the only interpretation of the relationship between National Socialism and modernity. Jeffrey Herf speaks of a "reactionary modernism" that "incorporated modern technology into the cultural system of modern German nationalism, without diminishing the latter's romantic and antirational aspects." See Jeffrey Herf, *Reactionary Modernism: Technology, Culture, and Politics in Weimar and the Third Reich* (Cambridge: Cambridge University Press, 1984), 2. One of the representatives of this movement as described by Herf is Ernst Jünger. In general, Herf's analysis of Jünger's works rings true, but it is difficult to accept his admiration for the latter's "unmatched literary flair" (70).

127. In a recent 1968 commemorative edition of the leftist *tageszeitung* (April 11, 1998), the '68ers' lack of political success was discussed. On April 9, the paper had published an article by Peter Gauweiler ("Kleiner großer Bruder") in which the conservative CSU politician claimed that the '68ers were no longer radical, or only verbally so. Instead of transforming the establishment, they have become part of it, said Gauweiler. In the same article, Gauweiler called the members of the '68 generation who were conservative back then "contras."

128. Herzinger's ideas will be scrutinized in the *Excursus* below.

129. Even Tilman Krause, a critic associated with the New Right, admits that the outlook is bleak: "No one has come forward. Many left, but no one came. Rightist authors have been rare since 1945. The irrational Brehms and Grimms, the Beumelburgs and Kolbenheyers — they simply died off. The German intellectual landscape has been redistributed [flurbereinigt]." Tilman Krause, "Der Sehnsüchtige im Fahndungsraster," *Deutsche Literatur 1994*, 299. Krause's article originally appeared in *Der Tagesspiegel* on September 25, 1994.

130. Some that come to mind are Syberberg's *Hitler*, Wolfgang Petersen's *Das Boot*, or Joseph Vilsmaier's *Stalingrad*. They all lend themselves more to ambivalence than one-dimensional interpretations, however.

Chapter 3

1. Christa Wolf, *Was bleibt* (Berlin, Weimar: Aufbau, 1990).

2. For a detailed exposition of this hypothesis, see Jay Rosellini, "Kahlschlag im Land der Dichter und (Polit-)Denker? Zum Hintergrund des Intellektuellenstreits in Deutschland," *Monatshefte* 86.4 (Winter 1994):480–499.

3. Karl Deiritz and Johannes Krauss, "Ein deutsches Familiendrama," *Der deutsch-deutsche Literaturstreit,* 8.

4. Frank Schirrmacher, "'Dem Druck des härteren, strengeren Lebens standhalten.' Auch eine Studie über den autoritären Charakter: Christa Wolfs Aufsätze, Reden und ihre jüngste Erzählung 'Was bleibt'." Cited in Anz, *"Es geht nicht um Christa Wolf,"* 89. Schirrmacher's article was originally published in the *Frankfurter Allgemeine Zeitung* of June 2, 1990.

5. Robert Leicht, "Vom Bockshorn und vom Bocksgesang," *Die Zeit,* no. 41, 1994. The subtitle of this editorial is "The '89ers against the '68ers — a new generational conflict or the old battle between myth and enlightenment?"

6. "Hausmitteilung: Betr.: Intellektuelle," *Der Spiegel,* no. 26, 1993, 3. The Strauß essay is found in no. 6 (202–207), Enzensberger's is in no. 25 (170–175), and Walser's concluding piece is in no. 26 (40–47). "Anschwellender Bocksgesang" is a "Polemik" listed under the rubric "Kultur," "Ausblicke auf den Bürgerkrieg" is categorized as "Zeitkritik," also under "Kultur," whereas "Deutsche Sorgen" is in the section "Deutschland" under the subheading "Intellektuelle." Page numbers of specific citations are provided in the text.

7. Analogous to this constellation, right wing Republicans of the Gingrich stripe in the U.S. House of Representatives portray themselves as revolutionaries, whereas the liberal establishment is branded as an obstacle to change.

8. Hans Magnus Enzensberger, "Gemeinplätze, die Neueste Literatur betreffend," *Kursbuch* 15 (1968): 197.

9. Cf. Rolf Warneke, "Kurswechselparade eines Intellektuellen. Konsequent inkonsequent: Hans Magnus Enzensberger," *text und kritik* 113, *Vom gegenwärtigen Zustand der deutschen Literatur* (January 1992): 97–105. See also Matthias Uecker, "Katastrophe und Normalität. Hans Magnus Enzensberger seit den siebziger Jahren," *Deutschsprachige Literatur der 70er und 80er Jahre,* ed. Walter Delabar and Erhard Schütz (Darmstadt: Wissenschaftliche Buchgesellschaft, 1997), 321–343.

10. Hermann Korte, "Hans Magnus Enzensberger" *Kritisches Lexikon zur deutschsprachigen Gegenwartsliteratur* (1978ff.), 39. Nachlieferung 1992, 20.

11. Holger-Heinrich Preuße, *Der politische Literat Hans Magnus Enzensberger. Politische und gesellschaftliche Aspekte seiner Literatur und Publizistik* (Frankfurt am Main, Bern, New York and Paris: Peter Lang, 1989), 191.

12. H. M. Enzensberger, *Aussichten auf den Bürgerkrieg* (Frankfurt am Main: Suhrkamp, 1993). For a wide-ranging discussion of Enzensberger's comments on the

state of the post-1989 world, see Gerhard Fischer, ed., *Debating Enzensberger.* Great Migration *and* Civil War (Tübingen: Stauffenburg, 1996).

13. H. M. Enzensberger, "Hitlers Wiedergänger," *Der Spiegel*, no. 6, 1991, 26–28. André Glucksmann, one of the so-called "new philosophers" in France, praised the essay on Saddam but castigated Enzensberger for his piece on the global civil war as an excuse for passivity in the face of barbarity. "Ein neuer Vogel Strauß," *Der Spiegel*, no. 37, 1993, 247–249.

14. In actuality, Enzensberger meant to say that the Germans should refrain from demonizing Saddam and his followers as some kind of foreign, premodern barbarians, since they themselves had engaged in the same behavior not long ago. This line of reasoning can be traced to traditional leftist internationalism and anti-imperialism, although the conclusion does not seem to fit into such a mode of thinking.

15. Hans Magnus Enzensberger, *Diderots Schatten* (Frankfurt am Main: Suhrkamp, 1994). In the afterword to this collection, he writes of Diderot: "He was responsible for everything and got involved in everything. . . . Diderot plunged into the adventure of helping not out of an ideological sense of duty or because of party discipline, but rather out of naive curiosity" (382–383).

16. "'Ich will nicht der Lappen sein, mit dem man die Welt putzt.' André Müller spricht mit Hans Magnus Enzensberger," *Die Zeit*, no. 4, 1995.

In his essay "Im Fremden das Eigene hassen?", Enzensberger refers to the Aryan as "an absurd construction" and speaks of Germany's "especially fragile national identity." *Der Spiegel*, no. 34, 1992, 176.

17. Martin Walser, "Treten Sie zurück, Erich Honecker!" *Der Spiegel*, no. 20, 1974, 136. In this letter, Walser is reacting to the Guillaume affair and Willy Brandt's resignation. He is upset that the rapprochement between the two German states has suffered a setback. In a way, he is calling for a kind of socialist nationalism, so this is clearly a foreshadowing of later developments in his thinking.

18. Martin Walser, *Dorle und Wolf* (Frankfurt am Main: Suhrkamp, 1987), 54. In his review of this book, Martin Lüdke wrote: "Walser confronts a problem that we, almost without exception, have repressed. . . . No one is still having sleepless nights over the division of Germany." "Nichts Halbes, nichts Ganzes. Martin Walsers deutsch-deutsche Novelle," *Die Zeit*, no. 13, 1987. In Peter Schneider's *The Wall Jumper* (*Der Mauerspringer*, 1982), the division of Berlin and Germany is really little more than a curiosity.

19. Martin Walser, "Über Deutschland reden. Ein Bericht," *Über Deutschland reden* (Frankfurt am Main: Suhrkamp, 1988), 88–89. It is interesting that Walser praises Enzensberger for pondering the German question in his "Katechismus zur deutschen Frage," which appeared in *Kursbuch* 4.

Enzenberger's fellow intellectuals are criticized sharply: "Leftist intellectuals and rightist ones are at the moment in agreement about nothing more than in the belief that the division [of Germany] is acceptable" (92). The inclusion of intellectuals on the right is worthy of note in the face of the New Right program of the 1990s.

20. "Viel Gefühl, wenig Bewußtsein. Der Schriftsteller Günter Graß über eine mögliche Wiedervereinigung Deutschlands," *Der Spiegel*, no. 47, 1989, 80: "I am no stranger to these feelings either, but that does not seduce me into breaking out in mawkishness." In the same interview, Grass describes several surprising flip-flops in Walser's world view: "When I met him, he was an enlightened conservative from Lake Constance with a certain careful leaning toward the SPD that became an affinity with the DKP [the orthodox West German Communist Party] via the student movement. He moved away from that later, and now he is chatting with Waigel [CSU member and cabinet minister] — there are one too many unexplained turns there that I don't like." (80) It is of course Grass himself who has remained steadfast in his support of the "Kulturnation" Germany as opposed to the geographically and politically unified version. Walser also used the term "feeling for history" in his article "Zum Stand der deutschen Dinge," which was published in the *Frankfurter Allgemeine Zeitung* on December 12, 1989.

21. Walser defended himself in the *tageszeitung* of January 16, 1989. Excerpts from his text were reprinted in *Die Zeit*, no. 4, 1989. He claimed there that he had maintained his independence: "I don't see any chance of being co-opted by someone as an author or intellectual." In the meantime, even ex-Communist poet and singer Wolf Biermann has participated in political discussions at the CSU retreat, and he seemed to feel more comfortable there than when mixing with the leftists who heap "totalitarian scolding" upon him like "pseudo-leftist Tartuffes." See Wolf Biermann, "Freundschaft mit dem Klassenfeind," *Der Spiegel*, no. 3, 1998, 32. The Berlin *Tagesspiegel* editorialized: "One would like to be there when the former anti-communist devourer Biermann and the former communist devourer Stoiber [the Bavarian premier] and his devotees encounter each other in January in Kreuth." See "Kreuther Kaminwunder," *Der Tagesspiegel*, December 12, 1997.

22. Some years ago, poet Erich Fried — hardly a conservative nationalist! — was vilified by Henryk M. Broder for daring to speak with skinheads.

23. Cf. Walser's letter "Lieber Herr Kinkel," *tageszeitung*, July 16, 1994. In this endeavor, Walser found himself in the company of Salman Rushdie and Elfriede Jelinek, among others. He inveighed against religious terror and "orders to kill given by fanatical monotheists," adding that "Europe has put its religious calamities behind her." Walser's support for Nasreen is exactly the kind of activity that A. Glucksmann had in mind when he criticized Enzensberger for his inactivity and cynicism (see note 13).

24. It should be emphasized that Enzensberger has a very different attitude toward Strauß than Walser does. The following quote from the 1995 interview (see note 16) illustrates this: "God, he [i.e., Strauß] is a very talented man, but his preoccupations are not mine. I find it indecent to portray oneself as a tragic figure. It is difficult to speak correctly of the tragic, since that can lead all too easily to self-stylization, self-heroization, and kitsch. I don't like any of these poses. . . . [A]ll this stuff from the '20s that he is constantly referring to, Ludwig Klages, Rudolf Borchardt, all of these leftover, faded motifs . . . I don't know why he keeps hanging on to these things. A gifted person has to recognize that those are no longer relevant themes."

25. Martin Walser, "Vormittag eines Schriftstellers. Über Deutschland reden—
und die Folgen: Warum einer keine Lust mehr hat, am Streit der Meinungen teil-
zunehmen," *Die Zeit*, no. 51, 1990. Reprinted in Martin Walser, *Vormittag eines
Schriftstellers* (Frankfurt am Main: Suhrkamp, 1994), 9–26. Walser is quoting from
Botho Strauß, *Diese Erinnerung an einen, der nur einen Tag zu Gast war* (München
and Wien: Hanser, 1985), 48. Here is the original German: "Kein Deutschland ge-
kannt zeit meines Lebens. / Zwei fremde Staaten nur, die mir verboten, / je im Na-
men des Volkes der Deutsche zu sein. / Soviel Geschichte, um so zu enden?"

26. I have discovered numerous parallels in the following editions: *Rumor*
(München: Hanser, 1980); *Paare, Passanten* (München and Wien: Hanser, 5th edition, 1982); *Der junge Mann* (München: Hanser, 1984); *Fragmente der Undeutlichkeit* (München: Hanser, 1989); *Beginnlosigkeit. Reflexionen über Fleck und Linie*
(München: Hanser, 1992);*Wohnen Dämmern Lügen* (München and Wien: Hanser,
1994); *Schlußchor* in *Theaterstücke II* (München and Wien: Hanser, 1991), and *Das
Gleichgewicht* (München and Wien: Hanser, 1993). These works demonstrate that
the development of Strauß's ideas has been a gradual one, not a sudden eruption.

27. One might also include Alice Schwarzer's afterword to the legendary volume
Frauen gegen den ¶ 218 (Frankfurt am Main: Suhrkamp, 1971), although Schwarzer
is a journalist rather than an imaginative writer.

28. Botho Strauß, *Versuch, ästhetische und politische Ereignisse zusammenzudenken.
Texte über Theater 1967–1986*, 2nd ed. (Frankfurt am Main: Verlag der Autoren,
1996).

29. In another essay, he uses the word "totalitarian" to describe both the left and
right avantgarde of art. *Versuch* 37.

30. "Internal Memo ("Hausmitteilung") Concerning Intellectuals," *Der Spiegel*,
no. 26, 1993, 3. The "entire critical intelligentsia," the memo goes on to say, "is on
the lookout for new values and orientations." If that were true, then the texts by Enzensberger, Strauß, and Walser would hardly have been criticized so sharply. (Some
observers of course consider the opponents of the three to be "uncritical," i.e., dogmatic intellectuals.)

31. *Der Pfahl. Jahrbuch aus dem Niemandsland zwischen Kunst und Wissenschaft* 7
(1993): 9–25.

32. In Schiller's poem "Dividing Up the Earth" ("Die Teilung der Erde," 1795–
96), the artist was still depicted as a dreamer who had no possessions on earth and was
thus allowed to live with Zeus in the heavens. Such modesty has been ebbing away
for the past two centuries.

33. Those with a historical memory or at least consciousness would also think of
Nazis or Communists. Their heirs are less given to "orderly" marching.

34. In "Hitler Reincarnated," Enzensberger theorized early in 1991 that the Iraqis
would willingly die for Saddam Hussein. The reality turned out to be quite different.
See "Hitlers Wiedergänger," *Der Spiegel*, no. 6, 1991, 27.

In the U.S., it is interesting to observe that not a restriction, but rather a limitless expansion of material needs is undergirded by religious beliefs ("God's own country"). There is no other country in the world where a widespread belief in God (demonstrated by regular attendance at church services) coexists so peacefully with the consumer society. A few conservative churches or sects have recognized the contradiction, but their criticism of it remains peripheral.

35. This has a problematic ring to it in German, since the verb "sich wehren," to defend oneself, contains the root of both "Wehrmacht" and "Wehrertüchtigung" (readying soldiers for battle). The present German army is the "Bundeswehr," perhaps named in such a way as to remove the term "Wehr" from initial position.

36. Historian Robert Darnton offers a refreshing and stimulating assessment of the "little" Enlightenment: The Enlightenment "has been blown up to such a size that it would not be recognized by the men who first created it." See "George Washington's False Teeth," *New York Review of Books*, March 27, 1997, 34. Defending the Enlightenment in this manner is more fruitful than attacking anyone who criticizes the West. It is possible to oppose the perversion and cooptation of the Enlightenment at the hands of the ruling classes without distorting the origins of the movement. This theme will be taken up in the *Excursus*.

37. For stylistic reasons, I have not translated this passage literally. Instead of "mocking, ridicule, and derision," Strauß uses the word "Verhöhnung" three times in one phrase. His version sounds more fanatical than mine.

38. Thirty years after 1968, the rise in youth crime has made antiauthoritarian pedagogy once again a target of criticism. See Rudolf Wassermann, "Wenn die moralischen Hemmschwellen fehlen. Das Versagen der Erziehung als entscheidender Grund für die wachsende Kinderkriminalität," *Die Welt*, April 23, 1998. Wassermann finds an "ethical vacuum" in society, with "little egotists" ignorant of the difference between "good and evil, right and wrong, yours and mine." According to Wassermann, much of the crime is committed by the children of immigrants, and those who speak openly about this are accused of antiforeigner sentiments. *Der Spiegel* has also weighed in with a lengthy report advertised in comic-book style on the cover of the magazine. See "Der Krieg der Kinder," *Der Spiegel*, no. 15, 1998, 126–137. A second article, discussing the psychological problems of today's youth ("Das Drama beginnt früh," 138–141), appeared in the same issue. The *Spiegel* journalists seem absolutely shocked that the kind of brutal acts that occurred in Jonesboro, Arkansas are also possible in Germany.

39. It seems inevitable that Joschka Fischer of the Greens will be immortalized in a novel or polemic entitled something like *From Sneakers to Double-Breasted Suits: The Transformation of a '68 Icon*.

40. I have translated "das Unsere" as "existing conditions." The German term, not really a political one, means "that which is ours," i.e., our civilization. The possessive is misleading, for it implies that there is consensus about what the civilization should be. There is no place for multiculturalism in Strauß's choice of words.

41. It is inexplicable that a sensitive person like Strauß could use a word like this

one. Anyone who has not forgotten the history of this century must be horrified by the author's callousness.

42. In this passage, Strauß speaks of scapegoats as objects of reverence rather than hate. When Green politician Antje Vollmer attempted to mediate in the debate about "Impending Tragedy," she discovered new, modern scapegoats: "Anyone who is clever can come out in Germany these days as anything—but not as a writer, filmmaker, and intellectual. The creative people are the noble animals, the scapegoats." "Woher kommt diese Wut?" *Der Spiegel*, no. 46, 1993, 255. German politicians, who are increasingly subjected to an American-style glare of publicity, might well dispute that statement. Resentments against the elite are, however, characteristic of contemporary Germany (although the economic and financial elite seems to be often disregarded).

43. This statement should not be interpreted to mean that it would be advisable to return to the old ubiquitous epithets "fascist" or "protofascist," but Strauß's characterization of antifascism as "ordered from above" or even "libertarian to the point of becoming psychopathological" (26) is the kind of frivolous rhetoric that could lead to Germany's stigmatization by the international community. That would be in no one's interest.

44. The following sentence recalls Nietzsche's disdain for the "semieducated:" "The illiterate with good writing skills is the typical paradox in today's newspapers" (29). Nietzsche, however, would not have expected anything else from journalists.

45. This particular sentence was—understandably—omitted from the *Spiegel* version of the essay.

46. At least one must hope that they were not his goal. If the opposite were true, one would have to write off Strauß completely as a political thinker (or a writer with an interest in politics). On the day after I wrote this footnote, the following sentence appeared in a German newspaper: "It is said of the Germans that in politics, they are receptive to everything that is nebulous, incomprehensible, and bombastic" ("verschwiemelt"). Michael Winter, "Triebkraft Angst. Über deutsche Nationaldenkmäler," *Süddeutsche Zeitung*, June 25, 1997.

47. Assuming that Strauß believed his own depiction of the German media as a leftist bastion, he must have known that "Impending Tragedy" would cause an outcry.

48. Others might turn to alternate pairs like Bettine von Arnim and Rachel Varnhagen, Annette von Droste-Hülshoff and Fanny Lewald, Marieluise Fleißer and Else Lasker-Schüler, or Ingeborg Bachmann and Christa Wolf.

49. Klaus R. Scherpe und Hans-Ulrich Treichel, "Vom Überdruß leben: Sensibilität und Intellektualität als Ereignis bei Handke, Born und Strauß," *Monatshefte* 73.2 (Summer 1981):189.

50. Lothar Pikulik, "Mythos und 'New Age' bei Peter Handke und Botho Strauß," *Wirkendes Wort*, no. 2 (1988), 236.

51. Pia Janke, *Der schöne Schein. Peter Handke und Botho Strauß* (Wien: Verlag Holzhausen, 1993), xi. Janke discovers several differences between the two figures, but in the end, she emphasizes—in her conclusion, for example—the common ele-

ments: "If in the works of Handke a new age is introduced, then in the works of Strauß the old one that once again is to reign is preserved. In the case of both authors, however, it is the sphere of literature that makes possible this (varied) invention of meaning" (214).

52. Susanne Marschall, *Mythen der Metamorphose—Metamorphose des Mythos bei Peter Handke und Botho Strauß* (Mainz: Gardez! Verlag, 1993), 11.

53. With regard to Handke, there are two exceptions to this rule. As a thirty-year-old, he published four so-called "political exercises" ("politische Versuche") from the years 1967 to 1969. Topics included socialism and the Springer publishing empire. See *Ich bin ein Bewohner des Elfenbeinturms* (Frankfurt am Main: Suhrkamp, 1972). It is noteworthy, however, that Handke attempted to depoliticize these texts in the preface that he wrote for this volume: "It would be nice if one could read most of these texts as stories." He added that it would not be possible to extract a coherent world view from the collection. "Vorbemerkung," 7–8.

In 1986, Handke published a polemic against Kurt Waldheim at the end of the latter's (successful) campaign to become president of Austria. This was not a real attempt to influence the outcome of the election, since Handke assumed that the "hideous dwarf" would be victorious. It is interesting that Handke emphasized at the time that he wanted to speak for the "real people of Austria." His text was first published in the Austrian journal *profil*. An English translation (from which the two citations were taken—cf. p. 177) can be found in Bernard Cohen and Luc Rosenzweig, *Waldheim*, trans. Josephine Bacon (New York: Adama Books, 1987). This volume is an English translation from the French original: *Le Mystère Waldheim* (Paris: Editions Gallimard, 1986). I am grateful to Matthias Konzett for making me aware of this episode in Handke's career.

54. Bernhard Sorg, "Erinnerung an die Dauer. Zur Poetisierung der Welt bei Botho Strauß und Peter Handke," *Peter Handke, Text und Kritik*, Heft 24 (5th rev. ed. 1989), 122.

55. In addition, one cannot assume that any insights that the imaginative writer might have will be formulated in such a way that the average reader, i.e., citizen, will be able to gain access to them.

56. *Süddeutsche Zeitung*, January 5–6 and 13–14, 1996. The title of the essay later became the subtitle.

The essays will be cited in the text using the following editions: Peter Handke, *Eine winterliche Reise zu den Flüssen Donau, Save, Morawa und Drina oder Gerechtigkeit für Serbien*, 2nd ed. (Frankfurt am Main: Suhrkamp, 1996) and *Sommerlicher Nachtrag zu einer winterlichen Reise* (Frankfurt am Main: Suhrkamp, 1996). The first volume will be abbreviated as "*WR*," the second as "*SN*."

57. Reinhard Mohr, "Eine böse Harmonie," *Der Spiegel*, no. 12, 1996, 216.

58. Karl-Ludwig Baader, "Aufbauscher und Abwiegler," *Hannoversche Allgemeine*, December 29, 1993. Cited in *Deutsche Literatur 1993. Jahresrückblick*, ed. Franz Josef Görtz et al. (Stuttgart: Reclam, 1994), 308.

59. "'Ich bin nicht hingegangen, um mitzuhassen.' Peter Handke antwortet seinen Kritikern. Ein ZEIT-Gespräch mit Willi Winkler," *Die Zeit,* no. 6, 1996. In the heading printed above the interview, the *Zeit* editors placed emphasis on the significance of the controversy: "Since 'Impending Tragedy' by Botho Strauß, no text has stirred up the public like Peter Handke's philippic ('Kampfschrift') 'Justice for Serbia.' Is this a political scandal or just a literature debate?"

60. Compare for example Handke's *Der kurze Brief zum langen Abschied* (1972) with his *Abschied des Träumers vom Neunten Land* [i.e., Slovenia] (1991).

61. The island Krk, formerly Croatian/Yugoslavian, is now Croatian. While on the island, Handke did not have the impression that the culture of then multiethnic Yugoslavia was a product of coercion. See his comments in the interview with *Die Zeit* (see note 59).

62. "'Nackter, blinder, blöder Wahnsinn'" (W. Reiter and C. Seiler interview Peter Handke), *profil,* no. 12 (1996), 81.

Handke has traveled through Slovenia on many occasions. Before greater Yugoslavia broke apart, he regarded the region as part of a larger country. It was the Slovenian contribution to the multicultural potpourri that fascinated him.

63. The phrase "need not continue to read" is also used on page 36. One Croatian reader who did not put the book down and went on to call for justice for *all* of the ethnic groups—including the Serbs, but not granting them special status—was journalist Branimir Soucek. See Branimir Soucek, *Eine Frühlingsreise zum Gedankenfluß eines verirrten Literaten oder Gerechtigkeit für Peter Handke* (Thaur, Wien, and München: Druck- und Verlagshaus Thaur, 1996), 31.

64. Already on the first page of *WR,* one finds the word "I" four times, "my" twice, and "me" once. In the *Spiegel* version of "Impending Tragedy," the word "I" appears only six times.

65. "Handke has always had two faces: the brooder and observer buried in the world of books and landscapes and the rebel and madman ('Amokläufer') . . . Handke was always good for a surprise. Sometimes he was a bit ahead of everyone else, but sometimes he was simply way off the mark." Volker Hage, "Dichters Winterreise. Peter Handkes Serbien-Reportage und die Intellektuellen," *Der Spiegel,* no. 6, 1996, 193.

66. Handke traveled with two companions (and, for a time, with his new wife—although that was not emphasized in the text).

67. A third volume about a journey to the Albanian region Kosovo is in the works. This would be an opportunity to work through some of the narrative difficulties described above. If the second volume is any indication, though, skepticism is in order.

68. Gerhard Stadelmaier, "Zittern und sagen. Szene Deutschland: Woran ist Botho Strauß schuld? (I)," *Frankfurter Allgemeine Zeitung,* April 11, 1994; Gustav Seibt, "Echo des Bocksgesangs. Was die Rechten lasen oder Woran ist Botho Strauß schuld? (II)," *Frankfurter Allgemeine Zeitung,* April 16, 1994.

69. Even the editors of *Der Spiegel* refer to "Impending Tragedy" as a "seismography" of the "growing tragedy . . . of a present shocked by xenophobia and disorien-

tation." See "Ein Unbekannter," *Der Spiegel*, no. 6, 1993, 203.

70. Bubis's *Tagesspiegel* interview was summarized in the article "Die gewaltige Schuld" in *Der Spiegel*, no. 16, 1994, 168–170.

71. Botho Strauß, "Der eigentliche Skandal," *Der Spiegel*, no. 16, 1994, 168.

72. As was discussed above, Enzensberger and Strauß are both critical of the status quo, but they have little else in common.

73. "'Wegbereiter wie Nolte.' Ignatz Bubis erläutert seine Intellektuellen-Schelte," *Der Spiegel*, no. 16, 1994, 170.

74. It is surely not coincidental that Strauß was moved to self-reflection after viewing a production of Goethe's play *Torquato Tasso* in 1969. That play thematizes the gap between real life in society and the esthetic sphere. Strauß comments on the plight of the title figure as follows: "Maintaining the consciousness of genius while producing in reality decorations for the status of the rulers must end in debilitating confusion." Botho Strauß, *Versuch,* 166.

75. Willi Winkler, "Ist Botho Strauß ein Faschist?" *tageszeitung*, February 13, 1993.

76. Peter Glotz, "Freunde, es wird ernst," *Deutsche Literatur 1993*, 273. Originally published in *Wochenpost* of February 25, 1993.

77. Andreas Kilb, "Anschwellende Geistesfinsternis," *Die Zeit*, no. 14, 1993. Kilb's title is a play on words with an apocalyptic tone like the one for which he criticizes Strauß.

78. Hilmar Hoffmann, "Sprachverwirrungen eines Unpolitischen," *Deutsche Literatur 1993*, 279. (Note the allusion to Th. Mann's *Reflections* in the title.) Originally published in *Die Welt*, March 29, 1993. For (much) more of the same, see Michael Maar, "Das Angerichtete: Botho Strauß oder die Unfähigkeit zum Stil," *Frankfurter Allgemeine Zeitung*, March 9, 1993. Strauß was later defended by Ulrich Greiner: "No one can write so badly that he deserves all these insults." See "Die Neunundachtziger," *Deutsche Literatur 1994*, 284.

79. Klaus Kreimeier, "Wiedergänger und Nachbereiter," *Deutsche Literatur 1994*, 266–268. Originally in *Freitag*, May 13, 1994. Looking back to a generation before Benn, Gustav Seibt spoke of Strauß as something like "a caricature of Stefan George": "Leere Truhen," *Deutsche Literatur 1994*, 277. Originally published in *Frankfurter Allgemeine Zeitung*, August 20, 1994.

80. Cited in the preface to the second edition of *Die selbstbewußte Nation* (also contained in the third edition). Strauß's letter was also published in the *Frankfurter Allgemeine Zeitung* on October 27, 1994.

81. Roland Müller, "Dichter im braunen Netz," *Deutsche Literatur 1994*, 319. Originally published in the *Stuttgarter Zeitung*, December 15, 1994.

82. Peter von Becker, "Abschied von Botho Strauß . . . ," *Deutsche Literatur 1994*, 324. Originally published in *Theater heute*, no. 12, 1994.

83. Michael Wachsmann, "Was darf ein Dichter denken dürfen?" *Deutsche Literatur 1994*, 300. Originally published in *Die Woche*, January 13, 1995.

84. Dietz Bering, who hopes to use "Impending Tragedy" to motivate the left to think about the destruction of the humanities and the general crisis of education in Germany, rejects the content of *Die selbstbewußte Nation* completely. He thus counsels his readers to forget about Strauß as a person (those who reprinted his essay were "usurpers," he claims) and to concentrate on his ideals. This stance is the opposite of the one that led to the "Literature Debate": "Die linke Lehre des Bocks," *Der Spiegel*, no. 29, 1995, 149. Here Strauß appears to be a *naif* who was hoodwinked.

85. Tilmann Krause, "Der Sehnsüchtige im Fahndungsraster," *Deutsche Literatur 1994*, 301. Originally published in *Der Tagesspiegel*, September 25, 1994.

86. Bodo Kirchhoff, "Die Mandarine werden nervös," *Deutsche Literatur 1993*, 277. Originally published in *Die Zeit*, February 26, 1993.

87. Eckhard Nordhofen, "Vor der Bundeslade des Bösen," *Deutsche Literatur 1993*, 291. Originally published in *Die Zeit*, April 9, 1993.

88. Sigrid Berka, ed., *Das Werk von Botho Strauß und die 'Bocksgesang'-Debatte*, *Weimarer Beiträge* 40.2 (1994). Berka provides a bibliography of the discussion of "Impending Tragedy" at the end of her introduction (175–177). She sees the essay as an integral part of Strauß's production, albeit with a different accent: "What is new in the 'Bocksgesang'-Essay is the articulation of that which was always present in Strauß's works in hermetic, allegorical, or parabolic form. The only partial translation of the coded message into the journalistic, i.e., polemical context and thus into the political context was at its conception thus doomed to failure" (167). This is in my view a problematic definition of the role of journalism in a democratic society. Page references from the special issue of *Weimarer Beiträge* are provided in the text.

89. In the May 7, 1993, edition of *Le Monde*, Jünger is quoted as saying: "il faudra que les élites deviennent puissantes, petites et puissantes" (203). (The elites will have to become powerful, small and powerful.)

90. See Volker Hage, "Dichter nach der Schlacht," *Der Spiegel*, no. 30, 1993, 140–146. Page references are taken from the *Spiegel* version.

91. Tilman Krause, "Ein guter Hasser, der lieben will," *Der Tagesspiegel*, July 20, 1997.

92. Strauß believes, according to Krause, that it was only in the early 1960s that German intellectuals played "a decisive role in changing consciousness."

93. One example: when the *New York Times* took up the Handke story, it was described as "a full-scale literary and political uproar." This is accurate, but the reporter went on to assert—referring indirectly to the "Historians' Debate"—that "[n]othing comparable has been seen here since a decade ago." In other words, Botho Strauß and his provocative essay were simply not noticed. See Stephen Kinzer, "German Writer Sets Off Storm over Balkan War," *New York Times*, March 18, 1996. Handke's works are definitely part of German literature, but he is an Austrian.

94. "'Gelassen wär' ich gern.'" *Der Spiegel*, no. 49, 1994, 170–176. Page references in the text. The interview was conducted by Volker Hage and Mathias Schreiber.

95. "'Ich bin nicht hingegangen, um mitzuhassen. Peter Handke antwortet seinen Kritikern.'" Handke later says that anyone who thinks that his description of Serbia

is "bucolic" or "idyllic" is simply an "oaf" ("Trottel"). In this regard, the affinity with Strauß is quite apparent.

In a preface written especially for American readers, Handke emphasized that his new work was no different from anything else that he had written: "I wrote about my journey through the country of Serbia [!] exactly as I have always written my books, my literature: a slow, inquiring narration; every paragraph dealing with and narrating a problem, of representation, of form, of grammar—of aesthetic veracity; that has always been the case with what I have written, from the beginning to the final period." Peter Handke, *A Journey to the Rivers: Justice for Serbia* (New York: Viking, 1997), vii–viii. The change in the title may reflect the publisher's belief that Americans are generally not very interested in geography.

96. *Noch einmal vom Neunten Land. Peter Handke im Gespräch mit Joze Horvat* (Klagenfurt, Salzburg: Wieser Verlag, 1993), 96, 98. Page references in the text.

97. "'Nackter, blinder, blöder Wahnsinn'" (W. Reiter and C. Seiler interview Peter Handke), *profil*, no. 12 (1996), 81–83. Page references in the text. The same issue also contains an article by Wolfgang Reiter about the "Handke affair": "'Der Journalismus hat versagt,'" 76–79.

98. Peter Schneider, "Ritt über den Balkan," *Der Spiegel*, no. 3, 1996, 163. Schneider also reminds his readers that Handke—"courageously and at the time almost alone" (164)—spoke out against German recognition of an independent Croatia at the beginning of the Balkan conflict. In the letters to the editor published in no. 5, 1996, Handke is both supported and criticized. One of Handke's supporters was the well-known Austrian writer Elfriede Jelinek. Schneider was one of the European writers sent to Sarajevo in 1994 to describe conditions there for European newspaper readers. In his report, Schneider railed against European "hypocrisy" in general and German denial in particular. See Peter Schneider, "Der Sündenfall Europas," *Der Spiegel*, no. 7, 1994, 140–146.

In 1992, the Viennese daily *Der Standard* asked Handke to write a reportage about Bosnia, but the author declined. See Michael Cerha, "Anregung einer gemeinsamen Erinnerung," *Der Standard*, March 20, 1996. Handke did, however, write an article for the Paris daily *Libération* ("My Slovenia in Yugoslavia," August 22, 1991) in which he denied that Serbia was oppressing the other ethnic groups in Yugoslavia. This article is mentioned in Mariam Niroumand, "Ils ne regrettent rien. Frankreichs Intellektuelle über ihr Engagement für Bosnien," *tageszeitung*, September 18, 1996.

99. It is perhaps not coincidental that Handke uses this word as a means of depersonalization, just as Strauß does in "Impending Tragedy" (see above). This is clearly not what one would expect from a sensitive artist and self-appointed peace ambassador. See *Winter Journey*, 47.

100. Andreas Kilb, "Das Neunte Land," *Die Zeit*, no. 4, 1996.

101. Michael Thumann, "Das andere Serbien," *Die Zeit*, no. 4, 1996.

102. Willi Winkler, "Am Stammtisch zum ewigen Krieg," *Deutsche Literatur 1996*, 289–290. Originally published in the *tageszeitung*, January 19, 1996.

103. Michael Scharang, "Erfahrung schrecklicher Fremdheit," *Der Standard*, January 24, 1996. This text was later reprinted in the German journal *konkret*, no. 3 (1996), 50–51.

104. Peter Vujica, "Ein Elfenbeinturm im Kreuzfeuer," *Der Standard*, February 3–4, 1996.

105. "'Lassen wir Peter Handke ein bißchen träumen.' Gespräch mit dem serbischen Schriftsteller Aleksandar Tisma," *Die Welt*, September 27, 1996.

106. Luc Rosenzweig, "Handke avocat pro-serbe," *Le Monde*, January 19, 1996. Quoted from excerpts published in the *Süddeutsche Zeitung*, January 27, 1996.

107. The discussion took place on March 19, 1996. The comments by Turrini and Handke were excerpted in "Die vierte Lesung und immer dasselbe," *Der Standard*, March 20, 1996. Already in 1995, Turrini had expressed sympathy with the viewpoints of Strauß and Handke, but not without reservations with regard to the former: "[T]he political right that he and others are getting close to has in the end just speculated about violence. The intellectual curiosity of the German rightists was always minimal, but the desire to murder great. It [the right] has never put up a program of thinking, but rather a program of acting—of violence. Sooner or later, any writer who sympathizes with the rightists will be hit on the head by rightists who are not at all sympathetic to him." See "'Wir sind explosive Wesen'" (Interview with Peter Turrini), *Der Spiegel*, no. 18, 1995, 196.

108. Reported by Rainer Stephan, "Zwischenzeit. Handke, umnachtet," *Der Standard*, March 26, 1996.

109. Reported by Peter Paul Wiplinger, "'Ein Affentheater, das die Würde des Hauses verletzt,'" *Der Standard*, May 29, 1996. For more on the anal tradition, see Alan Dundes, *Life Is Like a Chicken Coop Ladder: A Portrait of German Culture through Folklore* (New York: Columbia University Press, 1984). The title of the German edition is a bit different: *Sie mich auch! Das Hinter-Gründige in der deutschen Psyche* (München: Deutscher Taschenbuch Verlag, 1985).

110. Reported by Bernhard Küppers, "Die Angst des Publikums vor der Beschimpfung," *Süddeutsche Zeitung*, June 5, 1996. Küppers's title recalls the title of the early Handke play "Publikumsbeschimpfung" ("Insulting the Audience").

111. Gustav Seibt, "Wahn von Krieg und Blut und Boden," *Frankfurter Allgemeine Zeitung*, January 16, 1996. Quoted from excerpts reprinted in the *Süddeutsche Zeitung*, January 27, 1996.

112. Marcus Pucnik, "Die Beleidigung der Opfer," *Der Standard*, January 29, 1996. A lawyer friend of Pucnik's told him that there were only two explanations for Handke's "Schreibtischtätertum," either that he was crazy ("ein Spinner") or trying to increase his market value by starting a nonsensical discussion.

113. Wolfgang Müller-Funk, "Perspektivische Blindheit," *Der Standard*, February 10–11, 1996. Müller-Funk sees in Handke a mixture of naiveté and inflexibility.

114. Reinhard Mohr, "Eine böse Harmonie," *Der Spiegel*, no. 12, 1996, 217. Mohr actually calls Handke not a prophet, but a "charlatan."

115. Rainer Stephan (see note 108) called Handke a fitting "guru" for the "irrationalist gang."

116. "'Es gibt kein literarisches Leben'" (Interview with Gustav Seibt), *tageszeitung*, October 12, 1996.

117. Seibt makes a point of saying that he is not critical of the role that his predecessor Frank Schirrmacher played in the "Literature Debate."

118. Tilman Zülch, ed., *Die Angst des Dichters vor der Wirklichkeit* (Göttingen: Steidl, 1996). Page references in the body of the text.

After this study was completed, a new collection of material on the Handke/Serbia controversy appeared in Germany: Thomas Deichmann, ed., *Noch einmal für Jugoslawien: Peter Handke* (Frankfurt am Main: Suhrkamp, 1999).

119. See Peter Schneider, *Lenz* ([West-]Berlin: Rotbuch, 1973), 79.

120. Grass has always treated historical and political themes in his works, and his political activity was tied for years to the left wing of the Social Democratic Party. Unlike Handke, he has never been a "politicized poet." He is a writer engaged with the society in which he lives. One may criticize his engagement, but not because it is one undertaken by a writer.

121. Caspary's own sense of history is a questionable one, since Handke describes not only homemade bread and home-brewed drinks, but also the necessity of filling gasoline tanks from plastic canisters—hardly a "medieval" activity.

122. Even Volker Hage, who defended Christa Wolf during the "Literature Debate" and, as we have seen, empathized with Strauß, has become impatient with Handke's posturing: "How naive can a writer in the prime of life ("im reifen Mannesalter") be?" "Dichters Winterreise. Peter Handkes Serbien-Reportage und die Intellektuellen," *Der Spiegel*, no. 6, 1996, 190.

123. Compare this to the recent statement by theater director Claus Peymann, who took over Brecht's Berliner Ensemble in 1999: "Theater must be a place for political debates. . . . Theater keeps an eye on the powerful and speaks for the powerless." Cited in "Peymann kündigt politisches Theater für Berliner Ensemble an," dpa/eu dispatch distributed by the online service *Germany Live* on May 1, 1998.

124. Dzevad Karahasan, "Bürger Handke, Serbenvolk," *Die Angst des Dichters*, 53. Further page references in the text. Karahasan's analysis was first published in *Die Zeit*, no. 8, 1996.

125. Karahasan claims that Handke does not know "a single word" of the languages spoken in the area. He deduces this from the fact that Handke needs a dictionary. Actually, the author read aloud (for forty-five minutes!) parts of the Serbian translation of *Winter Journey* in Serbian when he visited Belgrade. This was reported by Andrej Ivanji in his article "Belgrad feiert Peter Handke," *Der Standard*, May 18–19, 1996.

126. This passage was misprinted in the book version—the preposition "of" ("von") was omitted. The problem might be the translation into German. I say "examples of" because the German phrase "Beiträge von" is incorrect. It would have to read either "contributions to" ("Beiträge zu") or examples of ("Beispiele für").

For an ethically based view of the Balkan conflict, see the book by American Peter Maass, *Love Thy Neighbor: A Story of War* (New York: Knopf, 1996). Compare Maass's description of Visegrad (8-15) with that of Handke (*Summer Supplement*, 30-60).

127. Marcel Ophuls, "Die Wut. Eine Antwort auf Peter Handkes Artikel 'Gerechtigkeit für Serbien,'" *Die Angst des Dichters*, 38. Originally published in the *tageszeitung*, January 22, 1996.

128. André Glucksmann, "Du bist ein Terrorist," *Süddeutsche Zeitung*, January 27, 1996. Excerpts from an article/interview printed in *Corriere della Sera* on January 6, 1996.

129. For insight into Grass's view of the Enlightenment, see his contributions to the symposium *Der Traum der Vernunft. Vom Elend der Aufklärung*, Eine Veranstaltungsreihe der Akademie der Künste, Berlin, 2 vols. (Darmstadt und Neuwied: Luchterhand, 1985-1986). In his speech "Der Traum der Vernunft," Grass sounds like an advocate for the "third path" between "a capitalism producing misery" and "a Communism ruling by force," 1:7. In his introductory remarks in the second volume, he mentions Gottfried Benn's "cowardly cynicism" (8).

130. In his rather positive review, Volker Hage takes it as a given that it is no longer possible to write a cohesive text with a clear structure. See "Vor allem die Liebe," *Der Spiegel*, no. 32, 1994, 158.

131. Botho Strauß, *Das Gleichgewicht* (München and Wien: Hanser, 1993). Page references in the body of the text.

132. Reported by Volker Hage in "Dichter nach der Schlacht," *Der Spiegel*, no. 30, 1993, 143. In the same article, it is reported that Claus Peymann, the then director of the Vienna Burgtheater, found the play a bit too nationalistic ("Das Stück riecht ein bißchen sehr nach Schwarz-Weiß-Rot."). Hage himself is amazed by Peymann's remark, as he views *Equilibrium* as "almost a summery play . . . devoid of the mystical" (143-146).

133. *Equilibrium* was not a great success in the former East Germany. Its diction was apparently too Westernized, too postmaterialistic for those whose lives of necessity continue to revolve around the basics of everyday life. See Ronald Richter, "Zen oder Die Kunst des hohen Klagetons," *Theater der Zeit*, July-August 1995, 66-68.

Not everyone in the West was enthusiastic, either. One well-known critic called *Equilibrium* "a mediocre play against mediocrity in society and art." See C. Bernd Sucher, "Gemogelt—und gewonnen. 'Das Gleichgewicht' von Botho Strauß in München," *Süddeutsche Zeitung*, October 5, 1996.

134. Reported by Sibylle Ahlers, "Die Odyssee, entstaubt und in 21 Happen," *Die Welt*, August 19, 1996. The American television version, which was broadcast in 1997, assumed no previous knowledge and reduced much of Homer's images to the level of comic books.

135. Botho Strauß, *Ithaka. Schauspiel nach den Heimkehr-Gesängen der Odyssee* (München and Wien: Hanser, 1996). Page references in the text.

136. See Wolfgang Höbel, "Ende einer Dienstfahrt," *Der Spiegel*, no. 30 (1996), 150. The title of this article is an allusion to a 1966 novel by Heinrich Böll about the

burning of a Bundeswehr jeep. The reference is meant to contrast Böll's pacifism with Strauß's alleged glorification of war.

137. It is ironic that the antimaterialist Strauß should echo Marx by using this phrase. Compare the following passage from Marx about the culture of ancient Greece: "Why should the historical childhood of humanity, where it had obtained its most beautiful development, not exert an eternal charm as an age that will never return?" Karl Marx, *Introduction to the Critique of Political Economy*, excerpted in *Marx and Engels on Literature and Art*, ed. Lee Baxandall and Stefan Morawski (St. Louis and Milwaukee: Telos Press, 1973), 135.

138. One observer reports that Strauß decided to work on an adaptation of the *Odyssey* after it was proposed to him by Swedish director Ingmar Bergman. See Peter Iden, "Wiederholung, Teilhabe, Erinnerung," *Deutsche Literatur 1996*, 97. Originally published in *Frankfurter Rundschau*, July 22, 1996.

139. Playwright Gerhart Hauptmann covered similar ground in his 1914 drama *Der Bogen des Odysseus* (Odysseus's bow). The early Hauptmann had been a naturalist interested in social problems. His "turn" was somewhat like that of Strauß.

140. Penelope is capable of resisting "the sirens of slime and passion" herself, but Odysseus must be tied to his ship's mast when passing by the Sirens and hearing their seductive song (14).

141. This reaction was quite clear when I attended a performance of the play at Berlin's Deutsches Theater in September 1997.

142. C. Bernd Sucher, "Zeige mir, Muse, die Gedanken, nicht Bilder nur!" *Süddeutsche Zeitung*, July 22, 1996.

143. Wolfgang Höbel (see note 136), 151.

144. Rolf Michaelis, "Der Bogen des Botho," *Die Zeit*, no. 31, 1996.

145. See the dpa dispatch "Bruno Ganz gefeierter Star in 'Ithaka' — Fast ungeteilte Zustimmung," July 21, 1996. The dispatch was distributed by *Germany Live*.

146. Gerhard Stadelmaier, "König Kinderleicht," *Frankfurter Allgemeine Zeitung*, July 22, 1996. In his review of the later Berlin production, Stadelmaier stated categorically that *Ithaka* is "not a drama of kingship . . . not a political play." See "König Schinderleicht oder Die Spaßarbeit am Mythos," *Frankfurter Allgemeine Zeitung*, April 7, 1997. In the Berlin theater program, one finds the following quotation (selected by Strauß) from Nicolás Gómez Dávila: "The reactionary is the guardian of the heritage. / Even of the heritage of the revolutionary." *Botho Strauß: Ithaka* (Berlin: Deutsches Theater und Kammerspiele, 1997), 25.

147. Richard Herzinger, "Die Rückkehr der romantischen Moderne," *Theater heute*, no. 8 (1996), 7. Further page references in the text.

148. See the following reviews of the premiere in Berlin: C. Bernd Sucher, "Das Weib als Wasserleiche und Weltanschauung," *Süddeutsche Zeitung*, April 23, 1998; Klaus Dermutz, "Ein Leben ohne Wahl," *Frankfurter Rundschau*, April 23, 1998; Günther Grack, "Von fern bellt der Welthund Hitler," *Der Tagesspiegel*, April 23,

1998; Reinhard Wengierek, "Ohnmenschliche Schönheit," *Die Welt,* April 23, 1998; Petra Kohse, "Aus dem Zwielicht ins Dunkel," *tageszeitung,* April 23, 1998; "Buhrufe für Botho Strauß' neues Stück 'Jeffers—Akt I und II,'" dpa dispatch, April 22, 1998 (distributed by *Germany Live*).

149. Eric Bentley gives Jeffers only a passing reference in his study *A Century of Hero Worship,* 2nd ed. (Boston: Beacon Press, 1957), 3. For a sympathetic portrayal of Jeffers, see Radcliffe Squires, *The Loyalties of Robinson Jeffers* (1956; Ann Arbor: University of Michigan Press, 1963). Squires's readers are called upon to make a leap of faith: "Eventually, when people cease to take his [Jeffers's] impersonal view of the species *homo sapiens* as an assault on humanity, he will be seen as one of our master poets" (vii). Another critic will have us believe that "the question whether Jeffers is pessimist or misanthropist . . . is really of no importance whatever." See William H. Nolte, *Rock and Hawk: Robinson Jeffers and the Romantic Agony* (Athens: University of Georgia Press, 1978), 15. For a broad selection of Jeffers's verse, see *The Selected Poetry of Robinson Jeffers* (New York: Random House, 1937). In his introduction, Jeffers compares his hideaway near California's Monterrey coast mountains to "Homer's Ithaca" (xvi). If Strauß adapted the *Odyssey,* he was following in the footsteps of Jeffers, who produced a verse adaptation of Euripides' *Medea* in 1946. See Robinson Jeffers, *Cawdor and Medea* (New York: New Directions, 1970).

150. Compare Martin Heidegger's lament: "Perhaps never before was the necessity of the *pure work* [i.e., œuvre] greater than today and in the future—for never before was the deforming and destructive force of announcing and chatting, of extolling and noise, of the addiction to spiritual dissection and dissolution greater and more unimpeded and more conscious than [it is] today. How much and [how] surely one succumbs to the illusion that one has comprehended and taken possession of the *work* if one knows the 'letters' and utterances of its creator and his psychology," "Ein Rückblick auf den Weg" (1937-38), *Besinnung,* Gesamtausgabe, vol. 66 (Frankfurt am Main: Klostermann, 1997), 416.

151. Botho Strauß, *Die Fehler des Kopisten* (München and Wien: Hanser, 1997). Page references in the text.

152. Willi Winkler, "Ich bin der Haß. Der Dichter Botho Strauß als Photoroman," *Süddeutsche Zeitung,* April 16, 1997.

153. "Wenn der Vater mit dem Sohne," *Der Spiegel,* no. 16, 1997, 192-193; Botho Strauß, "Wo der Geist Knecht ist," 194-200. Here are some reviews of the book: Ronald Pohl, "Die Firma Botho Strauß und Sohn," *Der Standard,* May 5, 1997; Hellmuth Karasek, "Ein Paar ohne Passanten," *Der Tagesspiegel,* April 24, 1997; Jörg Magenau, "Wege des Berührten," *tageszeitung,* April 26, 1997.

154. In his newest play, *Die Ähnlichen* (*The Similar Ones*), which had its premiere in the summer of 1998, people have become indistinguishable "androids." See Ronald Pohl, "Das Menschen-Ballett der Androiden," *Der Standard,* May 2-3, 1998. In *The Copyist's Errors,* these creatures are described as technical intellectuals who may eventually eliminate all of the problematic and yet enriching aspects ("consolation, desperation . . . , reflection and blind rage") from life (55). It may be that Strauß is

not offering these glimpses into his private life to the masses, but rather to the "second-class intellectuals," whose number, he claims, has grown tremendously. See *The Copyist's Errors*, 88.

155. Peter Handke, *Zurüstungen für die Unsterblichkeit. Ein Königsdrama* (Frankfurt am Main: Suhrkamp, 1997). Page references from this edition in the text.

156. The program for the performance at Berlin's Deutsches Theater has the following words printed on its back cover: "Remain true to the words of your childhood; / every other word would be false." *Peter Handke. Zurüstungen für die Unsterblichkeit. Ein Königsdrama* (Berlin: Deutsches Theater und Kammerspiele, 1997).

The Deutsches Theater marketed the plays by Handke and Strauß as a weekend package in fall, 1997. Participants in the "Strauß Handke Wochenende: Die Rückkehr der Könige II" had the opportunity to not only attend performances of the two plays on successive evenings, but also to hear a lecture by a professor, hear readings of other works by the two authors, and discuss the productions with the ensemble.

157. Peter Handke, *Mein Jahr in der Niemandsbucht — Ein Märchen aus den Neuen Zeiten* (Frankfurt am Main: Suhrkamp, 1994).

158. Ulrich Greiner, "Die ganze Welt, das ganze Leben," *Die Zeit*, no. 49, 1994.

159. The character Felipe Vega in *Preparations* refers to himself as a "Taugenichts," i.e., a good-for-nothing (79). Handke is of course familiar with Eichendorff's famous 1826 novel *Aus dem Leben eines Taugenichts*.

160. "'Gelassen wär' ich gern.' Der Schriftsteller Peter Handke über sein neues Werk, über Sprache, Politik und Erotik," *Der Spiegel*, no. 49, 1994, 170.

161. It is the women's father who says this of his "idiotic" (9) daughters, who confirm its accuracy later. Why Handke felt the need to include such sarcasm is unclear.

162. In German leftist culture, this sentiment is reflected in the popular bumper sticker "Foreigners! Don't leave us alone with the Germans!" (Ausländer! Laßt uns mit den Deutschen nicht allein!) Space permitting, it would be interesting to discuss how the purchasers of that bumper sticker explain to themselves and others that they are not "German." The New Right intellectuals would surely wish to participate in such a discussion.

163. This is a favorite term of Handke's ("Zwischenräume") denoting the spaces between "normal" perceptions that are the homeland of the writer. See the volume *"Aber ich lebe nur von den Zwischenräumen." Peter Handke im Gespräch mit Herbert Gamper* (Zürich: Ammann, 1987).

164. See the recent scholarly book on the ideology of childhood: Yvonne-Patricia Alefeld, *Die Kindheitsideologie in der Romantik* (Paderborn: Schöningh, 1996). In his review of this book, Karl Menges states the following: "Childhood utopia . . . coincides with poetic visions of the sovereignty of the poet who, incidentally, does not retreat from the world but embraces it with an advanced consciousness that combines 'universal' Romantic sensuality with contemporary (Kantian) transcendentalism." The review appeared in *Monatshefte* 90.1 (Spring 1998): 111–112.

165. Why must this be stated and repeated in both German and Spanish?

244 /// Notes to Chapter 3

("Traum und Arbeit. Arbeit und Traum. Sueño y trabajo. Trabajo y sueño.") This is, once again, excess ballast. Similarly, why must we be told that the storyteller's festive garb is that of a "Landarbeiterin oder labradora" (66)?

166. She does repeatedly say how "ugly" the Space Eliminators are, and she systematically goes about erasing their ugliness (102-103). Antinoos (see above) used the same word in *Ithaka*.

167. One critic described *Preparations* as a mixture of fairy tales, the magic plays ("Zauberstücke") of the Austrian *Biedermeier*, the *commedia dell'arte*, and Samuel Beckett. The eclecticism apparently did not disturb him, since he spoke of "the production of the year." See Lothar Schmidt-Mulisch, "Abenteuer im Zaubergarten der Phantasie," *Die Welt*, February 10, 1997. In the fall of 1997, this observer found the Berlin production of *Preparations* absolutely deadening. The mass of verbiage overwhelmed the audience in the Deutsches Theater.

168. Thomas Assheuer, "Die Ornamente der Ordnung," *Die Zeit*, no. 10, 1997. Assheuer actually uses the term "scandalous" to describe the essays.

169. Wolfgang Höbel, "Sag dem König leise Servus," *Der Spiegel*, no. 8, 1997, 210-211; "'Die Banalität bestimmt das Bewußtsein.' Claus Peymann über Wien, Berlin, und seine Liebe zu den Dichtern," *Der Spiegel*, no. 8, 1997, 211-214.

170. Ronald Pohl, "Zurüstungen für die Verlängerung" [Interview with Claus Peymann], *Der Standard*, February 6, 1997.

171. Benjamin Henrichs, "Ein Königreich für ein Kind," *Die Zeit*, no. 8, 1997. See the similar formulation in note 65.

172. Dietmar N. Schmidt, "Bald wird kaum einer noch wissen, wer Schiller war," *Die Welt*, May 12, 1997. Another critic discovered a quite different similarity: both plays, he said, were "boring" and (especially in the case of Handke) "sickeningly German" ("zum Kotzen deutsch"). See Lorenz Tomerius, "'Zurüstungen' als Zumutungen," *Der Standard*, June 17, 1997.

173. Gerhard Stadelmaier, "König Schinderleicht . . ." (see note 146).

174. Peter von Becker, "Unser aller Mitternachtsblues?" *Der Tagesspiegel*, June 17, 1997.

175. Thomas Assheuer, "Die Ornamente der Ordnung" (see note 168). Richard Herzinger (see note 147) portrays the author of *Ithaka* as the major heir of Ernst Jünger. See Strauß's own paean to Jünger, "Refrain einer tieferen Aufklärung," *Magie der Heiterkeit. Ernst Jünger zum Hundertsten*, ed. Günter Figal and Heimo Schwilk (Stuttgart: Klett-Cotta, 1995), 323-324. Strauß asserts here that Jünger is becoming a prototype of the art of the future for the younger generations, an art that will replace the "subversive radical, the Jacobin-'Hölderlinian' hero of the age" (324).

176. C. Bernd Sucher, "Aus dem Königreich der Kunst in die Welt," *Süddeutsche Zeitung*, February 10, 1997.

177. Peter Handke, *In einer dunklen Nacht ging ich aus meinem stillen Haus* (Frankfurt am Main: Suhrkamp, 1997).

178. Peter Handke, *Am Felsfenster morgens und andere Ortszeiten 1982–1987* (Salzburg and Wien: Residenz, 1998).

Notes to Excursus

1. Theodor Fontane, *Der Stechlin* (1898; Leipzig: Reclam, 1973), 323. [34. Kapitel.] The title character in this novel is a traditional conservative who does not automatically reject anything that is new.

2. See Klaus Schwabe, "Anti-Americanism within the German Right 1917–1933," *Amerikastudien* 21.1 (1976):89–107.

3. Rudolf Kayser, "Americanism," *The Weimar Republic Sourcebook*, 395. The text originally appeared in the *Vossische Zeitung* (Theodor Fontane's sometime employer!) on September 27, 1925.

4. Johann Wolfgang Goethe, "Den Vereinigten Staaten," *Gedichte — Versepen*, ed. Walter Höllerer, *Werke* (Frankfurt am Main: Insel, 1965), 1:224.

5. Stefan Zweig, "The Monotonization of the World," *The Weimar Republic Sourcebook*, 398–399. Originally published in the *Berliner Börsen-Courier*, February 1, 1925. Ironically, Rudolf Kayser had not seen America when he enthused about its merits.

6. The elites invented derogatory terms for such diversions: "Schmutz und Schund, Hintertreppenroman, Kitsch, Gassenhauer, Traumfabrik; pulp fiction, dime novel, soap opera, trashy literature; camelote, toc, littérature de bas étage, littérature de gare, etc." See Kaspar Maase, *Grenzenloses Vergnügen. Der Aufstieg der Massenkultur 1850–1970* (Frankfurt am Main: Fischer, 1997), 27.

7. "The *Bildungsbürgertum* as a hegemonial social stratum may have died off. However, the *Bildungsbürger*, in his ethos and habits dedicated to knowledge and cultural experience, lives on. And here's to him!" Tilman Krause, "Ohne Arbeit kein Genuß," *Der Tagesspiegel*, October 25, 1996. Krause credits these people for helping to transcend the gap between high and low culture, overcoming nationalistic narrow-mindedness (by often traveling abroad), and combining a sense of esthetics with the work ethic and a capacity to broaden one's horizons. This portrait applies more to the liberal *Bildungsbürger* than his conservative counterpart.

8. Botho Strauß, *Beginnlosigkeit. Reflexionen über Fleck und Linie* (München and Wien: Hanser, 1992), 122.

9. Ina Hartwig, "Politik und Landschaft. Über die Veränderung eines Motivs bei Peter Handke," *Frankfurter Rundschau*, April 25, 1998. In fall 1997, Peter Schneider returned from a nine-month stay in Washington, D.C., as a Woodrow Wilson Fellow. His published comments on the nature of U.S. society are astonishingly naïve. "Das mutlose Land," *Der Spiegel*, no. 46, 1997, 59–67 and "Sie irren, ich bin typisch deutsch" (interview with Peter Schneider), *Der Tagesspiegel*, October 7, 1997.

10. Richard Pells, *Not Like Us: How Europeans Have Loved, Hated, and Transformed American Culture Since World War II* (New York: Basic Books, 1997), xiv, 41, 239. In the fall of 1997, Prof. Pells was a Fulbright American Studies professor at the Universität Bonn. In an article entitled "Cinéma Vérité in Europe: Rejecting U.S. Culture" (*International Herald Tribune*, December 16, 1997), he described how European students reacted to his book and lectures. He was disappointed about "European youth's continuing apathy to the marketplace mentality of American culture" and observed that the "hostile attitudes" of students were still linked to "a Marxist analysis of capitalism." Although he hoped that his audiences would still "grow up to be dedicated capitalists," he stated that "policymakers in London, Paris, and Bonn have failed to convince large numbers of people crucial to the future economic health of Europe that the American model is worth following." (He should have known that it is dangerous to make generalizations about all of Europe on the basis of encounters with students interested in the humanities, who are hardly a representative group in Europe or the U.S.) The *IHT* printed highly critical letters responding to Pells's laments on December 19 and 24–25.

For other material on postwar reeducation, see the following: James F. Tent, *Mission on the Rhine: Reeducation and Denazification in American-Occupied Germany* (Chicago and London: The University of Chicago Press, 1982), and Nicholas Pronay and Keith Wilson, eds., *The Political Re-Education of Germany and Her Allies after World War II* (Totowa, N.J.: Barnes and Noble Books, 1985).

11. Rob Kroes, *If You've Seen One, You've Seen the Mall: Europeans and American Mass Culture* (Urbana and Chicago: University of Illinois Press, 1996), 178. In Kroes's view, European intellectuals "turned feelings of envy and inferiority toward America, the country that had twice saved Europe from its worst excesses, into a sense of intellectual superiority" (182).

12. Kroes, *If You've Seen*, 173.

13. Roger Rollin, "Introduction. On Comparative Popular Culture, American Style," *The Americanization of the Global Village*, ed. Roger Rollin (Bowling Green, Ohio: Bowling Green State University Popular Press, 1989), 1.

14. Rollin, "Introduction," 2.

15. Stephen Haseler, *The Varieties of Anti-Americanism: Reflex and Response* (Washington, D.C.: Ethics and Public Policy Center, 1985), 21. Another book in the same series is Uwe Siemon-Netto's *On the Brink: The Myth of German Anti-Americanism*.

16. Paul Hollander, *Anti-Americanism: Critiques at Home and Abroad 1965–1990* (New York, Oxford: Oxford University Press, 1992), xi. Hollander mentions the "tradition of romantic anti-modernism" as one reason behind the German critique of the American model (383).

17. Hollander, *Anti-Americanism*, 468. My emphasis.

18. For some Germans, the possibility has already become reality. One study done for the European Commission shows that there are now approximately 490,000 homeless people in reunified Germany. See Henning Lohse, "Deutschland hat die

meisten Obdachlosen. Hier lebt fast jeder zweite wohnungslose Europäer—Immer mehr jungen Leuten fehlt ein Dach über dem Kopf," *Die Welt*, October 21, 1995.

19. Dan Diner, *Verkehrte Welten. Antiamerikanismus in Deutschland. Ein historischer Essay* (Frankfurt am Main: Eichborn, 1993). The citations above are taken from the American translation: *America in the Eyes of the Germans: An Essay on Anti-Americanism*, with an introduction by Sander L. Gilman (Princeton: Markus Wiener, 1996). One wonders to what extent Diner shares Gilman's view of the Germans as expressed in the introduction: "the Nazi identity, accepted by most, internalized *by all*; . . . the socialist identity of the GDR, prized by few, accepted by most" (xvii). (My emphasis.)

20. See for example the following two volumes edited by Diner: *Ist der National-sozialismus Geschichte? Zu Historisierung und Historikerstreit* (Frankfurt am Main: Fischer, 1987); *Zivilisationsbruch. Denken nach Auschwitz* (Frankfurt am Main: Fischer, 1988).

21. Together with Armin Mohler, Schrenck-Notzing founded the right-wing journal *Criticón* in 1970.

22. It is interesting to contrast this analysis with another observer's comment that in France, anti-Semitism and *anti-intellectualism* are "never far apart." [My emphasis.] See Jeremy Jennings, "Of Treason, Blindness and Silence. Dilemmas of the Intellectual in Modern France," *Intellectuals in Politics: From the Dreyfus Affair to Salman Rushdie*, ed. Jeremy Jennnings and Anthony Kemp-Welch (London and New York: Routledge, 1997), 69. In France, many intellectuals are highly critical of American mass culture, and not a few of these intellectuals are Jewish.

23. See Rolf Winter, *Ami go home. Plädoyer für den Abschied von einem gewalttäti-gen Land* (Hamburg: Rasch und Röhring, 1989).

24. This passage is taken from the essay "Über die Schwierigkeiten, ein Inländer zu sein," *Deutschland, Deutschland unter anderem. Äußerungen zur Politik* (Frankfurt am Main: Suhrkamp, 1968), 12.

25. See for example the following: "Der neue Kulturnationalismus," *Die Zeit*, no. 34, 1993; (with Hannes Stein) "Hiroschima gleich Auschwitz?" *Der Spiegel*, no. 31, 1995, 146–149; "Die Moral als Sahnehäubchen," *Die Zeit*, no. 40, 1996; "In der Gemeinschaftsfalle," *Die Zeit*, no. 15, 1997; "Böse ist das Nicht-Denken," *Der Tagesspiegel*, July 22, 1997; "Gutmenschen in Talkshow-gewittern," *Der Tagesspiegel*, September 19, 1997. See also Herzinger's memorial essay for Isaiah Berlin, "Wider die Einhegung der Freiheit," *Der Tagesspiegel*, November 9, 1997.

26. Richard Herzinger and Hannes Stein, *Endzeit-Propheten oder Die Offensive der Antiwestler* (Reinbek: Rowohlt, 1995). Page references in the body of the text. Herzinger was born in 1955, Stein in 1965, making both of them representatives of post-1968 generations.

27. Herzinger and Stein provide a German translation of this passage. This is my retranslation back in to English.

28. Among the targets are Rousseau, Herder, Fichte, Novalis, Nietzsche, Georges Sorel, Oswald Spengler, Moeller van den Bruck, Carl Schmitt, Martin Heidegger,

Ernst Jünger, Arnold Gehlen, Ernst Nolte, Rudolf Bahro, Christa Wolf, Heiner Müller, Günter Grass, Edgar Reitz (and his epic film *Heimat*), Botho Strauß, Alice Schwarzer, Luise Rinser, Simone de Beauvoir, Frantz Fanon, Jacques Derrida, Alain de Benoist, Alexander Solzhenitsyn, Eugen Drewermann, Louis Farrakhan, Patrick Buchanan, and even German-American Germanist Jost Hermand.

Herzinger and Stein deny that they "throw cultural-elitist hotheads, cold-blooded intellectual historical revisionists and extremist murders into one pot." They are, they assert, merely interested in the "common ferment around which a new discourse is being formed in Europe" (17). In the book, they are anything but disinterested analysts.

29. Israel is not described as a "paradise on earth" (42)—discrimination against Palestinian Israelis and the torture of prisoners is criticized—but its status as an "open society" is emphasized. The authors are pleased that the original Zionist dream of creating the "new man" and realizing socialism in the desert (43) did not succeed.

In another passage, the relationship between the U.S. and Israel is reversed: "The fundamental American idea, universalism, is a necessary consequence of Jewish monotheism" (39).

30. The authors relate a joke told by Allen: He never attends a performance of a Wagnerian opera, because afterwards, he always feels "an irresistible urge to march into Poland" (69). This retelling speaks volumes about the authors' relationship to German culture.

31. Herzinger and Stein sound like Goldhagen (whose book appeared a year after their own) when they say the following: "National Socialism . . . was the most extreme, the most extremist culmination of a project anchored deep in German intellectual history" (167).

32. Roland Bubik (cf. *Die selbstbewußte Nation*) might have been the real-life model for this passage. In a 1996 interview, a former comrade described his life style: "Bubik as the big anti-Americanist eats at McDonald's every day, and his brand of cigarettes is Western. That's what I never have been able to understand about Bubik—how he can write these articles and live very differently." "Auf eine Art wollte ich Ernst machen" (Interview with Gerlinde Gronow), *tageszeitung*, June 8, 1996.

33. A very different interpretation of this world is found in Ariel Dorfman, *How to Read Donald Duck: Imperialist Ideology in the Disney Comic* (New York: International General, 1975). The title of the Spanish original is *Para leer al Pato Donald*.

34. Their image of the U.S. needs updating, however. They seem to think that the civil rights movement has removed all obstacles to a race-blind society, and they have the impression that multiculturalism has been accepted by almost everyone (108–109).

35. There is of course a historical dimension to the Herzinger/Stein position as well. It has been said of earlier critics of modern Germany that "[a]bove all, these men loathed liberalism." See Fritz Stern, *The Politics of Cultural Despair: A Study in the Rise of the Germanic Ideology* (Garden City: Anchor Books, 1965), 2. Stern is referring to Lagarde, Langbehn, and Moeller van den Bruck. His own position is clear: "As moralists and as the guardians of what they thought was an ancient tradition, they attacked the *progress*

of modernity— the growing power of liberalism and secularism" (1; my emphasis).

Herzinger himself has published a longer work on the nature of liberalism. See Richard Herzinger, *Die Tyrannei des Gemeinsinns. Ein Bekenntnis zur egoistischen Gesellschaft* (Berlin: Rowohlt, 1997). The title is characteristically tongue in cheek.

36. Gustav Sichelschmidt, *Deutschland— eine amerikanische Provinz. Der große Seelenmord* (Berg: VGB-Verlagsgesellschaft, 1996). Page references in the body of the text.

37. Sichelschmidt (b. 1913), a retired librarian, is the author of over sixty books. He is a member of the editorial staff of the right-wing journal *Nation. Das politische Magazin für Deutschland.* He has been characterized as a "neofascist journalist" (see *Antifaschistische Nachrichten* 4[1998]). Among his books are *Verblöden die Deutschen? Analyse und Bilanz eines Niveauabstiegs* (Herford: Nicolai, 1969) and *Deutschland verblödet. Wem nutzt der dumme Deutsche?* (Kiel: Arndt-Verlag, 1995). Both books lament German culture's descent into mediocrity. See also *Der ewige Deutschenhaß. Hintermänner und Nutznießer des Antigermanismus* (Kiel: Arndt, 1992) and his study of patriotic literature: *Verschwiegen und vergessen. Nationale deutsche Autoren im 20. Jahrhundert* (Berg: VGB-Verlagsgesellschaft, 1997). His publisher VGB is categorized as "right-wing extremist" by the German Office for the Protection of the Constitution. Sichelschmidt has also written for the *Deutsche National-Zeitung,* published by the DVU's Gerhard Frey. See Jens Mecklenburg, ed., *Antifa Reader. Antifaschistisches Handbuch und Ratgeber* (Berlin: Elefanten Press, 1996) 127.

38. Heimo Schwilk, *Was man uns verschwieg. Der Golfkrieg in der Zensur* (Frankfurt am Main, Berlin: Ullstein, 1991). Page references in the body of the text. Ullstein was also the publisher of *Die selbstbewußte Nation.*

39. It is instructive to compare the rhetorical styles of a Schwilk and a Sichelschmidt, however. Whereas the former portrays General Schwarzkopf as a cynic (120), the latter says that he is "equipped with the belly of an oil sheik and the jaw of a professional brawler" (113). This does not necessarily mean that Schwilk is more familiar with the U.S. He refers to CBS as the "Central Broadcasting Service" (67) and calls the commanding general "Stormy [instead of Stormin'] Norman" (120).

40. This stance is changing ever so slowly, as evidenced by the debate in the Green Party about using the Bundeswehr, or at least air support and medical teams, in Bosnia. In 1999, the SPD-Green coalition government survived a heated debate about whether to send German ground troops to Kosovo. The debate did leave deep divisions within the Greens, however.

41. This word is part of the title of yet another recent book condemning the U.S.: Karlheinz Deschner, *Der Moloch. Eine kritische Geschichte der U.S.A.* [The moloch: a critical history of the USA] (München: Heyne, 1992). Deschner explains how he came to write such a book: "I never had thought of writing a history of the United States, even though I had occasionally concerned myself with the topic while pursuing other projects. It was only the Gulf War that drove me to it, whether I wanted to or not; [it was] perhaps less its barbarism, as bad as it was, than the outrageous hypocrisy with which it operated. At first, I wanted to write a diary of the Gulf War, but

events came too thick and fast. Also, it soon seemed to me to be more illuminating to for once show the entire gruesome weave of violence and mendacity in the context of its history" ("Why?" [9]).

When another critical book appeared in 1997, a reviewer began his comments with the following statement: "There is probably hardly another country that suffers so much from [emulating] its great model America as Germany does." Jürgen Scheunemann, "Das Land der Vorbilder," *Der Tagesspiegel*, April 6, 1998. The book is Peter Loesche's *Die Vereinigten Staaten. Innenansichten. Ein Versuch, das Land der unbegrenzten Widersprüche zu begreifen* (Hannover: Fackelträger, 1997). In this title, the U.S. is transformed from the "land of endless opportunities" to the "land of endless contradictions."

Notes to Conclusions & Prospects

1. Jonathan Sperber, *The Kaiser's Voters. Electors and Elections in Imperial Germany* (Cambridge: Cambridge University Press, 1997), 1.

2. See the dpa/eu dispatch "Hooligans wecken in Frankreich Erinnerungen an finstere Vergangenheit," June 27, 1998. Distributed by *Germany Live*. The dispatch contains the following assessment of skinhead violence from the conservative French newspaper *Le Figaro:* "The German brutes who on Sunday terrorized Lens and seriously injured a policeman are the heirs of a minority, but tolerated neo-Nazi ideology."

This was not the only such news on that day: At about the same time, but much closer to home, about a dozen right-wing youths, armed with chains and bottles, attacked the guests at a garden party in Oebisfelde (Sachsen-Anhalt), injuring five. See dpa/eu, "Rechtsextremistische Jugendliche überfielen Gartenparty," June 27, 1998, *Germany Live*. In Saal (Mecklenburg-Vorpommern), a twenty-year-old asylum seeker from Algeria was beaten by six youths as he left a discotheque with friends. See dpa/eu, "20jähriger Algerier in Ostdeutschland niedergeschlagen," June 27, 1998, *Germany Live*. The day afterward, young supporters of the right-wing NPD—who were outnumbered by protesters—staged a demonstration in Berlin. See dpa/eu, "NPD-Aufmarsch in Berlin unter großem Polizeiaufgebot," June 27, 1998, *Germany Live*.

3. Not all Europeans would agree with Brigitte Seebacher-Brandt, for example: "The Germans do not have it in their power to make themselves smaller and poorer than they really are and to be spectators at the great global theater." See Seebacher-Brandt, *Die Linke und die Einheit* (Berlin: Corso bei Siedler, 1991), 80. She sees powerful nations as a prerequisite for a powerful United Europe.

4. Stefan Breuer, *Anatomie der Konservativen Revolution* (Darmstadt: Wissenschaftliche Buchgesellschaft, 1993). Page references in the body of the text.

5. Rolf Peter Sieferle, *Die Konservative Revolution. Fünf biographische Skizzen* (Frankfurt am Main: Fischer, 1995). Page references in the body of the text.

6. Michael Rupprecht, *Der literarische Bürgerkrieg. Zur Politik der Unpolitischen in Deutschland* (Frankfurt am Main: Knecht, 1995). Page references in the body of the text. The design of the book cover includes photographs of Botho Strauß, Günter Grass, Thomas Mann (in the middle), Ernst Nolte, Ernst Jünger, and Martin Heidegger.

7. Kurt Lenk, Günter Meuter, and Henrique Ricardo Otten, *Vordenker der Neuen Rechten* (Frankfurt am Main and New York: Campus, 1997). Page references in the body of the text.

8. Jürgen Habermas, *A Berlin Republic: Writings on Germany,* trans. Steven Rendall (Lincoln: University of Nebraska Press, 1997), 81. This is a translation of the 1995 book *Die Normalität einer Berliner Republik* (Frankfurt am Main: Suhrkamp).

9. Iris Weber, *Nation, Staat und Elite. Die Ideologie der Neuen Rechten* (Köln: PapyRossa, 1997). Page references in the body of the text.

10. See also Johannes Klotz and Ulrich Schneider, eds., *Die selbstbewußte Nation und ihr Geschichtsbild. Geschichtslegenden der Neuen Rechten* (Köln: PapyRossa, 1997). In the preface to this volume, the authors—after quoting from *Die selbstbewußte Nation* —offer the following statement of purpose: "[C]onservative and new-right historians and journalists are rewriting history: historicization of National Socialism and relativization of its crimes, description of the Federal Republic from 1949 to 1989 as a special path, etc. The point of this is to systematically revise the insights that have been developed and painstakingly established by critical historiography. Their place is to be taken by a view of history according to which it would be a return to normalcy if Germany would finally emerge from the shadow of the past, take on its responsibility as a major power, and once again play the international role that it is entitled to—also in a military sense. In order to counter such regression, the debate with the apologists of the self-confident nation and their view of history must finally be carried out." ("Vorwort," 7.)

11. Dirk von Petersdorff, "200 Jahre deutsche Kunstreligion!" *Neue Rundschau* 108.4 (1997): 67–87. Page references in the body of the text.

12. See Stefan Breuer, *Ästhetischer Fundamentalismus. Stefan George und der deutsche Antimodernismus* (Darmstadt: Wissenschaftliche Buchgesellschaft, 1995). I did not obtain a copy of this book until after finishing my own study. Breuer actually rejects the religion of art without denying that some of its insights (about environmental destruction, for example) are well worth considering. (There are parallels to Karl Heinz Bohrer's *Die Ästhetik des Schreckens* here, although Breuer does not list the Bohrer book in his bibliography.) In his introduction, Breuer expresses his disgust with those critics of Botho Strauß's "Impending Tragedy" who mindlessly make use of the "fascism club" rather than engaging in a historically based analysis.

13. Grass's advocacy for asylum seekers and his support for critical Turkish writer Yasar Kemal are documented in *Zeit sich einzumischen. Die Kontroverse um Günter Grass und die Laudatio auf Yasar Kemal in der Paulskirche,* ed. Manfred Bissinger and Daniela Hermes (Göttingen: Steidl, 1998).

Elfriede Jelinek, the 1998 winner of the prestigious Büchner Prize, would be a fitting heir to Grass, except for the fact that she is still, at age fifty-two, more interested in confrontation and polemics than dialogue. See the following interview done after the announcement of the prize: Peter von Becker, "Alles ist ein Spiel um den blutigen Ernst," *Der Tagesspiegel*, May 20, 1998.

14. Breuer, *Anatomie*, 28. In the American context, Todd Gitlin's recent defense of the humanities as a vital component of democracy was given a rather cold reception: "The Liberal Arts in the Age of Info-Glut," *The Chronicle of Higher Education*, May 1, 1998, and the letters to the editor about Gitlin in the June 5 edition.

15. Hermann Rauschning, *Die Konservative Revolution. Versuch und Bruch mit Hitler* (New York: Freedom Publishing, 1941), 63. Further page references in the body of the text. See also the author's analysis of Nazism in *The Revolution of Nihilism: Warning to the West* (New York: Alliance Book Corporation, 1939).

16. According to historian Lothar Kettenacker, a meeting of minds has already occurred. He calls it "a curious alliance of right- and left-wing critics against the so-called 'Coca-Cola' or 'McDonalds' culture": *Germany Since 1945* (Oxford and New York: Oxford University Press, 1997), 172. Kettenacker's aim here, one close to Herzinger/Stein, is to discredit all criticism of the American model. The use of the word "curious" demonstrates that he has not given much thought to the various critiques of Westernization since Romanticism. Like Pells, he states: "The so-called Americanization of West Germany is a very superficial description, which does not stand up to scrutiny" (172).

17. He also adds that the contributions of the German Jews are in no way a "foreign infiltration" ("Überfremdung") of the German mind (240).

18. One critic may have exaggerated, however, when he declared, in a review of the Schacht/Schwilk volume *Für eine Berliner Republik*, that the movement was already moribund. See Jan Ross, "Das schnelle Altern der Neuen Rechten," *Berliner Zeitung*, February 14–15, 1998. This political obituary was written two months before the state elections in Sachsen-Anhalt (seen below).

19. Those who wish to get a taste of this activity should begin with the "Thule-Netz" (<http://www.thulenet.com>). Among the offerings are a chat room for "discussion among nationalists." According to information provided on the website, over 171,000 visitors called up more than three million web pages between July 5, 1996, and April 4, 1998. A listing of right-wing sites on the web is provided in "Die Rechten im Internet" (<http://www.bnr.de/rechts.htm>). See also the contribution by Christian Flatz, "Rechtsextremismus im World Wide Web" (<http://www.gfpa. uibk.ac.at/art/0007.htm>).

20. The rising popularity of the populist Danish Folkeparti in a country so proud of its progressive policies and tolerance is especially troubling. The results of the March 1998 national elections in Denmark are summarized and analyzed in *Politiken Weekly*, March 18, 1998.

For a general introduction to the politics of the New Right in Europe, see Geoffrey Harris, *The Dark Side of Europe: The Extreme Right Today* (1990; Edinburgh: Edinburgh University Press, 1994). See also Mark Wegierski, "The New Right in Europe," *Telos* 98–99 (Winter 1993–Spring 1994): 55–69; Martina Kirfel and Walter Oswalt, eds., *Die Rückkehr der Führer. Modernisierter Rechtsradikalismus in Westeuropa*, 2nd rev. ed. (Wien and Zürich: Europaverlag, 1991).

21. Evelyn Roll, "Demokratiefreier Raum im Osten," *Süddeutsche Zeitung*, May 9, 1998.

22. For an example of Benoist's writing in English translation, see "Confronting Globalization," *Telos* 108 (1996): 117–137. See also *Telos* 98–99 (Winter 1993–Spring 1994), special double issue on "The French New Right." It is puzzling that students of French culture can ignore the impact of Benoist. There is, for example, not a single reference to him in *French Cultural Studies: An Introduction*, ed. Jill Forbes and Michael Kelly (Oxford and New York: Oxford University Press, 1995). In general, very little attention is paid to conservative intellectuals in this volume. Le Pen is also only mentioned once (6).

23. It is ironic that this institution is misspelled in the program: "Akadémie francaise."

24. For a brief, but thoughtful recent contribution to this discussion about the comparative horror of the gulag and the death camps, see Timothy Garton Ash's review of the French *Black Book of Communism* (1997) that appeared in the British journal *Prospect* in June 1998 (Online edition). For the response of a German historian to the German edition of the *Black Book*, see Manfred Hildermeier, "Das 'Schwarzbuch des Kommunismus' und die Fakten der historischen Forschung," *Die Zeit*, no. 24, 1998.

25. There is no objection to food shipments used to combat hunger in the "Third World," however.

26. For a thought-provoking discussion of Buchanan et al., see Michael Lind, "Why Intellectual Conservatism Failed," *Dissent* (Winter 1995), 42–47.

27. There is of course also a large number of unemployed young females in the former GDR, but they are less inclined to resort to violence as a way to vent their anger.

28. See the dpa dispatch "Katholikentag—Kritik an ungehemmten und schamlosen Egoismus," June 12, 1998. Distributed by *German Live* on the Internet. Merkel is now the CDU party chairperson (the first woman in this post), and Fischer is the foreign minister.

29. See the following reports about Habermas's support for the SPD and his theses about global democracy: Ullrich Fichtner, "Verschwommene Thesen, aber jede Menge Wirkung," *Frankfurter Rundschau*, June 6, 1998; Dieter Rulff, "Das Wagnis namens Habermas," *tageszeitung*, June 6, 1998; Günter Hofmann, "Der Philopolitiker," *Die Zeit*, no. 25, 1998.

30. Sibylle Tönnies, *Die Feier des Konkreten. Linker Salonatavismus* (Göttingen: Steidl, 1996), 122, 128. The bulk of this book consists of a critique of the "leftist atavism" of Adorno and its purported similarities with "rightist atavism."

31. See Sibylle Tönnies, "Gemeinschaft von oben. Der amerikanische Kommuni-

tarismus, eine antiliberale Bewegung?" *Frankfurter Allgemeine Zeitung*, December 30, 1994. In this article, Tönnies asserts that an attack on liberalism would play into the hands of the New Right and its project of political restoration. Instead, she proposes the following: "We really need a reawakened sense of the value of the family, true friendship, [and] unqualified, spontaneous attention to one another. We need a new sense of the value of all that which is not connected to money, but rather to the heart." See also her recent article calling for the Germans to finally shed their fear of the state, one based on the (misinterpreted) experience of National Socialism: Sibylle Tönnies, "Save the Whale! Rettet den Leviathan!" *tageszeitung*, June 13, 1998. This article is part of a series on the left's relationship to the state.

32. Antonia Grunenberg, *Der Schlaf der Freiheit. Politik und Gemeinsinn im 21. Jahrhundert* (Reinbek: Rowohlt, 1997), 242–243. This book was selected as the non-fiction book of the month by the *Süddeutsche Zeitung* and the *Norddeutscher Rundfunk* in August 1997. In a brief positive review, Rita Süssmuth, the then president of the German parliament, characterized the book as being "against the grain of the spirit of our time" ("quer zum Zeitgeist"). "Der Schlaf der Freiheit," *Der Tagesspiegel*, October 15, 1997.

33. Benjamin Barber, *Jihad vs. McWorld* (New York: Random House, 1995), 6, 8. My emphasis. Barber's comments on reunified Germany, which are found in a chapter entitled "The Colonization of East Germany by McWorld," are hardly music to the ears of the (West) German political establishment: "[W]hat the German case suggests is exactly what the Russian case establishes: that McWorld's markets, tied here to the West German political and economic leviathan, have not and probably cannot produce a democratic civil society; indeed, in East Germany, they helped to destroy one in its infancy. McWorld is the problem, not the solution" (267). This chapter should be required reading for Germanists, even though Barber makes one small error, namely the inclusion of apparatchik writer Hermann Kant in a list of dissident authors (266).

34. Tönnies, *Die Feier des Konkreten*, 128. A similar, but not identical vision is found at the end of Christophe Charle's study *Vordenker der Moderne. Die Intellektuellen im 19. Jahrhundert* (Frankfurt am Main: Fischer, 1997): "The new idea of the coming century is possibly that of the European intellectual: the emancipatory claim of the early nineteenth century, complemented by the cosmopolitanism of the Enlightenment and the strict rationalism of the late nineteenth century, but freed from the dogmatism that put its stamp on the first half of the twentieth century" (217).

35. It will, however, be interesting to follow the career of Bodo Morshäuser (b. 1953), who has taken it upon himself to examine both xenophobic violence in reunified Germany and the left's reaction to it: *Hauptsache Deutsch* (Frankfurt am Main: Suhrkamp, 1992) and *Warten auf den Führer* (Frankfurt am Main: Suhrkamp, 1993).

36. Matthias Altenburg, "Lullaby vor der Schlacht," *Der Spiegel*, no. 52, 1994, 151. This essay appeared not quite two years after Strauß's "Impending Tragedy."

37. For a summary of these and a differentiated portrayal of Syberberg, see Leonardo Quaresima, "Hans Jürgen Syberberg: Die neue 'Aura' des Films," *Neonationalismus. Neokonservatismus*, ed. Michael Kessler et al., 127–140.

In *A Dubious Past*, Elliot Neaman is more critical of Syberberg than I am. Neaman views Syberberg's 1990 book *Vom Unglück und Gluck der Kunst in Deutschland nach dem letzten Kriege* (München: Matthes und Seitz) as "openly anti-Semitic" (220). Syberberg does say, however, that "Auschwitz and the exodus of the European Jews to Israel and America" must be one of the central themes of art in our time (*Vom Unglück*, 33). Neaman's assessment of Syberberg appears to have been influenced at least in part by his reading of Eric Santner, to whose book *Stranded Objects: Mourning, Memory, and Film in Postwar Germany* (Ithaca and London: Cornell University Press, 1990) he refers. See Santner's chapter "Allegories of Grieving: The Films of Hans Jürgen Syberberg" (103–149).

38. Hans Jürgen Syberberg, *Die freudlose Gesellschaft. Notizen aus dem letzten Jahr* (München, Wien: Hanser, 1981). Page references in the body of the text.

39. One forerunner who proposed an "International of the Religious Intelligentsia" was author, essayist, and Dadaist Hugo Ball (1886–1927). See Hugo Ball, *Zur Kritik der deutschen Intelligenz* (1918; Frankfurt am Main: Suhrkamp, 1991), 10. In that same volume, Ball sees a "German mentality" that consists of a lack of "principles, feeling, logic and precision [and] instinctive morality" (12). He agrees with Bakunin that "if a tenth of their [the Germans'] rich intellectual consciousness had found its way into their lives, they would be glorious people" (32). Ball was a leftist who often sounded like a rightist, and he was not free of anti-Semitism. Anson Rabinbach examines the pitfalls inherent in Ball's "inverted nationalism" in *In the Shadow of Catastrophe: German Intellectuals between Apocalypse and Enlightenment* (Berkeley: University of California Press, 1997), 66–96. His analysis was originally published as the introduction to the English translation of Ball's work: *Critique of the German Intelligentsia* (New York: Columbia University Press, 1993).

See also Seth Taylor's discussion of Ball's *Critique* in *Left-Wing Nietzscheans*, 183–186. In my opinion, the way in which the East German dramatist Heiner Müller (1929–1995) and the theater director Frank Castorf (both associated with the cultural left) toyed with the ideas of Ernst Jünger in recent years is hardly an intellectual or political path worthy of emulation. For background on this, see the following: István Eörsi, "'Massaker als Sinnsuche.' Über die seltsame Allianz von Heiner Müller und Botho Strauß," *Der Spiegel*, no. 37, 1994, 215–220; Peter Zadek, "'Den Killern ein Alibi.' Über Frank Castorf, Heiner Müller und andere rechte Linke," *Der Spiegel*, no. 4, 1995, 183; Stephan Lebert, "Der Fall Frank Castorf: Verwirrende Rollenspiele eines deutschen Intellektuellen," *Süddeutsche Zeitung*, February 20, 1995; "'Theater ist feudalistisch.' Dramatiker Heiner Müller über das Berliner Ensemble, DDR—Nostalgie und Rechts-links-Verwirrungen," *Der Spiegel*, no. 12, 1995, 224–226. In this interview, Müller denies that he and Castorf ever were involved in "anything like neo-Nationalism" (225).

Richard Herzinger has described the intention of Müller's critique of civilization as "mobilization of resistance against a Westernization that is portrayed as a danger that threatens the development, even the existence of the human race." He shows that Müller "explicitly and implicitly links up with traditional modes of thought of the German critique of 'Western civilization.'" See *Masken der Revolution. Vitalistische Zivilisations- und Humanismuskritik in Texten Heiner Müllers* (München: Fink, 1992), 15-16.

40. For a reaction from the U.S., see David Binder, "Ernst Jünger, Contradictory German Author Who Wrote about War, Is Dead at 102," *New York Times*, February 18, 1998. This obituary is free of glossing over, unlike many of the German ones.

41. One could also postulate that Kohl, in expressing his respect for Jünger, knew that he would be applauded by those extremely conservative voters that the Christian Democrats invariably court in election years.

42. The views of Waigel and Lafontaine were reported by *Germany Live* ("Stimmen zum Tod von Ernst Jünger") on February 18, 1998.

43. See "Stimmen zum Tod von Ernst Jünger," *Germany Live*, February 18, 1998. Gadamer's comments were originally published in the *Frankfurter Allgemeine Zeitung*, February 18, 1998.

44. For *Libération* and *Le Figaro*, see "Ausländische Presse würdigt Ernst Jünger: 'Nationalist, aber kein Nazi,'" *Germany Live*, February 18, 1998. For Mitterand, Lang, and Tournier, see Jochen Hehn, "Ein Freund Frankreichs: Ernst Jünger," *Die Welt*, February 19, 1998.

45. Cited in Martina Meister, "Ungebrochen. Frankreichs Reaktionen auf den Tod Ernst Jüngers," *Frankfurter Rundschau*, February 19, 1998. Le Pen's opposite number, André Glucksmann, who has been extremely critical of Hans Magnus Enzensberger, brought Jünger's *War as an Inner Experience* to the attention of publisher Christian Bourgois and wrote the preface to the French edition. See Christian Bourgois, "Von Dauer," *Süddeutsche Zeitung*, February 18, 1998.

46. Cited in "Stimmen zum Tod von Ernst Jünger," *Germany Live*, February 18, 1998.

47. Ernst Jünger, "'Wer hat nicht Fehler gemacht im Leben,'" *Süddeutsche Zeitung*, February 21, 1998. See also Klaus Podak, "Immer bereit zu neuen Ausfahrten. Zum Tode von Ernst Jünger," *Süddeutsche Zeitung*, February 18, 1998.

48. Curt Hohoff, "Ein Augenmensch, der bis ins Innerste sehen wollte," *Die Welt*, February 18, 1998.

49. Harro Segeberg, "Wege und Irrwege einer Epochenaneignung," *Frankfurter Rundschau*, February 18, 1998.

50. Wolfram Schütte, "Jahrhundert-Gestalt. Zum Tode Ernst Jüngers," *Frankfurter Runschau*, February 18, 1998.

51. Thomas Assheuer, "Der beste Feind der Moderne," *Die Zeit*, no. 9, 1998. The online edition of *Die Zeit* offers a collection of materials about Jünger at <www.zeit.de/links/juenger_ernst.html>.

52. Rolf Schneider, "Er war niemals besser, als wenn er nur über sich selber schrieb," *Die Welt*, February 21, 1998. The only thoroughly negative eulogy that I discovered was printed in the Viennese daily *Die Presse*. It was excerpted in *Germany Live* on February 18, 1998.

53. How can one write—and correctly so—that democracy needs "intellectual deviation" to survive and then set up Ernst Jünger as a model of such deviation? See the comments from the February 21, 1998, edition of the *Berliner Zeitung* on the occasion of Jünger's funeral as excerpted by *Germany Live* on the day of their publication. As stated previously, "leftist deviation" has never been truly acceptable in Germany.

54. Gerhard Schulz, *Romantik* (München: Beck, 1996), 136. Further page references in the body of the text.

55. Werner Schneiders, *Das Zeitalter der Aufklärung* (München: Beck, 1997), 86. Further page references in the body of the text.

56. On this topic, see also W. Daniel Wilson, "Enlightenment's Alliance with Power: The Dialectic of Collusion and Opposition in the Literary Elite," *Impure Reason*, 364–384.

57. Annemarie Pieper, *Gut und Böse* (München: Beck, 1997), 121. This does not mean that the search for explanations is fruitless, she adds. Page references in the body of the text.

Notes to Epilogue

1. Anne Sa'adah, *Germany's Second Chance: Trust, Justice, and Democratization* (Cambridge, Mass., and London: Harvard University Press, 1998), ix. Sa'adah goes on to amplify this opening statement from her preface: "When I was a graduate student, Nazi Germany was not where I wanted to be late at night; even living in the shadow of the Third Reich seemed depressing. . . . Some of my closest friends now are German, but we sometimes come up hard against a wall of misunderstanding that can be explained only by radically different political experiences and cultures. And yet I now occasionally slip into the first-person plural when I speak about the problems and possibilities of contemporary Germany. The Federal Republic is indeed *ein schwieriges Vaterland* [a difficult fatherland], but it is a country in which I feel implicated" (ix-x). My own feelings are quite similar, even though I did ponder Nazi Germany—and several other manifestations of Germanness—as a graduate student, both "late at night" and during the day.

2. Schröder was never a "street fighting man," although photos from the 1970s show him in the requisite leather jacket with beer in hand. Unlike many more radical leftists, he comes from rather humble circumstances, and he grew up in a household devoid of the cultural artifacts of the *Bildungsbürgertum*. He thus did not rebel by rejecting bourgeois culture out of hand. In this, he resembles Bill Clinton more than

Tony Blair, with whom he has been compared. It was hardly a political statement when he gave an interview to the *Washington Post* while "puffing on a Cuban cigar." See "Schroeder: 'Decision to Stay Is . . . Right'," *Washington Post*, April 18, 1999.

3. Mathias Döpfner, "Sieg der Achtundsechziger," *Die Welt*, September 28, 1998. It has been said that Schröder was "not a '68er himself, but a sympathizer of this movement that ranged from rebellious to revolutionary." Gerfried Sperl, "Der große Wechsel," *Der Standard*, September 28, 1998.

4. I am translating here from excerpts published by the *Süddeutsche Zeitung* and the *Frankfurter Rundschau* (both of November 11, 1998).

5. One observer has put it this way: "The passages in the *Regierungserklärung* about cultural policy were the colorful prospectus of a Social-Democratic enterprise whose products are to be quickly put on the market." Christian Thomas, "Be Er De. Gerhard Schröders 'Republik der Neuen Mitte,'" *Frankfurter Rundschau*, November 12, 1998.

6. Heribert Prantl, "Der große Kommunikator," *Süddeutsche Zeitung*, November 11, 1998. Prantl's title is an homage to Ronald Reagan, whose ability to speak directly to the people is shared by Schröder, he thinks.

7. Richard Meng, "Aufbruch wohin?" *Frankfurter Rundschau*, November 11, 1998.

8. As reported by Robin Alexander and Eberhard Seidel-Pielen, "Rechte mußte draußen bleiben," *tageszeitung*, September 29, 1998. Few reports focused on this aspect of the election. Typical headlines were "The ghost of the right is done for" (Jens Schneider, "Aus für das rechte Gespenst," *Süddeutsche Zeitung*, September 29, 1998) or "No extreme-right parties in the German parliament" ("Keine rechtsextremen Parteien im deutschen Parlament," dpa dispatch distributed by *Germany Live*, September 27, 1998). Paul Geitner's article in the *Washington Post* (September 27, 1998) was entitled "Extremists Run Strong in E. Germany," but Geitner was referring to the PDS, the successor to the East German communists, who barely overcame the 5 percent hurdle in 1998.

9. As reported by Ada Brandes, "Schily besorgt über den Zulauf zur rechten Szene. Innenminister stellt Verfassungsschutzbericht vor . . ." *Berliner Zeitung*, March 25, 1999. In the Office's report, the number of left-wing extremists prone to violence is set at 7,000. See also the following articles: hjh, "Zulauf bei rechtsextremen Organisationen," *Süddeutsche Zeitung*, March 26, 1999; Thorsten Denkler, "Verfassungsschutzbericht vorgelegt," *tageszeitung*, March 26, 1999; Martina Fietz, "Zulauf für Rechtsextreme. Aber mehr linke Gewalt," *Die Welt*, March 26, 1999. A later article about the report ran under a headline that was a true slap in the face for East Germans: Peter Blechschmidt, "Im Osten nichts Neues," *Süddeutsche Zeitung*, May 4, 1999. This is a variation of the title of Erich Remarque's famous novel "Im Westen nichts Neues." The article suggests the opposite of what would be the English translation of the headline, i.e.: "All Quiet on the Eastern Front."

In Brandenburg, the federal state that surrounds Berlin, the number of attacks against foreigners went up almost 30 percent in 1999, even though the total number of crimes perpetrated by right-wing extremists went down somewhat. During the same year, the DVU increased its membership from 200 to 400, the NPD from 50 to 200. Only the Republicans lost members. See Jan Thomsen, "Fremdenfeindliche Gewalt nahm 1999 stark zu," *Berliner Zeitung*, May 13, 2000. The increase in xenophobic violence comes at a time when the number of people requesting asylum in Germany is at its lowest point since 1988. This means that there is a gap between the perception of the foreign presence and the actual social reality. See "Asylanträge. Tiefster Stand seit 1988 - Meiste Bewerber aus Jugoslawien," *Der Tagesspiegel*, May 13, 2000.

10. Cited by Helmut Lölhöffel, "Verfassungsschutz registriert starken Zulauf bei Rechtsextremisten," *Frankfurter Rundschau*, March 26, 1999. That edition of the newspaper contained an editorial by the same author ("Auffallende Neuerung") criticizing the continuing surveillance of the PDS by the Office.

Those critical of the provincialism and racism found in the East tend to downplay the fact that half of the violent attacks on foreigners do take place in the old West Germany. There are fewer per capita, to be sure, but one could argue that the ones that take place in a stable democracy are even more troubling.

11. A compilation of the most egregious acts from January 1996 to March 1999 can be found in an Associated Press dispatch of March 29, 1999, that was distributed by the online service Pipeline. More abbreviated summaries were printed in the *Berliner Zeitung* of February 16, 1999, and *Die Welt* of February 15, 1999.

12. Maku, "Dann geh doch gleich rüber!" *Süddeutsche Zeitung*, April 28, 1999. See also "Ghanaische Autorin auf Rügen angegriffen," *Frankfurter Rundschau*, April 27, 1999. In May, Darko returned to Mecklenburg-Vorpommern to finish her reading tour, after she was asked to do so by the state parliament (*Landtag*). The original incident was clearly an embarrassment to the area. It was reported that skinheads had imitated monkeys and called her "nigger." See adi, "Afrikanische Autorin Darko setzt Lesereise fort," *Süddeutsche Zeitung*, May 22, 1999.

13. "Ausländische Studenten in Greifswald angegriffen," *Frankfurter Rundschau*, April 30, 1999.

14. Ute Frings, "'Bündnis gegen Fremdenhaß.' Bonn will sich für Toleranz und Demokratie stark machen," *Frankfurter Rundschau*, April 30, 1999. Already in the fall of 1998, the government of Brandenburg had unveiled a new action program entitled "Tolerant Brandenburg." See Otto Jörg Weis, "Stolpe zeigt Flagge gegen rechts," *Frankfurter Rundschau*, October 7, 1998. In this context, it is interesting to note that Brandenburg had the highest rate of economic growth in the former GDR in 1998. See the ADN dispatch "Brandenburg ein Spitzenreiter im Wirtschaftswachstum" reprinted in the *Frankfurter Rundschau* of April 14, 1999.

15. "Sie hetzten ihn zu Tode," *Bildzeitung*, February 15, 1999. See also "Algerier von Neonazis zu Tode gehetzt," *tageszeitung*, February 15, 1999; Otto Jörg Weis, "Rechtsextreme hetzen Asylbewerber in den Tod," *Frankfurter Rundschau*, February 15, 1999; Karin Zimmermann and Jürgen Schwenkenbecher, "Entsetzen nach dem Tod eines Asylbewerbers in Guben," *Berliner Zeitung*, February 15, 1999; Dorit Kowitz, "Jetzt hat der Helfer Angst," *Süddeutsche Zeitung*, February 15, 1999.

16. See Claus-Dieter Steyer, "Der Trauerzug fand unter Polizeischutz statt," *Der Tagesspiegel*, February 15, 1999. In November 1998, the efforts of the two towns were singled out for recognition by the EU Commission. Additional social workers were hired in the early 1990s after a series of attacks on Poles. In March 1999, the Department of Economic and Social History at the Europa-Universität Viadrina in Frankfurt/Oder advertised a half-time position for a historian to work on the section "Guben/Gubin (1945–1990)" in the project "History of the German-Polish Border Region in the European Framework." Given recent events, an extension of the project's scope to include the present day would not be difficult to justify.

17. "'Vertrauen in Rechtsstaat unterentwickelt.' CDU-Landeschef Schönbohm zweifelt am Konzept für tolerantes Brandenburg," *Der Tagesspiegel*, February 15, 1999.

18. "Fremdenfeindlichkeit verprellt Investoren," dpa dispatch printed in the *Frankfurter Rundschau*, February 18, 1999.

19. Hans-Joachim Maaz, "Über den Nutzen des häßlichen Ostlers. Die wachsende Gewalt im Osten ist ein Hinweis auf die Verhältnisse in ganz Deutschland," *tageszeitung*, April 12, 1999. Maaz was reacting to the theses of the West German criminologist Christian Pfeiffer about socialization and the causes of xenophobia in the former GDR. See "Familienkultur der Intoleranz und des Hasses" [interview with C. Pfeiffer], *tageszeitung*, March 22, 1999; and Nick Reimer, "Angriff auf die ostdeutsche Volksseele," *tageszeitung*, March 25, 1999. For Maaz's analysis of the East German mentality, see Hans-Joachim Maaz, *Gefühlsstau. Ein Psychogramm der DDR* (Berlin: Argon Verlag, 1990).

20. Quoted in Ulrich Clewing, "Sir Foster hilft nicht beim Aufbau des Sozialismus," *tageszeitung*, August 19, 1998. The tongue-in-cheek title refers to the decision by Sir Norman Foster, the architect of the renovated Reichstag, not to participate. He was bothered by the partisan (i.e., pro SPD) nature of the event.

21. Given the immediate goal of unseating Kohl, it is no surprise that the question of Helmut Schmidt's coolness toward the *literati* was not emphasized. Willy Brandt's successor was no more prone to fireside chats with critical intellectuals than Ludwig Erhard, famous for his dismissal of activist writers.

One intellectual who praised Kohl's influence on cultural affairs was Christoph Stölzl, the founding director of the German Historical Museum in Berlin: "Kohl tut wohl," *Die Zeit*, no. 40, 1998. In 2000, Stölzl became the head of cultural affairs in Berlin.

22. "Eurovisionen" [Interview with Jack Lang], *Die Zeit*, no. 40, 1998. Lang also recalled how he had engaged in discussions with Hollywood executives: "One has to hammer into such people again and again that we [i.e., the Europeans] exist, and that they cannot do what they want in Europe without respecting certain rules." Criticism of the U.S. was not absent from the "Eurovisions" meeting either. See Jakob Augstein, "Ist Montesquieu in der SPD? Wie die Sozialdemokraten nach 'Eurovisionen' suchten," *Süddeutsche Zeitung*, August 21, 1998.

23. Cited in Moritz Rinke, "Vom Training des aufrechten Gangs," *Der Tagesspiegel*, August 21, 1998. Rinke, for one, found Schröder to be "pleasantly unpretentious," since he did not "constantly quote Ernst Jünger [!] or claim to be a bookworm."

24. Walser has been a visiting professor at Middlebury, Texas, West Virginia, Dartmouth, and Berkeley.

25. It was reported in a dpa dispatch that Walser had chosen Schirrmacher himself. This does not necessarily mean that Walser agreed in toto with the cultural-political agenda of his younger admirer. See "Friedenspreis an Walser—Gnade für Top-Spion 'Topas' gefordert," distributed by the online service *Germany Live*, October 12, 1998.

26. My translations refer to the online version of Schirrmacher's talk (entitled "Sein Anteil" ["His Share"], which was distributed by the Börsenverein des deutschen Buchhandels on its website: <http://www.boersenverein.de/fpreis/fs_laude. htm>. Walser's own talk—"Erfahrungen beim Verfassen einer Sonntagsrede" ["Experiences While Writing a Sunday Speech"]—will also be cited according to the version on the same website: <http://www.boersenverein.de/fpreis/mw_rede.htm>. For book versions, see *Friedenspreis des deutschen Buchhandels 1998. Martin Walser* (Frankfurt am Main: Verlag Buchhändler-Vereinigung, 1998) and *Erfahrungen beim Verfassen einer Sonntagsrede. Friedenspreis des deutschen Buchhandels 1998* (Frankfurt am Main: Suhrkamp, 1998). Lengthy excerpts from Walser's speech were also published in the *Frankfurter Rundschau*, the *Süddeutsche Zeitung*, the *tageszeitung*, and many other dailies on October 12, 1998. Two brief passages that Walser did not read in Frankfurt are included in the version found in the journal *Universitas*, December 1998, 1122–1132. The extra passages are briefly discussed by the editors on p. 1132.

After this epilogue was completed, the following collection appeared: Frank Schirrmacher, ed., *Die Walser-Bubis-Debatte. Eine Dokumentation* (Frankfurt am Main: Suhrkamp, 1999). The volume contains the speeches by Walser and Bubis, numerous responses to both (including personal letters), and the transcript of the December 13, 1998, meeting of Walser and Bubis at the *Frankfurter Allgemeine Zeitung*. The collection is organized chronologically, with one exception: The first document is not Schirrmacher's speech introducing Walser, but rather the honoree's Peace Prize Speech. This will probably be viewed by most German observers as an example of false modesty.

27. Martin Walser, *Ein springender Brunnen* (Frankfurt am Main: Suhrkamp, 1998).

28. Here are just two examples: In "Praktiker, Weltfremde und Vietnam" ["Practical Types, Otherwordly Ones and Vietnam"—Munich, 1966], he said: "[I]f we can't do anything about the decline of the U.S.A. and against our own enslavement to this system that has been rapidly decaying for ten years, then it can't be meaningless to at least speak of this decline [Verfall] and our enslavement [Verfallenheit]. . . . It can't be meaningless to call a crime a crime. . . . I call upon the parties represented in parliament to place Vietnam on the agenda of the German Bundestag." In "Amerikanischer als die Amerikaner" [More American than the Americans –Munich, 1967], he declared: "We have obviously chosen to put up with watching this brutalization of America like drugged sycophants. A Europeanization of our politics is no longer conceivable, although that would perhaps help the better America in its battle against the lousy and

bloody Texas style [of politics]." These passages are found in Martin Walser, *Ansichten, Einsichten. Aufsätze zur Zeitgeschichte, Werke in zwölf Bänden*, ed. Helmuth Kiesel (Frankfurt am Main: Suhrkamp, 1997)11:182, 186, and 259.

29. In a 1995 interview, Walser criticized the "glorification of violence" on television and said that he could no longer watch "certain American films" because of their depiction of brutality. These comments put his reference to television in the Frankfurt speech in a different light. See "'Man bleibt wunschbereit'" [interview with Martin Walser], *Der Spiegel*, no. 36, 1995, 209. Ignatz Bubis claimed that Walser had never become agitated about violence in "advertising or crime shows," so his opposition to violent documentaries about the Holocaust had nothing to do with violence and everything to do with his desire to make the Holocaust disappear. See "'Walser will, daß der Holocaust verschwindet.' Gespräch mit Ignatz Bubis und Peter Schneider," *Die Welt*, October 14, 1998.

30. See for example "Unser Auschwitz" (1965) and "Auschwitz und kein Ende" (1979). Both have been reprinted in *Ansichten, Einsichten*, 158–172 and 631–636.

31. Compare the feelings of Anne Sa'adah as quoted at the beginning of this epilogue.

32. There is a linguistic "slip" in this passage of which the author might not have been aware: "Everyone knows our historical burden, the interminable shame. [N]ot a day [passes] on which it is not held up before us. Could it be that the intellectuals who hold it up before us . . . for a second succumb to the illusion that they . . . are for a moment closer to the victims than to the perpetrators?" In this construction, the "intellectuals" are not part of the German people, but rather outside agents. This is too close to the fascist viewpoint for comfort.

33. See Martin Walser, "Über freie und unfreie Rede," *Der Spiegel*, no. 45, 1994. On that occasion, Walser spoke at the University of Heidelberg to express his gratitude for the Dolf-Sternberger-Preis. Prefigurations of the Frankfurt comments on the nature of conscience can be found in that speech: "For my part, I would rather be ashamed without being asked rather than after being asked. I do not blush on command. . . . Cultivating taboos in the service of enlightenment. Exercise of power that regards itself as enlightenment" (138). The full text of the speech was published in *Ansichten, Einsichten*, 1046–1061.

34. Schröder was one of the few dignitaries not to attend Walser's speech. In a later interview, he said that it was not his place to provide a public commentary on the speech. He did, however, deny that Walser wanted to provide ammunition for those who would rather forget the past ("den Verdrängern"). Although he thought that some of Walser's formulations were "exaggerated" ("überspitzt"), he defended their use: "A poet can do things like that. I would not be permitted to [do so]." See "Eine offene Republik" [interview with Gerhard Schröder], *Die Zeit*, no. 6, 1999. In Frankfurt, Walser expressed his hope that he would not be giving succor to "contemporary obscurantists with an aversion to guilt feelings." Such a statement shows that he was hardly as naïve as the Strauß of "Impending Tragedy" or the Handke of *Justice for Serbia*.

35. He uses the term "Denkmal" rather than "Mahnmal," ignoring usage in the

debate about the edifice. The former is a neutral word, whereas the latter has only negative connotations with regard to admonishing present and future generations. Already in September 1998, Walser had referred to the project as a "monument of shame" and "a monument as big as a soccer field." See "Martin Walser gegen Holocaust-Denkmal," *Der Tagesspiegel,* September 8, 1998.

For an anthology of contributions to the debate about the memorial, see Michael S. Cullen, *Das Holocaust-Mahnmal. Dokumentation einer Debatte* (Zürich: Pendo-Verlag, 1999). In an article about this debate, Cullen stated that it had at times "been enriched and simultaneously blanketed by the Walser-Bubis dispute." See Michael S. Cullen, "Aller Anfang ist lang," *Der Tagesspiegel,* January 6, 1999.

36. Before the publication of Goldhagen's book, Walser had used a similar formulation about the relationship between German and Jews. See Martin Walser, "'Wir werden Goethe retten,'" *Der Spiegel,* no. 52, 1995, 143. This article discusses Victor Klemperer's diaries, which were discovered by Walser in the Saxony State Library (Dresden) in the fall of 1989. He not only praises the diaries as the best vehicle for "making the reality of the NS dictatorship more comprehensible to us" but also agrees with Klemperer's view of the conscience: "One can learn from Klemperer how to deal with one's own conscience instead of paying attention to that of other people" (146). A German journalist has postulated that Klemperer's diaries will affect the American view of Nazi terror more than Goldhagen's book. See Robert von Rimscha, "Der Holocaust auf Augenhöhe," *Der Tagesspiegel,* January 13, 1999. For Klemperer in English, see *I Will Bear Witness: A Diary of the Nazi Years, 1933-1941* (New York: Random House, 1998). The *New York Times* published not one, but two reviews of this book: Richard Bernstein, "How the Little Things Add Up to Horror," November 11, 1998, and Peter Gay's assessment in the *New York Times Book Review* of November 22, 1998 (featured on the cover).

37. See Ignatz Bubis (with Peter Sichrovsky), *"Damit bin ich noch längst nicht fertig." Die Autobiographie* (Frankfurt and New York: Campus, 1996), 134. In another book, Bubis described the Fassbinder work as "a bad play" and the author as a "prime example of leftist anti-Semitism," even a "protofascist leftist." Ignatz Bubis, *Juden in Deutschland* (Berlin: Aufbau, 1996), 41, 45.

Fassbinder's play has never been performed in Germany (a planned production at the Maxim Gorki Theater in Berlin was cancelled in the autumn of 1998); it had its premiere in New York and has been performed in Denmark and Sweden. A performance in Milan in November 1998 was not controversial. See Henning Klüver, "Alles nur Verlierer," *Süddeutsche Zeitung,* November 20, 1998. When a small theater in Tel Aviv put it on in April 1999, the assistant director was quoted as saying: "After all, it is not the play itself that propagates anti-Semitism, but the situation in which it is set." Fassbinder himself had said that the characters in the play "do not express the views of the author." Both citations are taken from Thorsten Schmitz, "Der Müll, die Stadt und ein anderer Ort," *Süddeutsche Zeitung,* April 6, 1999. The successful 1985 protest has been described as "the only big theater scandal that has happened in the Federal Republic . . . the only case in which the principle of artistic freedom was not upheld." See

Stephan Speicher, "Ein reicher Jude. Ist Fassbinders *Der Müll, die Stadt und der Tod* antisemitisch?" *Berliner Zeitung*, September 2, 1998. To my knowledge, there has never been a successful protest against an anti-German play or film since 1945, even though there has been no lack of symbolic German self-mutilation on the stage and screen. This demonstrates that, at least in the cultural sphere, one cannot speak of a "normal" situation. (The only other country in which performance of the play has been prevented is normally liberal Holland.) The figure of the "rich Jew" in the play—which is more grotesque than realistic—is a manifestation of every imaginable anti-Semitic stereotype, and the character who wishes that he had been gassed (Hans von Gluck) is also hardly an appealing individual. As a whole, Fassbinder's play may well disgust many people, but it is hardly an example of anti-Semitic propaganda. See R. W. Fassbinder, *Der Müll, die Stadt und der Tod* (Frankfurt am Main: Verlag der Autoren, 1981).

38. "Bubis beschuldigt Walser 'geistiger Brandstiftung'," *Frankfurter Rundschau*, October 13, 1998. Educated Germans would associate Bubis's choice of words with Max Frisch's 1958 play *Biedermann and the Arsonists* (Biedermann und die Brandstifter). That work is a warning against tyranny in general and fascism in particular. The allusion was surely not lost on Walser.

39. This citation and others are taken from Ignatz Bubis, "Wer von der Schande spricht" ["He who speaks of shame"], *Frankfurter Allgemeine Zeitung*, November 10, 1998.

40. French intellectual Bernard-Henri Lévy has described Bubis as a "prototype . . . of those German Jews [who are] more German than the Germans." ["Prototype . . . de ces juifs allemands, plus allemands que les Allemands."] This dictum is found in Lévy's two-part series on Germany in the Schröder era. Although the tone is generally not polemical, the announcement of the series on the front page of *Le Monde* ("The New Germany of Gerhard Schröder or the Temptation to Forget") and the inclusion of gruesome photographs from the Wehrmacht Exhibition give it a strange flavor. See Bernard-Henri Lévy, "Allemagne, Année Zero?" *Le Monde*, February 6, and 7-8, 1999. At one point, Lévy says that "Schröder wants to change remembrance . . . [and Walser] claims the right to change the channel" when he has seen enough images of the Shoah.

41. For a recent study of Jewish assimilation in the educated middle class, see Klaus Kempter, *Die Jellineks 1820-1955. Eine familienbiographische Studie zum deutsch-jüdischen Bildungsbürgertum* (Düsseldorf: Droste 1998).

42. In 1994, Bubis drew attention to what he called the "phenomenon of intellectual right-wing radicalism." At first, he put Strauß and Enzensberger in that camp. When asked about the justification for this, he issued a retraction. He then maintained that he differentiated between the "mental arsonists" Frey, Schönhuber, and Deckert on the one hand and the "spiritual trailblazers of intellectual right-wing radicalism" like Ernst Nolte. In November 1999, he did not hesitate to use the arsonist label for Walser, only to retract it later (see below). See "'Wegbereiter wie Nolte.' Ignatz Bubis erläutert seine Intellektuellen-Schelte," *Der Spiegel*, no. 16, 1994, 170. In late 1998, he returned to Strauß and Enzensberger, claiming that they had a certain

"national[istic] touch," even though they were not "right-wing extremists." See "Bubis nennt Walser und Dohnanyi 'latente Antisemiten,'" *Frankfurter Allgemeine Zeitung*, November 30, 1998. This headline was printed at the top of the first page of that edition. (Writers are not usually given that kind of attention, even in the *FAZ*.) The ability of a public figure like Bubis to command attention in the media despite his history of vacillation and *ad hominem* attacks is significant, because it demonstrates how "abnormal" German society still is. No well-known non-Jewish German would be taken seriously if he were to act as Bubis did. His special status was a direct result of the official philosemitism, which restricts Jews to the status of "other" in postwar Germany. Seen in this light, the criticism of Bubis by non-Jewish Germans in the wake of the "Walser-Bubis debate" may well be a sign that a more "normal" dialogue and dispute will be possible in the future.

43. Those who would like a brief summary with selected quotations should peruse the materials assembled by Lutz Hagestedt in the online journal *literaturkritik*, no. 1, 1999 (<http://www.literaturkritik.de>). *Der Spiegel* published a long interview with Ignatz Bubis and a provocative editorial by publisher Rudolf Augstein in no. 49, 1998, an interview with German-Jewish students in no. 50, and a fascinating collection of letters to the editor in no. 51. The journal *Universitas* dedicated most of the December 1998 issue to the topic "Normales Deutschland?" including Walser's speech and several accompanying pieces (one of which was an interview with political scientist Antonia Grunenberg—see *Conclusions and Prospects* above.)

44. Klaus von Dohnanyi, "Eine Friedensrede. Martin Walsers notwendige Klage," *Frankfurter Allgemeine Zeitung*, November 14, 1998.

45. "'Walser will, daß der Holocaust verschwindet.' WELT-Gespräch mit Ignatz Bubis und Peter Schneider," *Die Welt*, October 14, 1998.

46. Probably the most frivolous and at the same time damaging answer came from scholar Saul Friedländer, an expert on the Nazi period: "That I would have become a member of a national resistance movement, seems to me not only conceivable, but probable." Saul Friedländer, "Über Martin Walsers Friedenspreis-Rede und die Aufgabe der Erinnerung," *Die Zeit*, no. 49, 1998. Many members of the German generation of 1968 spoke in this way with their parents, whom they considered to have been cowards, collaborationists, or worse. The actual reality was, at least in many cases, much more complicated.

47. See Ignatz Bubis, "Ich bleibe dabei," *Frankfurter Allgemeine Zeitung*, November 16, 1998.

48. See Elie Wiesel, "Ohne Schande. Offener Brief von Elie Wiesel an Martin Walser," *Die Zeit*, no. 51, 1998: "Do you not understand that you have opened a door through which others can storm in who pursue completely different political ends and are dangerous in a very different way?" This was also Bubis's main criticism of Walser. Outside observers would have the impression that the "hordes" are simply waiting for the right signal before unleashing their wrath.

49. "Primor fordert Klarstellung von Walser," *Die Welt*, December 7, 1998.

50. Richard von Weizsäcker, "Der Streit wird gefährlich. Mußte Walser provozieren?" *Frankfurter Allgemeine Zeitung*, November 20, 1998. A short article on the front page of that edition had the title: "Weizsäcker: Streit um Walser gerät außer Kontrolle." The phrase "out of control" could be interpreted as signifying a situation in which certain codes and taboos were no longer being maintained, and that is exactly what happened. From whose perspective was this "dangerous"? Aiming to avoid more controversy, the German Book Trade Association announced that the winner of the 1999 Peace Prize would be German-Jewish-American historian Fritz Stern. He has the advantage of being not only Jewish, but also having advocated the reunification of Germany, an "intellectual Bubis" as it were. See Ulrich Raulff, "Eine Chance. Friedenspreis für Fritz Stern," *Frankfurter Allgemeine Zeitung*, April 30, 1999.

51. "Wir brauchen eine neue Sprache für die Erinnerung. Das Treffen von Ignatz Bubis und Martin Walser: Vom Wegschauen als lebensrettender Maßnahme, von der Befreiung des Gewissens und den Rechten der Literatur," *Frankfurter Allgemeine Zeitung*, December 14, 1998. Another article summarizing the main points of the discussion appeared at the top of the front page.

52. "Rede von Bundespräsident Roman Herzog bei der Gedenkveranstaltung aus Anlaß des 60. Jahrestages der Synagogenzerstörung am 9./10. November 1938 ('Reichskristallnacht')," *Die Welt*, November 10, 1998.

53. One of the quirkiest aspects of the peace-prize speech was Walser's appeal to President Herzog to pardon the "idealistic" East German spy Rainer Rupp, who supposedly had only engaged in espionage in order to help maintain the peace in Europe.

54. The only other case of abrasiveness came when Bubis declared that he was satisfied with Walser's clarifications and would now retract the accusation of "mental arson." Walser, who had earlier said that he would not speak with Bubis unless he made such a retraction, now said that Bubis did not need to do so. Walser's arrogance in this instance might well have been no more than a mask hiding his insecurity. One sign of this is the fact that he made a point of citing four Jews (Salomon Korn, writer Rafael Seligmann, religious scholar Jakob Taubes, and journalist Henryk M. Broder) who, he asserted, shared his views about the dangers of over-ritualized remembrance.

Bubis's successor as president of the Central Council of Jews in Germany, Paul Spiegel, has said that the consequences of Walser's speech are enormous ("unübersehbar"), and that Bubis did not have to retract his accusation of "mental arson." Spiegel has even gone one step further, claiming that Walser has ignited a "wildfire" [Flächenbrand] in Germany. This type of rhetoric could hardly be characterized as a contribution to the promotion of German-Jewish dialogue. See ing, "Paul Spiegel rügt den Chef der Unionsfraktion," *Frankfurter Rundschau*, May 13, 2000.

55. Despite other disagreements, Walser and Goldhagen share the belief that contemporary Germany has nothing to do with this past.

56. It must be said, however, that the pacifistic left often ignored conflicts outside of Europe (e.g., in Afghanistan) or idealized "wars of liberation" in the Third World (as it was called then).

57. Fischer was splattered with red paint before he took the podium, but he went on speaking anyway.

58. See "Rede an meinen Sohn," *Der Stern*, no. 17, 1999, 36 and 38.

59. "Ein Territorium des Hasses" [collected statements by German writers about the NATO bombing], *Der Spiegel*, no. 15, 1999, 264. On the same page, one finds a rather strange statement by Walser: "A policy that leads to a war must have been a completely wrong policy. One cannot win a war, especially not this one—just as one could not win the Vietnam War." Contrast this with Enzensberger's praise for the allies in World War II!

60. "Grass billigt Nato-Einsatz," *Focus Online*, May 13, 1999.

61. Reinhard Mohr, "Krieg der Köpfe," *Der Spiegel*, no. 15, 1999, 258–259.

62. See "Die Nato-Bomben und die Intellektuellen," *Der Standard*, April 17–18, 1999.

63. See for example the article by novelist Gerhard Köpf, "In den Schuhen des Fischers. Der Prediger, der uns die Leviten liest—Eine Einführung in die geistliche Rhetorik des Schriftstellers Martin Walser," *Süddeutsche Zeitung*, October 10, 1998. Note that this piece was written before Walser's peace-prize speech.

Richard Herzinger seems puzzled that the Germans still enjoy the "anarchistic ritual" of sermonizing writers, dubbing it "an ancient burden that one has become fond of, [one] that weighs down the otherwise unbearable lightness of postmodern existence." See Richard Herzinger, "Sinn um Untergang? Identitätsstiftung in der Literatur," *Universitas*, March 1999, 220. In this article, he rejects Walser's supposed Heideggerian conservative cultural criticism, but does so with much irony. His coauthor Hannes Stein (see the *Excursus* above), who also criticizes Walser, uses not a rapier, but a club, and his methods are questionable, to say the least. Stein has discovered that Walser is a character ("Christoph") in Ruth Klüger's fictionalized autobiography *Weiter leben*, and he presents us with harsh judgments about this character. Aside from the fact that this is "Christoph," and not Walser, Stein ignores more positive aspects about the character. Klüger writes for instance: "What I am writing here, simplifies [matters]. We [i.e., the narrator and "Christoph"] were not at all that different." See Ruth Klüger, *Weiter leben* (Göttingen: Wallstein, 1992), 213. Stein also sees similarities between Walser as a "raving old man" ("polternder Greis") and as an "insolent young man" ("Schnösel") in the postwar years. The use of such language is no credit to the commentator. See Hannes Stein, "Geübt im Wegdenken. Wie sich Martin Walser treu blieb. Der Auftritt des Schriftstellers in einer Nachkriegserinnerung," *Berliner Zeitung*, November 16, 1998.

64. "Handke's defenders like to emphasize that 'poets know better,' as Bob Dylan once put it: that their fresh view enables us to see through journalistic manipulation. But if there is any lesson from the Balkan war, then it is that poets don't know better." Slavoj Zizek, "Der Balkan im Auge. Was Peter Handke nach Ruritanien treibt," *Süddeutsche Zeitung*, March 17, 1999.

65. According to *Stern Online* (May 16, 1999), the *Süddeutsche* was to publish

Handke's essay about his trip to Serbia on May 29, 1999. It actually appeared a week later. See Peter Handke, "Der Krieg ist das Gebiet des Zufalls," *Süddeutsche Zeitung*, June 5-6, 1999. The essay, consisting of excerpts from a larger piece, appeared after the completion of this epilogue. It has now appeared in book form: Peter Handke, *Unter Tränen fragend. Nachträgliche Aufzeichungen von zwei Jugoslawien-Durchquerungen im Krieg, März und April 1999* (Frankfurt am Main: Suhrkamp, 2000). Handke has also written a play about the Balkans, which had its premiere performance at the Viennese Burgtheater in June 1999. For a book version, see Peter Handke, *Die Fahrt im Einbaum oder Das Stück zum Film vom Krieg* (Frankfurt: Suhrkamp, 1999). The play cannot be discussed here. Suffice it to say that, as in the case of Botho Strauß's *Ithaka*, the text caused a scandal long before its first performance. Despite all legitimate criticism of Handke's political utterances, his literary works should not be read as mere editorials.

66. Cited in Nataly Bleuel, "Mars attacks!" *Spiegel Online*, April 1, 1999.

67. Handke's letter was printed in *Focus*, March 15, 1999, 290. I am quoting from a report about it ("Peter Handke zieht umstrittene Aussage zurück") in the *Berliner Zeitung* of March 15, 1999. In *Focus*, he had asserted: "My place is in Serbia if the NATO criminals bomb the country." Cited in "Aroma des Krieges," *Süddeutsche Zeitung*, April 3, 1999.

68. Cited in "Handke, Serbien, Marsianer," *Die Presse*, March 27, 1999.

69. Cited in "Ritter Handke," *Die Presse*, April 3, 1999.

70. See for example his dispute with Jürgen Habermas about using bombs to guarantee human rights. In the interview cited in note 72 below, Handke accuses Habermas of being an apologist of "raging violence." The philosopher had expressed the hope that the war in Kosovo could accelerate the transition from the "classic international law of the states to the cosmopolitan law of a global civil society." See Habermas, "Bestialität und Humanität. Ein Krieg an der Grenze zwischen Recht und Moral," *Die Zeit*, no. 18, 1999. He answered Handke's sharp criticism in "Zweifellos. Eine Antwort auf Peter Handke," *Süddeutsche Zeitung*, May 18, 1999.

71. "Handke im Interview," *NEWS* [Austria], May 11, 1999. Further quotations in the body of the text.

72. Willi Winkler, "Moral ist ein anderes Wort für Willkür" [Interview with Peter Handke], *Süddeutsche Zeitung*, May 15, 1999. In this interview, Handke refers to the '68ers again: "Does not all the suffering of [this] war stem from the fact that the '68ers are in power in the entire Western world?

73. See "Wer sind die willigen Vollstrecker? Ein Interview mit Daniel Goldhagen zum Krieg im Kosovo," *Frankfurter Rundschau*, April 20, 1999. For a description of a heated debate between Goldhagen and German intellectuals (moderated by American Andrei Markovits), see "Wie im 'Dritten Reich?' Goldhagens Holocaust-Vergleich," *tageszeitung*, May 10, 1999. When Goldhagen published his essay on Serbia in the *Süddeutsche*, the paper took the unusual step of adding an editorial critical of his the-

ses. See Daniel J. Goldhagen, "Eine 'deutsche Lösung' für den Balkan," and jj, "Die unwilligen Vollstrecker," *Süddeutsche Zeitung*, April 30, 1999. Echoing his book, Goldhagen calls Milosevic's policies "eliminatory" and describes the Serbs as being just as "fanatical" as the Germans and Japanese once were.

74. The full passage reads: "Reeducate Serbia? No, reeducate America together with its chairman and the Pimpf Goldhagen." Another advocate of Serbian reeducation is the Albanian author Ismail Kadaré. See "'Ein unheilbarer Haß mit tiefen Wurzeln'" [Interview with Ismail Kandaré], *tageszeitung*, May 26, 1999.

75. For now, analysis is taking a back seat to polemics. Handke has been denounced by such well-known figures as Salman Rushdie, Susan Sontag, and Alain Finkielkraut. Handke responded to Rushdie in "Une lettre de Peter Handke," *Le Monde*, May 20, 1999. To emphasize his—splendid—isolation, Handke signed the letter "ecrivain-sans-parlament." (Rushdie is president of the Parliament of European Writers.) Rushdie's pairing of Handke with National Rifle Association president Charleton Heston is witty, but a bit far-fetched. See Salman Rushdie, "De Pristina à Littleton," *Le Monde*, May 11, 1999. Susan Sontag's essay in support of the NATO bombing contains a passage that could have been taken from Botho Strauß's "Impending Tragedy": "How helpless 'our' Europe feels in the face of all this irrational slaughter and suffering taking place in the other Europe." See Susan Sontag, "Why Are We in Kosovo?" *The New York Times Magazine*, May 2, 1999.

76. See the following reports about the vote: Peter Pragal and Christine Richter, "Bundestag beschließt Bau des Holocaust-Mahnmals in Berlin," *Berliner Zeitung*, June 26, 1999; Wulf Schmiese, "Das Parlament hat gesprochen, die Sache ist entschieden," *Die Welt*, June 26, 1999; Hermann Rudolph, "Das Mahnmal: Ein Kraftakt ohne Kraft," *Der Tagesspiegel*, June 26, 1999; "Bubis: Eine Entscheidung des deutschen Volkes," *Der Tagesspiegel*, June 26, 1999; Roderich Reifenrath, "Das Mahnmal," *Frankfurter Rundschau*, June 26, 1999; Stefan Reinecke, "Ein Spiegel, keine Antwort. Der Bundestag votiert für Eisenmans Stelenfeld," *tageszeitung*, June 26, 1999; Claus Leggewie, "'. . . denn, Entschuldigung, der Bundestag ist ja souverän.' Ein deutsches Denkmal: Das Parlament in Bonn und die Abstimmung über das Holocaust Memorial in Berlin," *Frankfurter Rundschau*, June 24, 1999.

77. See hjh, "Bundesrat billigt neues Staatsbürgerschaftsrecht," *Süddeutsche Zeitung*, May 22, 1999. The law took effect on January 1, 2000.

78. "Rechtsextreme preisen den Holocaust," *Stern Online*, May 24, 1999.

Selected Bibliography

"Aber ich leben von den Zwischenräumen." Peter Handke im Gespräch mit Herbert Gamper. Zürich: Ammann, 1987.

Alefeld, Yvonne-Patricia. *Die Kindheitsideologie in der Romantik.* Paderborn: Schöningh, 1996.

Aly, Götz. *Macht—Geist—Wahn. Kontinuitäten deutschen Denkens.* Berlin: Argon, 1997.

André Müller im Gespräch mit Peter Handke. Weitra (Austria): Bibliothek der Provinz, 1993.

Ansell, Amy Elizabeth. *New Right, New Racism: Race and Reaction in the United States and Britain.* New York: New York University Press, 1997.

Anz, Thomas, ed. *"Es geht nicht um Christa Wolf." Der Literaturstreit im vereinten Deutschland.* München: Edition Spangenberg, 1991.

Ardagh, John. *Germany and the Germans.* Rev. ed. London: Penguin, 1995.

Aschheim, Steven E. *The Nietzsche Legacy in Germany 1890–1990.* Weimar and Now: German Cultural Criticism, vol. 2. Ed. Martin Jay and Anton Kaes. Berkeley, Los Angeles and London: University of California Press, 1992.

———. *Culture and Catastrophe: German and Jewish Confrontations with National Socialism and Other Crises.* New York: New York University Press, 1996.

Ash, Timothy Garton. *In Europe's Name: Germany and the Divided Continent.* New York: Random House, 1993.

Bala, Heike Catrin, and Christian Scholz, eds. *'Deutsch-jüdisches Verhältnis? Fragen, Betrachtungen, Analysen.* Essen: Klartext Verlag, 1997.

Baldwin, Peter, ed. *Reworking the Past: Hitler, the Holocaust, and the Historians' Debate.* Boston: Beacon Press, 1990.

Ball, Hugo. *Der Künstler und die Zeitkrankheit. Ausgewählte Schriften.* Ed. Hans Burkhard Schlichting. Frankfurt am Main: Suhrkamp, 1984.

———. *Zur Kritik der deutschen Intelligenz.* (1919) Bibliothek Suhrkamp 690. 2nd ed. Frankfurt am Main: Suhrkamp, 1991.

Ball, Hugo. *Critique of the German Intelligentsia.* Intro. by Anson Rabinbach. New York: Columbia University Press, 1993.

Barber, Benjamin. *Jihad vs. McWorld.* New York: New York Times Books, 1995.

Baring, Arnulf, and Dominik Geppert. *Scheitert Deutschland? Abschied von unseren Wunschwelten.* Stuttgart: Deutsche Verlags-Anstalt, 1997.

Barkai, Avraham, and Paul Mendes-Flohr. *Aufbruch und Zerstörung 1918–1945. Deutschjüdische Geschichte in der Neuzeit.* Vol. 4. Ed. Michael A. Meyer. München: C. H. Beck, 1997.

Barner, Wilfried, et al. *Geschichte der deutschen Literatur von 1945 bis zur Gegenwart.* Geschichte der deutschen Literatur von den Anfängen bis zur Gegenwart. Ed. Helmut de Boor and Richard Newald. Vol. 12. München: C. H. Beck, 1994.

Baum, Rainer C. *The Holocaust and the German Elite: Genocide and National Suicide in Germany, 1871–1945.* Totowa, N.J.: Rowman and Littlefield; and London: Croom Helm, 1981.

Bauschinger, Sigrid, et al., eds. *Nietzsche heute. Die Rezeption seines Werks nach 1968.* Amherster Kolloquium zur Deutschen Literatur no. 15. Bern und Stuttgart: Francke, 1988.

Baxandall, Lee, and Stefan Morawski, eds. *Marx and Engels on Literature and Art.* Milwaukee: Telos Press, 1973.

Benda, Julien. *Der Verrat der Intellektuellen.* (1927.) Trans. Arthur Merin. Frankfurt am Main: Fischer, 1988.

Benn, Gottfried. *Gesammelte Werke in vier Bänden.* Ed. Dieter Wellershoff. Wiesbaden: Limes, 1959–1961.

Bentley, Eric. *A Century of Hero-Worship. A Study of the Idea of Heroism in Carlyle and Nietzsche, with Notes on Wagner, Spengler, Stefan George, and D. H. Lawrence.* 2nd ed. Boston: Beacon Press, 1957.

Benz, Wolfgang, ed. *Rechtsradikalismus: Randerscheinung oder Renaissance?* Frankfurt am Main: Fischer, 1980.

Berka, Sigrid. *Mythos-Theorie und Allegorik bei Botho Strauß.* Wien: Passagen-Verlag, 1991.

Berka, Sigrid, ed. *Das Werk von Botho Strauß und die 'Bocksgesang'-Debatte. Weimarer Beiträge* 40.2 (1994).

Berlin, Isaiah. *The Crooked Timber of Humanity: Chapters in the History of Ideas.* New York: Vintage, 1990.

———. *The Roots of Romanticism.* Ed. Henry Hardy. Princeton: Princeton University Press, 1999.

Berman, Russell. "Goldhagen's Germany." *Telos* 109 (1996): 131–140.

Betz, Hans-Georg. "*Deutschlandpolitik* on the Margins: On the Evolution of Contemporary New Right Nationalism in the Federal Republic." *New German Critique.* Special issue on the *Historikerstreit.* 44 (Spring/Summer 1988): 127–157.

Betz, Hans-Georg, and Stefan Immerfall, eds. *The New Politics of the Right: Neo-Populist Parties and Movements in Established Democracies.* New York: St. Martin's Press, 1998.

Bissinger, Manfred, and Daniela Hermes, eds. *Zeit sich einzumischen. Die Kontroverse um Günter Grass und die Laudatio auf Yasar Kemal in der Paulskirche.* Göttingen: Steidl, 1998.

Bjørgo, Tore, ed. *Terror from the Extreme Right.* London: Frank Cass, 1995.

Blackbourn, David, and Geoff Eley. *The Peculiarities of German History: Bourgeois Society and Politics in Nineteenth-Century Germany.* Oxford and New York: Oxford University Press, 1984.

Blackbourn, David, and Richard J. Evans, eds. *The German Bourgeoisie.* London and New York: Routledge, 1997.

Bohrer, Karl Heinz. *Die Ästhetik des Schreckens. Die pessimistische Romantik und Ernst Jüngers Frühwerk.* München, Wien: Hanser, 1978.

Bormann, Alexander von, and Horst Albert Glaser, eds. *Weimarer Republik — Drittes Reich: Avantgardismus, Parteilichkeit, Exil.* Deutsche Literatur. Eine Sozialgeschichte. Ed. Horst Albert Glaser. Vol. 9. Reinbek: Rowohlt, 1983.

Bottomore, Tom. *Élites and Society.* 2nd rev. ed. London and New York: Routledge, 1993.

Bracher, Karl Dietrich. *Die deutsche Diktatur. Entstehung, Struktur, Folgen des Nationalsozialismus.* 4th ed. Köln: Kiepenheuer & Witsch, 1972.

Braun, Aurel, and Stephen Scheinberg, eds. *The Extreme Right: Freedom and Security at Risk.* Boulder: Westview Press, 1997.

Breuer, Stefan. *Anatomie der Konservativen Revolution.* Darmstadt: Wissenschaftliche Buchgesellschaft, 1993.

———. *Ästhetischer Fundamentalismus. Stefan George und der deutsche Antimodernismus.* Darmstadt: Wissenschaftliche Buchgesellschaft, 1995.

———. "Ein Mann der Rechten? Thomas Mann zwischen 'konservativer Revolution', ästhetischem Fundamentalismus und neuem Nationalismus." *Politisches Denken. Jahrbuch 1997.* Stuttgart, Weimar: Metzler, 1997. 119-140.

Brinkley, Alan. *Liberalism and Its Discontents.* Cambridge: Harvard University Press, 1998.

Brockmann, Stephen. "A Literary Civil War." *The Germanic Review* 68.2 (Spring 1993): 69-78.

———. "German Literary Debates after the Collapse." *German Life and Letters* 47.2 (April 1994): 201-210.

Bruck, Moeller van den. *Das dritte Reich.* Hamburg, Berlin: Hanseatische Verlagsanstalt, 1931.

Brunkhorst, Hauke. *Der Intellektuelle im Land der Mandarine.* Frankfurt am Main: Suhrkamp, 1987.

Brzezinski, Zbigniew. *The Grand Chessboard: American Primacy and Its Strategic Imperatives.* New York: Basic Books, 1997.

Bubik, Roland. *Wir '89er. Wer wir sind und was wir wollen.* Berlin, Frankfurt am Main: Ullstein, 1995.

Bubis, Ignatz. *Juden in Deutschland.* Berlin: Aufbau, 1996.

Bubis, Ignatz (with Peter Sichrovsky). *"Damit bin ich noch längst nicht fertig."* Die Autobiographie. Frankfurt am Main and New York: Campus, 1996.

Bullivant, Keith. "The Conservative Revolution." *The Weimar Dilemma: Intellectuals in the Weimar Republic.* Ed. Anthony Phelan. Manchester, England and Dover, N.H.: Manchester University Press, 1985. 47-70.

———. *The Future of German Literature.* Oxford and Providence: Berg, 1994.

Bullivant, Keith, ed. *Beyond 1989. Re-reading German Literature since 1945.* Modern German Studies 3. Providence and Oxford: Berghahn Books, 1997.

Bullock, Marcus Paul. *The Violent Eye: Ernst Jünger's Visions and Revisions on the European Right.* Kritik: German Literary Theory and Cultural Studies. Ed. Liliane Weissberg. Detroit: Wayne State University Press, 1992.

Burns, Rob, ed. *German Cultural Studies: An Introduction.* New York: Oxford University Press, 1995.

Butterwege, Christoph, ed. *NS-Vergangenheit, Antisemitismus und Nationalismus in Deutschland: Beiträge zur politischen Kultur der Bundesrepublik und zur politischen Bildung.* Mit einem Vorwort von Ignatz Bubis. Baden-Baden: Nomos Verlagsgesellschaft, 1997.

Capra, Fritjof, and Charlene Spretnak. *Green Politics: The Global Promise.* New York: Dutton, 1984.

Carey, John. *The Intellectuals and the Masses: Pride and Prejudice among the Literary Intelligentsia, 1880-1939.* New York: St. Martin's Press, 1993.

Charle, Christophe. *Vordenker der Moderne. Die Intellektuellen im 19. Jahrhundert.* Trans. Michael Bischoff. Europäische Geschichte. Ed. Wolfgang Benz. Frankfurt am Main: Fischer, 1997.

Claussen, Johann Hinrich. "Politik der Unpolitischen. Konservative Revolution: Hofmannsthal und Thomas Mann." *Frankfurter Allgemeine Zeitung.* June 4, 1997.

Cohn-Bendit, Daniel, and Thomas Schmid. *Heimat Babylon. Das Wagnis der multikulturellen Demokratie.* Hamburg: Hoffmann und Campe, 1993.

Conradt, David P., et al., eds. *Germany's New Politics.* Tempe, Ariz.: German Studies Review, 1995.

Corino, Karl, ed. *Intellektuelle im Bann des Nationalsozialismus.* Hamburg: Hoffmann und Campe, 1980.

Craig, Gordon L. *The Germans.* New York: Meridian, 1991.

———. "Good Germans." *New York Review of Books.* December 17, 1992, 38-44.

Cullen, Michael S. *Das Holocaust-Mahnmal. Dokumentation einer Debatte.* Zürich Pendo-Verlag, 1999.

Darnton, Robert. "George Washington's False Teeth." *New York Review of Books,* March 27, 1997.

Deichmann, Thomas. *Noch einmal für Jugoslawien: Peter Handke.* Frankfurt am Main: Suhrkamp, 1999.

Deiritz, Karl, and Hannes Krauss. *Der deutsch-deutsche Literaturstreit oder "Freunde, es spricht sich schlecht mit gebundener Zunge." Analysen und Materialien.* Hamburg and Zürich: Luchterhand Literaturverlag, 1991.

Delabar, Walter, and Erhard Schütz, eds. *Deutschsprachige Literatur der 70er und 80er Jahre.* Darmstadt: Wissenschaftliche Buchgesellschaft, 1997.

Denham, Scott, Irene Kacandes, and Jonathan Petropoulos. *A User's Guide to German Cultural Studies. Social History, Popular Culture, and Politics in Germany.* Ed. Geoff Eley. Ann Arbor: University of Michigan Press, 1997.

Denken im Zwiespalt. Über den Verrat von Intellektuellen im 20. Jahrhundert. Frankfurter Historik-Vorlesungen no. 3. Ed. Werner von Bergen and Walter H. Pehle. Frankfurt am Main: Fischer, 1996.

Deschner, Karlheinz. *Der Moloch. Eine kritische Geschichte der USA.* München: Heyne, 1992.

Deutsche Literatur 1996. Jahresrückblick. Ed. Franz Josef Görtz et al. Stuttgart: Reclam, 1997.

Deutsche Literatur 1995. Jahresrückblick. Ed. Franz Josef Görtz et al. Stuttgart: Reclam, 1996.

Deutsche Literatur 1994. Jahresrückblick. Ed. Franz Josef Görtz et al. Stuttgart: Reclam, 1995.

Deutsche Literatur 1993. Jahresrückblick. Ed. Franz Josef Görtz et al. Stuttgart: Reclam, 1994.

Dewey, John. *German Philosophy and Politics.* New York: Holt, 1915.

Dictionary of the History of Ideas. Ed. Philip P. Wiener. 4 vols. New York: Charles Scribner's Sons, 1973.

Dictka, Norbert. *Ernst Jünger—vom Weltkrieg zum Weltfrieden. Biographie und Werkübersicht 1895-1945.* Keimers Abhandlungen zur deutschen Sprache und Kultur 6. Bad Honnef: E. Keimer; Zürich: Herbsacker, 1994.

Diner, Dan. *America in the Eyes of the Germans: An Essay on Anti-Americanism.* Trans. Allison Brown. Princeton: Markus Wiener, 1996.

Diner, Dan, ed. *Ist der Nationalsozialismus Geschichte? Zu Historisierung und Historikerstreit.* Frankfurt am Main: Fischer, 1987.

———. *Zivilisationsbruch, Denken nach Auschwitz.* Frankfurt am Main: Fischer, 1988.

"'Dissidenten?' Texte und Dokumente zur DDR-Exil-Literatur." *Deutschunterricht* 43.10 (1990).

Dorfman, Ariel. *How to Read Donald Duck: Imperialist Ideology in the Disney Comic.* New York: International General, 1975.

Dorrien, Gary. *The Neoconservative Mind: Politics, Culture, and the War of Ideology.* Philadelphia: Temple University Press, 1993.

Dürr, Volker, et al., eds. *Nietzsche. Literature and Values.* Monatshefte Occasional Volumes. Madison: University of Wisconsin Press, 1988.

Dundes, Alan. *Life Is Like a Chicken Coop Ladder: A Portrait of German Culture through Folklore.* New York: Columbia University Press, 1984.

Dujmic, Daniela. *Literatur zwischen Autonomie und Engagement. Zur Poetik von Hans Magnus Enzensberger, Peter Handke und Dieter Wellershoff.* Konstanz: Hartung-Gorre, 1996.

Eickhoff, Volker, and Ilse Korotin, eds. *Sehnsucht nach Schicksal und Tiefe. Der Geist der konservativen Revolution.* Wien: Picus Verlag, 1997.

Eley, Geoff, ed. *Society, Culture, and the State in Germany, 1870–1930*. Ann Arbor: University of Michigan Press, 1996.

Engelmann, Bernt. *Deutschland ohne Juden. Eine Bilanz.* Köln: Pahl-Rugenstein, 1988.

Enzensberger, Hans Magnus. *Deutschland, Deutschland unter anderem. Äußerungen zur Politik.* Frankfurt am Main: Suhrkamp, 1967.

———. "Hitler's Wiedergänger." *Der Spiegel,* no. 6, 1991, 26–28.

———. "Ausblicke auf den Bürgerkrieg." *Der Spiegel,* no. 25, 1993, 170–175.

———. *Aussichten auf den Bürgerkrieg.* Frankfurt am Main: Suhrkamp, 1993.

———. *Diderots Schatten.* Frankfurt am Main: Suhrkamp, 1994.

Erb, Andreas, ed. *Baustelle Gegenwartsliteratur. Die neunziger Jahre.* Opladen: Westdeutscher Verlag, 1998.

Evans, Richard J. *Rereading German History 1800–1996.* London and New York: Routledge, 1997.

Farías, Victor. *Heidegger and Nazism.* Trans. Paul Burrell and Gabriel R. Ricci. Philadelphia: Temple University Press, 1989.

Fassbinder, Rainer Werner. *Der Müll, die Stadt und der Tod.* Frankfurt am Main: Verlag der Autoren, 1981.

Feit, Margret. *Die "Neue Rechte" in der Bundesrepublik. Organisation—Ideologie—Strategie.* Frankfurt am Main and New York: Campus, 1987.

Fellinger, Raimund, ed. *Peter Handke.* Frankfurt am Main: Suhrkamp, 1985.

Fetz, Gerald A. *Martin Walser.* Stuttgart and Weimar: J. B. Metzler, 1997.

Figal, Günter, and Heimo Schwilk, eds. *Magie der Heiterkeit. Ernst Jünger zum Hundertsten.* Stuttgart: Klett-Cotta, 1995.

Fischer, Bernd. *Das Eigene und das Eigentliche: Klopstock, Herder, Fichte, Kleist. Episoden aus der Konstruktionsgeschichte nationaler Intentionalitäten.* Philologische Studien und Quellen 135. Ed. Hugo Steger and Hartmut Steinecke. Berlin: Erich Schmitt, 1995.

Fischer, Gerhard, ed. *Debating Enzensberger: Great Migration and Civil War.* Studien zur deutschsprachigen Gegenwartsliteratur 5. Ed. Paul Michael Lützeler. Tübingen: Stauffenburg, 1996.

Fischer, Jörg. *Ganz rechts. Mein Leben in der DVU.* Hamburg: Rowohlt, 1999.

Flinker, Martin. *Thomas Mann's politische Betrachtungen im Lichte der heutigen Zeit.* 's-Gravenhage: Mouton and Co., 1959.

Forbes, Jill, and Michael Kelly, eds. *French Cultural Studies.* Oxford: Oxford University Press, 1995.

Friedenspreis des deutschen Buchhandels 1998: Martin Walser (Frankfurt am Main: Verlag Buchhändler-Vereinigung, 1998).

Fritsche, Martin. *Hans Magnus Enzensbergers produktionsorientierte Moral. Konstanten in der Ästhetik eines Widersachers der Gleichheit.* Bern, Berlin, Frankfurt am Main, New York, Paris, and Wien: Peter Lang, 1997.

Fukuyama, Francis. *The End of History and the Last Man.* New York: The Free Press, 1992.

Fulbrook, Mary. *A Concise History of Germany.* Rev. ed. Cambridge: Cambridge University Press, 1994.

George, Stefan. *Werke. Ausgabe in zwei Bänden.* München und Düsseldorf: Helmut Küpper, 1958.

———. *Das Neue Reich.* Gesamt-Ausgabe der Werke. Endgültige Fassung. Vol. 9. Berlin: Georg Bondi, 1937.

Der George-Kreis. Eine Auswahl aus seinen Schriften. Ed. Georg Peter Landmann. Stuttgart: Klett-Cotta, 1980.

Giddens, Anthony. *Beyond Left and Right: The Future of Radical Politics.* Stanford: Stanford University Press, 1994.

Giesen, Bernhard. *Intellectuals and the German Nation: Collective Identity in an Axial Age.* Trans. Nicholas Levis and Amos Weisz. Cambridge: Cambridge University Press, 1998.

Glaser, Hermann. *Spießer-Ideologie. Von der Zerstörung des deutschen Geistes im 19. und 20. Jahrhundert und dem Aufstieg des Nationalsozialismus.* Rev. ed. Frankfurt am Main: Fischer, 1985.

———. *Die Kulturgeschichte der Bundesrepublik Deutschland.* 3 vols. Frankfurt am Main: Fischer, 1990.

Glotz, Peter. *Die deutsche Rechte. Eine Streitschrift.* Stuttgart: Deutsche Verlagsanstalt, 1985.

Goldhagen, Daniel Jonah. *Hitler's Willing Executioners: Ordinary Germans and the Holocaust.* Rev. ed. New York: Vintage, 1997.

Golsan, Richard J. *Fascism's Return: Scandal, Revision, and Ideology since 1980.* Lincoln and London: University of Nebraska Press, 1998.

Gooch, G. P., et al. *The German Mind and Outlook.* Issued under the auspices of the Institute of Sociology. London: Chapman and Hall, 1945.

Grass, Günter. *Ein Schnäppchen namens DDR. Letzte Reden vorm Glockengeläut.* (1990.) München: Deutscher Taschenbuch Verlag, 1993.

Gross, David. *The Writer and Society: Heinrich Mann and Literary Politics in Germany, 1890–1940.* Atlantic Highlands, N.J.: Humanities Press, 1980.

Große, Jürgen. "Politische Verantwortung und moralische Schuld: Aspekte des intellektuellen Diskurses." *German Studies Review.* Special Issue "Totalitäre Herrschaft—totalitäres Erbe." Fall 1994. 173–186.

Grunenberg, Antonia. *Antifaschismus—ein deutscher Mythos.* Reinbek: Rowohlt, 1993.

———. *Der Schlaf der Freiheit. Politik und Gemeinsinn im 21. Jahrhundert.* Reinbek: Rowohlt, 1997.

Habermas, Jürgen. *Philosophisch-politische Profile.* Rev. ed. Frankfurt am Main: Suhrkamp, 1984.

———. *Die nachholende Revolution. Kleine Politische Schriften VII.* Frankfurt am Main: Suhrkamp, 1990.

———. *Vergangenheit als Zukunft.* pendo profile. Ed. Michael Haller. Zürich: pendo, 1990.

Habermas, Jürgen. *Die Moderne—ein unvollendetes Projekt. Philosophisch-politische Aufsätze.* Leipzig: Reclam, 1990.

———. *The Past as Future.* Trans. and ed. Max Pensky. Lincoln and London: University of Nebraska Press, 1994.

———. *Die Einbeziehung des Anderen. Studien zur politischen Theorie*. Frankfurt am Main: Suhrkamp, 1996.

———. *A Berlin Republic. Writings on Germany.* Trans. Steven Rendall. Lincoln: University of Nebraska Press, 1997.

Hallberg, Robert von, ed. *Literary Intellectuals and the Dissolution of the State: Professionalism and Conformity in the GDR*. Trans. Kenneth J. Northcott. Chicago and London: University of Chicago Press, 1996.

Hamilton, Nigel. *The Brothers Mann: The Lives of Heinrich and Thomas Mann 1871-1950 and 1875-1955*. New Haven: Yale University Press, 1979.

Hammersen, Nicolai. *Politisches Denken im deutschen Widerstand. Ein Beitrag zur Wirkungsgeschichte neokonservativer Ideologien 1914-1944*. Beiträge zur Politischen Wissenschaft, vol. 67. Berlin: Duncker and Humblot, 1993.

Handke, Peter. *Ich bin ein Bewohner des Elfenbeinturms*. Frankfurt am Main: Suhrkamp, 1972.

———. *Der kurze Brief zum langen Abschied*. Frankfurt am Main: Suhrkamp,1972.

———. *Abschied des Träumers vom Neunten Land*. Frankfurt am Main: Suhrkamp, 1991.

———. *Die Theaterstücke*. Frankfurt am Main: Suhrkamp, 1992.

———. *Mein Jahr in der Niemandsbucht—Ein Märchen aus den neuen Zeiten*. Frankfurt am Main: Suhrkamp, 1994.

———. *Die Tage gingen wirklich ins Land. Ein Lesebuch*. Ed. Heinz Schafroth. Stuttgart: Reclam, 1995.

———. *Eine winterliche Reise zu den Flüssen Donau, Save, Morawa und Drina oder Gerechtigkeit für Serbien*. 2nd ed. Frankfurt am Main: Suhrkamp, 1996.

———. *Sommerlicher Nachtrag zu einer winterlichen Reise*. Frankfurt am Main: Suhrkamp, 1996.

———. *A Journey to the Rivers: Justice for Serbia*. Trans. Scott Abbott. New York: Viking, 1997. Translation of *Eine winterliche Reise zu den Flüssen Donau, Save, Morawa und Drina oder Gerechtigkeit für Serbien*.

———. *Zurüstungen für die Unsterblichkeit. Ein Königsdrama*. Frankfurt am Main: Suhrkamp, 1997.

———. *In einer dunklen Nacht ging ich aus meinem stillen Haus*. Frankfurt am Main: Suhrkamp, 1997.

———. *Am Felsfenster morgens und andere Ortszeiten 1982-1987*. Salzburg, Wien: Residenz, 1998.

———. *Die Fahrt im Einbaum oder Das Stück zum Film vom Krieg*. Frankfurt am Main: Suhrkamp, 1999.

———. *Unter Tränen fragend. Nachträgliche Aufzeichnungen von zwei Jugoslawien-Durchquerungen im Krieg, März und April 1999*. Frankfurt am Main: Suhrkamp, 2000.

Harpprecht, Klaus. *Thomas Mann. Eine Biographie*. Reinbek: Rowohlt, 1995.

Harris, Geoffrey. *The Dark Side of Europe: The Extreme Right Today.* 2nd ed. Edinburgh: Edinburgh University Press, 1994.

Haseler, Stephen. *The Varieties of Anti-Americanism: Reflex and Response.* Washington, D.C.: Ethics and Public Policy Center, 1985.

Haslinger, Josef. *Die Ästhetik des Novalis.* Literatur in der Geschichte, Geschichte in der Literatur. Ed. Friedbert Aspetsberger et al. Vol. 5. Königstein: Hain, 1981.

Haupt, Jürgen. *Heinrich Mann.* Sammlung Metzler 189. Stuttgart: Metzler, 1980.

Heidegger, Martin. *Wegmarken.* Ed. Friedrich-Wilhelm von Herrmann. *Gesamtausgabe,* Abt. 1, Band 9. Frankfurt am Main: Klostermann, 1976.

———. *Besinnung.* Ed. Friedrich Wilhelm von Herrmann. *Gesamtausgabe,* Abt. III, Band 66. Frankfurt am Main: Klostermann, 1997.

Heine, Heinrich. *Heines Werke in fünf Bänden.* Ed. Helmut Holtzhauer. Bibliothek deutscher Klassiker. Berlin and Weimar: Aufbau, 1974.

Heller, Erich. *The Importance of Being Nietzsche: Ten Essays.* Chicago and London: University of Chicago Press, 1988.

Hepp, Corona. *Avantgarde. Moderne Kunst, Kulturkritik und Reformbewegungen nach der Jahrhundertwende.* Deutsche Geschichte der neuesten Zeit, ed. Martin Broszat et al. München: Deutscher Taschenbuch Verlag, 1987.

Herf, Jeffrey. *Reactionary Modernism: Technology, Culture, and Politics in Weimar and the Third Reich.* Cambridge: Cambridge University Press, 1984.

Hermand, Jost. *Old Dreams of a New Reich: Volkish Utopias and National Socialism.* Trans. Paul Levesque and Stefan Soldovieri. Bloomington and Indianapolis: Indiana University Press, 1992.

Hermann, Hans Peter, Hans-Martin Blitz, and Susanna Moßmann. *Machtphantasie Deutschland. Nationalismus, Männlichkeit und Fremdenhaß im Vaterlandsdiskurs deutscher Schriftsteller des 18. Jahrhunderts.* Frankfurt am Main: Suhrkamp, 1996.

Herrmann, Wolfgang. *Der neue Nationalismus und seine Literatur* (1933). *Ein besprechendes Auswahlverzeichnis.* Ed. Markus Josef Klein. Schriftenreihe zur Konservativen Revolution, Nr. 1. 2nd rev. ed. Limburg a.d. Lahn: San Casciano Verlag, 1994.

Herz, Thomas, and Michael Schwab-Trapp. *Umkämpfte Vergangenheit. Diskurse über den Nationalsozialismus seit 1945.* Opladen: Westdeutscher Verlag, 1997.

Herzinger, Richard. *Masken der Lebensrevolution. Vitalistische Zivilisations- und Humanismuskritik in Texten Heiner Müllers.* München: Fink, 1992.

———. "Die Rückkehr der romantischen Moderne." *Theater heute,* no. 8, 1996, 6-12.

———. *Die Tyrannei des Gemeinsinns: Ein Bekenntnis zur egoistischen Gesellschaft.* Berlin: Rowohlt, 1997.

Herzinger, Richard. "Sinn im Untergang? Identitätsstiftung in der Literatur." *Universitas,* March 1999, 205-220.

Herzinger, Richard, and Hannes Stein. *Endzeit-Propheten oder Die Offensive der Antiwestler. Fundamentalismus, Antiamerikanismus und Neue Rechte.* Reinbek: Rowohlt, 1995.

Himmelstein, Jerome L. *To the Right: The Transformation of American Conservatism.* Berkeley, Los Angeles, and Oxford: University of California Press, 1990.

Hobsbawm, Eric. *The Age of Empire, 1875-1914.* New York: Pantheon, 1987.

Hochhuth, Rolf. *Und Brecht sah das Tragische nicht. Plädoyers, Polemiken, Profile.* Ed. Walter Homolka and Rosemarie von Knesebeck. München: Knesebeck, 1996.

Hofmannsthal, Hugo von. "Das Schrifttum als geistiger Raum der Nation." *Gesammelte Werke in Einzelbänden.* Ed. Herbert Steiner. Vol. 6. Frankfurt am Main: Fischer, 1955. 390-413.

Hofmannsthal, Hugo von, ed. *Deutsches Lesebuch. Eine Auswahl deutscher Prosastücke aus dem Jahrhundert 1750-1850.* (1923.) Frankfurt am Main: Fischer, 1952.

Hollander, Paul. *Anti-Americanism: Critiques at Home and Abroad 1965-1990.* New York: Oxford University Press, 1992.

Hollingdale, R. J. *Nietzsche.* Routledge Author Guides. London and Boston: Routledge and Kegan Paul, 1973.

Huch, Ricarda. "Die Romantik." *Gesammelte Werke.* Ed. Wilhelm Emmerich. Vol. 6. Köln and Berlin: Kiepenheuer & Witsch, 1969. 17-646.

Huyssen, Andreas. "Fortifying the Heart—Totally: Ernst Jünger's Armored Texts." *Twilight Memories: Marking Time in a Culture of Amnesia.* New York and London: Routledge, 1995. 127-143.

Jäckh, Ernst. *Amerika und Wir. Amerikanisch-deutsches Ideen-Bündnis.* Stuttgart, Berlin, Leipzig: Deutsche Verlags-Anstalt, 1929.

Jäger, Andrea. *Schriftsteller aus der DDR. Ausbürgerungen und Übersiedlungen von 1961 bis 1989. Autorenlexikon und Studie.* 2 vols. Frankfurt am Main: Peter Lang, 1995.

Jameson, Fredric. *Fables of Aggression: Wyndham Lewis, the Modernist as Fascist.* Berkeley, Los Angeles, London: University of California Press, 1979.

Janka, Franz. *Die braune Gesellschaft. Ein Volk wird formatiert.* Stuttgart: Quell, 1997.

Janke, Pia. *Der schöne Schein. Peter Handke und Botho Strauß.* Wien: Verlag Holzhausen, 1993.

Jeffers, Robinson. *The Selected Poetry of Robinson Jeffers.* (1927.) New York: Random House, 1937.

———. *Cawdor and Medea.* New York: New Directions, 1970.

Jennings, Jeremy, and Anthony Kemp-Welch, eds. *Intellectuals and Politics: From the Dreyfus Affair to Salman Rushdie.* London and New York: Routledge, 1997.

Jochimsen, Maren. *Die Poetisierung der Ökonomie. Novalis' Thesen im* Heinrich von Ofterdingen *als Anregungen zu einer ökologieorientierten Ökonomie.* Stuttgarter Arbeiten zur Germanistik 297. Stuttgart: Hans-Dieter Heinz, 1994.

Joll, James. "Nietzsche vs. Nietzsche." *The New York Review of Books.* February 11, 1993, 20-23.

Joppke, Christian. *East German Dissidents and the Revolution of 1989: Social Movement in a Leninist Regime.* New York: New York University Press, 1995.

Jost, Dominik. *Stefan George und seine Elite. Eine Studie zur Geschichte der Eliten.* Zürich: Speer, 1949.

Jünger, Ernst. *Storm of Steel.* Trans. Basil Creighton. Garden City: Doubleday, Doran and Company, 1929.

————. *Jahre der Okkupation.* Stuttgart: Klett, 1958.

————. *Strahlungen. Erster Teil.* Werke. Vol. 2. Stuttgart: Klett-Cotta, 1960–1965.

————. *Sämtliche Werke.* Stuttgart: Klett-Cotta, 1978–83.

Junge, Barbara, Julian Naumann, and Holger Stark. *RechtsSchreiber. Wie ein Netz in Medien und Politik an der Restauration des Nationalen arbeitet.* Berlin: Elefanten Press, 1997.

Kaempfer, Wolfgang. *Ernst Jünger.* Sammlung Metzler 201. Stuttgart: Metzler, 1981.

Kaes, Anton, et al., eds. *The Weimar Republic Sourcebook.* Weimar and Now: German Cultural Criticism. Ed. Martin Jay and Anton Kaes. Vol. 3. Berkeley, Los Angeles, and London: University of California Press, 1994.

Keller, Ernst. *Der unpolitische Deutsche. Eine Studie zu den "Betrachtungen eines Unpolitischen" von Thomas Mann.* Bern and München: Francke, 1965.

Kemper, Peter, ed. *Martin Heidegger—Faszination und Erschrecken. Die politische Dimension einer Philosophie.* Frankfurt am Main and New York: Campus, 1990.

Kempter, Klaus. *Die Jellineks 1820–1855. Eine familienbiographische Studie zum deutschjüdischen Bildungsbürgertum.* Düsseldorf: Droste, 1998.

Kessler, Michael, Wolfgang Graf Vitzthum, and Jürgen Wertheimer, eds. *Neonationalismus. Neokonservatismus. Sondierungen und Analysen.* Stauffenburg Discussion, vol. 6. Tübingen: Stauffenburg, 1997.

Kettenacker, Lothar. *Germany Since 1945.* Oxford and New York: Oxford University Press, 1997.

Kielmansegg, Peter Graf. *Lange Schatten. Vom Umgang der Deutschen mit der nationalsozialistischen Vergangenheit.* Berlin: Siedler, 1989.

Kirfel, Martina, and Walter Oswalt, eds. *Die Rückkehr der Führer. Modernisierter Rechtsradikalismus in Westeuropa.* 2nd rev. ed. Wien and Zürich: Europaverlag, 1991.

Klemperer, Victor. *I Will Bear Witness: A Diary of the Nazi Years, 1933–1941.* New York: Random House, 1998.

Klinger, Cornelia. *Flucht Trost Revolte. Die Moderne und ihre ästhetischen Gegenwelten.* München and Wien: Hanser, 1995.

Klinkowitz, Jerome, and James Knowlton. *Peter Handke and the Postmodern Transformation.* Columbia: University of Missouri Press, 1983.

Klotz, Johannes, and Ulrich Schneider, eds. *Die selbstbewußte Nation und ihr Geschichtsbild. Geschichtslegenden der Neuen Rechten.* Köln: PapyRossa, 1997.

Klotz, Johannes, and Gerd Wiegel, eds. *Geistige Brandstiftung? Die Walser-Bubis-Debatte.* Köln: PapyRossa Verlag, 1999.

Koebner, Thomas. "Die Erwartung der Katastrophe. Zur Geschichtsphilosophie des 'neuen Konservatismus' (Oswald Spengler, Ernst Jünger)." *Unbehauste. Zur deutschen Literatur in der Weimarer Republik, im Exil und in der Nachkriegszeit.* München: Edition Text und Kritik, 1992.

Koenen, Andreas. *Der Fall Carl Schmitt. Sein Aufstieg zum "Kronjuristen des Dritten Reiches."* Darmstadt: Wissenschaftliche Buchgesellschaft, 1995.

Kohn, Hans. *The Mind of Germany: The Education of a Nation.* Harper Torchbooks / The Academy Library. New York: Harper and Row, 1960.

Konitzer, Martin. *Ernst Jünger.* Reihe Campus Einführungen 1071. Frankfurt am Main and New York: Campus, 1993.

Konzett, Matthias. *The Rhetoric of National Dissent in Thomas Bernhard, Peter Handke, and Elfriede Jelinek.* Columbia, S.C.: Camden House, 2000.

Koopmann, Helmut. *Thomas-Mann-Handbuch.* Stuttgart: Kröner, 1990.

Koselleck, Reinhart. *Critique and Crisis: Enlightenment and the Pathogenesis of Modern Society.* Studies in Contemporary German Social Thought. Ed. Thomas McCarthy. Cambridge: MIT Press, 1988.

Koshar, Rudy. *Germany's Transient Pasts: Preservation and National Memory in the Twentieth Century.* Chapel Hill and London: University of North Carolina Press, 1998.

Kraft, Werner, *Stefan George.* München: Edition Text und Kritik, 1980.

Kreutzer, Helmut, ed. *Pluralismus und Postmodernismus. Zur Literatur- und Kulturgeschichte in Deutschland 1980-1995.* Forschungen zur Literatur- und Kulturgeschichte 25. Ed. Helmut Kreuzer and Karl Riha. 4th ed. Frankfurt am Main: Peter Lang, 1996.

Krispyn, Egbert. *Anti-Nazi Writers in Exile.* Athens: University of Georgia Press, 1978.

Kritisches Lexikon zur deutschsprachigen Gegenwartsliteratur. München: Text und Kritik. 1978ff.

Krockow, Christian Graf von. *Die Entscheidung. Eine Untersuchung über Ernst Jünger, Carl Schmitt, Martin Heidegger.* (1958.) Rev. ed. Frankfurt am Main and New York: Campus, 1990.

———. *Die Deutschen in ihrem Jahrhundert 1890-1990.* Reinbek: Rowohlt, 1992.

———. *Von deutschen Mythen. Rückblick und Ausblick.* München: Deutscher Taschenbuch Verlag, 1997.

Kroes, Rob. *If You've Seen One, You've Seen the Mall: Europeans and American Mass Culture.* Urbana: University of Illinois Press, 1996.

Kroes, Rob, and Maarten van Rossem, eds. *Anti-Americanism in Europe.* Amsterdam: Free University Press, 1986.

Kunst oder Pornographie? Der Prozess Grass gegen Ziesel. München: Lehmann, 1969.

Kurthen, Hermann, Werner Bergmann, and Rainer Erb, eds. *Antisemitism and Xenophobia in Germany after Unification.* New York and Oxford: Oxford University Press, 1997.

Kurzke, Hermann. *Auf der Suche nach der verlorenen Irrationalität. Thomas Mann und der Konservatismus.* Epistemata. Würzburger wissenschaftliche Schriften, Reihe Literaturwissenschaft. Vol. 1. Würzburg: Königshausen und Neumann, 1980.

———. *Romantik und Konservatismus. Das "politische" Werk Friedrich von Hardenbergs (Novalis) im Horizont seiner Wirkungsgeschichte.* München: Fink, 1983.

Lacoue-Labarthe, Philippe. *Heidegger, Art and Politics: The Fiction of the Political.* Trans. Chris Turner. Oxford: Blackwell, 1990.

Langguth, Gerd, ed. *Autor, Macht, Staat. Literatur und Politik in Deutschland. Ein notwendiger Dialog.* Düsseldorf: Droste, 1994.

Lasch, Christopher. *The Revolt of the Elites*. New York: Norton, 1995.

Leeder, Karen. *Breaking Boundaries: A New Generation of Poets in the GDR*. Oxford: Clarendon Press, 1996.

Leggewie, Claus. *Die Republikaner. Phantombild der Neuen Rechten*. Berlin: Rotbuch, 1989.

———. *Die 89er. Portrait einer Generation*. Hamburg: Hoffmann und Campe, 1995.

———. *America First? Der Fall einer konservativen Revolution*. Frankfurt am Main: Fischer, 1997.

Lenk, Kurt. *Deutscher Konservatismus*. Frankfurt am Main and New York: Campus, 1989.

Lenk, Kurt, et al. *Vordenker der Neuen Rechten*. Reihe Campus Einführungen 1094. Frankfurt am Main and New York: Campus, 1997.

Lennartz, Franz. *Deutsche Schriftsteller des 20. Jahrhunderts im Spiegel der Kritik*. 3 vols. Stuttgart: Kröner, 1984.

Lermen, Birgit, and Matthias Loewen. "Ulrich Schacht." *Lyrik aus der DDR. Exemplarische Analysen*. Paderborn, München, Wien, Zürich: Schöningh, 1987. Uni-Taschenbücher 1470. 404–424.

Lilla, Mark. "A Tale of Two Reactions." *New York Review of Books*, May 14, 1998, 4–7.

Lind, Michael. "Why Intellectual Conservatism Died." *Dissent* (Winter 1995): 42–47.

Linse, Ulrich. *Ökopax und Anarchie. Eine Geschichte der ökologischen Bewegungen in Deutschland*. München: Deutscher Taschenbuch Verlag, 1986.

Linstead, Michael. *Outer World and Inner World: Socialisation and Emancipation in the Works of Peter Handke, 1964–1981*. European University Studies, vol. 1024. Frankfurt am Main, Bern, and New York: Peter Lang, 1988.

Lippmann, Heinz. *Honecker and the New Politics of Europe*. Trans. Helen Sebba. New York: Macmillan, 1972.

Loesche, Peter. *Die Vereinigten Staaten. Innenansichten. Ein Versuch, das Land der unbegrenzten Widersprüche zu begreifen*. Hannover: Fackelträger, 1997.

Löwith, Karl. *From Hegel to Nietzsche: The Revolution in Nineteenth-Century Thought*. Trans. David E. Green. Garden City, N.Y.: Doubleday Anchor, 1967.

Lützeler, Paul Michael, ed. *Plädoyers für Europa. Stellungnahmen deutschsprachiger Schriftsteller 1915–1949*. Frankfurt am Main: Fischer, 1987.

Lukács, Georg. *The Destruction of Reason*. Trans. Peter Palmer. Atlantic Highlands, N.J.: Humanities Press, 1981.

Lunzer, Heinz. *Hofmannsthals politische Tätigkeit in den Jahren 1914–1917*. Europäische Hochschulschriften, Reihe I, Deutsche Sprache und Literatur, vol. 380. Frankfurt am Main, Bern, and Cirencester: Peter Lang, 1981.

Maass, Peter. *Love Thy Neighbor: A Story of War*. New York: Knopf, 1996.

———. *Die Sache mit dem Krieg. Bosnien von 1992 bis Dayton*. Aus dem Amerikanischen von Barbara Scriba-Sethe. München: Knesebeck, 1997.

Maase, Kaspar. *Grenzenloses Vergnügen. Der Aufstieg der Massenkultur 1850–1970*. Europäische Geschichte. Ed. Wolfgang Benz. Frankfurt am Main: Fischer, 1997.

Maaz, Hans-Joachim. *Gefühlsstau. Ein Psychogramm der DDR.* Berlin: Argon Verlag, 1990.

Maclean, Ian, Alan Montefiore, and Peter Winch, eds. *The Political Responsibility of Intellectuals.* Cambridge: Cambridge University Press, 1990.

Mähl, Hans-Joachim. *Die Idee des goldenen Zeitalters im Werk des Novalis. Studien zur Wesensbestimmung der frühromantischen Utopie und zu ihren ideengeschichtlichen Voraussetzungen.* (1965.) Rev. ed. Tübingen: Max Niemeyer, 1994.

Mahrholz, Werner. *Deutsche Literatur der Gegenwart. Probleme—Ergebnisse—Gestalten.* Berlin: Stäbe-Verlag, 1930.

Maier, Charles S. *The Unmasterable Past: History, Holocaust, and German National Identity.* Cambridge: Harvard University Press, 1988.

Malsch, Wilfried. *"Europa." Poetische Rede des Novalis. Deutung der Französischen Revolution und Reflexion auf die Poesie in der Geschichte.* Stuttgart: Metzler, 1965.

Mann, Heinrich. *Geist und Tat. Essays über Franzosen.* Bibliothek Suhrkamp 732. Frankfurt am Main: Suhrkamp, 1981.

Mann, Thomas. *Gesammelte Werke in zwölf Bänden.* Ed. Hans Bürgin. Frankfurt am Main: Fischer, 1960.

———. *Betrachtungen eines Unpolitischen.* Frankfurt am Main: Fischer, 1988.

———. *Reflections of a Nonpolitical Man.* Trans. with an introduction by Walter D. Morris. New York: Frederick Ungar, 1983.

Mannheim, Karl. *Conservatism: A Contribution to the Sociology of Knowledge.* Trans. David Kettler and Volker Meja. International Library of Sociology. Ed. John Rex. London and New York: Routledge and Kegan Paul, 1986.

Marschall, Susanne. *Mythen der Metamorphose—Metamorphose des Mythos bei Peter Handke und Botho Strauß.* Mainz: Gardez! Verlag, 1993.

Marx, Karl, and Friedrich Engels. *Über Kunst und Literatur.* 2 vols. [East] Berlin: Dietz Verlag, 1967.

Mayer, Arno J. *The Persistence of the Old Regime: Europe to the Great War.* New York: Pantheon, 1981.

Mayer, Matthias. *Hugo von Hofmannsthal.* Sammlung Metzler 273. Stuttgart: Metzler, 1993.

Mayer-Tasch, Peter Cornelius. *Aus dem Wörterbuch der Politischen Ökologie.* München: Deutscher Taschenbuch Verlag, 1985.

Mecklenburg, Jens, ed. *Antifa Reader. Antifaschistisches Handbuch und Ratgeber.* Berlin: Elefanten Press, 1996.

———. ed. *Handbuch deutscher Rechtsextremismus.* Berlin: Elefanten Press, 1996.

Meier, Heinrich. *The Lesson of Carl Schmitt: Four Chapters on the Distinction between Political Theology and Political Philosophy.* Trans. Marcus Brainard. Chicago and London: University of Chicago Press, 1998.

Meinecke, Friedrich. *Die deutsche Katastrophe. Betrachtungen und Erinnerungen.* Zürich: Aero-Verlag, 1946.

———. *The German Catastrophe: Reflections and Recollections.* Cambridge: Harvard University Press, 1950.

————. *Cosmopolitanism and the National State.* Trans. Robert B. Kimber. Princeton: Princeton University Press, 1970.

Mendelssohn, Peter de. *Der Geist in der Despotie. Versuche über die moralischen Möglichkeiten des Intellektuellen in der totalitären Gesellschaft.* Frankfurt am Main: Fischer, 1986.

Merkl, Peter H., and Leonard Weinberg, eds. *The Revival of Right-Wing Extremism in the Nineties.* London and Portland, Ore.: Frank Cass, 1997.

Mertz, Peter, ed. *Und das wurde nicht ihr Staat. Erfahrungen emigrierter Schriftsteller mit Westdeutschland.* München: C. H. Beck, 1985.

Meyer, Martin. *Ernst Jünger.* München and Wien: Hanser, 1990.

Meyer, Thomas. *Identitäts-Wahn. Die Politisierung des kulturellen Unterschieds.* Berlin: Aufbau, 1997.

Milchman, Alan, and Alan Rosenberg, eds. *Martin Heidegger and the Holocaust.* Atlantic Highlands, N.J.: Humanities Press International, 1996.

Mitscherlich, Alexander and Margarete. *Die Unfähigkeit zu trauern. Grundlagen kollektiven Verhaltens.* München: Piper, 1970.

Möller, Horst. *Vernunft und Kritik. Deutsche Aufklärung im 17. und 18. Jahrhundert.* Neue historische Bibliothek. Ed. Hans-Ulrich Wehler. Frankfurt am Main: Suhrkamp, 1986.

Mohler, Armin. *Die Konservative Revolution in Deutschland 1918–1932. Grundriß ihrer Weltanschauungen.* Stuttgart: Friedrich Vorwerk, 1950.

————. *Die konservative Revolution in Deutschland 1918–1932. Ein Handbuch.* 2nd rev. ed. Darmstadt: Wissenschaftliche Buchgesellschaft, 1972.

————. *Die konservative Revolution in Deutschland 1918–1932. Ein Handbuch.* 3rd rev. ed. 2 vols. Darmstadt: Wissenschaftliche Buchgesellschaft, 1989.

Mommsen, Hans. "Die deutschen Eliten und der Mythos des nationalen Aufbruchs von 1933." *Merkur* 38.1 (1984): 97–102.

Morshäuser, Bodo. *Hauptsache Deutsch.* Frankfurt am Main: Suhrkamp, 1992.

————. *Warten auf den Führer.* Frankfurt am Main: Suhrkamp, 1993.

Moser, Tilmann. *Politik und seelischer Untergrund.* Frankfurt am Main: Suhrkamp, 1993.

Mosse, George L. *The Crisis of German Ideology: Intellectual Origins of the Third Reich.* New York: Grosset and Dunlap, 1964.

Mouffe, Chantal, ed. *The Challenge of Carl Schmitt.* London and New York: Verso, 1999.

Müller, Hans-Harald, and Harro Segeberg, eds. *Ernst Jünger im 20. Jahrhundert.* München: Fink, 1995.

Neaman, Elliot. "A New Conservative Revolution? Neo-Nationalism, Collective Memory, and the New Right in Germany since Unification." *Antisemitism and Xenophobia in Germany after Unification.* Ed. Hermann Kurthen, Werner Bergmann, and Rainer Erb. New York and Oxford: Oxford University Press, 1997. 190–208.

————. *A Dubious Past: Ernst Jünger and the Politics of Literature after Nazism.* Berkeley, Los Angeles, and London: University of California Press, 1999.

Neske, Günther, and Emil Kettering, eds. *Martin Heidegger and National Socialism: Questions and Answers.* Trans. Lisa Harries. New York: Paragon House, 1990.

Neuhaus, Volker, ed. *Günter Grass. Die Blechtrommel. Erläuterungen und Dokumente.* Stuttgart: Reclam, 1997.

Nevin, Thomas. *Ernst Jünger and Germany: Into the Abyss, 1914–1945.* Durham: Duke University Press, 1996.

Nicht alle Grenzen bleiben. Gedichte zum geteilten Deutschland von Reiner Kunze, Wolf Biermann, Peter Huchel, u.a. Ed. with a foreword by Ulrich Schacht. Dortmund: Harenberg Edition, 1989.

Nicolas, M.-P. *From Nietzsche Down to Hitler.* (1938.) Trans. E. G. Echlin. Port Washington, New York and London: Kennikat Press, 1970.

Nicolaus, Ute and Helmut. "Hofmannsthal, der Staat und die 'konservative Revolution.' Aktuelle Bemerkunen anläßlich einer parlamentarischen Anfrage." *Politisches Denken. Jahrbuch 1997.* Stuttgart and Weimar: Metzler, 1997. 141–174.

Nietzsche, Friedrich. *The Philosophy of Nietzsche.* New York: Modern Library, 1954.

———. *The Portable Nietzsche.* Ed. Walter Kaufmann. New York: Viking, 1968.

———. *Philosophical Writings.* Ed. Reinhold Grimm and Caroline Molina y Vedia. The German Library 48. New York: Continuum, 1995.

Noack, Paul. *Ernst Jünger: Eine Biographie.* Berlin: Alexander Fest Verlag, 1998.

Noch einmal vom Neunten Land. Peter Handke im Gespräch mit Joze Horvat. Klagenfurt-Salzburg: Wieser, 1993.

Nolte, Ernst. *Der europäische Bürgerkrieg 1917–1945. Nationalsozialismus und Bolschewismus.* Frankfurt am Main and Berlin: Propyläen and Ullstein, 1987.

Nolte, William H. *Rock and Hawk: Robinson Jeffers and the Romantic Agony.* Athens: University of Georgia Press, 1978.

Novalis. *Werke, Tagebücher und Briefe Friedrich von Hardenbergs.* Ed. Hans-Joachim Mähl and Richard Samuel. 3 vols. München and Wien: Hanser, 1978–1987.

———. *Pollen and Fragments: Selected Poetry and Prose of Novalis.* Trans. with an introduction by Arthur Versluis. Grand Rapids, Mich.: Phanes Press, 1989.

Oswald, Ansgar. "Die Drahtzieher. Neue rechte Eliten." *Zitty,* No. 18, 1997, 28–31.

Ott, Hugo. *Martin Heidegger: Unterwegs zu seiner Biographie.* Frankfurt am Main and New York: Campus, 1988.

———. *Martin Heidegger: A Political Life.* Trans. Allan Blunden. New York: Basic Books, 1993.

Parkes, Stuart. *Understanding Contemporary Germany.* London and New York: Routledge, 1997.

Pascal, Roy. *From Naturalism to Expressionism: German Literature and Society 1880–1918.* New York: Basic Books, 1973.

Paulsen, Wolfgang, ed. *Das Nachleben der Romantik in der modernen deutschen Literatur.* Poesie und Wissenschaft XIV. Heidelberg: Lothar Stiehm, 1969.

Pells, Richard. *The Liberal Mind in a Conservative Age: American Intellectuals in the 1940's and 1950's.* New York: Harper and Row, 1985.

———. *Not Like Us: How Europeans Have Loved, Hated, and Transformed American Culture Since World War II.* New York: Basic Books, 1997.

Peter, Klaus. *Stadien der Aufklärung. Moral und Politik bei Lessing, Novalis und Friedrich Schlegel.* Wiesbaden: Athenaion, 1980.

Peter, Klaus, ed. *Die politische Romantik in Deutschland. Eine Textsammlung.* Stuttgart: Reclam, 1985.

Petersdorff, Dirk von. "200 Jahre deutsche Kunstreligion!" *Neue Rundschau* 108.4 (1997): 67–87.

Petrow, Michael. *Der Dichter als Führer? Zur Wirkung Stefan Georges im "Dritten Reich."* Marburg: Tectum Verlag, 1995.

Pfahl-Traughber, Armin. *Rechtsextremismus in der Bundesrepublik.* München: C. H. Beck, 1999.

Piccone, Paul, Gary Ulmen, and Paul Gottfried, "Ostracizing Carl Schmitt: Letters to *The New York Review of Books*." *Telos* 109 (1996): 87–97.

Pieper, Annemarie. *Gut und Böse.* Wissen in der Beck'schen Reihe 2077. München: C. H. Beck, 1997.

Pikulik, Lothar. "Mythos und 'New Age' bei Peter Handke und Botho Strauß." *Wirkendes Wort*, 2/1988, 235–252.

Pinkert, Ernst Ullrich, ed. *Deutschlands 'innere Einheit.' Traum oder Alptraum, Ziel oder Zwangsvorstellung?* Kopenhagen and München: Wilhelm Fink, 1998.

Politisches Denken. Jahrbuch 1997. Ed. Karl Graf Ballestrem et al. Stuttgart, Weimar: Metzler, 1997.

Post, Ken. *Communists and National Socialists: The Foundations of a Century, 1914–39.* New York: St. Martin's Press, 1997.

Preuße, Holger-Heinrich. *Der politische Literat Hans Magnus Enzensberger. Politische und gesellschaftliche Aspekte seiner Literatur und Publizistik.* Frankfurt am Main, Bern, New York, and Paris: Peter Lang, 1989.

Pronay, Nicholas, and Keith Wilson, eds. *The Political Re-Education of Germany and Her Allies after World War II.* Totowa, N.J.: Barnes and Noble Books, 1985.

Pross, Harry, ed. *Die Zerstörung der deutschen Politik. Dokumente 1871–1933.* Frankfurt am Main: Fischer, 1983.

Pütz, Peter. *Friedrich Nietzsche.* Stuttgart: Metzler, 1967.

Rabinbach, Anson. *In the Shadow of Catastrophe: German Intellectuals between Apocalypse and Enlightenment.* Weimar and Now. Ed. Martin Jay and Anton Kaes. Berkeley, Los Angeles, and London: University of California Press, 1997.

Raschel, Heinz. *Das Nietzsche-Bild im George-Kreis.* Monographien und Texte zur Nietzsche-Forschung 12. Ed. Ernst Behler et al. Berlin and New York: Walter de Gruyter, 1984.

Raschke, Joachim. *Die Grünen. Wie sie wurden, was sie sind.* Köln: Bund Verlag, 1993.

Rauschning, Hermann. *The Revolution of Nihilism: Warning to the West.* New York: Alliance Book Corporation, 1939.

———. *Die Konservative Revolution. Versuch und Bruch mit Hitler.* New York: Freedom Publishing (Freiheit-Verlag), 1941.

Reimann, Bruno W., and Renate Haßel. *Ein Ernst Jünger-Brevier. Jüngers politische Publizistik 1920 bis 1933. Analyse und Dokumentation.* Forum Wissenschaft Studien 31. Marburg: BdWi-Verlag, 1995.

Reiss, H. S., ed. *The Political Thought of the German Romantics 1793-1815.* Oxford: Blackwell, 1955.

Renner, Rolf Günter. *Peter Handke.* Stuttgart: J. B. Metzler, 1985.

Richter, Ronald. "Zen oder Die Kunst des hohen Klagetons." *Theater der Zeit,* July–August 1995, 66–68.

Riedel, Sabine. *Ende der Ausgangssperre. Sarajevo nach dem Krieg.* Frankfurt am Main: Schöffling and Co., 1997.

Ringer, Fritz K. *The Decline of the German Mandarins: The German Academic Community 1890-1933.* Cambridge: Harvard University Press, 1969.

Rockmore, Tom. *Heidegger and French Philosophy: Humanism, Antihumanism, and Being.* London and New York: Routledge, 1995.

Rockmore, Tom, and Joseph Margolis, eds. *The Heidegger Case: On Philosophy and Politics.* Philadelphia: Temple University Press, 1992.

Rohloff, Joachim. *Ich bin das Volk. Martin Walser, Auschwitz und die Berliner Republik.* Hamburg: Konkret, 1999.

Rollin, Roger, ed. *The Americanization of the Global Village: Essays in Comparative Popular Culture.* Bowling Green: Bowling Green State University Popular Press, 1989.

Roos, Peter, ed. *Die wilden 40er. Porträt einer pubertären Generation.* 2nd ed. Düsseldorf: Econ, 1992.

Rosellini, Jay. "Kahlschlag im Land der Dichter und (Polit-)Denker? Zum Hintergrund des Intellektuellenstreits in Deutschland." *Monatshefte* 86.4 (1994): 480–499.

———. "The Cult(ure) of Violence: Recent German Reflections." *Glossen* 2 (1997): 24 pages. Online.

———. "A Revival of Conservative Literature? The '*Spiegel*-Symposium 1993' and Beyond." *Beyond 1989. Re-reading German Literature since 1945.* Ed. Keith Bullivant. Modern German Studies 3. Ed. Gerald R. Kleinfeld. Providence and Oxford: Berghahn Books, 1997. 109–128.

Ross, Werner. *Der ängstliche Adler. Friedrich Nietzsches Leben.* 2nd ed. München: Deutscher Taschenbuch Verlag, 1994.

Rudolph, Hermann. *Kulturkritik und konservative Revolution. Zum kulturell-politischen Denken Hofmannsthals und seinem problemgeschichtlichen Kontext.* Tübingen: Max Niemeyer, 1971.

Rüther, Günther, ed. *Literatur in der Diktatur. Schreiben im Nationalsozialismus und DDR-Sozialismus.* Paderborn: Schöningh, 1997.

Rupprecht, Michael. *Der literarische Bürgerkrieg. Zur Politik der Unpolitischen in Deutschland.* Frankfurt am Main: Josef Knecht, 1995.

Sa'adah, Anne. *Germany's Second Chance. Trust, Justice, and Democratization.* Cambridge, Mass., and London: Harvard University Press, 1998.

Safranski, Rüdiger. *Schopenhauer and the Wild Years of Philosophy.* Trans. Ewald Osers. Cambridge: Harvard University Press, 1990.

———. *Ein Meister aus Deutschland. Heidegger und seine Zeit.* München, Wien: Hanser, 1994.

————. *Martin Heidegger: Between Good and Evil.* Trans. Ewald Osers. Cambridge: Harvard University Press, 1998.

————. *Das Böse oder Das Drama der Freiheit.* München and Wien: Hanser, 1997.

Saul, John Ralston. *Voltaire's Bastards: The Dictatorship of Reason in the West.* Toronto: Penguin, 1993.

Schacht, Ulrich. *Gewissen ist Macht. Notwendige Reden, Essays, Kritiken zur Literatur und Politik in Deutschland.* Serie Piper 1464. München and Zürich: Piper, 1992.

Schacht, Ulrich, and Heimo Schwilk. *Für eine Berliner Republik. Streitschriften, Reden, Essays nach 1989.* München: Langen Müller, 1997.

Schacht, Ulrich, ed. *Hohenecker Protokolle. Aussagen zur Geschichte der politischen Verfolgung von Frauen in der DDR.* Zürich: Ammann, 1984.

Schädlich, Hans Joachim, ed. *Aktenkundig.* Reinbek: Rowohlt, 1993.

Schelsky, Helmut. *Die skeptische Generation. Eine Soziologie der deutschen Jugend.* Düsseldorf and Köln: Diederichs, 1958.

Scherpe, Klaus R., and Hans-Ulrich Treichel, "Vom Überdruß leben: Sensibilität und Intellektualität als Ereignis bei Handke, Born und Strauß." *Monatshefte* 73.2 (Summer 1981): 187-206.

Scheuer, Helmut, ed. *Dichter und ihre Nation.* Frankfurt am Main: Suhrkamp, 1993.

Schildt, Axel. *Konservatismus in Deutschland. Von den Anfängen im 18. Jahrhundert bis zur Gegenwart.* München: C. H. Beck, 1998.

Schirrmacher, Frank. *Die Stunde der Welt. Fünf Dichter—Ein Jahrhundert.* Berlin: Nicolai, 1996.

Schirrmacher, Frank, ed. *Die Walser-Bubis-Debatte. Eine Dokumentation.* Frankfurt am Main: Suhrkamp, 1999.

————. *Der westliche Kreuzzug. 41 Positionen zum Kosovo-Krieg.* Stuttgart: Deutsche Verlags-Anstalt, 1999.

Schmiedt, Helmut, and Helmut J. Schneider, eds. *Aufklärung als Form. Beiträge zu einem historischen und aktuellen Problem.* Würzburg: Königshausen und Neumann, 1997.

Schmitt, Hans-Jürgen, ed. *Die Expressionismus-Debatte. Materialien zu einer marxistischen Realismuskonzeption.* Frankfurt am Main: Suhrkamp, 1976.

Schmitz, Michael. *Wendestress. Die psychosozialen Kosten der deutschen Einheit.* Berlin: Rowohlt, 1995.

Schneider, Peter. *Lenz.* (West-)Berlin: Rotbuch, 1973.

Schneider, Peter. *The German Comedy: Scenes of Life after the Wall.* Trans. Philip Boehm and Leigh Hafrey. New York: Farrar, Straus, and Giroux, 1991.

————. *Extreme Mittellage. Eine Reise durch das deutsche Nationalgefühl.* Reinbek: Rowohlt, 1992.

————. *Vom Ende der Gewißheit.* Berlin: Rowohlt, 1994.

Schneiders, Werner. *Das Zeitalter der Aufklärung.* Wissen in der Beck'schen Reihe 2058. München: C. H. Beck, 1997.

Schoeps, Julius H., ed. *Ein Volk von Mördern? Die Dokumentation zur Goldhagen-Kontroverse um die Rolle der Deutschen im Holocaust.* 3rd ed. Hamburg: Hoffmann und Campe, 1996.

Schopenhauer, Arthur. *Philosophical Writings*. Ed. Wolfgang Schirmacher. The German Library 27. New York: Continuum, 1994.

Schröder, Burkhard. *Rechte Kerle. Skinheads, Faschos, Hooligans*. Reinbek: Rowohlt, 1992.

Schultz, Sigrid. *Germany Will Try It Again*. New York: Reynal and Hitchcock, 1944.

Schulz, Gerhard. *Romantik. Geschichte und Begriff*. Wissen in der Beck'schen Reihe 2053. München: C. H. Beck, 1996.

Schumacher, Hans. "Exkurs über Ernst Jünger." *Deutsche Literatur im 20. Jahrhundert. Strukturen und Gestalten*. Ed. Otto Mann and Wolfgang Rothe. Vol. 1. Bern and München: Francke, 1967. 285–296.

Schwab-Trapp, Michael. *Konflikt, Kultur und Interpretation. Eine Diskursanalyse des öffentlichen Umgangs mit dem Nationalsozialismus*. Opladen: Westdeutscher Verlag, 1996.

Schwan, Gesine. *Politik und Schuld. Die zerstörerische Macht des Schweigens*. Frankfurt am Main: Fischer, 1997.

Schwarz, Hans-Peter. *Der konservative Anarchist. Politik und Zeitkritik Ernst Jüngers*. Freiburg: Rombach, 1962.

Schwarzer, Alice, ed. *Frauen gegen den ¶ 218*. Frankfurt am Main: Suhrkamp, 1971.

Schwilk, Heimo. *Wendezeit—Zeitenwende. Beiträge zur Literatur der achtziger Jahre*. Bonn and Berlin: Bouvier, 1991.

———. *Was man uns verschwieg. Der Golfkrieg in der Zensur*. Frankfurt am Main and Berlin: Ullstein, 1991.

Schwilk, Heimo, ed. *Das Echo der Bilder. Ernst Jünger zu Ehren*. Stuttgart: Klett-Cotta, 1990.

Schwilk, Heimo, and Ulrich Schacht, eds. *Die selbstbewußte Nation. "Anschwellender Bocksgesang" und weitere Beiträge zu einer deutschen Debatte*. 3rd rev. ed. Frankfurt am Main and Berlin: Ullstein, 1995.

Seebacher-Brandt, Brigitte. *Die Linke und die Einheit*. Berlin: Corso bei Siedler, 1991.

Seferens, Horst. *"Leute von übermorgen und von vorgestern." Ernst Jüngers Ikonographie der Gegenaufklärung und die deutsche Rechte nach 1945*. Bodenheim: Philo Verlagsgesellschaft, 1998.

Seyhan, Azade. *Representation and Its Discontents. The Critical Legacy of German Romanticism*. Berkeley, Los Angeles, and Oxford: University of California Press, 1992.

Shandley, Robert R., ed. *Unwilling Germans? The Goldhagen Debate*. With essays translated by Jeremiah Riemer. Minneapolis and London: University of Minnesota Press, 1998.

Sichelschmidt, Gustav. *Deutschland—eine amerikanische Provinz. Der große Seelenmord*. Berg: VGB-Verlagsgesellschaft, 1996.

Siedler, Wolf Jobst. "Afterword." ("Die wahren Abenteuer finden im Herzen statt.") *Das abenteuerliche Herz. 2. Fassung*. By Ernst Jünger. Stuttgart: Klett-Cotta, 1979.

Sieferle, Rolf Peter. *Die konservative Revolution. Fünf biographische Skizzen.* Frankfurt am Main: Fischer, 1995.

Sie kommen aus Deutschland. DDR-Schriftsteller in der Bundesrepublik. Ed. Detlev Johannes. Ausstellung 10. Oktober bis 7. November 1989. Worms: Stadtbibliothek Worms, 1989.

Soergel, Albert. *Dichtung und Dichter der Zeit. Eine Schilderung der deutschen Literatur der letzten Jahrzehnte.* Leipzig: Voigtländer, 1911.

Sontheimer, Kurt. *Thomas Mann und die Deutschen.* München: Nymphenburger, 1961.

Sorg, Bernhard. "Erinnerung an die Dauer. Zur Poetisierung der Welt bei Botho Strauß und Peter Handke." *Peter Handke. Text und Kritik,* Heft 24 (5th rev. ed. 1989). 122–130.

Soucek, Branimir. *Eine Frühlingsreise zum Gedankenfluß eines verirrten Literaten, oder, Gerechtigkeit für Peter Handke.* Thaur, Wien and München: Druck- und Verlagshaus Thaur, 1996.

Sowell, Thomas. *Migrations and Cultures: A World View.* New York: Basic Books, 1996.

Spender, Stephen. *European Witness.* New York: Reynal and Hitchcock, 1946.

Spengler, Oswald. *Der Untergang des Abendlandes. Umrisse einer Morphologie der Weltgeschichte.* (1918 1922.) Ungekurzte Sonderausgabe in einem Band. Stuttgart, Hamburg, München: Deutscher Bücherbund, n.d.

Sperber, Jonathan. *The Kaiser's Voters: Electors and Elections in Imperial Germany.* Cambridge: Cambridge University Press, 1997.

Squires, Radcliffe. *The Loyalties of Robinson Jeffers* (1956). Ann Arbor: University of Michigan Press, 1963.

Städtler, Thomas. *Von den Schwierigkeiten, ein Konservativer zu werden. Über den idealen und den real-existierenden Konservatismus. Eine Streitschrift.* Hamburg: Rasch und Röhring, 1996

Stern, Fritz. *The Politics of Cultural Despair: A Study in the Rise of the Germanic Ideology.* (1961.) Garden City: Anchor Books, 1965.

———. *The Failure of Illiberalism: Essays on the Political Culture of Modern Germany.* New York: Knopf, 1972.

Stern, J. P. *Ernst Jünger.* Studies in Modern European Literature and Thought. Ed. Erich Heller. New Haven: Yale University Press, 1953.

Stern, J. P. *Friedrich Nietzsche.* Penguin Modern Masters. Ed. Frank Kermode. New York: Penguin, 1978.

———. *The Heart of Europe: Essays on Literature and Ideology.* Oxford: Blackwell, 1992.

Stojanovic, Svetozar. *The Fall of Yugoslavia: Why Communism Failed.* Amherst, N.Y.: Prometheus Books, 1997.

Stöss, Richard. *Politics against Democracy: Right-Wing Extremism in West Germany.* Trans. Lindsay Batson. German Studies Series. Ed. Eva Kolinsky. New York and Oxford: Berg, 1991.

Strasser, Peter. *Der Freudenstoff. Zu Handke eine Philosophie.* Salzburg and Wien: Residenz, 1990.

Strauß, Botho. *Rumor.* München and Wien: Hanser, 1980.

————. *Paare, Passanten.* 5th edition. München and Wien: Hanser, 1982.

————. *Diese Erinnerung an einen, der nur einen Tag zu Gast war.* München and Wien: Hanser, 1985.

————. *Fragmente der Undeutlichkeit.* München and Wien: Hanser, 1989.

————. *Theaterstücke.* 2 vols. München and Wien: Hanser, 1991.

————. *Beginnlosigkeit. Reflexionen über Fleck und Linie.* München and Wien: Hanser, 1992.

————. "Anschwellender Bocksgesang." *Der Spiegel,* no. 6, 1993, 202–207.

————. *Das Gleichgewicht. Stück in drei Akten.* München and Wien: Hanser, 1993.

————. *Wohnen Dämmern Lügen.* München and Wien: Hanser, 1994.

————. *Versuch, ästhetische und politische Ereignisse zusammenzudenken. Texte über Theater 1967–1986.* 2nd ed. Frankfurt am Main: Verlag der Autoren, 1996.

————. *Ithaka. Schauspiel nach den Heimkehr-Gesängen der Odyssee.* München and Wien: Hanser, 1996.

————. *Die Fehler des Kopisten.* München and Wien: Hanser, 1997.

Strauß lesen. Ed. Michael Radix. München and Wien: Hanser, 1987.

Syberberg, Hans Jürgen. *Die freudlose Gesellschaft. Notizen aus dem letzten Jahr.* München and Wien: Hanser, 1981.

————. *Vom Unglück und Glück der Kunst in Deutschland nach dem letzten Kriege.* München: Matthes and Seitz, 1990.

Taylor, Seth. *Left-Wing Nietzscheans: The Politics of German Expressionism.* Berlin and New York: Walter de Gruyter, 1990.

Tent, James. *Mission on the Rhine: "Re-education" and Denazification in American-Occupied Germany.* Chicago: University of Chicago Press, 1982.

Theweleit, Klaus. *Männerphantasien.* Vol. 1: *Frauen, Fluten, Körper, Geschichte.* Frankfurt am Main: Verlag Roter Stern, 1977. Vol. 2: *Männerkörper—zur Psychoanalyse des weißen Terrors.* 1978. Reinbek: Rowohlt, 1980.

Thies, Christian. *Die Krise des Individuums. Zur Kritik der Moderne bei Adorno und Gehlen.* Rowohlts Enzyklopädie 55590. Reinbek: Rowohlt, 1997.

Thomas, Gina, ed. *The Unresolved Past: A Debate in German History.* Introduction by Ralf Dahrendorf. New York: St. Martin's Press, 1990.

Tönnies, Sibylle. *Der westliche Universalismus. Eine Verteidigung klassischer Positionen.* Opladen: Westdeutscher, 1995.

————. *Die Feier des Konkreten. Linker Salonatavismus.* Göttingen: Steidl, 1996.

Torpey, John. *Intellectuals, Socialism, and Dissent: The East German Opposition and Its Legacy.* Minneapolis: University of Minnesota Press, 1995.

Der Traum der Vernunft. Vom Elend der Aufklärung. Eine Veranstaltungsreihe der Akademie der Künste, Berlin. 2 vols. Darmstadt und Neuwied: Luchterhand, 1985–1986.

Trommler, Frank, ed. *Jahrhundertwende: Vom Naturalismus zum Expressionismus 1880–1918.* Deutsche Literatur. Eine Sozialgeschichte. Ed. Horst Albert Glaser. Vol. 9. Reinbek: Rowohlt, 1987.

Uerlings, Herbert. *Friedrich von Hardenberg, genannt Novalis. Werk und Forschung.* Stuttgart: Metzler, 1991.

Uerlings, Herbert, ed. *Novalis und die Wissenschaften*. Tübingen: Max Niemeyer, 1997.

Ulmen, Gary. "Toward a New World Order: Introduction to Carl Schmitt's 'The Land Appropriation of the New World'." *Telos* 109 (1996): 3–27.

Ulrich, Bernd. *Deutsch, aber glücklich. Eine neue Politik in Zeiten der Knappheit*. 2nd ed. Berlin: Alexander Fest, 1997.

Von einem Land zum andern. Gedichte zur deutschen Wende 1989/1990. Ed. Karl Otto Conrady. Frankfurt am Main: Suhrkamp, 1993.

Vondung, Klaus, ed. *Das wilhelminische Bildungsbürgertum. Zur Sozialgeschichte seiner Ideen*. Göttingen: Vandenhoek and Ruprecht, 1976.

Vuksanovic, Mladen. *Pale—Im Herzen der Finsternis. Tagebuch 5.4.–15.7.1992*. Aus dem Serbokroatischen von Detlef I. Olof. With a preface by Joschka Fischer and an afterword by Roman Arens and Christiane Schlötzer-Scotland. Wien, Bozen: Folio Verlag, 1997.

Wacker, Bernd, ed. *Die eigentlich katholische Verschärfung . . . Konfession, Theologie und Politik im Werk Carl Schmitts*. München: Fink, 1994.

Walser, Martin. *Dorle und Wolf*. Frankfurt am Main: Suhrkamp, 1987.

———. *Über Deutschland reden*. Frankfurt am Main: Suhrkamp, 1988.

———. "Deutsche Sorgen." *Der Spiegel*, no. 26, 1993, 40–47.

———. *Vormittag eines Schriftstellers*. Frankfurt am Main: Suhrkamp, 1994.

———. *Ansichten, Einsichten. Aufsätze zur Zeitgeschichte*. Werke in zwölf Bänden. Ed. Helmuth Kiesel and Frank Barsch. Vol. 11. Frankfurt am Main: Suhrkamp, 1997.

———. *Erfahrungen beim Verfassen einer Sonntagsrede: Friedenspreis des deutschen Buchhandels 1998*. Frankfurt am Main: Suhrkamp, 1998.

———. *Ein springender Brunnen*. Frankfurt am Main: Suhrkamp, 1998.

Warneke, Rolf. "Kurswechselparade eines Intellektuellen. Konsequent inkonsequent: Hans Magnus Enzensberger." *text und kritik* 113 (Januar 1992): 97–105.

Weber, Frank. *Die Bedeutung Nietzsches für Stefan George und seinen Kreis*. Europäische Hochschulschriften, Reihe 1, Deutsche Sprache und Literatur 1140. Frankfurt am Main, Bern, New York and Paris: Peter Lang, 1989.

Weber, Iris. *Nation, Staat und Elite. Die Ideologie der Neuen Rechten*. PapyRossa Hochschulschriften 15. Köln: PapyRossa, 1997.

Wegierski, Mark. "The New Right in Europe." *Telos* 98–99 (Winter 1993–Spring 1994): 55–69.

Weimars Ende. Ed. Thomas Koebner. Frankfurt am Main: Suhrkamp, 1982.

Weißmann, Karlheinz. *Der Weg in den Abgrund: Deutschland unter Hitler, 1933 bis 1945*. München: Herbig, 1997.

Weizsäcker, Richard von. *Von Deutschland aus. Reden des Bundespräsidenten*. Berlin: Siedler, 1985.

Wellershoff, Dieter. *Gottfried Benn. Phänotyp dieser Stunde*. Frankfurt am Main and Berlin: Ullstein, 1964.

Weninger, Robert, and Brigitte Rossbacher, eds. *Wendezeiten. Zeitenwenden. Positionsbestimmungen zur deutschsprachigen Literatur 1945–1995*. Studien zur deutschsprachigen Gegenwartsliteratur, ed. Paul Michael Lützeler. Vol. 7. Tübingen: Stauffenburg, 1997.

Wetzels, Walter D., ed. *Myth and Reason: A Symposium.* Austin and London: University of Texas Press, 1973.

Weyergraf, Berhard. *Literatur der Weimarer Republik 1918-1933.* Hansers Sozialgeschichte der deutschen Literatur vom 16. Jahrhundert bis zur Gegenwart. Vol. 8. München and Wien: Hanser, 1995.

Wiegand, Julius, et al. *Deutsche Geistesgeschichte im Grundriß.* Frankfurt am Main: Diesterweg, 1932.

Willett, Ralph. *The Americanization of Germany, 1945-1949.* London: Routledge, 1989.

Williams, Arthur, and Stuart Parkes, eds. *The Individual, Identity and Innovation: Signals from Contemporary Literature and the New Germany.* Berlin, Frankfurt am Main, New York, Paris, and Wien: Peter Lang, 1994.

Wilson, W. Daniel, and Robert C. Holub, eds. *Impure Reason: Dialectic of Enlightenment in Germany.* Detroit: Wayne State University Press, 1993.

Winkler, Michael. *Stefan George.* Sammlung Metzler 90. Stuttgart: Metzler, 1970.

———. *George-Kreis.* Sammlung Metzler 110. Stuttgart: Metzler, 1972.

Winter, Lorenz. *Heinrich Mann and His Public: A Socioliterary Study on the Relationship between an Author and His Public.* Trans. John Gorman. Coral Gables: University of Miami Press, 1970.

Winter, Rolf. *Ami go home. Plädoyer für den Abschied von einem gewalttätigen Land.* Hamburg: Rasch und Röhring, 1989.

Wippermann, Wolfgang. *Totalitarismustheorien. Die Entwicklung der Diskussion von den Anfängen bis heute.* Darmstadt: Primus, 1997.

———. *Wessen Schuld? Vom Historikerstreit zur Goldhagen-Kontroverse.* Berlin: Elefanten Press, 1997.

Wittek, Bernd. *Der Literaturstreit im sich vereinigenden Deutschland. Eine Analyse des Streits um Christa Wolf und die deutsch-deutsche Gegenwartsliteratur in Zeitungen und Zeitschriften.* Marburg: Tectum Verlag, 1997.

Woelk, Ulrich. *Amerikanische Reise.* Frankfurt am Main: Fischer, 1996.

Wolff, Rudolf, ed. *Heinrich Mann. Das essayistische Werk.* Sammlung Profile 24. Bonn: Bouvier, 1986.

Wolffsohn, Michael. *Meine Juden—Eure Juden.* München and Zürich: Piper, 1997.

Wulf, Joseph, ed. *Literatur und Dichtung im Dritten Reich. Kultur im Dritten Reich.* (1982.) Ed. Joseph Wulf. Vol. 2. Frankfurt am Main and Berlin: Ullstein, 1989.

Wuthenow, Ralph-Rainer, ed. *Stefan George in seiner Zeit. Dokumente zur Wirkungsgeschichte.* Vol. 1. Stuttgart: Klett-Cotta, 1980.

Zimmerman, Michael. *Martin Heidegger's Confrontation with Modernity: Technology, Politics and Art.* Bloomington: Indiana University Press, 1990.

Zimmermann, Clemens. *Die Zeit der Metropolen. Urbanisierung und Großstadtentwicklung.* Europäische Geschichte. Ed. Wolfgang Benz. Frankfurt am Main: Fischer, 1996.

Zitelmann, Rainer. *Adolf Hitler. Eine politische Biographie.* Persönlichkeit und Geschichte, vol. 21/22. Göttingen and Zürich: Muster-Schmidt, 1989.

Zitelmann, Rainer, Karlheinz Weißmann, and Michael Großheim, eds. *Westbin-dung. Chancen und Risiken für Deutschland*. Frankfurt am Main and Berlin: Ull-stein/Propyläen, 1993.

Zuckermann, Moshe. *Zweierlei Holocaust. Der Holocaust in den politischen Kulturen Israels und Deutschlands*. Göttingen: Wallstein Verlag, 1998.

Zülch, Tilman, ed. *Die Angst des Dichters vor der Wirklichkeit. 16 Antworten auf Peter Handkes Winterreise nach Serbien*. Göttingen: Steidl, 1996.

Bibliography

Index